Understanding Difficulties in Literacy Development: Issues and Concepts

This Reader, along with the companion volume *Approaching Difficulties in Literacy Development: Assessment, Pedagogy and Programmes,* forms part of *Difficulties in Literacy Development* (E801), a course belonging to the Open University MA in Education programme.

The Open University Masters in Education

The Open University Masters in Education is now firmly established as the most popular postgraduate degree for education professionals in Europe, with over 3000 students registered each year. It is designed particularly for those with experience of advisory service, educational administration or allied fields. Specialist lines in management, applied linguistics, special needs/inclusive education and lifelong learning are available within the programme. Successful study on the MA entitles students to apply for entry into the Open University Doctorate in Education programme.

Details of this and other Open University courses can be obtained from the Student Registration and Enquiry Service, The Open University, PO Box 197, Milton Keynes MK7 6BJ, United Kingdom; telephone: +44 (0) 845 300 6090; e-mail: general-enquiries@open.ac.uk.

Alternatively, you may wish to visit the Open University website at http://www.open.ac.uk, where you can learn more about the wide range of courses and packs offered at all levels by The Open University.

Understanding Difficulties in Literacy Development: Issues and Concepts

Edited by
Janet Soler, Felicity Fletcher-Campbell and Gavin Reid

Los Angeles | London | New Delhi
Singapore | Washington DC

The Open University
Walton Hall
Milton Keynes
MK7 6AA
United Kingdom
www.open.ac.uk

SAGE Publications Ltd
1 Oliver's Yard
55 City Road
London EC1Y 1SP

SAGE Publications Inc.
2455 Teller Road
Thousand Oaks, California 91320

SAGE Publications India Pvt Ltd
B 1/I 1 Mohan Cooperative Industrial Area
Mathura Road
New Delhi 110 044

SAGE Publications Asia-Pacific Pte Ltd
33 Pekin Street #02-01
Far East Square
Singapore 048763

Library of Congress Control Number: 2008944005

British Library Cataloguing in Publication data

A catalogue record for this book is available from the British Library

ISBN 978-1-84860-772-9
ISBN 978-1-84860-773-6 (pbk)

Typeset by C&M Digitals (P) Ltd, Chennai, India
Printed and bound in Great Britain by TJ International Ltd, Padstow, Cornwall
Printed on paper from sustainable resources

Contents

Acknowledgements

We should like to thank the authors who contributed their chapters, as well as colleagues within and outside The Open University who helped with the preparation of the manuscripts. Special thanks are due to the following people for their assistance in the production of this book:

Kathy Simms (course secretary)
Theresa Nolan (course manager)
Gill Gowans (copublishing executive)

Chapter 1
From: Rassool, N., 'Literacy: In Search of a Paradigm', in *Literacy for Sustainable Development in the Age of Information*, pp. 25–53 (Clevedon, OH: Multilingual Matters, 1999). Reprinted by permission of the publisher Multilingual Matters.

Chapter 2
From: Johnson, D. and Kress, G., 'Globalisation, Literacy and Society: Redesigning Pedagogy and Assessment', *Assessment in Education: Principles, Policy and Practice* 10 (1), 2003, pp. 5–14. Reprinted by permission of the publisher (Taylor & Francis Group, http://www.informaworld.com).

Chapter 4
From: Stuart, M., Stainthorp, R. and Snowling, M., 'Literacy as a Complex Activity: Deconstructing the Simple View of Reading', *Journal of Research in Literacy*, 42 (2), 2008, pp. 59–66. A journal of the United Kingdom Literacy Association.

Chapter 5
From: Purcell-Gates, V., 'The Irrelevancy – and Danger – of the "Simple View" of Reading to Meaningful Standards', in R. Fisher, G. Brooks and M. Lewis (eds) *Raising Standards in Literacy*, pp. 121–32 (London: RoutledgeFalmer, 2002). Copyright © 2002. Reproduced by permission of Taylor and Francis Books UK.

Chapter 6
From: Beech, J.R., 'Ehri's Model of Phases of Learning to Read: A Brief Critique', *Journal of Research in Reading*, 28 (1), 2005, pp. 50–8. A journal of the United Kingdom Literacy Association.

Chapter 7
From: Williams, A. and Gregory, E., 'Siblings Bridging Literacies in Multilingual Contexts', *Journal of Research in Reading*, 24 (3), 2001, pp. 248–65. A journal of the United Kingdom Literacy Association.

Chapter 8
From: Burns, J. and Bracey, P., 'Boys' Underachievement: Issues, Challenges and Possible Ways Forward', *Westminster Studies in Education*, 24 (2), 2001, pp. 155–66. Reprinted by permission of the publisher (Taylor & Francis Group, http://www.informaworld.com).

Chapter 9
From: Payne, G., 'Re-Counting "Illiteracy": Literacy Skills in the Sociology of Inequality', *The British Journal of Sociology*, 57 (2), 2006, pp. 219–40. Copyright © 2006 London School of Economics and Political Science. Reproduced with permission of Blackwell Publishing Ltd.

Chapter 10
From: Beard, R., 'Research and the National Strategy', *Oxford Review of Education*, 26 (3 & 4), 2000, pp. 421–36. Reprinted by permission of the publisher (Taylor & Francis Group, http://www.informaworld.com).

Chapter 11
From: Hall, K., 'Literacy Policy and Policy Literacy: A Tale of Phonics in Early Reading in England', in J. Soler and R. Openshaw (eds) *Reading Across International Boundaries: History, Policy and Politics*, pp. 55–67 (Charlotte, NC: Information Age Publishing, 2007). Reprinted with permission of the publisher, Information Age Publishing.

Chapter 13
From: Hamilton, M., Macrae, C. and Tett, L. (2001) 'Powerful Literacies: The Policy Context', in M. Hamilton, L. Tett and J. Crowther and National Institute of Adult Continuing Education, *Powerful Literacies*, pp. 23–42. Reproduced with kind permission of the authors and NIACE. Copyright © NIACE 2001. www.niace.org.uk/publications

Chapter 14
From: Burden, R., 'The Self-concept and its Relationship to Educational Achievement', in *Dyslexia and Self-concept: Seeking a Dyslexic Identity*, pp. 5–14 (London and Philadelphia, PA: Whurr, 2005). Copyright © 2005. Reproduced with permission of John Wiley & Sons Ltd.

Chapter 15
Pollak, D., 'The Self-concept and Dyslexia', in *Dyslexia, the Self and Higher Education: Learning Life Histories of Studies Identified as Dyslexic*, pp. 31–42 (Stoke on Trent and Sterling: Trentham Books, 2005).

Chapter 16
From: Artiles, A.J., 'Special Education's Changing Identity: Paradoxes and Dilemmas in Views of Culture and Space', *Harvard Educational Review*, 73 (2) (Summer 2003), pp. 164–202. Copyright © by the President and Fellows of Harvard College. All rights reserved. For more information, please visit www.harvardeducationalreview.org

Introduction

Janet Soler

This book is one of two readers adopting a cross-disciplinary approach to understanding and working with those who experience difficulties with literacy. Both readers highlight current political and research-based issues in an area of education which is currently under intense political, professional and public scrutiny. This book, *Understanding Difficulties in Literacy Development: Issues and Concepts*, adopts a broader view of difficulties in literacy and related educational and curriculum learning issues across a range of ages, phases and settings.

The authors of the chapters challenge ways of thinking about current policy- and research-based debates and issues related to the addressing and assessment of literacy difficulties. They argue for practices that take into account the need to build bridges between learners' experience and wider political concerns and tensions when determining the efficacy of literacy programmes and curriculum policy. They also cover current debates and concerns in relation to socially negotiated ideas, programmes and policies intended to address literacy and literacy difficulties across the phases and ages from early childhood to adulthood. The book's authors draw upon different disciplinary and methodological perspectives to bring together policy analysis, research and professional perspectives from different international educational settings and contexts to raise and address the background and broader questions and issues related to recent developments intended to address literacy difficulties.

Brought together in one volume, these chapters demonstrate that educators, professionals, policy makers and the public need to move beyond a focus upon the acquisition of individual skills and views of the teaching of reading as a neutral, technical process. These chapters also collectively provide a greater understanding of the political and socially embedded nature of literacy and literacy difficulties and associated curriculum policies and programmes, and how they impact upon the identity and agency of literacy learners. The companion reader, *Approaching Difficulties in Literacy Development: Assessment, Pedagogy and Programmes,* takes up the themes raised in this book to examine in greater detail the implications of these issues for specific pedagogies, literacy programmes and assessment.

The first section of the book considers 'What is literacy?' and 'What are difficulties in literacy?' These questions are examined in chapters which unpack the contemporary and changing understandings of literacy and the nature of learning to read in relation to developments in technology and understandings related to literacy difficulties and dyslexia.

The first piece is the introductory chapter from Naz Rassool's seminal book *Literacy for Sustainable Development in the Age of Information* (Rassool, 1999). In this chapter, he explores the 'multidimensional' nature of literacy in order to reveal the social purposes which underpin literacy and can be seen to drive everyday practices and the way people engage with literacy. Rassool highlights the way literacy studies have provided answers to the question 'What is literacy?' which stretch beyond viewing literacy as a set of neutral skills related to the decoding and production of text. He highlights the need to understand literacy in relation to social practices linked to ideology, culture, knowledge and power. This enables him to explore the politics and interdisciplinary struggles between experimental psychologists, psycholinguists and New Literacy Studies and critical literacy theorists. In this chapter, and in the original book, Rassool demonstrates how the use of an interdisciplinary approach enables us to view literacy in relation to both the individual and broader contextual issues which are key to shaping both policy and practice.

The second chapter in this section is by David Johnson and Gunther Kress who are founding academics in the emerging field of 'New Literacy Studies'. This chapter draws upon three central themes within New Literacy Studies to argue that we need to re-evaluate how literacy is conceptualized, taught and assessed. Johnson and Kress examine the way in which assessment is increasingly driven by unitary standards with an emphasis on 'basic skills', rather than meaning and understanding in an age when we are experiencing immense changes in our work and everyday life, increasing diversity and plurality and rather than 'basic literacy skills' currently highlighted in our literacy curricula. The chapter concludes by considering how new understandings of cognition and learning can be drawn upon to redesign pedagogy and assessment.

The last chapter in Part 1 uses a very different disciplinary lens to illustrate the different ways we may examine, understand and conceptualize literacy. This chapter has been specifically written for this book by Janet Soler. It draws upon a social history perspective to trace the development of current definitions and understandings of dyslexia and to reveal how their historical construction and changing and contested definitions of dyslexia have had an impact upon public and professional views in the higher education sector. Her chapter relates the historical development and changing definitions of dyslexia to social justice issues that are emerging in higher education. This is an area where assessments and the diagnosis of dyslexia has come to the fore, with recent legislation resulting in funding being linked to the diagnosis of dyslexia.

The second section of this book considers the major issues and concepts in public debates which arise from differing conceptions of literacy. The teaching of reading and the improving of literacy standards are currently the subject of intense national and international interest, which has led to high-profile public and professional debates. Concerns over how to address difficulties in literacy have become the focus of government, policy makers and the public in general, as attention over the past decade has increasingly focused on the raising of literacy standards. This has given rise to specific policy initiatives, national literacy strategies, interventions and programmes related to preventing and addressing literacy difficulties and developing reading skills.

The authors of the first chapter in this section, Morag Stuart, Rhona Stainthorp and Maggie Snowling, are arguing for the 'Simple View of Reading' as a new framework. The Rose Report in England recommended the 'reconstruction' of the Searchlights model which underpinned the National Literacy Strategy. Stuart et al. relate the Simple View of Reading to the Searchlights model of reading, and argue that the Simple View of Reading can account for, and contribute to, understandings of reading as a complex activity.

Victoria Purcell-Gates debates the 'Simple View of Reading' from a different disciplinary and national perspective. Purcell-Gates argues for 'embracing complexity' given her analysis of socio-cultural factors, and the complexities of literacy development revealed by a socio-cultural view. She is concerned that a 'one size fits all' which is currently being emphasized in the United States does not take into account the diversity of socio-cultural contexts. She therefore advocates the collection of empirical data that covers cognitive skills related to literacy development and the contexts and interactions within which literacy practices take place in everyday lives.

John Beech focuses upon another issue related to learning. His critique of Ehri's influential four phases of reading development demonstrates, as we have seen in the chapters above, that there can be as many differences amongst literacy researchers based within disciplines as between those from different disciplinary perspectives. Anne Williams and Eve Gregory draw upon a socio-cultural view to provide further insights into the complexity surrounding literacy. While reading difficulties have been attributed to cultural differences between home and school literacy practice, this chapter provides evidence of the ways in which literacy practices can also be blended practices which reflect the values of both the community and the school.

Joe Burns and Paul Bracey use case study research to look at the issue of boys' under-achievement. They argue that their evidence shows that raising literacy levels is a key element for all the schools in their case studies. Geoff Payne in the final chapter in this section focuses upon adult education in his exploration of the conceptualization, issues and debates surrounding illiteracy.

The third section of the book explores examples of the development of nationally based literacy curriculum policy initiatives and the way in which they reflect responses to public debates, research and professionally based issues, and conceptions of learning to read for those who experience difficulties with literacy. Roger Beard outlines the research evidence which influenced the 1998 National Literacy Strategy. His chapter highlights the research contexts which forged the strategy and the influence of literacy studies research as well as other perspectives, drawn from areas from beyond literacy studies such as school effectiveness based research.

Kathy Hall examines the debates surrounding the role of phonics, which have arisen with the review of early reading in the 2006 Rose Report. Hall's chapter picks up themes related to phonics and synthetic phonics, which have been explored in Part 2. Her analysis in this chapter examines the research literature underpinning the Rose report and associated debates. She balances this with an examination of the policy contexts which have fostered the ascendancy of synthetic phonics.

Janet Soler and Roger Openshaw pick up the themes related to the teaching of reading and early literacy acquisition and provide evidence which clearly indicates that although both countries draw upon the same body of international research, there has been a marked difference in policy responses to the teaching of phonics in England and New Zealand. They argue that the highly politicized debates over the teaching of phonetic knowledge are linked to alliances and struggles between different interest groups in the professional, academic and political spheres. This section concludes with a chapter by Mary Hamilton, Catherine Macrae and Lyn Tett, who provide an overview of the policy contexts which have recently shaped basic adult education (ABE) in the UK and Ireland and relate these to wider issues and themes.

In the fourth section, we examine how these issues and conceptualizations of the process of learning to read and becoming literate transcend the educational settings and extend into the school/place home and school. This section emphasizes the ways in which experiences of difficulties in becoming literate impact upon agency, identity and participation with others, and the ways in which individual agency and learners' identities can be enhanced and extended to transform the experiences of literacy learners.

Bob Burden reviews the literature to examine issues associated with the identities and self-concepts of dyslexic children. He concludes that there is a lack of research into how dyslexic children and adults 'make sense' of their disability. His review shows that there is a clear association between early and continuing literacy difficulties and that these have serious consequences for those who experience reading difficulties. David Pollak draws upon New Literacy Studies in the following chapter to provide a New Literacies based perspective on the themes raised in Burden's literature review. Pollak examines the constituent parts of the self-concept and relates them to dyslexia.

The fifth and final section picks up the themes and issues explored in the previous sections and considers the tensions arising from the social construction and historical development of literacy difficulties as learning disabilities and the implications for social justice and equity. Alfredo Artiles argues from a socio-cultural and cultural theory perspective in this chapter that inclusion in education systems deals with 'difference' in contexts which are 'highly charged' political and cultural climates. In order to infuse a social justice dimension that moves beyond merely addressing disability at the individual level to a much wider social inclusion of disability, he notes that we must take into account the dynamics, complexities and nuances of social and cultural interactions.

Ray McDermott, Shelley Goldman and Hervé Varenne, who are based in the United States, pick up the themes explored in Artiles' *Learning disabilities* chapter and relate them specifically to learning disabilities (LD). Learning Disabilities are the equivalent of specific learning difficulties (SpLD) in the United Kingdom and include dyslexia. Like Artiles, they draw upon cultural theory to explore ways of thinking about LD/SpLD. Their chapter provides us with some insights from a socio-cultural viewpoint regarding the politics surrounding LD/SpLD and claims that they are a 'middle-class' phenomenon. Above all, their analysis provides insights into the way in which the social production of learning disabilities may be perpetuated by the conditions and culture of the school as an institution and educational setting.

Reference

Rassool, Naz (1999) *Literacy for Sustainable Development in the Age of Information.* Clevedon: Multilingual Matters.

Part 1

What is Literacy? What are 'Difficulties in Literacy'?

1

Literacy: In Search of a Paradigm

Naz Rassool

Literacy in academic discourse

Considerable developments have taken place in the broad area of literacy studies during the past two decades. Within this ongoing debate, the idea that literacy cannot be regarded as an autonomous set of technical skills is gaining support amongst many critical theorists. Literacy is now more generally regarded as a social practice that is integrally linked with ideology, culture, knowledge and power. Moreover [...] reference is being made increasingly to different literacies or, as Gee (1996) and the New London Group (NLG) (1996) put it, 'multiliteracies' suited to a range of context-related situations. In consequence, the concept of literacy has lost much of the rigidity and linearity associated with it in the traditional, decontextualised, skills-oriented framework.

Instead, literacy is perceived to be *organic* because it is seen as a cultural activity that involves people in conscious and reflexive action within a variety of situations in everyday life. Much of this has been reflected in various interpretations of Freire's approach to critical literacy, and its impact on adult literacy programmes internationally. Barton and Hamilton's (1998) description of community literacies provides another excellent account of the ways in which literacy practices shape people's lives. Community literacies as described by Barton and Hamilton (1998) illustrate the self-defining principles of literacy. They show how, through participating in literacy events, people can interrogate the narrative of everyday life and, in the process, redefine themselves in relation to the social world. Barton and Hamilton's ethnographic documentation of individual 'literacy histories and literacy lives', provides evidence of the ways in which people can change things in their everyday lives, and also transform the consciousness of others. Within this framework, emphasis shifts from concerns about *process,* or individual behaviours during reading, to that of *agency,* or active involvement, within a defined context.

Literacy is regarded also as being *multidimensional* because it is seen as serving a variety of social, economic, ideological and political purposes. The *social purposes,* referred to here, derive from the literacy practices that feature in everyday life such as reading for information, learning, pleasure, recreation and religion. *Economic purposes* can be seen in relation to the literacy skills and knowledge demands made on people in the workplace. People seek to enhance their capabilities as workers as those who are literate are perceived to have better job opportunities in the labour market, and thus literacy obtains an exchange value. In this sense, literacy is regarded as an investment in 'human capital'. Human capital

From: Rassool, N., *Literacy for Sustainable Development in the Age of Information*, pp. 25–53 (Clevedon: Multilingual Matters, 1999).

ses the direct relationship between education, worker productivity and the
is underscored by the principle that people need to invest in themselves in
of skills to make them more employable. [...] [T]his view of literacy has
votal position in the discourse on societal development. Economic purposes
seen as relating to the specific value attached to 'formal' literacies associated
nt professions and social roles.

purposes refer to the literacy practices in which people engage in their multiple
roi... izens, activists or community members allowing them to take up positions in relation to the social world. At the same time, they also describe the broader relationship between
literacy and specific interests in society. These revolve around social structure and different
power interests that shape definitions of literacy, and influence levels of access to the types
and forms of literacy for different groups of people in society. *Ideological purposes* relate to
the values, assumptions, beliefs and expectations that frame dominant literacy discourse
within particular social contexts. Together, these different aspects and the criteria that define
them, frame the 'normal' levels of literacy 'competence' for everyday living, and thus they
influence our commonsense understandings of 'personal efficacy'.

Literacy as a site of struggle over meaning/ literacy wars in education

Alongside this dynamic debate, we have had an ongoing critique within the educational
terrain, from within the framework of experimental behavioural psychology (henceforth
referred to as experimental psychology). Experimental psychology provides a view of literacy that is primarily concerned with the de-coding of texts involving the perceptual process
(phonological and graphic), word structure (morphological) and technical writing (spelling)
skills. Of significance to this perspective are the *cognitive processes that underlie skilled
reading and learning how to read* (Stanovich, 1986; Goswami & Bryant, 1990). For these
writers, 'teaching literacy is about teaching the skills of reading and writing' per se (Oakhill &
Beard, 1995: 69).

That is, teaching children 'how to analyse the sounds in words [one word at a time] and
how alphabetic letters symbolise these sounds' (Bryant, 1994), otherwise referred to as
sound–symbol correspondences, or graphic–phoneme correspondences. Providing a 'scientific' approach to literacy, this approach presents literacy as a neutral technology. As
Gough (1995: 80) puts it:

> I confess to subscribing to the autonomous model, 'a literacy narrowly conceived as
> individual, psychological skills'. I believe that literacy is a single thing ... that texts
> have independent meanings ... that readers can be separated from the society that
> gives meaning to their uses of literacy, and that their cognitive skills, importantly
> including their ability to read and write, can be assessed, and thus abstracted from
> social persons and cultural locations.

Experimental psychology represents the subject-discipline which, at least until the 1970s,
influenced the dominant literacy meanings incorporated into educational policy frameworks.
It is also the subject-discipline that has contributed greatly to discussions about literacy

within the social terrain. When literacy is discussed in, for example, the media or in political rhetoric, reference is often made to the learning of 'basic' literacy skills or the 'three Rs', direct instruction and rote learning.

Literacy outcomes are measured in terms of skills acquisition, and the personal and social benefits derived from being literate. Being able to read and write is viewed as central to increasing or enhancing individuals' 'life chances'. Again, Gough (1995: 80) underlines this in his statement that, 'I believe that learning to read and write does contribute to social progress, to personal improvement and mobility, perhaps to better health, almost certainly to cognitive development'. This is in line with the views expressed by cognitive and social psychologists such as Goody and Watt (1968) and Ong (1982), regarding the intrinsic value of literacy to the development of the intellect and, relatedly, the development of society. Views of literacy as an 'autonomous' set of skills decontextualised from society and culture have been critiqued in considerable detail elsewhere (Street, 1984, 1993).

Experimental psychology versus psycholinguistics

What has been referred to polemically as the 'literacy wars' (Stanovich & Stanovich, 1995) first started as an attack by experimental psychologists on the orthodoxy that evolved during the 1970s around the emphasis placed by psycholinguists on the reading *process* and the production of meaning through the use of contextual cues. Psycholinguists hold the view that:

> three language systems interact in written language: the graphophonic [sound and letter patterns], the syntactic [sentence patterns], and the semantic [meanings]. We can study how each one works in reading, and writing, but they can't be isolated for instruction without creating non-language abstractions. (Goodman, 1986: 38–9)

Readers construct meaning during reading by drawing on their prior learning and knowledge in order to make sense of texts (Goodman, 1986). As such, literacy is defined in terms of the range of meanings produced at the interface of person and text, and the linguistic strategies and cultural knowledges used to 'cue' into the meanings embedded in the text. I will return to this discussion later in the chapter.

A further critique was subsequently mounted against advocates of the 'whole language' and 'real book' approach who argue that children *learn to read by reading* (Smith, 1971, 1979; Goodman, 1986). The 'whole language' approach draws on key elements in the psycholinguistic perspective of reading discussed here, and research on writing within the broader framework of applied linguistics, notably the work of Britton (1975), Wells (1986) and Wilkinson (1965). Of significance is the 'language experience' approach that emerged within the Schools Council Initial Literacy Project, *Breakthrough to Literacy* (Mackay *et al.*, 1978), and the writing process. The 'language experience approach' and 'process writing' emphasise learners' active involvement in the construction of texts, as opposed to placing a reliance on textbooks. Overall emphasis is placed on the *meaning* that learners want to communicate.

This approach represents a top-down model of literacy development, that is, it is seen to develop 'from whole to part [meaningful units of language], from vague to precise, from gross to fine, from highly concrete and contextualised to more abstract' (Goodman, 1986: 39, information in brackets added). Goodman (1986: 26) summarises the principles of this approach in the argument that:

language development is empowering: the learner 'owns' the process, makes the decisions about when to use it, what for and with what results ... literacy is empowering too, if the learner is in control with what's done with it ... language learning is learning how to mean: how to make sense of the world in the context of how our parents, families, and cultures make sense of it. (Quoted in Weaver, 1990: 5)

This philosophical approach to literacy, which involves both text and context, has been criticised within experimental psychology as operating on broad assumptions and not having sufficient empirical data. As such, it is viewed as lacking scientific validity (Stanovich & Stanovich, 1995).

A comparative analysis

Although the *foci* are different within the psycholinguistics and experimental psychology paradigms, they do share some similarities. For instance, their overall analyses are located within the individual child and developmental processes in which 'the child is seen as progressing through successively more complex stages, each building on the other, each characterised by a particular structuring of component cognitive and affective capabilities' (Cole & Scribner, 1981: 12). Similarly, literacy within both paradigms has an exclusively individual, child-focused, pedagogic orientation. Much of the emphasis in the psycholinguistic approach to literacy also centres on perceptual skills and orthographic knowledge although this is approached from a different perspective.

But there are also differences. The one emphasises context and meaning, whilst the other stresses individual skills in isolation. Experimental psychologists have as their central goal:

that children should learn how their writing system works. This means, for alphabetic writing systems, making sure [that] they learn the alphabetic principle, something that requires some attention to fostering students' phonemic awareness. (Perfetti, 1995: 112)

This involves a significant measure of direct teaching and skills reinforcement. It is only once basic literacy skills have been acquired that they can be 'applied and extended in a wealth of ways which might come within the remit of the broader definitions of reading' (Oakhill & Beard, 1995: 69). For psycholinguists, on the other hand:

language learning is easy when it's whole, real, and relevant; when it makes sense and is functional; when it's encountered in the context of its use; when the learner chooses to use it ... language is learned as pupils learn through language and about language, all simultaneously in the context of authentic speech and literacy events ... (Goodman, 1986: 29)

Risk-taking involving readers in predicting and guessing as part of the meaning-making process, and writers in clarifying ideas and experimenting in spelling and punctuation, is seen as an essential part of the literacy process in this paradigm.

Stanovich and Stanovich (1995: 98) summarise the basis of the disagreement between the two camps as being:

selectively focused around the necessity of explicit analytic instruction in word decoding in the early years of schooling. The current differences between the camps are all traceable to differing underlying assumptions about the process of reading that were present in the debates about top-down versus bottom-up models of reading that began over twenty years ago. Two decades of empirical research have largely resolved these debates in favour of bottom-up models.

Bottom-up models lay stress on the need for children to build 'word knowledge' proceeding from part-to-the-whole and thus would emphasise the need for children to know common letter-strings, initial sound blendings, phonics and to have phonological awareness as an integral part of learning to read and write.

This one-dimensional skills-based view is problematised by Hasan (1996) who, arguing from an applied linguistics perspective, suggests that reading and writing constitute complex processes that fundamentally involve the ability to grasp the principle of representation. She argues that:

> becoming literate in the sense of being able to read/write presupposes the ability to 'see' a phenomenon as 'standing for' something other than itself … the fundamental attribute for the onset of literacy is the ability to engage in acts of meaning: to be an initiate in literacy is to be able to make sense. (Hasan, 1996: 379)

In other words, children learn that words represent actions, emotions and concrete elements in the social world; they stand for something other than themselves. Literacy is integrally linked with a semiotic system that is grounded in language, culture and society. Signification is important in relation to making sense of any representational text […].

Experimental psychology versus the New Literacy Studies

Recently, criticisms from experimental psychologists have also extended to the views expressed by adherents of the 'New Literacy Studies' (NLS) whose focus is on the *socio-cultural aspects of literacy* (Barton & Ivanic, 1991; Barton & Padmore, 1991; Street, 1993; Barton, 1994). This paradigm argues against a universal concept of literacy and proposes an acceptance of different 'literacies' within various social and cultural contexts. The NLS draws on a range of conceptual-analytic frameworks including social anthropology, sociology, critical linguistics and discourse theory.

Of these, social anthropology has been very influential historically in shaping the overall literacy discourse. Social anthropology draws on key motifs in cognitive psychology but interpretations of the intellectual and social 'consequences' of literacy are related to large groups of people within particular societies. Thus, they will include 'the study of kinship organisation, conceptual systems, political structures, economic processes' (Street, 1993: 14). Since literacy issues are discussed in relation to social and cultural practices within the context of social change, some anthropological analyses draw also on sociological concepts and sociolinguistics as well as historical relations. In this regard, the NLS draw on a range of research traditions and build on previous critical discussions on literacy. This includes the writings of Cole and Scribner (1981), Brice Heath (1983) and Scollon and Scollon (1981) whose work has challenged previous theories based on superficial and biased assumptions about literate and oral cultures. These writers stress the need to take account of the different ways of making sense of the world reflected within different cultures and communities.

To give an example, the approach advocated in the psycholinguistic paradigm is not applicable to the acquisition of Quranic literacy in non-Arabic speaking societies as described by Cole and Scribner (1981) in their study of the Vai in West Africa. Quranic literacy is learned initially 'by rote-memorisation since the students can neither decode the written passages nor understand the sounds they produce. But students who persevere, learn to read [that is, sing out] the text and to write passages – still with no understanding of the language' (Scribner & Cole, 1988: 246). As a student of Quranic literacy myself in my early years, I recall that whilst we did not know the language (classical Arabic) we, never-theless, did learn sound–symbol correspondence, we did learn to decode and we also learned about the rules and conventions of classical Arabic script. Technically then, we *did* learn to read as described by experimental psychologists. But we learned really only to 'bark' at print. Our reading purpose (prayer) did not necessitate comprehension as textual interpretation is traditionally performed by the Ulamah (learned scholars) (see Rassool, 1995). This bears out Cole and Scribner's (1981) view that specific uses of literacy have specific implications, and that particular practices promote particular skills.

A comparative analysis

Many of the differences between the NLS and experimental psychology paradigms relate to the particular *focus* of the disciplines in which literacy is articulated. The latter's concern about the teaching of reading and writing skills relates to a significant extent to their primary involvement with the diagnosis of reading ability and the remediation of specific literacy problems amongst individual children in schools. Oakhill and Beard (1995: 72) summarise the differences in research approach between the subject-disciplines in their argument that:

> experimental research by psychologists adopts 'stipulative' [or 'operationalised'] def-initions, in order to facilitate 'controlled and circumscribed' studies. Ethnographic and other sociological studies tend to adopt or seek to establish 'descriptive' [or 'essen-tialist'] definitions, advancing particular constructs to enable them to discuss different 'literacies'. Thus the New Literacy Studies can be said to be developing new philo-sophical lines of enquiry, rather than seeking to replace 'old' notions of literacy.

There is some validity in this view and I return to this discussion again later in the chapter.

Literacy as a bounded discourse

Other subject-disciplines involved with theorisation and research into literacy include *cognitive psychology* which is concerned mainly with the impact of literacy on intellectual development – and, particularly, abstract thinking skills. Although there is some congru-ence with the views held in experimental psychology, the overall focus of research is dif-ferent. Whilst emphasis within the latter is mainly on decoding skills, the former is concerned with the development of higher-order reading skills and cognitive processes.

Social psychology, on the other hand, draws on elements of cognitive psychology, namely, the relationship between language and thought but locates its arguments within particular environments, cultures and societies. A variety of views of literacy prevail within this framework. Most influential has been the level of importance attached to the 'great divide' between literate and oral cultures by writers such as Goody and Watt (1968), Hildyard and Olson (1978) and Ong (1982). Others including Vygotsky (1962) and Luria (1979) emphasised the development of cognition and consciousness in relation to 'the social relations with the external world' (Luria, 1979: 43). Their emphasis was particularly on the cognitive consequences and the political and ideological dimensions of literacy acquisition during a period of social change in the USSR. This included the economic transition from a predominantly agrarian society to post-revolutionary industrialism as well as the sociocultural and ideological transition from the semi-feudalism of Tsarist Russia towards the modernist ideals of the new 'socialist' milieu. The underlying thesis was that 'sociocultural changes formed the basis for the development of higher memory and thinking processes and more complex psychological organisation' (Cole & Scribner, 1981: 10).

Overall, social psychology is primarily concerned with educational and cultural practices and the 'impact' and 'effects' of literacy on larger groups of people, and much emphasis is placed on the transference of cognitive literacy skills to the process of living in society. More recently, social psychology has also focused on the uses to which basic literacy knowledges are applied and, accordingly, centres on '*what* people read, the *amount* of reading that is done, the *purposes* and *effects* of reading' (Edwards, 1997: 119, original emphases).

Literacy theorised within *sociolinguistics* generally takes account of the different forms and functions of written and spoken language within a variety of social and cultural contexts. Emphasis is placed on the communicative functions of speech and written language within different language communities. With regard to literacy, it also considers the communicative functions of 'text' including different textual forms and conventions, and their embeddedness in different language and cultural systems. As is the case with psycholinguistics, both readers and writers bring meaning to the text in terms of their knowledge of the language system as well as the sociocultural context. Stubbs (1980: 15) states that in order to:

> make sense of written material we need to know more than simply the 'linguistic' characteristics of the text: in addition to these characteristics we need to recognise that any writing system is deeply embedded in attitudinal, cultural, economic and technological constraints … People speak, listen, read and write in different social situations for different purposes.

Its focus on appropriateness in relation to context incorporates a consideration of 'communicative competence' in oral discourse. 'Communicative competence' is defined as:

> a synthesis of knowledge of basic grammatical principles, knowledge of how language is used in social settings to perform communicative functions, and knowledge of how utterances and communicative functions can be combined according to the principles of discourse (Canale & Swain, 1980; quoted in Verhoeven, 1994: 8)

Verhoeven (1994: 6) incorporated this notion of 'communicative competence' into the concept of 'functional literacy' which he appropriated from the UNESCO framework, reinterpreted and redefined in terms of 'the demands of literacy in the complex world'.

This redefined notion of functional literacy involves the development of different levels of competence including 'grammatical competence' relating to phonological, lexical and morpho-syntactic abilities; 'discourse competence' relating to cohesion and coherence within the text; 'de-coding competence' involving code conventions and automisation, that is, 'grasping the essentials of the written language code itself'; 'strategic competence' centring on the meta-cognitive abilities involved in the planning, execution and evaluation of written texts; and 'sociolinguistic' competence revolving around understanding of literacy conventions, and cultural background knowledge (Verhoeven, 1994: 9).

The notion of 'grammatical competence' described here by Verhoeven shares similarities with the overall emphasis in the experimental psychology paradigm, on developing linguistic awareness/competence as part of the process of learning to read. The model of communicative competence that he advances overall also includes knowledge of discourse and subject register. Discourse here refers to appropriate language use within a specific communicative event and thus involves role relationships, cultural norms and values, different textual conventions including content, form (schemata) and style as well as knowledge and understanding of the context. Subject register describes the language categories and forms of description particular to certain subjects or genre, for example, the language of science, history, music or art. [...]

On a different level, although multilingualism and issues of bi-literacy have been discussed within sociolinguistics, analysis has been limited to language policy and language programmes within particular societies. Issues related to local and subjugated literacies have not generally been theorised in this paradigm. Hymes (1973) and Labov (1972), concentrating mostly on speech communities, foregrounded the importance of going beyond the linguistic perspective in order to transcend inequalities between language and competence. These writers argued that linguistic inequalities needed to be analysed in relation to people and their location within the social structure. This perspective has been incorporated into the work of, inter alia, Kress *et al.* (1997), Fairclough (1992), Gee (1996), Halliday (1996) and Hasan (1996).

Research approaches

Within a macro-perspective, the research approaches adopted in social anthropology and sociolinguistics employ a variety of measurement instruments including descriptive interpretive approaches, participant observation, field notes and taped transcripts in ethnographic case studies and, in the instance of sociolinguistics, also textual analysis. In contrast, in the micro-perspective adopted by psycholinguistics and experimental psychology, the measurement of literacy includes, largely, psychometric testing, checklists, reading inventories, analysis of writing samples, observation quantification, interviewing and the classification of behaviour. Important emphases are reading diagnosis, instructional techniques and strategies, although these derive from very different views of the literacy process.

Definitions and models of literacy

Definitions of literacy relevant to teaching contexts tend to be implied rather than stated in the macro-perspective adopted in some of the paradigms. As is already highlighted in the UNESCO discourse [...] the issue of definition extends beyond the rhetorical. Indeed, Scribner (1984: 6) suggests that definitional problems have more than academic significance. She argues that:

each formulation of an answer to the question 'What is literacy?' leads to a different evaluation of the scope of the problem (i.e. the extent of *ill*iteracy) and to different objectives

for programs aimed at the formation of a literate citizenry ... A chorus of class
answers also creates problems for literacy planners and educators. (Original emph

Account needs to be taken also of the fact that research paradigms or theoretical frameworks that take the individual as the unit of analysis, argue outside a consideration of the fact
that literacy is a primary means of cultural transmission, which is essentially a social
achievement (Scribner, 1984). Although the literacy act in itself is often a private experience, as is suggested by experimental psychologists (Gough, 1995), it obtains its meaning
ultimately within society and culture; it is a means of social communication, of knowledges,
thoughts and ideas. As is argued by Hasan (1996: 378), 'the goals of literacy can hardly have
a value in and of themselves: they need to be seen in the context of the wider social environment which is at once the enabling condition and the enabled product of literacy pedagogy'.

With the exception of psycholinguistics, and the Freirean approach [...], *models of literacy*
are not clarified; they are understood at the level of commonsense, that is to say, they tend
to feature as taken-for-granted variables in literacy analysis. Models of literacy refer to
pedagogic frameworks in which theories about the literacy process are generated. They
would therefore include the range of meanings produced in literacy practices as well as
conceptions of how and what meanings can be obtained in texts – and contexts. Thus,
models of literacy make explicit the range of knowledges or literacies that they frame –
and the process through which they are accessed. Models of literacy do not constitute
instructional techniques, although they may frame them. If we are to assess the value of
literacy, we cannot do so effectively without taking account of the knowledges that they
make available, and the contexts in which they are situated.

Many of these views also originate within different ideological frameworks. For example,
literacy theorised as a sociocultural practice emphasises ideology, politics and power. In contrast, literacy theorised within the cognitive and behavioural psychology framework regards
literacy as a value-free, autonomous set of skills, a neutral technology that can be applied to
different literacy demands in everyday life. Similarly, literacy theorised within psycholinguistics makes a variety of assumptions about what literacy *is* (e.g. print-text based). Its
primary focus on the literacy *process* also implicitly underscores a de-ideologised view of literacy. According to Luke (1996: 311), in psycholinguistics:

> language and literacy are theorised by reference to the internal states of human subjects –
> for example, ... models of language acquisition, developmental stage theories, schema
> theory, and humanist models of personal response and expression.

In other words, each perspective brings with it not only its own particular view of what
literacy is and what it is for, but also a particular world view.

Table 1.1 provides a brief and schematic outline of a selection of *subject-disciplines* in order
to highlight the distinct nature of the literacy meanings produced within each framework.

What I am concerned with here are not the substantive or methodological differences
between these perspectives per se. Rather, the point that I want to make is that because
the *foci* are different within these subject-disciplines, and because their research
approaches differ, they yield a wide variety of information on literacy within a broad
context. This discreteness supports Stubbs' view that each subject-discipline advances a
particular analytical and research framework yielding different views on what constitutes important knowledge about literacy.

Table 1.1   Literacy as a bounded discourse

Subject-discipline	Literacy foci
Experimental behavioural psychology	Focus on the individual Perceptual process Logographic knowledge Phonological awareness Technical writing skills Decoding of texts Functional literacy Methods of instruction
Cognitive psychology	Focus on individuals and groups Impact of literacy on intellectual development Abstract thinking skills
Social psychology	Focus on groups Variety of positions taken: (a) great-divide theory – differences between oral and literate cultures (e.g. Goody & Watt; Hildyard & Olson) (b) emphasis on development of cognition and consciousness in relation to social relations within external world – ideological and political aspects of literacy (e.g. Luria; Vygotsky) (c) emphasis on need to understand various ways in which different societies and cultures make sense of their world – challenge great-divide theory (Scribner; Cole & Scribner)
Psycholinguistics	Focus on the individual Reading and writing *process* Internal relations between perceptual processes, orthographic systems and reader's knowledge of language Meaning production at interface of person and text
Sociolinguistics	Focus on individuals and groups Different forms and functions of written and spoken language within variety of social contexts Bilingualism and multilingualism Discourse and subject registers Communicative competence
Social anthropology	Focus on groups Interpretations of social consequences of literacy related to groups of people within their sociocultural contexts Social change

Boundaries, knowledge and power

With the exception of the integrated approach adopted by the New Literacy Studies and social anthropology, the divergent views on literacy discussed here lend support to Stubbs' contention that the field of literacy studies is marked by a lack of integration. The theorisation of literacy in different subject-disciplines, he argues, has resulted in the development of a variety of conceptual-analytic frameworks. Stubbs (1980: 3) identified this problem in his argument that:

one reason why the literature on reading is so vast and unintegrated is that topics have been approached from different directions from within disciplines, including psychology, education and linguistics. Often these approaches have been largely self-contained, making little reference to work within other approaches, and, in fact, putting forward contradictory definitions of *reading* and *literacy*. (Original emphases)

Whilst the sociocultural approach (NLS) and social anthropology derive their terms of reference across disciplinary boundaries, the rest of the views discussed here, to a large extent, rely on the frame and terms of reference of specific subject-disciplines as the basis of their interpretation and analysis.

Bernstein (1990: 156) defines a discipline as 'a specialised, discrete discourse, with its own intellectual field of texts, practices, rules of entry, modes of examination and principles of distributing success and privileges'; they are 'oriented to their own development rather than to applications outside themselves'. Each subject-discipline frames 'a domain of objects, a set of methods, a corpus of propositions considered to be true, a play of rules and definitions, of techniques and instruments' (Foucault, 1970: 59). And, as we could see in the different research approaches discussed earlier, each subject-discipline projects a particular view of what constitutes research, and different sets of variables operate within each frame of reference to define selected aspects of literacy as foci for research. As a result, different sets of data emerge that are analysed using subject-specific terms of reference and arguments to arrive often at conclusions that, generally, are not integrated in a meaningful way within the educational terrain. This bears out Scribner's (1984) argument regarding difficulties in educational planning. It also bears out the views expressed by Oakhill and Beard (1995, referred to earlier), regarding the nature of the differences in the conceptual-analytic frameworks of NLS and experimental psychology.

Conceptual-analytical frameworks derive from the subject-discipline that provides the frame and terms of reference to the analysis. This includes subject-specific terminology, relational concepts as well as the range of assumptions, questions and problematics that can be engendered within this context. They refer also, at a meta-level, to the ways in which discourses are structured as well as how meanings are produced and reproduced.

Conceptual-analytical frameworks grounded in subject-disciplines, according to Bernstein (1990), are not neutral; they are constituted in 'self-interest' with their own subject-specific views of the 'truth' – which implicitly support a particular view of the world. Thus, they constitute what Foucault (1980: 133) refers to as 'regimes of truth':

'truth' is to be understood as a system of ordered procedures for the production, regulation, distribution, circulation and operation of statements … [and] is linked in a circular relation with systems of power which produce and sustain it, and to effects of power which it induces and which extend it. A 'regime' of truth.

Together, these frame what are legitimate knowledges and ways of knowing in research. Some of this professional interest is expressed in Oakhill and Beard's (1995: 69) argument that:

[w]hilst acknowledging the undoubted contribution of language, motivation and cultural factors to literacy acquisition, *we should not forget the contribution of scientific experimental research to our understanding of reading and its development*. (Emphasis added)

Oakhill and Beard sought to reinforce the scientific validity of their 'language-as-system' and empirical research paradigm over and against the ethnographic and theoretical-analytical approaches adopted in what they term as 'sociological perspectives on literacy' (1995: 72), and the broad assumptions that they associate with psycholinguistic research.

Conceptual-analytic frameworks are ultimately embedded in particular ideologies and, as such, each represents a distinctive view of 'what is legitimate knowledge'. Without acknowledging the ideology with which their own perspective of literacy (reading) is imbued, Oakhill and Beard (1995: 72) call for counter-critiques of the 'ideological influences on how misplaced orthodoxies become so widely accepted', and why it takes so long for them to 'receive critical scrutiny'.

Literacy discourses in society

In addition to hierarchies constructed between subject-knowledges, different levels of importance are also attached to selected forms of knowledge within the social and political terrain. This relates, to a large extent, to prevailing (dominant) ideologies that underscore policy frameworks as well as particular hegemonic projects pursued by political and economic interest groups. Thus it is that some literacy knowledges are chosen for inclusion in educational policy frameworks, whilst others are marginalised, excluded or derided in social and political debate at specific moments in societal development.

For instance, the argument for *basic skills* and *rote learning* derives its scientific legitimacy largely from the positivism of behavioural psychology and, for a long time, constituted (and in many instances continue to be) the dominant view of 'what literacy is' in education. Moreover, as we could see [...] during the Apartheid years, 'official' literacies are inscribed into national language policy. In Foucauldian terms, 'knowledge and power are inseparable, ... forms of power are imbued within knowledge, and forms of knowledge are permeated by power relations' (Ball, 1990: 17). Ideologically, definitions of literacy can then be seen as constituting 'power/knowledge' discourses (Foucault, 1980). According to Foucault, discourse defined in terms of power/knowledge constitutes the means by which power is exercised through relations of dominance established within the social terrain. [...]

Border crossings

Some critiques of the unitary subject-discipline approach have come from what has become known as *critical literacy discourse* and include a diverse range of research approaches and conceptual frameworks.

Street (1984, 1993), one of the most significant contributors to the debate about adult literacy research in the UK during the past two decades, has made important inputs towards a re-conceptualisation of literacy within an inter-disciplinary framework. In his research conducted in Iran during the 1970s, Street analysed literate behaviours and the way meanings are produced in the reading process amongst the peasants of the village of Chesmeh. He identified two different forms of literacy that prevailed in Iran at the time, namely 'commercia' literacy (economic) and 'Maktab' (religious) literacy. Of major importance was the fact that Street was identifying different forms of literacy for specific social and economic purposes. Moreover, his critique of the 'autonomous' model of literacy adhered to by Goody (1968) and his identification of the 'ideological' model of literacy were major contributions to the way in which literacy has been theorised during the past decade.

The significance of this research in both methodological and conceptual terms was the way in which micro-social processes were linked with broader developments within society – whilst taking account also of historical relations. In his critique of the 'psychologistic' paradigm, Street (1984, 1993) challenges the claims made of the role of literacy in fostering rationality and abstract-thinking capabilities. Instead, he argues that literacy should be understood as a social practice in which there is an interplay of different ideologies. Street also stresses the importance of analysing literacy within its institutional as well as the wider sociopolitical and economic context. As such, it is argued that

> the uses, consequences and meanings of literacy; the differences and similarities between written and spoken registers and inter-register variation with spoken and written modes; and the problem of what is culture specific and what [is] universal in literacy practices – must be answered with reference to close descriptions of the actual uses and conceptions of literacy in specific cultural contexts. (Street, 1993: 3)

Street's views on the theorisation of literacy have been central to the development of the New Literacy Studies discussed earlier. In pedagogical terms, this paradigm supports the development of different literacies, the centrality of the learner to the teaching and learning context, 'the politicisation of content in literacy instruction, and the integration of the voices and experiences of learners with critical social analysis' (Auerbach, 1992, quoted in Verhoeven, 1994: 7). This framework also takes account of the often neglected complex issue of literacy within multilingual social settings – the disappearance of minority languages, subjugated literacies and the importance of maintaining local literacies.

Critical linguists such as Phillipson and Skutnabb-Kangas (1995), similarly, carry this thread through their analysis of linguistic imperialism which refers to the imposition of colonial languages historically. These writers address the issue of linguistic human rights within which the concept of local literacies is grounded. Writers within this broad framework identify the inter-relationship between literacy, national language planning policies and power processes.

Social historians such as Graff (1979, 1987) and Williams (1961), analysing the political economy of literacy programmes, explore the importance attached in social policy to specific ideologies during different historical periods. Within a macro-perspective, these writers draw on sociological concepts in their emphasis on the sociocultural, political and structural variables that contribute to literacy inequalities and, *de facto,* sociocultural and economic inequalities. Significant contributions have come also from writers who focus on the political economy of textbooks and texts (Apple, 1982, 1986, 1993; De Castell *et al.,* 1989). In addition, important new developments have come from writers who locate their analyses within a *'postmodern' analytical framework.*

Border pedagogies

Drawing on Gramscian cultural theory centred on the role of language in maintaining hegemonic relations – and the contestation and resistance that this intrinsically generates, writers such as Giroux (1993; Giroux and Macedo, 1987) and McLaren (1995) emphasise the links between knowledge, ideology and power. These writers extend the concept of 'conscientisation' advanced within the Freirean framework and propose concepts that they term *'critical pedagogy'* and *'border pedagogies'*. Outlining a 'postmodern' framework which borrows concepts from feminist research and cultural theory, Giroux (1993: 75) stresses the need for a language:

> that allows for competing solidarities and political vocabularies that do not reduce the issues of power, justice, struggle, and inequality to a single script, a master narrative that suppresses the contingent, the historical, and the everyday as serious objects of study.

This approach emphasises agency, difference, contestation and the relationship between these and social structures and ideological forces. Giroux argues further that 'critical pedagogy needs to create new forms of knowledge through its emphasis on breaking down disciplinary boundaries and creating new spheres in which knowledge can be produced' (Giroux, 1993: 76).

Critical pedagogies or 'border' pedagogies draw on aspects of feminist theory, cultural studies and the sociology of knowledge and, in this sense, constitute politicised discourses. Most of the writers within the cross-disciplinary paradigm ground their analyses in the 'specificities of peoples' lives, communities, and cultures' (Giroux, 1993: 67) and place relative emphasis on the time–space dimensions of specific literacy knowledges. Significantly though, only a few (Giroux, 1993; McLaren, 1995) embed their analyses in an exposition of the complexity of social theory that incorporates the variables of gender, 'race' and social position as analytic categories.

As was the case with the discussion on subject-disciplines earlier, at the level of practice, the views of literacy highlighted in the critical literacy paradigm continue to raise qualitative questions about: (a) definitions of literacy, (b) models of literacy, (c) criteria for and, relatedly, the level of importance attached to local variables in the measurement of societal literacy levels, (d) what literacy in relation to human rights means in concrete terms and (e) the real and symbolic impact and effects of particular forms of literacy on individual 'empowerment' and social development. Account also needs to be taken of the fact that literacy meanings are in a constant state of flux – and thus are subject to alteration within different social milieux. Scribner (1984: 8) underlines this point in her argument that

> since social literacy practices vary in time and space, what qualifies as individual literacy varies with them. At one time, ability to write one's own name was the hallmark of literacy; today in some parts of the world, the ability to memorise a sacred text remains the modal literacy act. Literacy has neither a static nor a universal essence.

This issue is highly pertinent at the moment as new technologies and, relatedly, new ways of living evolve within society. [...]

Summary

The different perspectives outlined here illustrate that, conceptually, literacy is multifaceted and thus requires different *levels* of analysis within a broad and flexible framework that incorporates complexities. These include, inter alia, historical relations, social practices and institutions, locality as well as individual and group subjectivities, and the tension that exists between agency and specific state-sanctioned political and hegemonic projects.

Luke (1996), for instance, arguing from a sociological perspective, critiques socially based models of literacy pedagogy including the Freirean approach […] and the new 'genre-based' literacies within sociolinguistics (van Leeuwen & Humphrey, 1996; Veel & Coffin, 1996). He contends that these approaches 'stop short of coming to grips with their assumptions about the relationship between literacy and social power' (Luke, 1996: 309). These views, he suggests, define agency as an individual property which is 'neither collective or inter-subjective, nor necessarily connected with political ideology or cultural hegemony' (p. 311). Luke maintains that the history of literacy education is about power and knowledge:

> But it is about power not solely in terms of which texts and practices will 'count' and which groups will have or not have access to which texts and practices. It is also about who in the modern state will have access to a privileged position in specifying what will count as literacy … Schooling and literacy are used to regulate and broker not just access to material wealth, but as well access to legally constituted 'rights', to cultural and subcultural histories and archives, to religious virtue and spiritual rewards, and to actual social networks, gendered desires and identities. (Luke, 1996: 310)

For Luke, a critical literacy approach extends beyond issues related to textual biases and representation: 'it is nothing less than a debate over the shape of a literate society, its normative relations to textual and discourse exchange, and the relative agency and power of the literate in its complex and diverse cultures and communities' (Luke, 1996: 145). […]

Literacy as a field of inquiry: levels, contexts and definitions

Since literacy spans such a broad terrain within various subject-disciplines, to address the complexities that surround literacy in the modern world necessitates an approach that incorporates many of the literacy meanings discussed earlier. In order to do so, I will explore the conceptualisation of literacy as a *regionalised field of inquiry*. A regional field of study according to Bernstein (1990: 156) represents a 'recontextualising of disciplines which operate both in the intellectual field of disciplines and in the field of practice'. Because literacy interpenetrates a wide range of subject-disciplines, we can argue that regions are the interface between subject-disciplines, and the literacy knowledges that are thus made available. These are illustrated in Figure 1.1.

The degree of overlap indicated in Figure 1.1 signifies the dialogical relationship between literacy knowledges and subject disciplines. This overlap, or interstices, represent the regionalised field of inquiry within which literacy will be conceptualised and discussed in the rest of the book.

The range of literacy meanings identified in the earlier critical paradigm highlight the fact that literacy constitutes, simultaneously, a *social practice,* an *ideological practice,* a *cultural practice* and an *educational practice.* Within the regionalised field identified here, discussion of these inter-related aspects would be able to draw on concepts and analytical categories across the disciplines. It would also be able to draw on analytic categories used in cross-disciplinary frameworks such as feminism and cultural studies. Crossing boundaries in this way provides opportunity to analyse the dynamic interplay that exists between

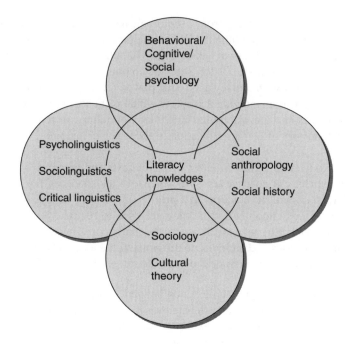

Figure 1.1   Literacy as a regionalised field of study

specific literacy practices and the social, cultural, economic and political structures in which they are grounded, as is suggested by Luke (1996). Thus it would be possible to address educational meanings, whilst at the same time, take account of the fact that meaning production takes place organically within the complex power relations that traverse the social terrain. Moreover, it can take account also of agency, contestation and struggle which make possible the production of alternative meanings and practices as highlighted in the critical literacy framework.

The different interlocking aspects of literacy to be explored as a regionalised field of study [...] are summarised in Table 1.2, and will be discussed in more detail below.

Literacy as a social practice

Working towards concretising this framework and identifying analytic categories, I start with the argument that literacy defined as a *social practice* has to be contextualised within a general theory of society. As is argued earlier, its permeation into the social body requires that literacy as a social practice needs to be analysed in terms of its relationship with institutions, structures and processes and the social system in which they are grounded. The importance of this lies in the fact that these contexts constitute the key defining sites of what literacy is, who it is for and what purposes it should serve for the individual, specific groups of people and society as a whole. Scribner (1984: 8) concretises the intrinsic link between literacy and structures in the argument that:

Table 1.2   Interlocking levels at which literacy needs to be theorised

Literacy as:	Variables
A social practice	Social life Institutions: state, industry, commerce, finance, media, education Social processes e.g. national language policy, educational policy, social policy (health, employment, economic) Social system: models of governance, social roles Structures e.g. social policy, language rights, ethnicity, gender, social position Religious-cultural practices
An ideological practice	Meanings produced in social discourse e.g. policy, media, political interest groups, industry, funding bodies Censorship Textual and contextual meanings Critical literacies/counter discourses
A cultural practice	Historical relationships Workplace literacy requirements Leisure/interest literacy requirements Literacy requirements to function in everyday life e.g. technologies, banking, health, social services, housing, civic engagement Range of cultural meanings produced and reproduced e.g. values, beliefs, expectations, aspirations Impact of religious-cultural beliefs on levels of access to literacy for particular groups e.g. women, religious minorities, ethnic groups
An educational practice	Models and forms of knowledge Technical literacy skills Technological skills and knowledges Theories of knowledge Pedagogical models Teaching methodologies Teaching and learning resources (including staffing; multimedia) Democratisation of sociopolitical structures and processes Literacy for democratic participation, e.g. decision-making, knowledge of rights and obligations, freedom of expression, freedom of access to information, knowledge of social system, citizenship, critical knowledges

grasping what literacy 'is' inevitably involves social analysis: What activities are carried out with written symbols? What significance is attached to them, and what status is conferred on those who engage in them? Is literacy a social right or a private power? … Does the prevailing distribution of literacy conform to standards of social justice and human progress? What social and educational policies might promote such standards?

Such considerations should inform policy frameworks. Clearly then, the inter-relationship between literacy and knowledge needs to be concretised and theorised in relation to specific conditions that exist within particular societies – and the diverse uses of literacy within different societies. In positioning literacy within the context of societal relations, analysis would draw on sociological concepts and theories to explain the complex interactions in which literacy meanings are shaped – as well as what their concrete effects are on the lives of people. In terms of the latter, analyses of societal literacy levels should therefore also include a consideration of sociocultural factors such as ethnicity, languages, religious-cultural practices, gender and social position. Transferred to practice, this means that within culturally and linguistically plural societies, issues of national language policy have to be considered in analysis of societal literacy levels.

It also means that literacy levels need to be discussed in relation to the role of women in society as is highlighted in the work of Rockhill (1987) and Stromquist (1990). These studies identify the fact that the social position of women and their differential levels of access to particular forms of literacy – or, literacy per se need to be addressed in relation to the social relations that inhere in particular religious-cultural practices within different societies. In relation to this, the emphasis in the UNESCO discourse currently on the need for higher literacy rates amongst women needs to be examined with regard to the particular value attached to the role of women in different societies.

Literacy defined in terms of 'individual empowerment' and 'social transformation' – and literacy defined as a 'fundamental human right' can only really be understood within the context of specific cultural formations and the diverse and complex power relations that traverse the social terrain. This incorporates political processes including models of governance and social policy (see Table 1.2). Ultimately, literacy policy and provision arise within the organisation of particular social systems and forms of governance as well as economic, social and political priorities identified within the context of the state. Related to this are issues that revolve around, for example:

- migration and the language rights of asylum seekers and refugees;
- routes of access to participation in the democratic process;
- fiscal policy as this affects approaches adopted to public expenditure – and thus funding for educational and/or language provision;
- social change related to technological developments;
- the linguistic and cultural rights of settled minority groups;
- the role and influence of external funding bodies.

Alongside these variables are issues that revolve around exclusion, subjugation and control exercised over particular forms of literacy – and the struggles and possibilities for transformation that these inequalities generate within the context of everyday life. Again, these multifaceted and inter-locking variables highlight the fact that because literacy is rooted in both the social and material world, discussions of societal literacy levels cannot be reduced to the level of discourse alone. To do so would be to present only a partial view of literacy as a dynamic social practice.

Literacy and technology issues

This is particularly important in the current period of technological change and rapid social transformation. Indeed, the organic links between microelectronics, and, especially, information technology and economic, social and political processes raise important questions regarding the conceptualisation of literacy as a social practice. The gains made in terms of time and space, facilitated by the new technologies, have resulted not only in the fact that the world is rapidly becoming smaller because of mass communication practices, but in the emergence of multifaceted networks of unequal social relations on a global scale. The new 'flexible accumulation' made possible by 'flexible' technologies enable not only speedier capital transfer to take place across the world but also contribute to new forms of control emerging within the restructured workplace. New realities are in the process of being constructed with the evolution of ever-newer, more adaptable and faster technologies. Thus, literacy defined as a social practice has also to address the effects of the uses of the new technologies on the social experience of people in their everyday social roles – as well as their quality of life as workers. This includes not only skills and knowledge requirements but also a consideration of the relationship between levels of technological literacy and broader social factors such as unemployment, intermittent on sporadic employment such as 'yearly work-time' and seasonal work – in addition to the variables of gender, race, their position as workers in the workplace as well as their everyday experiences as workers.

In definitional terms then, other than the necessary technical skills and knowledges required to function on an everyday basis, we need to move towards a re-conceptualisation of, inter alia, how we interpret the world, think on our lived realities and analyse the essence of power and control inherent in the technologies themselves – and the social processes through which they operate.

Literacy as an ideological practice

Literacy defined as an *ideological practice* needs to address the multiple meanings ascribed to literacy by different interest groups. First, this refers not only to the views of literacy legitimated in policy discourse, but also those articulated within other defining sites such as funding bodies, social institutions and political interest groups within society. For instance, UNESCO's current concerns with the breakdown of moral values in society and its growing emphasis on the role of education in inculcating 'those principles which are conducive to peace, human rights and democracy that finally must constitute the fabric of the "intellectual and moral solidarity of mankind"' (UNESCO, 1995: 17) signify a clear move towards re-establishing a link between literacy and a moral economy. This, in turn, has to be seen in juxtaposition with the overall emphasis within the UNESCO framework, at least since the 1970s, on the principles of technological modernisation. It also includes a consideration of the mechanisms of control of information or censorship and the subjugation of local and critical literacies. Examples here can be taken from the particular forms of censorship that prevailed in pre-revolutionary Iran in the Shah's modernisation programme during the 1970s (see Street, 1984; Rassool, 1995). Within that context at the time, whilst the mass literacy programme launched by the Shah sought to increase literacy rates amongst the peasants, different forms of censorship affected those who could read and write. According to Kamrava (1992: 138–9), in Iran at that time: '[p]eople were encouraged to read and write the alphabet, but reading and trying to understand books that were suspected of being threatening to the state was punishable by long sentences'. Oppositional literature, film, novels and essays were banned and the literati came under state surveillance by the notorious secret police, the SAVAK (Rassool, 1995).

Elsewhere, in Eastern Europe, Bulgaria pursued the same model of literacy that prevailed in the UNESCO framework; that is, literacy as a central part of societal modernisation, despite the fact that it was grounded in a different ideological framework. Yet alongside this process of rapid modernisation, the rights of ethnic Turkic and Roma people to become literate in their own languages were systematically repressed under the Zhivkov regime's policy of 'Bulgarisation' (Rassool & Honour, 1996). Again, what is highlighted here, first, is the overall ideological 'package' in which literacy is inscribed into state policy and practices – and the specific purposes that dominant forms of literacy served within these contexts within a specific time-frame – and as part of a specific hegemonic project of the state to assimilate minority cultural groups.

Second, the case of pre- and post-revolutionary Iran illustrates the point made earlier that literacy meanings are contingent; that they are subject to change within different sociohistorical frameworks – as well as in relation to the emergence of new technologies within the social terrain. Analysis thus has to draw on social history as well as the political economy of literacy programmes. Third, account has to be taken of the fact that literacy is also a signifier of cultural, social and individual aspirations – some of which may conflict with one another – as is the case for women in post-revolutionary Iran, and the empowering meanings inscribed into the revolutionary Nicaraguan literacy programme. [...]

Literacy and technology issues

Fourth, the impact of the new technologies on the reconstruction of our social reality requires a re-conceptualisation of the literacy process. Apple (1987: 171), for example, argues that the new technologies are not only 'an assemblage of machines and their accompanying software', they also have potent symbolic power. Embedded within the communications industry, the new technologies make possible the construction of – and, relatedly, they have the capacity to sustain 'second order universes that increasingly are our experience of the cultural and social world' (Hall, 1989: 43). Applied to literacy, this refers to the reality that we live today in a world dominated by the television advert defining our consumer needs, wants and desires; computer games in homes, shops, pubs and amusement arcades; and video equipment in family homes having access to video libraries providing boundless popular entertainment. Alongside this is the power of communication contained in the almost unlimited textual interaction possibilities provided by the Internet as well as the multiple realities that inhere in CD-ROM facilities. Computers form part of the taken-for-granted values, beliefs, material aspirations and expectations that we have of our everyday lives and thus they have been incorporated as hegemonic cultural capital. That is to say, technology has become an unquestioned, taken-for-granted 'must have' in order to function in everyday life.

In real terms then, we have already moved beyond a one-dimensional view of text within our experience of everyday life. Indeed, because of the organic links between the new technology, the state and other power processes such as corporate business and the microelectronics industry, the concept of literacy today transcends written and other representational texts such as visual art, television, information technologies and photography to include also the social and political contexts in which communication practices are grounded. In other words, to be a literate citizen in the age of high technology means to be able to read not only the word and image, but as is argued by Freire and Macedo (1987), also the world in its fullest sense.

Literacy as a cultural practice

As a *cultural practice*, literacy has to be theorised in a conceptual-analytic framework that makes it possible to consider the subordinating meanings, values and beliefs that inhere not only in dominant discourse but also in traditional cultural practices. This refers to the maintenance of gender and political power elites legitimated in religious-cultural beliefs and practices, through which access to literacy can be controlled to exclude women and minority groups from acquiring particular forms of literacy. Dominant literacy practices also serve to subjugate local cultural literacies. The current rise of religious fundamentalism in countries such as Algeria, Egypt, Turkey and Afghanistan has implications for the range and types of literacy that would be made available to women within these societies.

In a more general sense, literacy as a cultural practice also refers to the relative importance attached to particular types and forms of literacy within the culture. These comprise not only religious-cultural literacies, but also the range of social literacies required within everyday life including the workplace and leisure. Collectively, these influence the literacy knowledges that people would aspire to have in order to survive and become 'useful' citizens. Analyses should therefore also include the ways in which cultural meanings are produced and reproduced within and through literacy practices.

Literacy as an educational practice

As an *educational practice,* literacy has to be theorised in terms of definitions and models including pedagogy, assessment and measurement. Moreover, literacy as an educational practice cannot, reasonably, be conceptualised outside a theory of knowledge, or the function that it will serve in terms of the multifaceted purposes in people's everyday lives within society. As has already been suggested earlier, this extends beyond a direct link between literacy and the functional skills and knowledges required within the workplace to include also social and political purposes.

Scribner (1984: 8), emphasising the fact that literacy is a 'many-meaninged thing', tries to overcome this difficulty by identifying three metaphors, namely, 'literacy as adaptation, literacy as power, and literacy as a state of grace' around which to articulate the multiple and multifaceted meanings that surround literacy for the individual. *Literacy as adaptation* involves the skills needed to function in a 'range of settings and customary activities' such as jobs, training and benefits and civic and political responsibilities. In this sense, she argues, literacy as adaptation is pragmatic and involves a range of competencies which should be broad enough to encompass new systems of literacy as is represented here in the new technologies. In this regard, account needs to be taken of the fact that literacy needs will not be the same for everyone; they may increase for some and reduce for others. *Literacy as power* is articulated around the 'relationship between literacy and community advancement' (Scribner, 1984: 11) and highlights the association between illiteracy and disempowerment grounded in the Freirean view of literacy. Scribner advocates mobilisation for literacy around local needs and small-scale activism. *Literacy as a state of grace* is defined in terms of the liberal tradition of intellectual, aesthetic and spiritual enhancement. Not all uses of literacy have a practical end. All these views of literacy, she argues, are inter-related and have validity for educational planning. Thus, although there are obvious boundaries between these metaphors, they are not inflexible.

Another integrated view of what literacy is, pertinent to the discussion here, can be derived from the range of discourses described by the Russian literary theorist Mikhail Bakhtin. According to Bakhtin, discourse is not a fixed communication; it is intertextual (Todorov, 1984: x). That is to say, it exists in a dialogical relationship with previous discourses on the same subject; meanings are transferred from one discourse to another within a particular social context. Emphasising language and communication thus in relation to the social world, he argues that 'language is not an abstract system of normative forms but a concrete heterological opinion on the world' (quoted in Todorov, 1984: 56). In other words, it is constituted in a diversity of languages and a diversity of voices. Thus, both plurality and difference are intrinsic to discourse.

Bakhtin identifies a typology of socially located discourses essential to functioning in everyday life:

> (1) the communication of production [in the factory, shop etc.]; (2) the communication of business [in offices, in social organisation etc.]; (3) familiar communication [encounters and conversations in the street, cafeteria, at home etc.]; [(4) artistic communication (in novels, paintings etc.]; and finally (5) ideological communication in the precise sense of the term: propaganda, school, science, philosophy, in all their varieties. (Bakhtin, quoted in Todorov [1984: 57], information in brackets added)

To this we can add communication of the classroom defined in terms of learning processes. Literacy located within this framework of socially based communication practices becomes linked with discursive sets of interaction in which a diversity of social and individual meanings are negotiated within the social terrain. What does this mean for education? I argue throughout the book that, first, in definitional terms, it would include a range of subject-registers in order to function within a variety of contexts – extending beyond those identified earlier in the OECD survey. Second, it also includes levels of access to adequate literacy provision which revolves around different forms of knowledge, cultural traditions, beliefs and values, resources and integrated teaching approaches as well as freedom of access to different forms of information. [...]

Third, with regard to pedagogy, it includes a consideration of goal-directed learning and the specification of criterion-referenced learning outcomes. [...] [L]iteracy for citizenship within a democratic framework is intrinsically bound up with access to different knowledges as well as with concepts of individual empowerment and social progress. Fourth, literacy, defined in terms of its role in facilitating social transformation, needs to extend to the democratisation of sociopolitical structures and processes. This, implicitly, includes a contextualisation of literacy within models of governance, the nature of decision-making and the possibilities that they provide for bottom-up influences on policy frameworks. Collectively, these factors impact on the range and levels of literacies that can be made available to different groups of people within society – and, relatedly, influence the assessment and measurement of literacy levels in terms of the range of competencies required to function within society. Thus, literacy as an educational practice is integrally linked with literacy defined as social and ideological practices.

Conclusion

Using these categories as guiding principles, literacy theorised within the regionalised field suggested here draws on all the major subject-disciplines without confining itself to the parameters of knowledge inscribed into them. Within this flexible and integrated framework constituted in a dynamic interchange of concepts, criteria and registers, literacy can be analysed and theorised in relation to both individual and broader contextual issues. These refer to social and individual development in relation to complex political, cultural, educational and ideological processes and practices. [...]

References

Apple, M.W. (1982) *Education and Power.* London: Routledge.

Apple, M.W. (1986) National reports and the construction of inequality. *British Journal of Sociology of Education* 7 (2), 171–190.

Apple, M.W. (1987) Mandating computers: The impact of the new technology on the labour process, students and teachers. In S. Walker and L. Barton (eds) *Changing Policies and Changing Teachers.* Milton Keynes: Open University Press.

Apple, M.W. (1993) *Official Knowledge: Democratic Education in a Conservative Age.* London: Routledge.

Auerbach, E. (1992) Literacy and ideology. *Annual Review of Applied linguistics* 12, 71–85.

Ball, S.J. (1990) *Politics and Policy Making in Education: Explorations in Policy Sociology.* London: Routledge.

Barton, D. (1994) *Literacy: An Introduction to the Ecology of Written Language.* Oxford: Blackwell.

Barton, D. and Hamilton, M. (1998) *Local Literacies: Reading and Writing in One Community.* London: Routledge.

Barton, D. and Ivanic, R. (1991) *Writing in the Community.* London: Sage.

Barton, D. and Padmore, S. (1991) Roles, networks and values in everyday writing. In D. Barton and R. Ivanic (eds) *Writing in the Community.* London: Sage.

Bernstein, B. (1990) *Class, Codes and Control, Vol. IV: The Structuring of Pedagogic Discourse.* London: Routledge.

Brice Heath, S. (1983) *Ways with Words.* Cambridge: Cambridge University Press.

Britton, J. (1975) *Language and Learning.* Harmondsworth, Middlesex: Penguin Books.

Bryant, P. (1994) Reading research update. *Child Education* (Oct.), 13–19.

Canale, M. and Swain, M. (1980) Theoretical bases of communicative approaches to second language teaching and testing. *Applied Linguistics* 1, 1–47.

Cole, M. and Scribner. S. (1981) *The Psychology of Literacy.* Boston, MA: Harvard University Press.

De Castell, S., Luke, A. and Luke, C. (1989) *Language, Authority and Criticism: Readings on the School Textbook.* Lewes: The Falmer Press.

Edwards, J. (1997) The social psychology of reading. In V. Edwards and D. Corson (eds) *Encyclopedia of Language and Education, Volume 2: Literacy* (pp. 119–26). Amsterdam: Kluwer.

Fairclough, N. (ed.) (1992) *Critical Language Awareness.* London: Longman.

Foucault, M. (1970) The order of discourse. Inaugural Lecture at the College de France, given 2 December, 1970. In R. Young (ed.) *Untying the Text: A Post-Structuralist Reader* (pp. 48–78). London: Routledge & Kegan Paul (1987).

Foucault M. (1980) *Power/Knowledge: Selected Interviews and Other Writings 1972–1977.* (Colin Gordon, Leo Marshall, John Mepham, Kate Soper, trans.) Brighton: The Harvester Press.

Freire, P. and Macedo, D. (1987) *Literacy: Reading the Word and the World.* London: Routledge and Kegan Paul.

Gee, J.P. (1996) *Social Linguistics and Literacies: Ideology in Discourses* (2nd edn). London: Taylor & Francis.

Giroux, H.A. (1993) *Border Crossings: Cultural Workers and the Politics of Education.* London and New York: Routledge.

Giroux, H.A. and Macedo, D. (1987) *Literacy: Reading the Word and the World.* London: Routledge and Kegan Paul.

Goodman, K. (1986) *What's Whole in Whole Language?* London: Scholastic.

Goody, J. (ed.) (1968) *Literacy in Traditional Societies.* Cambridge: Cambridge University Press.

Goody, J. and Watt, I. (1968) The consequences of literacy. In J. Goody (ed.) *Literacy in Traditional Societies* (pp. 27–68). Cambridge: Cambridge University Press.

Goswami, U. and Bryant, P. (1990) *Phonological Skills and Learning to Read.* London: Lawrence Erlbaum.

Gough, P.B. (1995) The New Literacy: caveat emptor. *Journal of Research in Reading* 18 (2), 79–86.

Graff, H.J. (1979) *The Literacy Myth: Literacy and Social Structure in Nineteenth Century Canada.* New York and London: Academic Press.

Graff, H.J. (1987) *The Labyrinths of Literacy: Reflections on Literacy Past and Present.* London: The Falmer Press.

Hall, S. (1989) Ideology and communication theory. In B. Dervin, L. Grossberg, B.J. O'Keefe and E. Wartella (eds) *Rethinking Communication, Vol. I: Paradigm Issues* (pp. 40–52). Newbury Park, CA: Sage.

Halliday, M.A.K. (1996) Literacy and linguistics: a functional perspective. In R. Hasan and G. Williams (eds) *Literacy in Society* (pp. 339–76). London and New York: Longman.

Hasan, R. (1996) Literacy, everyday talk and society. In R. Hasan and G. Williams (eds) *Literacy in Society* (pp. 377–424). London and New York: Longman.

Hildyard, A. and Olson, D. (1978) Literacy and the specialisation of language. Unpublished MS, Ontario Institute for Studies in Education.

Hymes, D. (1973) On communicative competence. In J.B. Pride and J. Holmes (eds) *Sociolinguistics.* Harmondsworth: Penguin.

Kamrava, M. (1992) *Revolutionary Politics.* New York: Praeger.

Kress, G., Leite-Garcia, R. and van Leeuwen, T. (1997) Discourse semiotics. In T. van Dijk (ed.) *Discourse as Structure and Process* (pp. 257–91). London: Sage.

Labov, W. (1972) *Language in the Inner City: Studies in Black English Vernacular.* Philadelphia: Philadelphia Press.

Luke, A. (1996) Genres of power? Literacy education and the production of capital. In R. Hasan and G. Williams (eds) *Literacy in Society.* London and New York: Longman.

Luria, A. (1979) The making of mind. In M. Cole (ed.) *Soviet Developmental Psychology.* Boston, MA: Harvard University Press.

Mackay, D., Thompson, B. and Schaub, P. (1978) *Breakthrough to Literacy: The Theory and Practice of Teaching Initial Reading and Writing.* London: Longman for the Schools Council.

McLaren, P. (1995) *Critical Pedagogy and Predatory Culture: Oppositional Politics in a Postmodern Era.* London: Routledge.

New London Group (NLG) (1996) A pedagogy of multiliteracies: designing social futures. *Harvard Educational Review* 66 (1), 60–92.

Oakhill, J. and Beard, R. (1995) Guest editorial. *Journal of Research in Reading* 18 (2), 69–73

Ong, W. (1982) *Orality and Literacy: The Technologizing of the Word.* London: Routledge.

Perfetti, C.A. (1995) Cognitive research can inform reading education. *Journal of Research in Reading* 18 (2), 106–15.

Phillipson, R. and Skutnabb-Kangas, T. (1995) Language rights in postcolonial Africa. In T. Skutnabb-Kangas and R. Phillipson (eds) *Linguistic Human Rights: Overcoming Linguistic Discrimination* (pp. 335–46). Berlin: Mouton de Gruyter.

Rassool, N. (1995) Language, cultural pluralism and the silencing of minority discourses in England and Wales. *Journal of Education Policy* 10 (3), 287–302.

Rassool, N. and Honour, L. (1996) Cultural pluralism and the struggle for democracy in post-communist Bulgaria. *Education Today* 46 (2), 12–23.

Rockhill, K. (1987) Gender, language and the politics of literacy. *British Journal of Sociology of Education* 8 (2), 153–67.

Scollon, R. and Scollon, S.B. (1981) *Narrative, Literacy, and Face in Interethnic Communication.* Norwood, NJ: Ablex.

Scribner, S. (1984) Literacy in three metaphors. *American Journal of Education* (Nov.), 6–21.

Scribner, S. and Cole, M. (1988) Unpackaging literacy. In N. Mercer (ed.) *Language and Literacy from an Educational Perspective Vol. I: Language Studies* (pp. 241–55). Milton Keynes: Open University Press.

Smith, F. (1971) *Understanding Reading: A Psycholinguistic Analysis of Reading and Learning to Read.* London: Holt, Rinehart & Winston.

Smith, F. (1979) *Reading.* Cambridge: Cambridge University Press.

Stanovich, K.B. and Stanovich, P.J. (1995) How research might inform the debate about early reading acquisition. *Journal of Research in Reading* 18 (2), 87–105.

Stanovich, K.E. (1986) Mathew effects in reading: some consequences of individual differences in the acquisition of literacy. *Reading Research Quarterly* (Fall), 360–406.

Street, B.V. (1984) *Literacy in Theory and Practice.* Cambridge: Cambridge University Press.

Street, B.V. (ed.) (1993) Introduction. *Cross-cultural Approaches to Literacy* (pp. 1–21) Cambridge: Cambridge University Press.

Stromquist, N.P. (1990) Women and illiteracy: the interplay of gender subordination and poverty. *Comparative Education Review* 34 (1), 95–111.

Stubbs, M. (1980) *Language and Literacy: The Sociolinguistics of Reading and Writing.* London: Routledge.

Todorov, T. (1984) *Mikhail Bakhtin: The Dialogical Principle.* (Wlad Godzich, trans.). Manchester: Manchester University Press.

UNESCO (1995) *World Education Report.* Paris: UNESCO.

Van Leeuwen, T. and Humphrey, S. (1996) On learning to look through a geographer's eyes. In R. Hasan and G. Williams (eds) *Literacy in Society* (pp. 29–49). London and New York: Longman.

Veel, R. and Coffin, C. (1996) Literacy learning across the curriculum: towards a model of register for secondary school teachers. In R. Hasan and G. Williams (eds) *Literacy in Society* (pp. 191–231). London and New York: Longman.

Verhoeven, L. (1994) Modeling and promoting functional literacy. In L. Verhoeven (ed.) *Functional Literacy: Theoretical Issues and Educational Implications* (pp. 3–34). Amsterdam: John Benjamins.

Vygotsky, L.S. (1962) *Thought and Language: Studies in Communication.* Cambridge, MA: Massachusetts Institute of Technology; Wiley.

Weaver, C. (1990) *Understanding Whole Language: From Principles to Practice.* Portsmouth, NH: Heinemann.

Wells, G. (1986) *The Meaning Makers.* London: Hodder & Stoughton.

Wilkinson, A. (ed.) (1965) *Spoken English.* With contributions by A. Davies and D. Atkinson. Educational Review Occasional Publications, No. 2, University of Birmingham.

Williams, R. (1961) *The Long Revolution.* Harmondsworth: Penguin Books in association with Chatto & Windus.

2

Globalisation, Literacy and Society: Redesigning Pedagogy and Assessment

David Johnson and Gunther Kress

[...]

Introduction

Globalisation is placing new demands on the kinds of 'literacies' we need in the workplace as much as in the communicational demands of everyday life. Globalisation is frequently thought about in economic terms alone, but there is equally a cultural globalisation which is no less, maybe even more potent in its shaping of the ways in which we communicate and represent meaning. In any case, the two go hand in hand. As different societies are increasingly multilinguistic and culturally diverse, new technologies and new media, such as the so-called 'new screens', make multilingualism a fact not just of local geography – a matter of my street and of the local school – but a fact of ordinary experience in the so-called virtual reality of the screen. British school-children surfing the internet to get materials for their next assignment seem as happy to go to a French site as to an English language one. Thus, in addition to the effects that globalisation has on the organisation of the workplace, the global economy and the discourses associated with these (Gee,1994), it is also producing new social situations at the local and community level – the level of the school – and therefore creating new demands on textual forms of all kinds, whether as genres or in their discursive form, or as we contend here, in forms of the increasing variety of modes of representation which are in use. Globalisation, we argue, prompts us to raise serious questions about what literacy is, how it is best developed within the curriculum and outside it, and how it is assessed. [...]

New economies, literacy and assessment

Amongst the most visible effects of globalisation is the structural reorganisation of big business and industry that has been termed variously, 'post-Fordism' (Piore & Sable, 1984) or 'fast capitalism' (Gee, 1994). The old 'Fordist' organisation of labour was divided so that some

From: *Assessment in Education*, 10 (1), 2003, pp. 5–14.

people planned and designed things while others worked on atomised tasks. In the 'new economy', flatter hierarchies are more common and larger numbers of the workforce take more responsibility for a bigger part of the production process including designing, producing and marketing. Such structural change has resulted in accompanying cultural changes to the practices, ethos, values and discourses of the world of business, but more importantly, it has also propelled to the fore discussions about new kinds of knowledge and new kinds of literacies, required for the new economy.

To answer the question, what kinds of knowledge are required for the twenty-first century, we need to understand the qualitative shifts in the means people use to represent meaning. There is undoubtedly a massive shift towards electronic communication, in the world of work, as well as in our private and public worlds. This is visible in the way people send in email messages to BBC Television during the morning news to comment on various topics, from news of domestic interests, for example whether Britain should accept more refugees, or a clip from the soap opera they watched the night before, to something of interest globally, such as the war against Iraq.

In the world of big business, electronic communication is intricately implicated in globalisation. The instantaneous flow of capital around the globe would not be possible without it and arguably, this would have a weighty effect on many societies. Demands on the education system in one locality, let us say in South Wales, are shaped in a profound fashion by the impact of South Korean capital, with its forms of management and its demands on the (local) labour force. From the perspective of representation, the literacy curriculum is affected in various ways. The demands of the economy, of course, have their impact, but there are also two divergent effects of electronic communication independent to some degree from the direct effects of the economy. Communicationally speaking, electronic communication obliterates both time and distance, and with that it unmakes some of the linguistic forms which had been developed as a response to both. Email and its 'informality', manifesting itself in what seem more 'speech-like' forms, is the example frequently cited. But another effect is the facility afforded by the 'new media' for the easy production and use of a multiplicity of modes of representation – sound, image, writing, moving image, speech – in the message-entities that populate the screen. The screen is now the culturally dominant medium in many parts of the world, and for many members of numerous societies around the globe. This is in no way to gloss over continuing and often even deepening facts of economic inequality, which makes access to the new media of electronic communication simply impossible for hundreds of millions of people around the globe. But those who are excluded from this form of participation are no less affected by all the forces of globalisation and its technologies than are those who participate in a variety of different ways.

In the ordinary world of those who inhabit our schools, the effects of globalisation are experienced as the normal co-presence of the most diverse forms of representation in many languages – whether as the wide variety of genres of film, of cartoon, of traditional written text, or whether as discourses of all kinds, as the modes of image, of music, of speech, of writing. It is a world where Hollywood and Bollywood mingle 'naturally'.

Schools find themselves at the confluence between the traditional and conventional approaches to meaning-making (Johnson et al., 2003) and assessment is the domain where all these pressures come home to roost. At the moment, too often new givens are met by recourse to old practices. New demands are countered by old certainties. In this context, we argue that in the rapidly changing global context in which the world of work, as much as our social and private world, is being re-configured, we need to re-think the nature of knowledge, of the school curriculum and pedagogy, and in particular we need to focus on the forms and – the concern of this issue – on the representational modes, the literacy aspects of assessment.

Kalantzis, Cope and Harvey [2003] make the case that knowledge today is highly situated, rapidly changing and more diverse than ever. The successful learner for the demands of today's economies and today's societies needs to be an autonomous, self-directed designer of their own learning experiences who uses multiple modes through which to represent meaning. Such modes include linguistic representation (text, oral presentation, etc.), visual representation (colours, foregrounding, backgrounding, etc.), audio representation (sound effects), spatial representation (perspective) and gesture (New London Group, 1996), and successful learners of a 'new' set of basic skills are those who are able to work at the nexus of these visual, aural, gestural and spatial patterns of meaning-making.

Kalantzis *et al.* [2003] argue that the learner for the new economy and new society is also a learner who uses different sets of tools to make meaning. The image of success most readily associated with the old world of work is of smoke billowing out of chimney stacks at industrial plants. The equivalent image of success at school is probably of the book – the written word. The image of the so-called new economy is of a worker sitting in front of a computer screen – a symbol of the dominance of information and communication technologies. New screen technologies are quickly becoming the dominant medium of communication and it is an important consideration for assessment of literacy, to take account of how these new technologies mediate students' learning.

Thus we argue here that we need to re-define what we mean by literacy, review how it is currently taught and assessed, and in particular, how it itself enters into forms of assessment. If in the science curriculum, the curriculum is largely taught by means of images (Kress & van Leeuwen, 2001; Kress *et al.*, 2001), if language as writing plays a less and less central role, if children do not come into contact with extended written texts as a matter of daily experience, then how can it be that so much assessment is conducted in the mode of writing, which is ceasing to be centrally present in the everyday experience of a student 'doing' science? In brief, in this issue literacy is seen as more than reading and writing and the acquisition of technical competencies and skills, and rather as a set of social practices, forms of knowledge, and variety of resources for representation and communication that enable individuals to participate and function fully in society.

Curriculum, democracy and the politics of assessment

We have argued above that the multilinguistic and multicultural nature of society as much as the culturally and representationally plural world of the screen and the Internet, requires us to think in new and different ways about what literacy is and how it ought to be considered 'successfully mastered'.

At the community level, cultural and linguistic pluralism demand new forms of literacy which allow people to negotiate diversity and difference and maximise these. There is a growing recognition of the need for new and different ways for people to arrive at shared meanings, and the current global discussions about 'war against terrorism' expose how the use of language can fragment and divide communities, even those that occupy the same geographical space. At the same time, it exposes the extent to which culturally diverse communities can be united through a discourse, which contains shared values and common positions.

For most societies, finding ways in which to harness linguistic and cultural difference has become imperative to building citizenship and furthering social justice and democracy. This commitment is reflected in the political rhetoric of many modern societies. We would have thought that such policy rhetoric might transform itself into ways of thinking about language and literacy and ways of acting (pedagogy and assessment). We would have thought that the design of new literacy curricula and literacy pedagogy would reflect a move away from the conception of literacy as a narrow, singular standard, to one which encourages people to learn a range of new discourses and modes of communication to enable them to deal with local diversity and the demands of local cultures. In the words of the New London Group (1996):

> The most important skills students need to learn is to negotiate regional, context; hybrid cross cultural discourses; the code switching often to be found within a text among different languages, dialects, or registers; different visual and iconic meanings; and variations in the gestural relationships among people, language and material objects. Indeed this is the only hope for averting the catastrophic conflicts about identities and spaces that now seem ever ready to flare up. (p. 65)

Ironically, in countries such as Britain, the United States of America, Australia and South Africa, to name but a few, educational policy response to increasing cultural and linguistic diversity has been to narrow the definitions of what constitutes 'legitimate literacy practice' (Meacham, 2002, p. 181). In the United States particularly, the Federal Government is being criticised for allowing dominant political interests to dictate literacy pedagogy and assessment. Meacham (2002) claims that literacy is being conceived of as a structurally singular and exclusively written language practice and that any mention of cultural and linguistic diversity is seen as a threat to 'conceptual coherence'. Anything other than 'strong text' is 'marginal and even detrimental, to effective literacy conception and practice' (p. 181).

For Gee, [2003], a conceptualisation of language or literacy that ignores or explicitly seeks to erase the cultural identities of learners is undemocratic. He argues in an earlier paper (Gee, 1994) that a coherent literacy practice like reading involves a coming together of the 'vernacular' identities cultivated in the homes of children and the language forms encountered in school.

Sadly, even though some educators are doing their best to recruit cultural and linguistic diversity into the way in which literacy is taught, not enough is known about the social contexts in which the literacy practices of children now in school are developed and what their characteristics and potential are (Freebody et al., 1995; Street, 1999). Consequently, literacy pedagogy does not build sufficiently on either linguistic or cultural pluralism. More important, different cultural and representational traditions give rise to different shapes of knowledge, and different ways of 'knowing' and 'making meaning'. To be truly democratic and fair, assessment of literacy needs to take account of this.

In his paper [2003], Gee discusses the issue of democracy in assessment in terms of opportunity to learn. He argues that a fundamental flaw in the way in which learning and assessment is conceptualised is the assumption that children who have had different 'opportunities to learn' are exposed to the same assessment, and that the assessment is unjust. He points to the assessment of reading as one example to argue that we never simply 'read', rather 'we always read something in some way' ([2003], p. 28).

Reading and literacy are embedded in social practice. For some children at least, they are expected to read and master texts that convey the knowledge and traditions of a particular community of practice, with no knowledge of the social practices within which those texts are used. Even where children are able to master the reading test (by answering factual questions), they often learn nothing of the genre or the social practices which are, Gee argues, 'the heart and soul of literacy' ([2003], p. 30). The problem is that assessment is geared to assessing the basics. Assessment of reading continues to emphasise general, factual and dictionary type questions about written texts. Many children who score well on these assessments might know the literal meaning of the text but cannot really read. To ensure that assessment is just, children need to have equivalent experiences with reading specific types of text in specific ways.

[O]ur argument then [is] that literacy first needs to be reconceptualised much more broadly, taking into account the many contexts in which it is in use and developed in our working, public and private lives, and evolving in line with these. This raises the question of redesigning the literacy curriculum which in itself involves asking three questions: what is the form of a literacy curriculum which will be adequate to the demands faced by young people as they move into their social lives? Who is it for, and what is it for? What are its 'contents'? Beyond that is the essential question of a theory of language, of meaning more broadly, and of learning that will go with such a conception of the curriculum. [...]

Our claim [is] that despite years of debate on the nature of the literacy curriculum and ensuing policy directions, it is assessment – its weighting in the political culture and the means of enforcing that culture, which will guide what is taught and how what is taught is taught. Assessment is therefore the key to directing and changing education's forms, its aims and its development (Broadfoot, 2002). This is never more so than in periods when 'performativity' in the sense of meeting targets and achieving standards is so much in the limelight, and supported by heavy sanctions of all kinds. So on the one hand there are the professed aims of moving school-based education in the (now clichéd) directions of change, creativity and innovation, and on the other hand there are the straightjackets of rigorously enforced and narrow criteria of performance.

In this context, forms of assessment probably have their most serious effects on forms of pedagogy. Assessment is the point of 'delivery' of 'performance' and pedagogy has to become its instrument. The need to 'ratchet up' standards in an environment of heavy sanctions on performance criteria makes any attempts at open, exploratory forms of pedagogy unlikely in the case of able students, and impossible in the case of weaker ones. (Of course the opposite holds equally true.) So in as far as the overt demands at the moment are for dispositions on the part of students towards innovation, assessment practices and forms should be designed to foster pedagogies which are likely to encourage, foster and develop such dispositions.

Emergent theories, new literacies and assessment

The issue then becomes one of elaborating our views of the mid-term futures of society in which people will need particular kinds of resources and dispositions in order to function fully.

If we are successful in arguing for a reconfiguration of the literacy curriculum, this has implications for assessment. The challenge then is for performance-based assessment to extend its conception of what is at issue. If curricular content is now communicated in specific forms, then assessment practices need to follow what curriculum does. Given that multimodal forms of representation exist in all curriculum subjects, leading to their specific configurations of knowledge, then the repertoire of techniques of assessment needs to include multimodal forms, including the recognition of gestural, visual and iconic modes (New London Group, 1996). An essential prerequisite and requirement will be that the shapers of the school curriculum subjects pose as serious and searching questions what the purposes of each curriculum subject are, how these purposes are realised as curriculum content, and how they are represented and communicated.

We would want to argue for a curriculum and forms of pedagogy that foster in a non-trivial way dispositions towards ease with difference, with change, creativity and inno-vation. This will be a curriculum that moves, beyond (mere) competence towards facility with design (Kress, 2000). Pedagogies of conformity, joined with curricula which do not engage with the representational world in its existing form cannot hope to foster innova-tion, creativity, ease with change. A conservative curriculum asks for conformity, and the competent performance of stable skills. By contrast, the rhetoric of politicians and the real-ity of present and developing demands require the competencies and dispositions to proj-ect the interests of individuals in their social worlds into designs that can realise those interests in social environments of diverse kinds.

What are the contents of such a curriculum? In many ways, they are entirely traditional, that is, they would encompass understanding of the resources of alphabetic writing, of speech, alongside the visual, and equally clear and well articulated sense of the potentials of all the resources in use. Included in this would be the understanding of how each mode – forms or technologies other than writing – deal with the world in their specific ways. Here understanding means a full awareness of the affordances – the potentials and limitations – of alphabetic writing, of image, of moving image, of action and movement, the aim usually articulated as 'critical literacy'. The contents of such a curriculum would place text-as-social process and entity as the central category from which other categories derive their sense, use and function in the text. A text-centred literacy curriculum would need – text being a socially produced entity – to include a strong sense of the interrelation of the social and the represen-tational. But above all, it would be a curriculum in which not only alphabetic writing but all the modes of representation are seen as resources which are constantly reshaped and trans-formed by those who use them in accord with their interests in the power-laden social envi-ronments in which they act. [...]

We hope that we have made our intention and aim clear in this [chapter]. Our central concern [...] is to think about what a 'new' literacy curriculum should look like, and how literacy should be taught and assessed in all sites in the curriculum. In considering the 'stuff' of literacy, we think that it is broader than reading and writing. While stressing the inescapable reality of the multimodal (and multimedial) communicational landscape – and we are insistent on the urgent need for the school to pay full attention to that fact – we urge at the same time an even greater seriousness of attention to the teaching of writing. Far from suggesting that we need no longer pay attention to these forms of literacy, we feel strongly that writing will remain the preferred form of the cultural and political élites, so that an equitable curriculum must pay the greatest attention to writing for the reason of 'access' alone. What we do argue is that in the new literacy curriculum, full and serious attention be given to all the modes which play their part in the representation and communication of the school curriculum overall.

If we seem to focus much more on curriculum, it does not mean that we are not aware of the equal significance of pedagogy. We see pedagogy as the instantiation of forms of social relations in the classroom (in a Bernsteinian sense). We could not possibly be content simply to provide children with technical skills. There is no possibility of fostering dispositions towards innovativeness and creativity – that is, of freedom in the domain of representation, of semiosis – in the environment of an authoritarian pedagogy. We recognise that children come to school as meaning-makers, and see it as the future task of the school to foster, enhance and value that disposition.

But our main focus here remains assessment. And in designing a new literacy curriculum, one cannot avoid the central question of assessment because of its effect, and particularly so in the era of narrowly conceived and economically enforced performativity.

References

Broadfoot, P. (2002) Editorial. Beware the consequences of assessment, *Assessment in Education: principles, policy and practice,* 9 (3), pp. 285–288.

Freebody, P., Ludwig, C. & Gunn, S. (1995) *Everyday Literacy Practices In and Out of Schools in Low Socio-economic Urban Communities* (Brisbane, Centre for Literacy in Education Research).

Gee, J.P. (1994) New alignments and old literacies: from fast capitalism to the canon, in: B. Shorthand-Jones, B. Bosich & J. Rivalland (Eds) Conference Paper: 1994 Australian Reading Association, Twentieth National Reading Conference (Carlton South, Australian Reading Association).

Gee, J.P. (2003) Opportunities to learn: language-based perspective on assessment, *Assessment in Education: principles, policy and practice*, 10 (1), pp. 27–46.

Johnson, D., Garrett, R. & Crossley, M. (2003) Global connectedness and local diversity: forging 'new' literacies at the point of confluence, in: G. Claxton, A. Pollard & R. Sutherland (Eds) *Learning and Teaching where Worldviews Meet.* (London, Trentham Books).

Kalantzis, M., Cope, B. & Harvey, A. (2003) Assessing multiliteracies and the new basics, *Assessment in Education: principles, policy and practice*, 10 (1), pp. 15–26.

Kress, G. (2000) Multimodality, in: B. Cope and M. Kalantzis (Eds) *Multiliteracies* (London, Routledge).

Kress, G. and Van Leeuwen, T. (2001) *Multimodal Discourse* (London, Edward Arnold).

Kress, G., Jewitt, C., Ogborn, J. & Tsatsarelis, C. (2001) *Multimodal Teaching and Learning: the rhetorics of the science classroom* (London, Continuum).

Meacham, S. (2002) Literacy at the crossroads: movement, connection, and communication within the research literature on literacy and cultural diversity, *Review of Research in Education,* 25, pp. 181–208.

New London Group (1996) A pedagogy of multiliteracies: designing social futures, *Harvard Educational Review,* 66 (1), pp. 60–92.

Piore, M. and Sable, C. (1984) *The Second Industrial Divide* (New York, Basic Books).

Street, B. (1999) *Multiple Literacies and Multilingual Society.* NALDIC Working Papers (Watford, NALDIC).

3

The Historical Construction of Dyslexia: Implications for Higher Education

Janet Soler

Introduction

It has been recently argued that there is a need for greater understandings of the way in which dyslexia has been historically constructed and embedded in medical and psychological discourses and the way in which this has shaped the conceptualization and diagnosis of learning disabilities (LD) in the USA and specific learning difficulties (SpLD) in the UK (Reid and Valle, 2004). This chapter explores the historical evolution of dyslexia and the debate surrounding LD/SpLD and how this has impacted upon professional and political struggles in relation to definitions, assessment, diagnosis classification and the allocation of funding, particularly in relation to higher educational contexts. This is particularly relevant for areas related to higher education as the need to address disabilities such as dyslexia has become enshrined in legislation in recent decades.

Historically, the professional and 'expert' discourses related to dyslexia can be traced from their roots in medicine and clinical studies in the 1860s to the emergence of broader psychologically and LD based understandings of dyslexia and their use by educationally based professionals in the 1980s. This chapter will examine the socio-historical legacies and influences which can be seen to have affected these understandings of dyslexia and the allocation of resources for individuals considered to be dyslexic.

Professional discourses related to the development of dyslexia as a construct, have drawn upon 'scientific' medically and psychologically based discourses that have in turn impacted upon their implementation in educational policy and practice. The academic field of dyslexia was formulated from pioneering research at the end of the nineteenth century which was grounded in medical approaches arising from early neurologists' investigations of the strange symptoms that were often exhibited by individuals who had survived traumatic head injuries. While in many cases brain disorders led to a loss of speech and the ability to translate words into speech, sometimes these brain-damaged patients might speak and understand English quite well but were unable to read. The latter were able to see and hear letters but they could not make sense of the specific language information contained in the text.

The interest in this field led to similarities being noted between these patients and uninjured school children who were considered to be of 'normal intelligence' in nearly every respect, except that they experienced difficulties in language and literacy skills. This initiated attempts to find the specific brain dysfunctions responsible for dyslexia. The pursuit of this agenda led to dyslexia emerging in the 1980s as a mainly psychologically based field inextricably linked to reading skills and the distribution of reading ability and disability in the school population and the use of the labels LD/SpLD.

While professional discourses surrounding dyslexia are rooted in medicine and clinical studies, there were, however, very early links to the development of mass education and its associated professions. Michael Gerber (2007) points out that the growing influence of dyslexia can be seen to be linked to an ongoing historical trend to promote mass reading and a perceived need for universal and ever higher literacy standards which originated in the institutionalization of mass education in the late 1800s. For example, in Great Britain, the Forster Education Act in 1870 brought mass education to all children, and with the establishment of compulsory schooling, the associated ability to identify and observe and begin to label children who had reading problems.

Recent work in a special 2007 international issue of *Learning Disabilities and Research International,* also highlights the complexities arising from the social construction of dyslexia and the later development of the labels LD and SpLD through their relationship to the social processes and objectives associated with mass schooling and the demands for mass literacy. Gerber argues that this demonstrates that 'learning disability exists – in fact, arises from – an inextricable transaction between characteristics of educational arrangements and characteristics of learners', that has led to 'years of productive science focused on the innate differences between learners', yet despite this and 'decades of policy formulation and reformulation', we have not been able to 'respond appropriately to those differences' (Gerber, 2007: 216).

This chapter draws upon an historical perspective to examine how changing and different understandings of dyslexia have contributed to difficulties in defining, diagnosing and addressing dyslexia. This historical legacy has important implications for the ways dyslexic individuals are identified and constructed in educational policy and associated practices.

The historical construction of dyslexia as a professional discourse

A German, R. Berlin, was the first person to use the term dyslexia, when he used it in 1862 to describe an adult who had lost the ability to read due to a brain lesion. In 1877, the term 'word blindness' which has been commonly used in association with the term dyslexia was used by A. Kussmaul to describe an adult patient who was unable to read due to aphasia. Charcot coined another word, alexia, commonly associated with dyslexia in its earlier periods of development, in 1887, and used it to describe 'a total loss of reading ability'. Bateman also used this word in 1890 to refer to a 'form of verbal amnesia in which the patient has lost the memory of the conventional meaning of graphic symbols' (Critchley, 1964, cited in Guardiola, 2001: 6).

The concepts of 'developmental dyslexia' and 'congenital world blindness' were developed in Great Britain during this period, in a series of articles published in the growing proliferation of academic and professional journals which encouraged academic debate and the publishing and dissemination of current scientific knowledge amongst physicians and ophthalmologists (Guardiola, 2001: 6). A key article in this series of articles was published in 1896, by Pringle-Morgan, a British physician, from Sussex, who published a report on 'congenital word blindness' in the *British Medical Journal*. This article focused on a boy of normal intelligence who had not learnt to read but appeared to be of above average intelligence as he had:

> ... always been a bright intelligent boy, quick at games, and in no way inferior to others of his age. His great difficulty has been – and is now – his inability to learn to read. This inability is so remarkable, and so pronounced, that I have no doubt it is due to some congenital defect ... In spite of ... laborious and persistent training, he can only with difficulty spell out words of one syllable. (Morgan, 1896: 1378, cited in Miles and Miles, 1999: 4)

James Hinshelwood, a Scottish opthalmologist and Glasgow eye surgeon, also published a series of articles which described similar cases of congenital word blindness during the 1890s and early 1900s. His articles emphasised the 'congenital' nature of 'word blindness' as a defect in children who had difficulties in reading, but could be seen to have 'normal' and undamaged brains. Hinshelwood also noted several other factors which were to become commonly associated with dyslexia. He thought the condition was sometimes hereditary and was more common in boys than girls, and was 'quite sure it was a pathological condition which was somehow related to damage to a "visual word-centre"' (Miles and Miles, 1999: 5).

During the 1920s and 1930s, the study of dyslexia mostly shifted from Great Britain to the USA. The American neurologist Samuel Orton's ideas, which were based on a different scientifically based disciplinary background from Hinshelwood, changed currently accepted views on dyslexia. Orton argued that it arose from an abnormality of psychological development rather than a specific area of the brain. He also argued against the use of Hinshelwood's term 'congenital', which, Orton felt, tended to overstress genetic and hereditary factors. However, as is evident in the quote below, Orton's psychologically influenced viewpoint heavily stressed the individualized nature of dyslexia:

> We feel that the use of the term congenital tends to overstress the inherent difficulty and to underemphasize the many environmental factors both specific – such as methods of teaching – and more general – such as emotional and social forces – and we therefore prefer the use of the term developmental to congenital since it may be said to include both the hereditary tendency and the environmental forces which are brought to play on the individual ... There is not word blindness in the ordinary sense of the term, nor indeed is there even blindness for words. (Orton, cited in Miles and Miles, 1999: 8)

Orton's ideas also signalled the replacement of the accepted notion of 'word blindness' with strephosymbolia theory, which means the twisting of symbols. He had noticed the tendency of people he had worked with to change the order in the way in which they recalled letters, and unusual patterns in their 'handedness' and 'eyedness' which he felt could be linked to genetic factors. This theory would be picked up in the 1940s by other researchers who would come to be linked to the Orton Dyslexia Society, which later become the International Dyslexia Society.

Orton, who was more strongly influenced by neuropathy and psychiatry, can be seen as influential in moving the discourse surrounding dyslexia. Prior to Orton, the field was influenced by clinicians focusing on the clinical classification of an isolated group of patients through investigation of biological and genetic factors. Orton's work signalled a move to broader-based psychologically influenced understandings of dyslexia.

After Orton, there was a stronger move to a consideration of environmental factors and their influence on the broader population. The focus which emerged drew upon the effi- cacy of educational methods and an analysis of dyslexics' abilities and disabilities, so that dyslexia came to be seen as a complex phenomenon that could be caused be a number of factors (Miles and Miles, 1999; Guardiola, 2001). While the literacy and language difficul- ties of dyslexics were still seen to be distinctive, there was thought to be too many differ- ences for this group of individuals to have any one label. This resulted in the terms 'word blindness' and 'strephosymbolia' being discarded and dyslexia becoming the commonly adopted term. The broader emphasis which was emerging in relation to dyslexia also linked it much more firmly to ideas of 'normality', and the 'distribution of intelligence' through the work of psychologists in the field in the 1940s and 1960s (Guardiola, 2001).

Javier Guardiola (2001) argues that, from the 1970s onwards, the causes of dyslexia have increasingly become seen as linguistically based rather than visual. Cognitive abilities related to the reading process have also been identified. Dyslexia assessments and teaching pro- grammes are therefore commonly linked to lexical problems and key related areas such as 'orientation, naming or repeating long words, arithmetic difficulties, list of items (forward or reverse), letter reversals etc.' (Guardiola, 2001: 19). While theories related to visual effects have continued in the work of Thomson (1984) and Stein and Fowler (1982), more influen- tial theories have focused upon deficits in phonological and isolated word recognition skills.

The historical construction of dyslexia from the mid-1800s onwards can, therefore, be seen to be closely linked to the fields of medicine and psychology. From the 1860s to the 1960s, it broadened and became much more strongly linked to psychology, and the narra- tives and meaning making surrounding definitions of 'normal' and the individualizing of difference. From the 1970s through the 1980s, it increasingly became underpinned by lin- guistics and forged stronger links to broader psychologically based fields related to educa- tion and neurobiology.

The social construction of learning disabilities

As discussed in the previous section, definitions of dyslexia were originally based upon medical models, and have from the time of Pringle-Morgan included the notion that dyslexia applies to individuals who have difficulties in reading and writing even though they are of 'normal' or 'above normal' intelligence. As dyslexia research moved towards system- atically identifying the differences between normal and 'dyslexic' readers, the definitions moved on to include environmental factors such as 'socio-cultural opportunity' as well as 'adequate intelligence' as shown by the definition reached by consensus at the 1968 Word Federation of Neurology:

> [Dyslexia is] a disorder manifested by difficulty in learning to read despite conventional instruction, adequate intelligence and socio-cultural opportunity. It is dependent upon fundamental cognitive disabilities, which are frequently of constitutional origin. (cited in Snowling, 2000: 15)

This definition fell out of use as it defined by exclusion and clinicians were unable to find objective data to 'diagnose' a person as dyslexic. For example, what is 'conventional instruction' and how much 'intelligence' and 'socio-cultural opportunity' is deemed to be 'adequate'?

Snowling (2000) argues that subsequent definitions of dyslexia have rested on differentiating between 'generally backward readers' and people who have specific reading difficulties. However, in 1996, Stanovich produced findings that questioned the usefulness of this distinction and it became evident that it was not possible to link discrepancies in IQ and reading attainment even if the concept of an Intelligence Quotient was accepted as a given:

> If the only substantial difference between 'dyslexic' or specifically retarded readers and generally backward readers is IQ (the very characteristic that defines the groups) and there is an imperfect correlation between IQ and reading skill in the normal population (Stanovich, 1986, reported that on average this was only 0.31), these findings call into question the usefulness of the distinction. The findings speak neither to the causes of reading difficulties nor to whether poor readers of different IQ require different forms of remediation. Thus there are distinct limitations inherent in the approach that seeks to define dyslexia as a discrepancy between a child's reading attainment and that predicted from their IQ. (Snowling, 2000: 23)

With this in mind, the International Dyslexia Association (IDA) offered a definition in 1994 which noted that dyslexia could be seen as only one kind of learning difficulty and that it often co-occurs with other disorders and that these disorders needed to be treated separately for clinical and theoretical purposes:

> Dyslexia is one of several distinct learning disabilities. It is a specific language-based disorder of constitutional origin characterized by difficulties in single-word decoding, usually reflecting insufficient phonological processing. These difficulties in single-word decoding are often unexpected in relation to age and other cognitive and academic abilities; they are not the result of generalized developmental disability or sensory impairment. Dyslexia is manifest by variable difficulty with different forms of language, often including, in addition to problems in reading, a conspicuous problem with acquiring proficiency in writing and spelling. (Snowling, 2000: 24–5)

This definition also stressed problems with word decoding rather than reading comprehension skills, and differentiated between children who have specific reading difficulties and those who have more global language impairments. However, despite these refinements, this definition of dyslexia also created problems for clinicians and those who wanted to positively assess and identify 'dyslexic' individuals as it was too vague and could not be falsified (Snowling, 2000: 23). By the late 1990s, it was being argued that it was not possible to have a changing and simple definition for dyslexia because dyslexia increasingly became seen as a disorder which operated on a number of levels which linked biological, cognitive, behavioural and environmental factors which can influence the causal pathway which influences the decoding of print (see, for example, Frith, 1997).

In 1999, the British Child Psychology Society of the British Psychological Society produced the definition which is still commonly used and forms the basis of much of LEA policy:

> Dyslexia is evident when accurate and fluent word reading and/or spelling develops very incompletely or with great difficulty.

This focuses on literacy learning at the 'word level' and implies that the problem is severe and persistent despite appropriate learning opportunities. It provides the basis for a staged process of assessment through teaching. (BPS, 1999: 64)

While this definition clarified the existence of dyslexia, it has been argued that there still remain problems regarding the continued existence of other definitions and positions and the way in which dyslexia is commonly perceived in a far less specific way. It also raises questions about how diagnosing dyslexia can be a totally objective process and it does not clearly indicate what the appropriate forms of treatment are (Elliott, 2005). As we shall see in the final section of this [chapter], this has had ramifications for diagnosis and for allocation of resources to meet the legal requirements and obligations to address it as a recognized disability in higher educational institutions.

The learning difficulties orientated definition of dyslexia was to have a lasting social and political impact as definitions of dyslexia became more inextricably linked to the more general LD label in the 1970s (McDermott et al., 2006: 13). A more generic term than dyslexia, LD refers to learning difficulties in a wider range of academic areas including maths and other subject areas. Dyslexia has come in recent decades, as suggested in the definitions above, to be referred to as a specific learning disability in the area of reading and writing.

Attempts to define learning difficulties also reflect the issues highlighted above in relation to definitions of dyslexia, as it has also been used to refer to children who despite appearing to be of normal 'cognitive capacity' had trouble learning in school settings because of assumed neurological functions (Zuriff, 2007). Children who gained the label of LD were thought to have problems with specific psychological processes that were related to academic success rather than lacking in 'intelligence':

Generally speaking, people with learning disabilities are of average or above average intelligence. There often appears to be a gap between the individual's potential and actual achievement. This is why learning disabilities are referred to as 'hidden disabilities': the person looks perfectly 'normal' and seems to be a very bright and intelligent person, yet may be unable to demonstrate the skill level expected from someone of a similar age. (cited on the Learning Disabilities Association of America website, 2008)

This definition implied that children with LDs, including dyslexia, who are deemed to be intelligent rather than intellectually disabled, could be helped by devising programmes and pedagogies that were designed to address these deficient psychological processes.

Recently, there have been a number of papers by authors in the United States which have stressed the historical and culturally negotiated meanings associated with the conceptualization and development of practices associated with the conceptualization and application of the concept of LD. For example, Reid and Valle note that:

… to examine and problematize the 'conventions that structure the meanings assigned to disability and the patterns of response to disability that emanate from, or are attendant upon, those meanings' (Linton, 1988, p. 8) is to reveal the discursive practices that both define people as having LD and determine what happens to them after they are so labelled. (Reid and Valle, 2004: 466)

Reid and Valle's paper draws upon historiography and Foucault's notion of discourse to argue that LDs have been culturally and socially produced through processes associated with their historical development. From this viewpoint, learning disabilities such as dyslexia cannot be seen as natural, solely biologically determined, individualized, personal attributes. Moreover, they argue that the discourses surrounding LD have a 'shifting nature' which can be constructed and reconstructed in relation to the culture within which it is embedded:

> Moreover, the LD discourse is, like all other discourses, a discourse that responds to the shifting nature of the culture in which it is embedded. Disability becomes constructed and reconstructed through the ways in which we speak about it and practice it. (Reid and Valle, 2004: 467)

The legal recognition of dyslexia in higher education: social justice issues

As the LD label in the USA and the SpLD label in the UK became adopted and taken up with national organizations, an associated industry and nationally and internationally based consultancies have emerged to diagnose, assess and treat LD and SpLD in areas such as dyslexia. In further and higher education, the lobbying of dyslexia groups has resulted in funding and policies designed to make 'reasonable' accommodation for students who are seen to have dyslexia. Such 'accommodations' can take a number of forms including computers and reader writers in examinations, and modification of examination standards. However, in the UK as well as in the USA, the increasing legal recognition of learning disabilities and the shifting nature of the discourses surrounding dyslexia has led to public debates over equity issues, the efficacy of the diagnosis of dyslexia and the role of vested interest groups in influencing assessments and distribution of resources.

In England, from 1970 onwards, there has been a series of acts, which have resulted in legal consequences in relation to the diagnosis of dyslexia. The Chronically Sick and Disabled Persons Act, 1970, section 27, was probably the first to refer to 'acute dyslexia'. This was followed by the Department of Education and Science's Tizard Report (1972) on Children with Specific Reading Difficulties which referred to the small group of children with reading and perhaps writing, spelling and number difficulties. The Bullock Report (1975) mentioned dyslexics' problems while the Warnock Report (1978) considered that dyslexic children had special educational needs, which led to a recommendation regarding this in the 1981 Education Act. In 1981, the Department of Education and Science's Tansley and Panckhurst Report advocated the use of the expression 'specific learning difficulties' (Guardiola, 2001: 15).

More recently, in the area of higher education, it was made unlawful for service providers to discriminate against disabled people in The Disability Discrimination Act (DDA) in 1995. While the Act covered areas of the university providing a service, such as public places, catering facilities, sports facilities, shops, etc., education provision was exempt from the requirements of the DDA. In May 2001, The Special Educational Needs and Disability Act was passed through parliament. This Act resulted in higher education establishments being expected to:

... anticipate the needs of students in a proactive way, and to make adjustments and provide support as appropriate. Adjustments and support might include changes to administrative procedure, teaching arrangements, the physical environment, as well as guidance and training for staff. The Act comes into force in stages from September 2002 to 2005, allowing HEIs time to make adjustments. (cited on the University of Sheffield website, 2008)

The Higher Education Funding Council for England (HEFCE) produced base level provision for disabled students in Higher Education Institutions (HEI) in 1999. These recommendations stated the minimum service levels that a HEI should be expected to provide to meet the requirements of disabled students and deal effectively with applications. A *Code of Practice for Assurance of Academic Quality and Standards in Higher Education: Students with Disabilities* was also produced by The Quality Assurance Agency for Higher Education. This outlined ways for universities to provide for students who have disabilities through the development of a framework of 'good practice' around which higher education institutions can base their provision for students with disabilities. In order to distribute funding and resources to 'meet the needs of students in a proactive way', and to demonstrate provision for students who have disabilities such as dyslexia, there has been an increased reliance in England on diagnosis and appeals to the Office of the Independent Adjudicator (OIA) set up by higher education institutions in March 2004 (see, for example, Garner, 2004; Hoare, 2007). This reliance on diagnosis and more specific identification of LD/SpLD dyslexic individuals has in turn raised key issues related to the prioritization of dyslexia over other literacy difficulties, and the 'over-diagnosis' of dyslexia in undergraduate students (see, for example, Davies, 2004; Garner, 2004).

As noted in the previous section, dyslexia has come to be socially and historically constructed as a specific learning difficulty, with the implicit assumption that the learner is of normal intelligence with a particular explanation for a neurological or brain dysfunction which is affecting literacy development. In the USA, this has had far reaching ethical and social justice and financial implications. For example, Zuriff (2007) argues that the student diagnosed as dyslexic and LD is seen to be intelligent and capable in many areas, but failing in areas related to literacy. This definition, however, excludes other students not included in the LD definition. Other students who have academic problems can be diagnosed and labelled as 'slow learners' rather than LD because they are seen to have 'low intelligence' and therefore their low performance is to be expected. These slow learners may not be considered disabled and therefore may not receive the funding and other benefits and access to help that LD diagnosed learners receive.

There are also difficulties associated with the measurement of 'normal' or above average intelligence and/or ability. There is evidence that IQ and other achievement tests can be ethnically and culturally biased which implies that certain groups in the population could be excluded from being diagnosed as dyslexic. If the concept of IQ has been challenged and is seen to measure only a narrow range of intellectual potential, how can we assess who is 'normal and above normal' as opposed to who is not, and where do we draw the line between being intelligent enough and not intelligent enough to confirm a diagnosis of dyslexia given that a diagnosis of dyslexia can have many benefits for a higher education student? There is also the problem that reading problems and language listening skills can depress IQ and achievement scores. This leads us to question how assessments can separate out the specific learning-disabled student from a student who is a 'slow learner' (Zuriff, 2007: 292–4). It also highlights what Zuriff (2007) calls the 'tortuous logic' that underpins LD/dyslexia definitions and the diagnosis of dyslexia.

There are also issues associated with what assessments, including standardized assessments, can reveal about literacy and learning difficulties. For example, the diagnosis of dyslexia is inferred by a process of elimination based on academic work and performance on psychological tests rather than a positive identification of a 'brain dysfunction' and a neurological condition. Standardized tests are commonly utilized to identify 'dyslexic' individuals when it has not been possible to establish a clear definition of dyslexia to underpin these assessment tools. In the USA, so-called slow learners are expected to be poor performers so there is nothing to be explained and no brain dysfunction to be inferred even though we may not know the biological explanation for either the dyslexic or slow learners' literacy difficulties (Zuriff, 2007: 292–4).

In the UK, there has been an increasing emphasis upon the diagnosis and assessment of dyslexia since the passing of The Disability Discrimination Act (DDA) in 1995. A report from the national working party on dyslexia in higher education drew attention to problems associated with resources and support for dyslexic students in UK universities in 1999 (Singleton, 1999). The report stressed the need for guidelines for correct diagnosis and for universities and colleagues to use a consistent test of dyslexia (Goddard, 1999). The demand for the diagnosis of dyslexia in the UK was increased further by the implementation of the May 2001, Special Educational Needs and Disability Act which led to special arrangements and the customization of the exam process for dyslexic students. Over the past decade, the UK media has continued to draw attention to the difficulties of diagnosing dyslexia and the potential for 'over-diagnosis' and the 'boosting of exam results' (see, for example, Garner, 2004).

In 2004, reports appeared in the *Times Higher Education Supplement* that dyslexia had become an issue on university campuses since the introduction of the 1995 Disability Act, because this Act legally required universities not to discriminate against disabled people, including those diagnosed with dyslexia, in admissions or in the services they provide. The report (Garner, 2004: 1) noted that this had created problems because there was 'no agreed definition of dyslexia', and that a very wide range of definitions was being used to diagnose dyslexia, which opened up opportunities for vested interests and local agendas to determine who was being diagnosed as dyslexic.

This situation was seen to result in a 'rising number of cases of students being diagnosed as dyslexic at university and then suing their local authority for not spotting the disability'. Brian Harrison-Jennings, the general secretary of the Association of Educational Psychologists, claimed that universities could be over-diagnosing undergraduates for their 'own gain'. He was quoted as stating that:

> Universities are not centres of altruism. They want to get more students on the roll and more course fees. And the dispensations with dyslexia help them to increase their pass rates in exams. It should not be possible to get dispensations by having a disability diagnosed by someone who is in the pay of an institution. (Garner, 2004: 10)

Claims that students who were seen to be incapable of working at higher education level 'are slipping through the net by claiming to be dyslexic' continued to highlight difficulties with the diagnosis of dyslexia. In September 2004, Ross Cooper wrote an article in the *Times Higher Education Supplement* which outlined his concerns over the proposed use of

IQ tests to diagnose dyslexia. In this article, entitled 'An Idea that Spells Inequality', Cooper warned about the consequences which could arise from the new recommendations being drafted by the Disabled Student Allowance Specific Learning Difficulties Working Group. He felt that these recommendations, which favoured the use of IQ to diagnose dyslexia, could lead to bitter battles because of the contentious nature of IQ testing. Cooper reported that there were continuing debates on who should diagnose dyslexia, with teachers being seen to have more practical training in recognizing dyslexia while educational psychologists were seen to rely on 'psychometric testing' to reach a diagnosis. He also argued that the difficulties associated with diagnosing dyslexia were leading to concerns that students were claiming to be dyslexic to gain access to higher education, when they were not capable of working at this level. Cooper felt that the issues over diagnosis would lead to increased bureaucracy and discrimination against dyslexics from lower socio-economic groups. He therefore called for challenges to the proposed changes to diagnosis on the grounds of the problems they posed for equal opportunities in Higher Educational Institutions (Cooper, 2004)

In September 2005, Julian Elliott's *Dispatches* film on Channel 4 directly attacked the scientific basis of dyslexia. In the *Times Higher Education Supplement*, it was interpreted by Katherine Hewlett who was the project director of AchieveAbility at Westminster University as denying the existence of dyslexia (Hewlett, 2005). Elliott however maintained that he was not arguing that dyslexia did not exist or was not 'real', but rather that he wanted to highlight the way that difficulties in the definition and understandings of dyslexia were leading to difficulties in its utilization rather than question its validity.

> My piece argued that there were so many different understandings and conceptualizations about what dyslexia is, or is not, that the term, as used in professional practice at least, had become almost meaningless. This turned into media headlines incorrectly reporting 'Academic claims that dyslexia doesn't exist'. Of course, the point was much more subtle than this although in talking with journalists, it proved hard to explain the difficulties of dealing with social constructs such as this and persuade them that the Manichean world that they wished to present was an oversimplification ... What I actually have said repeatedly is that there are multiple understandings of dyslexia, and as a result, this has rendered the term meaningless. I guess I'm questioning the utility rather than the validity of the construct as it is popularly conceived. (Shaughnessy, 2005)

In this interview, Elliott argued that he was drawing attention to the difficulties resulting from the lack of consensus and multiple definitions of dyslexia. He also commented on the gap that has emerged between researchers in the field of 'developmental dyslexia' and teachers, educators and the general public. Many commentators and dyslexia action groups, however, interpreted his message as denying the existence of dyslexia (Shaughnessy, 2005).

While Elliott's comments and documentary created a furious reaction amongst dyslexia campaigners (Camber, 2007), other experts, as well as Elliott, have continued to express concerns about the issues surrounding the definition of dyslexia and the 'flourishing industry' which has sprung up around dyslexia assessment in higher education. From 2005 to the end of 2008, newspaper articles have continued to report concerns over policies surrounding the diagnosis of dyslexia and allocation of resources in higher education which have echoed those raised in earlier newspaper reports (see, for example, Bee, 2007; Camber, 2007; Hoare, 2007; Bennett, 2008; Sampson, 2008).

Conclusion

The current issues surrounding dyslexia and its legal recognition in higher education highlight the definitional and diagnostic problems which can be associated with dyslexia's historical origins and its links to medical and psychological discourses. The medical and psychological discourses which are embedded in the socio-historical development of dyslexia tend to reinforce the view of dyslexia as a biologically based disorder, existing independently of historical, political, social and cultural contexts. However, an examination of the historical constructions of meanings associated with dyslexia and LD/SpLD, and the resulting issues associated with its legislative recognition, supports the contention that the efficacy and usefulness of the dyslexia diagnosis is inherently linked to the wider political processes associated with the evolution of education in representative democracies (Artiles, 2003; Reid and Valle, 2004). This is particularly evident in the public debates resulting from the implementation of legislation and resulting pressures to diagnose dyslexia in higher education which has been examined in the section above.

Like Julian Elliott, I am not denying the existence of specific learning difficulties such as dyslexia here. My intention in writing this chapter is to examine how the shaping of our understandings and conceptualizations of dyslexia over the past century are linked to contemporary political issues and debates which have arisen as a result of the recognition of dyslexia in higher education. The examination of recent debates surrounding the definitions, diagnosis and funding access to resources in higher education also draws attention to the way in which the historical narratives and discourses surrounding dyslexia have associated visions and beliefs about how we address and categorize literacy difficulties. From this viewpoint, the linking of the past to the present in order to forge future directions in relation to dyslexia, SpLD and LD must take account of the way the historical construction of literacy difficulties can create equity issues and impact upon aspects of education such as credentialing and access to, and distribution of, educational resources.

References

Artiles, A.J. (2003) Special Education's Changing Identity: Paradoxes and Dilemmas in Views of Culture and Space, *Harvard Educational Review,* 73(2): 164–202.

Bee, P. (2007) A Label to get You Off the Hook?, *The Times,* 28 May, p. 9.

Bennett, C. (2008) Comment: I'd Prefer to have a Doctor who can tell Left from Right: A Medical Student Says she's Discriminated Against because she's Dyslexic. Is it Really the Profession for Her?, *The Observer,* 3 August, p. 35.

BPS (1999) Dyslexia, Literacy and Psychological Assessment: Report by the Working Party of the Division of Educational and Child Psychology of the British Psychological Society. Leicester: BPS.

Camber, R. (2007) Dyslexia 'Is Just a Middle-class Way to Hide Stupidity', 28 May, *Mail Online,* http://www.dailymail.co.uk/news/article-458160/Dvslexia-just-middle-class-way-hide-stupidity.html (accessed 27 November 2008).

Cooper, R. (2004) An Idea that Spells Inequality, *The Times Higher Education Supplement,* 17 September, p. 16.

Critchley, M. (1964) *Developmental Dyslexia.* London: Heinemann.

Davies, C. (2004) Cynicism Won't Help Dyslexics, Letters to the Editor, *The Times Higher Education Supplement,* 17 September, p. 17.

Elliott, J. (2005) The Dyslexia Debate Continues, *The Psychologist,* 18(12): 728–9.

Frith, U. (1986) A Developmental Framework for Developmental Dyslexia, *Annals of Dyslexia, and Dyspraxia*, 36: 69–81.

Frith, U. (1997) Brain, Mind and Behaviour in Dyslexia, in C. Hulme and M. Snowling (eds) *Dyslexia: Biology, Cognition and Intervention*, London: Whurr. pp. 1–19.

Garner, M. (2004) Universities Exaggerate Dyslexia Epidemic for Own Gain, Expert Claims, *The Times Higher Education Supplement*, 10 September, http://www.timeshighereducation.co.uk/story.asp?storyCode=191053& section code=26 (accessed 27 November 2008).

Gerber, M.M. (2007) Globalization, Human Capital, and Learning Disabilities, *Learning Disabilities Research and Practice*, 22(3): 216–17.

Goddard, A. (1999) Report Questions Dyslexic Claims, *The Times Higher Education Supplement*, 19 February, http://www.timeshighereducation.co.uk/story.asp?storyCode=145162&sectioncode=26 (accessed 27 November 2008).

Guardiola, J.G. (2001) The Evolution of Research on Dyslexia, *Annuario de Psicologia,* 32(1): 3–30. English version cited, http://ibgwww.colorado.edu/~gayan/ch1.pdf (accessed 27 November 2008).

Hewlett, K. (2005) Why I Believe that Dyslexia is not a Myth, *The Times Higher Education Supplement*. Opinion, 16 September, p. 16.

Hoare, S. (2007) Education: Turning Points: What to do When Things Go Wrong: The Resolution of Student Complaints Used to be a Hit-and-Miss Process. It's Now a Lot Easier, Thanks to a New Judicial Review, *The Guardian*, 20 February, p. 4.

Learning Disabilities Association of America website (2008) *Learning Disabilities: Signs, Symptoms and Strategies*, http://www.Idaamerica.org/aboutId/parents/Id_basics/Id.asp (accessed 27 November 2008).

McDermott, R., Goldman, S. and Varenne, H. (2006) The Cultural Work of Learning Disabilities, *Educational Researcher,* 35(6): 12–17.

Miles, T.R. and Miles, E. (1999) *Dyslexia a Hundred Years On* (2nd edn). Buckingham: Open University Press.

Morgan, W.P. (1896) A Case Study of Congenital Word Blindness, *British Medical Journal,* 2: 1378.

Reid, D.K. and Valle, J.W. (2004) The Discursive Practice of Learning Disability: Implications for Instruction and Parent-School Relations, *Journal of Learning Disabilities,* 37(6): 466–81.

Sampson, G. (2008) British Graduates' Problems are Home-grown, Letters to the Editor, *The Daily Telegraph*, 2 January, p. 21.

Shaugnessy, M. (2005) An Interview with Julian Elliott: About 'Dyslexia', *EdNews*, 12 September, http://www.ednews.org/articles/431/1/An-lnterview-with-Julian-Elliott-About-quotDyslexiaquot/Page1.html (accessed 27 November 2008).

Singleton, C.H. (Chair) (1999) Dyslexia in Higher Education: Policy, Provision and Practice. Report of the National Working Party on Dyslexia in Higher Education. Hull: University of Hull on behalf of the Higher Education Funding Councils of England and Scotland.

Snowling, M.J. (2000) *Dyslexia*. Oxford: Blackwell.

Stanovich, K.E. (1986) Matthew Effects in Reading: Some Consequences of Individual Differences in the Acquisition of Literacy, *Reading Research Quarterly,* 21(4): 360–407.

Stein, J. and Fowler, S. (1982) Diagnosis of Dyslexia by Means of a New Indicator of Eye Dominance, *British Journal of Opthalmology*, 66(5): 69–73.

Thomson, M.E. (1984) *Developmental Dyslexia*. Baltimore, MD: Edward Arnold.

University of Sheffield website (2008) http://www.shef.ac.uk/disability/extrain/2_legislation.html (accessed 27 November 2008).

Zuriff, G.E. (2007) The Myths of Learning Disabilities, in R. Curren (ed.), *Philosophy of Education*. Oxford: Blackwell. pp. 291–7.

Part 2

Issues and Concepts in Public Reading Debates

4

Literacy as a Complex Activity: Deconstructing the Simple View of Reading

Morag Stuart, Rhona Stainthorp and Maggie Snowling

[...]

Remit and recommendations of the Rose Review

The Rose Review (DfES, 2006) into the teaching of early reading was commissioned by the government in 2005, following publication of the House of Commons Education and Skills Select Committee report on the teaching of reading. The remit given for the review required Rose to consider and report on five aspects, including: 'What best practice should be expected in the teaching of early reading and phonics' and 'How this relates to the development of the birth to five framework and the development and renewal of the National Literacy Strategy *Framework for Teaching*'. Throughout the review, the emphasis is on beginner readers, as might be expected, given that the remit of the review was to consider 'the teaching of early reading'. The recommendation from the review which is of particular relevance to the present [chapter] is that:

> The searchlights model should be reconstructed to take full account of word recognition and language comprehension as distinct processes related one to the other.

In recommending reconstruction of the Searchlights model, the review drew attention to some of the problems inherent in this model, notably that 'the searchlights model does not best reflect how a beginner reader progresses to become a skilled reader'. It also drew attention to the fact that there are at least four sources of evidence of the validity of the conceptual framework of a theory known as 'The Simple View of Reading' (Gough and Tunmer, 1986; Hoover and Gough, 1990), which the review recommended as the reconstruction of the Searchlights model. These are that (1) different factors predict word reading from those that predict comprehension (Muter et al., 2004; Oakhill et al., 2003); (2) there are children who have word recognition[1] difficulties in the absence of language comprehension difficulties (Catts et al., 2006; Spooner et al., 2004); (3) there are children who have language comprehension difficulties in the absence of word recognition difficulties (Bishop and Adams, 1990;

From: *Literacy*, 42 (2), 2008, pp. 59–66.

Grigorenko et al., 2003; Nation, 2005; Snowling and Frith, 1986; Stothard and Hulme, 1992); and (4) there are differences between the effects of context that operate at word and at text levels (Paul and Kellas, 2004); children with poor word recognition skills rely more on context to decipher words (Briggs et al., 1984; Perfetti et al., 1979; Pring and Snowling, 1986; Schwantes, 1985, 1991; Stanovich et al., 1981); whereas children with fluent word recognition skills use context to construct a coherent mental representation of the text (Baker and Brown, 1984; Stanovich and Cunningham, 1991).

Adoption of the Simple View of Reading as the new conceptual framework within which the teaching of reading is to be situated has evidently caused some disquiet in some quarters, as witnessed by the current Call for Papers, which claims the Simple View signifies 'a regression to an age before the work of Shirley Brice Heath, Ann Bussis and Ted Chittenden et al., Marie Clay, Emilia Ferreiro and Ana Teberosky, Usha Goswami, Eve Gregory, Kenneth and Yetta Goodman, Margaret Meek, Judith Solsken and many others who had shown what a complex process becoming literate actually is'.

We agree entirely that becoming literate is complex: many processes are involved in becoming literate, and the same sets of processes are not necessarily involved in becoming a reader as are involved in becoming a writer. In what follows, we limit ourselves (as do both the Searchlights model and the Simple View of Reading) to a consideration of what reading involves, and how reading develops.

From Searchlights to the Simple View

The Searchlights model is derived from proposals advanced in Clay and Cazden (1990), that strategic use of multiple sources of information is necessary in order to derive understanding from written texts. Clay and Cazden write that all readers:

> need to use, and check against each other, four sources of information: semantic (text meaning), syntactic (sentence structure), visual (graphemes, orthography, format and layout) and phonological (the sounds of oral language) (Clay and Cazden, 1990, pp. 206–207).

The Searchlights model formalised these proposals in the diagram portrayed in Figure 4.1. In this model, the 'semantic' information source was depicted as 'knowledge of context', the 'syntactic' information source as 'grammatical knowledge', the 'visual' information source as 'word recognition and graphic knowledge' and the 'phonological' information source as 'phonics (sounds and spelling)'.

These proposals and their formulation in the Searchlights model make clear that a range of different types of knowledge are used in reading, and that these different types of knowledge all need to be acquired if children are to develop into skilled readers. However, in attempting to account for the complexity of reading as it develops over time within a single diagram, the Searchlights model introduced a serious confound between word reading and text comprehension, because word reading is a prerequisite for text comprehension. Thus, although phonics and word recognition (as depicted in the vertical dimension of Figure 4.1) impact on reading comprehension, their influence is mediated through the ability to read the words on the page. Similarly, semantic context and grammatical knowledge (as depicted in the horizontal dimension of Figure 4.1) contribute to reading the words on the page, but their major influence is on understanding the text (Nation and Norbury, 2005).

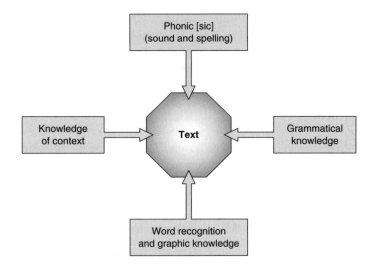

Figure 4.1   The Searchlights model

The substantive issue that we wish to consider here is how the Searchlights model relates to the Simple View of Reading. That is, where within the Simple View of Reading might we find the four information sources conceptualised in the NLS Framework for Teaching (DfEE, 1998) as four searchlights, and what is their role in reading and its development? In other words, how does reading happen, and how is the development of reading differently conceptualised in the Searchlights model and the Simple View?

A good starting point from which to consider how reading happens is to imagine a written text, and a reader who wishes to understand what is written in that text. First and foremost, the reader must decipher the words on the page in order to begin to gain access to the meanings contained within the text. To illustrate the non-contentious nature of this statement, imagine that your pre-school years had been spent in China, where you learned to speak but not to read Chinese. Faced with a page of Chinese characters, you would have no way to begin to understand the meanings presented on that page:

刻舟求剑

楚国有个人乘船渡江。剑从船上掉进水里了。这个人便急忙在船边刻下一个记
号，说：“这是我的剑掉下去的地方。”然后就悠闲地等着船靠岸。船靠岸停下来以
后，他就从刻记号的地方跳进水里去找剑，可是再也没有找到剑。[2]

– although, if someone read the text aloud to you, your knowledge of spoken Chinese would allow you to understand the story.

Similarly, pre-reading children brought up to speak English in the United Kingdom cannot begin to access for themselves the meanings presented in English printed texts until they learn to decipher the printed words that convey those meanings. So the starting point for reading is printed word recognition and this will be true irrespective of the language you are learning. Children need to acquire two sets of processes in order to become proficient readers who can link the orthographic forms of words to their meanings and pronunciations (Coltheart et al., 2001; Plaut et al., 1996). The first process is one of sight word recognition, the other is a phonically based decoding process. Once the reader can decode printed words using a combination of these two processes, their meanings are activated in the language system. The language system contains all the stored knowledge about language so far acquired (e.g., the meanings of words, and the ways in which words can be combined to form meaningful clauses and sentences). The language system, with its stored vocabulary and syntactic and semantic structures, is within the mind and thus able to draw on memory and real-world knowledge to interpret what is heard in oral communication and what is read in written communication.

It follows that in every act of reading, once word meanings are activated in the language system, semantic and syntactic processes (combined with the reader's relevant real-world background knowledge) allow the reader to start to determine the literal meaning of the sentences and to build a mental representation of the situation described in the text. Oakhill and Garnham (1988) give the example of a very simple text:

> Jane was invited to Jack's birthday party. She wondered if he would like a kite. She went to her room and shook her piggy bank. It made no sound. (Oakhill and Garnham, 1988, pp. 21–22)

The application of background knowledge about birthdays is essential to make the inferences necessary to link the first two sentences and create a coherent mental representation: if you do not know that it is expected that those invited to a birthday party will bring a present for the person whose birthday it is, then why on earth should Jane be wondering if Jack would like a kite? Background knowledge about piggy banks is necessary to link and understand the next two sentences. Cultural influences are inevitably brought to bear in understanding written texts, and they are implicit in the Simple View of Reading.

Access to the language system confers another benefit. Within this system, word meanings are stored in associative networks. This means that words within the language system whose meanings are associated with meanings of words read in the text also receive some activation within the language system. This is the origin of context effects: words with associated meanings are read more quickly because their meanings are already partially activated in the reader's mind. There is an important distinction to be drawn here between this automatic contextual speeding of word reading, and deliberate use of context to aid in deciphering unfamiliar printed forms of words. Contextual facilitation is not necessary for the skilled reader to decipher the printed word – skilled readers can do that using the fluent and automatic word recognition processes they have at their disposal. Words are simply read faster in context than out of context, and this has been amply demonstrated in priming[3] experiments over many years (see, e.g., Hutchison, 2003; Masson, 1995; McRae and Boisvert, 1998; Shelton and Martin, 1992; Smith and Besner, 2001). However, beginner readers who rely on deliberate use of context to predict what the next word might be would be unable to read words necessitating such deliberate prediction if they were presented out of context. This is why the Simple View of Reading assigns the major influence of context to its role in understanding written text: successful readers do not need to use context to read words. It is also one of the reasons underlying the decision to replace the Searchlights model with the Simple View of Reading: diligently encouraging beginner readers to use the 'four cueing' system misleads these beginners into thinking that predicting what a word might be (educated guessing) is of equal value to deciphering the words on the page either by accessing sight vocabulary or through the process of applying phonic rules. It is clearly not; sight word recognition and phonic decoding must take precedence to ensure reading fluency,

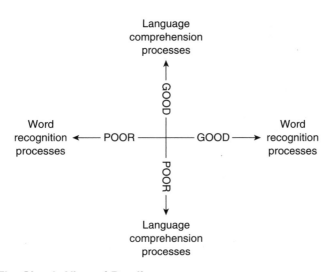

Figure 4.2   The Simple View of Reading

the first step to successful text comprehension. Encouraging prediction from context is leading the beginner up a blind alley, as skilled readers do not need to employ the strategy of deliberately predicting from context.

Importantly, it has also been proposed (Share, 1995) that successful beginner readers rapidly start to develop a 'self-teaching' system, whereby the application of phonic rules to decipher unfamiliar printed words results in storage of those unfamiliar items in sight vocabulary (Bowey and Muller, 2005; Cunningham et al., 2002; Nation et al., 2007; Share, 1999, 2004). In turn, a knock-on effect of this is that as the store of words that can be immediately recognised on sight expands, so it becomes a database from which children can infer previously unknown phonic rules (Stuart et al., 1999; Thompson et al., 1999). Thus, the word recognition system becomes self-sustaining: the child no longer needs to be taught how to decipher the words on the page. This is what the Rose Review means by stating that development of word reading skills is time limited. It also clearly entails that for children to continue to develop as readers, they need to continue to develop and perfect their ability to understand written texts in a variety of genres and topic areas. Again, no loss here of any previously recognised insights into literacy.

Arguably, therefore, it is possible to reassign the four 'searchlights' to just two dimensions of reading: word recognition processes (comprising sight word and phonic decoding processes), and language comprehension processes (comprising spoken vocabulary, semantic and syntactic processes). Each of the processes within these two dimensions operate in text comprehension and there is convincing evidence that different factors underlie performance on each of these two dimensions. Phonological processing best predicts word recognition whereas language comprehension processes are underpinned by lexical knowledge (vocabulary), semantics and syntactic processes. To emphasise, both word recognition and language comprehension are essential at all levels of reading skill, but they are not one and the same. Moreover, children can have relatively well-developed skills in one dimension, combined with relatively poorly developed skills in the other. The interdependence of the two dimensions and the possibility of differential ability in each is portrayed by presenting the two dimensions in the form of a cross, as in Figure 4.2 which shows the Simple View of Reading. Rotating this figure by 90° aligns each dimension with the relevant 'searchlights' from the Searchlights model.

We hope to have made clear that all elements of the Searchlights model are also represented in the Simple View of Reading. The Simple View is preferable because it better accommodates research evidence as to the nature and operation of cognitive and linguistic processes in reading, the processes which it aims to depict. By limiting itself to cognitive and linguistic processes, it does not deny that reading development takes place within a socio-cultural background, which can be different for different learners. Nor does it deny the importance of educational input, which also can be different for different learners. It simply portrays, in stark skeletal form, the essential elements of reading which have to be developed whatever the socio-cultural and educational context within which a particular learner is situated, if that learner is to become a fluent and skilled reader. It does not imply that beginner readers should first be taught to read the words on the page and should only be encouraged to turn their attention to understanding what they read once they are fluent in deciphering written words. If that were its implication then the two dimensions would be portrayed as succeeding each other in linear fashion. Presentation in the form of a cross is intended to indicate the complete interdependence of the two dimensions in skilled reading and at all the points on the way from beginner reader to skilled reader. Nor does the Simple View imply that word recognition skills are all that need to be taught; that once children can read and understand words, comprehension will automatically follow. The time-limited nature of the development of word recognition skills and the increasing contribution of language factors to reading performance over time (Catts et al., 2005; Gough et al., 1996; Leach et al., 2003) make clear that children's ability to understand written texts in a variety of genres and topic areas develops more slowly than their word recognition skills and is never completed. It develops more slowly because of its dependence on the continuing development of language comprehension. It can never be completed, because of its dependence on the continuing acquisition, storage and organisation of real-world knowledge. The Simple View is therefore embedded within the socio-cultural milieu that characterises readers' lives.

How might adoption of the Simple View of Reading serve to further improve the teaching of reading? The Simple View clearly delineates word recognition and language comprehension as two components of reading, and thus encourages us to analyse the development of each in detail. So, what do we know about how children develop word reading skills, and how children develop their ability to understand texts?

Developing word recognition skills

All recent theories of the development of word reading skills in alphabetic orthographies propose that children must at some point begin to use a decoding strategy, which is based on the relationship between graphemes and phonemes. This is best described in Ehri's theory (e.g., Ehri, 1992, 1995), which proposes four phases[4] in the development of accurate fast word reading skills: pre-alphabetic, partial alphabetic, full alphabetic and consolidated alphabetic.

Pre-alphabetic phase

Children characterised as being in the pre-alphabetic phase might recognise some printed words, but have not yet realised that there are systematic relationships between the print and the sounds of the words that are represented by the 'squiggles on the page'. Their word reading is therefore entirely dependent on visual memory. Experimental evidence indicates that children in this phase can make only arbitrary and unsystematic links between printed words and their meanings. For example, Gough et al. (1992) conducted a word learning experiment in which a thumbprint deliberately placed on one of the word cards acted subsequently as the cue by which the word was recognised. Thus, the visual cues used may not be letters, and sometimes, where the child might appear to be using letters as cues, these are not in fact treated as letters by the child. For example, Seymour and Elder (1986) describe a child who read the word 'ball' as 'yellow', and commented 'it's "yellow", because it's got two sticks'. She had remembered the word 'yellow' presumably by forming a connection between the two sticks and the word's meaning. On seeing the word 'ball', she identified two sticks and so concluded the word was 'yellow'.

Though Ehri (1992, 1995), Frith (1985), Gough (1993), Marsh et al. (1981) and Seymour and Elder (1986) have all provided evidence that some children begin to try to recognise words using this pre-alphabetic strategy, Stuart and Coltheart (1988), Wimmer and Hummer (1990) and Jackson and Coltheart (2001, p. 97) suggest that this is not a necessary phase in learning to read words. For these authors, use of visual cues is simply a default strategy used by children who do not have the necessary knowledge and understanding of the alphabetic principle that enables development of more productive and systematic word reading processes.

Partial alphabetic phase

Children whose reading is characterised as being partial alphabetic are able to identify initial and final phonemes in spoken words and are beginning to show some ability to use their knowledge of letter–sound correspondences to decipher printed words. This typically results in the formation of systematic connections between letters and those phonemes which the child can identify in the words's pronunciation. Because children do not as yet have full alphabetic knowledge and mature decoding skills, their attempts are not perfect, but they are no longer arbitrary. They make informed approximations. Stuart and Coltheart (1988) showed that being able to use the first and last letters to make a constrained attempt at the word was indicative of the five- or six-year-old child who was about to take off in reading. One reason why this might be so is that the ability to link some of the graphemes with some of the phonemes in words facilitates the development of sight vocabulary (Ehri, 1992; Rack et al., 1994; Savage et al., 2001; Stuart et al., 2000; Wright and Ehri, 2007). However, although these attempts at working out the word are not arbitrary, they are unlikely to yield fast, accurate word reading: there are simply too many words at each letter length that have the same beginnings and ends for this to support accurate word reading.

Full alphabetic phase

In the full alphabetic phase, children are characterised as being able to use a complete decoding strategy for analysing new words. The letters are mapped sequentially onto sounds, resulting in a sequence of sounds that can be blended into a word. When a new word that they are attempting has a regular spelling pattern (e.g., 'saf', 'boat'), they successfully come up with the correct pronunciation. However, words which do not obey the phonic rules the child knows will be 'regularised'.[5] This means that if they do not know 'swan', they are likely to read it to rhyme with 'ran' (Coltheart and Leahy, 1992; Sprenger-Charolles et al., 2003). Here we can see how this account of the development of word reading articulates with adult models: during these second and third phases, children are establishing sight vocabulary and phonic decoding processes. Note that development of both sets of processes depends on phoneme awareness, and knowledge of grapheme–phoneme correspondences. The research evidence presented above, combined with evidence of the benefits of early systematic structured phonics teaching (National Reading Panel report, NICHHD, 2000), has informed the additional emphasis on the importance of teaching phoneme awareness and phonics to children at the start of reading tuition in the renewed National Strategy for Literacy.

Consolidated alphabetic phase

The more children read, the greater exposure to print they get, so they become more skilled in the use of their decoding strategy to form the links between the letters and the pronunciations, with the caveat that they need to have the complete range of knowledge of grapheme–phoneme correspondences. Thus, this final consolidated alphabetic phase of word reading development is characterised by an ability to decode unknown words on the basis of multi-letter units. When children have reached this point, they have become successful word readers and just need to continue to read as much as possible so that their word reading becomes fast and fluent as well as accurate. The more they read, the larger their sight vocabulary becomes, so word reading per se is no longer a limiting factor and comprehension then drives the system.

Developing comprehension

It is interesting that children who experience difficulty in understanding written texts also, as predicted by the Simple View, experience listening comprehension difficulties (Nation et al., 2004). Indeed, Gernsbacher et al. (1990) showed that adults with comprehension difficulties were unable to build adequate representations of meaning for narratives whether these were presented in spoken or written language, or pictorially, which also is in keeping with the Simple View, that a single language system underlies both reading and listening comprehension. Although there are clearly some differences in the task demands of reading and listening comprehension, a review by Catts et al. (2005) found that, typically, word recognition skills and listening comprehension scores accounted for between 65% and 85% of the variance in reading comprehension scores. Moreover, there are increasingly large correlations between the two measures as children progress through the education system (Gough et al., 1996).

The Simple View of Reading overtly acknowledges what research studies suggest to be true: the foundations of word recognition processes and of text comprehension processes are different. It is therefore imperative to develop children's language comprehension abilities before and alongside the development of their word recognition skills. There is good evidence that reading to children in certain interactive ways (e.g., using dialogic reading) facilitates vocabulary development (see, e.g., Cunningham, 2005; Elley, 1989; Hargrave and

Senechal, 2000) and the development of narrative skills (see, e.g., Allor and McCathren, 2003; Heath, 1983; Jordan et al., 2000; Paris and Paris, 2007; Whitehurst et al., 1988). The ways in which parents and caregivers talk with and to children also significantly affect children's language development in terms of vocabulary, syntax and semantics (see, e.g., de Rivera et al., 2005; Dockrell et al., 2006; Rice and Wilcox, 1995; Wasik and Bond, 2001; Wasik et al., 2006). Vocabulary is one of the most consistent predictors of reading comprehension: children with good vocabularies understand texts better, and the predictive relationship between vocabulary and reading comprehension increases through the primary grades (Snow, 2002; Torgesen et al., 1997), However, children can fail to understand texts even when vocabulary knowledge is controlled for (Cain et al., 2004; Erlich and Rémond, 1997): language processes beyond the lexical level are clearly involved in text comprehension.

Recent research comparing children who are skilled or less skilled comprehenders shows differences between the two groups in listening comprehension, lexical semantics, morphology and syntax (Nation et al., 2004). Skilled comprehenders also do better than less skilled when asked to reassemble scrambled sentences, a further indication that their syntactic and semantic abilities are better developed (Nation and Snowling, 2000). Skilled comprehenders are better able to integrate information from different parts of a text (Markman, 1979), and thus better able to monitor their own comprehension (Hacker, 1997). They are better able to draw inferences necessary to constructing an accurate mental model of the situation described in a text (Cain and Oakhill, 1999).

We would like to finish by suggesting that insight into the nature of the difficulties experienced by children who find it hard to understand what they read is essential to developing teaching methods designed to overcome these difficulties. The Simple View of Reading provides a clear conceptual framework within which teachers can organise their thoughts. Teaching word reading skills is relatively easy and, when children are given insight into the alphabetic principle (which they inevitably gain through systematic phonics teaching) and encouraged to use their phonic knowledge to decode unfamiliar words, most children acquire word reading skills very rapidly. Enabling children to understand what they read across a variety of different topics and genres is much more difficult and requires much more in-depth knowledge of processes involved in language comprehension if teachers charged with this important task are to be better able to accomplish it. It is important now to ensure that language development is given the pride of place it requires throughout the foundation, primary and secondary stages of education if we want to ensure that children acquire the reading skills they need to be included in an increasingly complex and technical society.

Acknowledgements

We are grateful to Dr Anna Law Faure, who recently completed her PhD at the Institute of Education, University of London, for her translation from the Chinese.

Notes

1   Throughout this article, the terms 'word reading' and 'word recognition' are used interchangeably to mean the ability to recognise, understand and pronounce written words.

2 In Search of a Sword by the Marking on the Side of the Boat in the State of Chu, a man crossed a river on a boat. While he was crossing it, his sword fell into the river. He quickly made a mark on the side of the boat, saying 'This is where my sword fell into the river'. Then unhurriedly he waited for the boat to reach the bank. When the boat was moored, he jumped into the river from the boat at the spot where he made the mark in search of his sword. He would never find his sword!

3 In priming experiments, participants are asked to read aloud a target word, or to decide whether it is a real word or not, as quickly as they can. When target words are preceded by semantically related words (primes – which are presented so briefly that participants have no awareness of having seen them), the target word is typically read or decided about faster than when no semantically related prime is presented.

4 The word 'phase' is chosen carefully in preference to 'stage' because there is no suggestion that a child reads all words in exactly the same way; instead there is a gradual acquisition of more advanced skills. Process through phases depends on cultural constraints of the timing and provision of literacy instruction and on individual differences in cognitive ability; the phases children pass through to read words are influenced both by the teaching they receive and by the level of cognitive development they have attained. In addition, as the Simple View shows, the level of reading performance is determined both by the word reading skills and by the level of language competence that has been acquired.

5 This over-regularisation can only happen in non-transparent orthographies like English.

References

Allor, J.H. and McCathren, R.B. (2003) Developing emergent literacy skills through storybook reading. *Intervention in School and Clinic,* 39, pp. 72–79.

Baker, L. and Brown, A.L. (1984) 'Metocognitive skills in reading', in P. D. Pearson (Ed.) *Handbook of Reading Research.* New York: Longman, pp. 353–394.

Bishop, D.V.M. and Adams, C. (1990) A prospective study of the relationship between specific language impairment, phonological disorders, and reading retardation. *Journal of Child Psychology and Psychiatry*, 31, pp. 1027–1050.

Bowey, J.A. and Muller, D. (2005) Phonological recoding and rapid orthographic learning in third-graders' silent reading: a critical test of the self-teaching hypothesis. *Journal of Experimental Child Psychology,* 92, pp. 203–219.

Briggs, P., Austin, S. and Underwood, G. (1984) The effects of semantic context on good and poor readers: a test of Stanovich's interactive-compensatory model. *Reading Research Quarterly,* 20, pp. 54–61.

Cain, K. and Oakhill, J.V. (1999) Inference making and its relation to comprehension failure. *Reading and Writing,* 11, pp. 489–503.

Cain, K., Oakhill, J.V. and Lemmon, K. (2004) Individual differences in the inference of word meanings from context: the influence of reading comprehension, vocabulary knowledge and memory capacity. *Journal of Educational Psychology,* 96, pp. 671–681.

Catts , H.W., Adlof, A.M. and Weismer, S.E. (2006) Language deficits in poor readers: a case for the Simple View of Reading. *Journal of Speech, Hearing and Language Disorders,* 49, pp. 278–293.

Catts, H.W., Hogan, T. P. and Adlof, S.M. (2005) 'Developmental changes in reading and reading disabilities', in H.W. Catts and A.G. Kamhi (Eds.) *The Connections between Language and Reading Disabilities.* Mahwah, NJ: Lawrence Erlbaum Associates, pp. 25–40.

Clay, M.M. and Cazden, C.B. (1990) 'A Vygotskian interpretation of reading recovery', in L. Moll (Ed.) *Vygotsky and Education.* New York: Cambridge University Press, pp. 206–222.

Coltheart, M., Rastle, K., Perry, C., Langdon, R. and Ziegler, J.C. (2001) DRC: a dual route cascaded model of visual word recognition and reading aloud. *Psychological Review,* 108, pp. 204–256.

Coltheart, V. and Leahy, J. (1992) Childrens and adults reading of nonwords – effects of regularity and consistency. *Journal of Experimental Psychology – Learning, Memory and Cognition*, 18, pp. 718–729.

Cunningham, A.E. (2005) 'Vocabulary growth through independent reading and reading aloud to children', in E.H. Hiebert and M.L. Kamil (Eds.) *Teaching and Learning Vocabulary: Bringing Research to Practice*. Mahwah, NJ: Lawrence Erlbaum Associates, pp. 45–68.

Cunningham, A.E., Perry, K.E., Stanovich, K. and Share, D.L. (2002) Orthographic learning during reading: examining the role of self-teaching. *Journal of Experimental Child Psychology*, 32, pp. 185–199.

De Rivera, C., Girolametto, L., Greenberg, J. and Weitzman, E. (2005) Children's responses to educators' questions in day care play groups. *American Journal of Speech and Language Pathology*, 14, pp. 14–26.

Department for Education and Employment (DfEE) (1998) *The National Literacy Strategy: A Framework for Teaching*. London: HMSO.

Department for Education and Skills (DfES) (2006) *Independent Review of the Teaching of Early Reading*. Nottingham: DfES Publications. http.www.teachernet.gov.uk / publications.

Dockrell, L.J., Stuart, M. and King, D. (2006) 'Implementing effective oral language interventions in preschool settings: no simple solutions', in J. Clegg and J. Ginsbourg (Eds.) *Language and Social Disadvantage: Theory into Practice*. Hoboken, NJ: John Wiley and Sons, pp. 177–187.

Ehri, I.C. (1992) 'Reconceptualising the development of sight word reading and its relationship to recoding', in P.B. Gough, L.C. Ehri and R. Treiman (Eds.) *Reading Acquisition*. Hillsdale, NJ: Erlbaum, pp. 107–143.

Ehri, L.C. (1995) Phases of development in learning to read words by sight. *Journal of Research in Reading*, 18, pp. 116–125.

Elley, W.B. (1989) Vocabulary acquisition from listening to stories. *Reading Research Quarterly*, 24, pp. 174–187.

Erlich, M. F. and Rémond, M. (1997) Skilled and less skilled comprehenders: French children's processing of anaphoric devices in written texts. *British Journal of Developmental Psychology*, 15, pp. 291–310.

Frith, U. (1985) 'Beneath the surface of developmental dyslexia', in K.E. Patterson, J.C. Marshall and M. Coltheart (Eds.) *Surface Dyslexia: Neuropsychological and Cognitive Studies of Phonological Reading*. London: Erlbaum, pp. 301–330.

Gernsbacher, M.A., Varner, K.R. and Faust, M. (1990) Investigating differences in general comprehension skill. *Journal of Experimental Psychology – Learning, Memory and Cognition*, 16, pp. 430–445.

Gough, P.B. (1993) The beginning of decoding. *Reading and Writing*, 5, pp. 181–192.

Gough, P.B. and Tunmer, W.E. (1986) Decoding, reading and reading disability. *Remedial and Special Education*, 7, pp. 6–10.

Gough, P.B., Hoover, W.A. and Peterson, C.L. (1996) 'Some observations on a simple view of reading', in C. Comoldi and J. Oakhill (Eds.) *Reading Comprehension Difficulties: Processes and Intervention*. Mahwah, NJ: Lawrence Erlbaum Associates, pp. 1–13.

Gough, P.B., Juel, C. and Griffith, P. (1992) 'Reading, spelling and the orthographic cipher', in P.B. Gough, L.C. Ehri and R. Trieman (Eds.) *Reading Acquisition*. Hillsdale, NJ: Erlbaum, pp. 35–48.

Grigorenko, E.L., Klin, A. and Volmar, F. (2003) Annotation: hyperlexia: disability or superability? *Journal of Child Psychology and Psychiatry*, 44, pp. 1079–1091.

Hacker, D.J. (1997) Comprehension monitoring of written discourse across early-to-middle-adolescence. *Reading and Writing*, 9, pp. 207–240.

Hargrave, A.C. and Senechal, M. (2000) A book reading intervention with preschool children who have limited vocabularies: the benefits of regular reading and dialogic reading. *Early Childhood Research Quarterly*, 15, pp. 75–90.

Hoover, W.A. and Gough, P.B. (1990) The simple view of reading. *Reading and Writing*, 2, pp. 127–160.

Heath, S.B. (1983) What no bedtime story means – narrative skills at home and at school. *Language in Society*, 11, pp. 49–76.

Hutchison, K.A. (2003) Is semantic priming due to association strength or feature overlap? A microanalytic review. *Psychonomic Bulletin and Review*, 10, pp. 785–813.

Jackson, N.E. and Coltheart, M. (2001) *Routes to Reading Success and Failure*. New York: Psychology Press.

Jordan, G.E., Snow, C.E. and Porche, M.V. (2000) Project EASE: the effect of a family literacy project on kindergarten students' early literacy skills. *Reading Research Quarterly*, 35, pp. 524–546.

Leach, J.M., Scarborough, H.S. and Rescorla, L. (2003) Late-emerging reading disabilities. *Journal of Educational Psychology*, 95, pp 211–224.

Markman, E.M. (1979) Realizing that you don't understand: elementary school children's awareness of inconsistencies. *Child Development*, 50, pp. 643–655.

Marsh, G., Friedman, M., Welch. V. and Desberg, P. (1981) 'A cognitive-developmental theory of reading acguisition', in G. MacKinoon and T. Waller (Eds.) *Reading Research: Advances in Theory and Practice*. Mahwah, NJ: Erlbaum, pp. 279–300.

Masson, M.E.J. (1995) A distributed memory model of semantic priming. *Journal of Experimental Psychology – Learning, Memory and Cognition*, 21, pp. 3–23.

McRae, K. and Boisvert, S. (1998) Automatic semantic similarity priming. *Journal of Experimental Psychology – Learning, Memory and Cognition*, 24, pp. 558–572.

Muter, V., Hulme, C., Snowling, M.J. and Stevenson, J. (2004) Phonemes, rimes, vocabulary and grammatical skills as foundations of early reading development: evidence from a longitudinal study. *Developmental Psychology*, 40, pp. 665–681.

Nation, K. (2005) 'Children's reading comprehension difficulties', in M. Snowling and C. Hulme (Eds.) *The Science of Reading: A Handbook*. Oxford: Blackwell, pp 248–265.

Nation, K. and Norbury, C.F. (2005) Why reading comprehension fails: insights from developmental disorders. *Topics in Language Disorders*, 25, pp. 21–32.

Nation, K. and Snowling, M.J. (2000) Factors influencing syntactic awareness skills in normal readers and poor comprehenders, *Applied Psycholinguistics*, 21, pp. 229–241.

Nation, K., Angell, P. and Castles, A. (2007) Orthographic learning via self-teaching in children learning to read English: effects of exposure, durability and context. *Journal of Experimental Child Psychology*, 96, pp. 71–84.

Nation, K., Clarke, P., Marshall, C.M. and Durand, M. (2004) Hidden language impairments in children; parallels between poor reading comprehension and specific language impairment? *Journal of Speech, Language and Hearing Research*, 47, pp. 199–211.

National Institute of Child Health and Human Development (NICHHD) (2000) *Report of the National Reading Panel: Teaching Children to Read*, pp. 99–176.

Oakhill, J. and Garnham, A. (1988) *Becoming a Skilled Reader*. Oxford: Blackwell.

Oakhill, J., Cain, K. and Bryant, P.E. (2003) The dissociation of word reading and text comprehension: evidence from component skills. *Language and Cognitive Processes*, 18, pp. 443–468.

Paris, A.H. and Paris, S.G. (2007) Teaching narrative comprehension strategics to first graders. *Cognition and Instruction*, 25, pp. 1–44.

Paul, S.T. and Kellas, G. (2004) A time course view of sentence priming effects. *Journal of Psycholinguistic Research*, 33, pp. 383–405.

Perfetti, C.A., Goldman, S.R. and Hogaboam, T.W. (1979) Reading skill and the identification of words in discourse context. *Memory and Cognition,* 7, pp. 273–282.

Plaut, D.C., McClelland, J.L. Seidenberg, M.S. and Patterson, K.E. (1996) Understanding normal and impaired word reading: computational principles in quasi-regular domains. *Psychological Review*, 103, pp. 765–805.

Pring, L. and Snowling, M. (1986) Developmental changes in word recognition: an information processing account. *Quarterly Journal of Experimental Psychology*, 38A, pp. 395–418.

Rack, J.P., Hulme, C., Snowling, M.J. and Wightman, J. (1994) The role of phonology in young children's learning of sight words: the direct-mapping hypothesis. *Journal of Experimental Child Psychology*, 57, pp. 42–71.

Rice, M. and Wilcox, K.A. (Eds.) (1995) *Building a Language-Focused Curriculum for the Pre-School Classroom, Volume 1: A Foundation for Lifelong Communication*. Baltimore, MD: Paul H. Brookes Publishing Co.

Savage, R., Stuart, M. and Hill, V. (2001) The role of scaffolding errors in reading development: evidence from a longitudinal and a correlational study. *British Journal of Educational Psychology*, 71, pp. 1–13.

Schwantes, E.M. (1985) Expectancy, integration, and interactional processes. Age differences in the nature of words affected by sentence context. *Journal of Experimental Child Psychology*, 39, pp. 212–229.

Schwantes, F.M. (1991) Children's use of semantic and syntactic information for word recognition and determination of sentence meaning. *Journal of Reading Behavior*, 23, pp. 335–350.

Seymour, P.H.K. and Elder, L. (1986) Beginning reading without phonology. *Cognitive Neuropsychology*, 1, pp. 1–36.

Share, D.L. (1995) Phonological recoding and self-teaching: sine qua non of reading acquisition. *Cognition*, 55, pp. 151–218.

Share, D.L. (1999) Phonological recoding and orthographic learning: a direct test of the self-teaching hypothesis. *Journal of Experimental Child Psychology*, 72, pp. 95–129.

Share, D.L. (2004) Orthographic learning at a glance: on the time course and developmental onset of self-teaching. *Journal of Experimental Child Psychology*, 87, pp. 267–298.

Shelton, J.R. and Martin, R.C. (1992) How semantic is automatic semantic priming? *Journal of Experimental Psychology – Learning, Memory and Cognition*, 18, pp. 1191–1210.

Smith, M.C. and Besner, D. (2001) Modulating semantic feedback in visual word recognition. *Psychonomic Bulletin and Review*, 8, pp. 111–117.

Snow, C.E. (2002). *Reading for Understanding: Toward a Research and Developmental Program in Reading Comprehension* (Rand Reading Study Group). http://www.rand.org/publications/MR/MR1465?MR1465.pdf

Snowling, M. and Frith, U. (1986) Comprehension in hyperlexic readers. *Journal of Experimental Child Psychology*, 42, pp. 392–415.

Spooner, A.L.R., Baddeley, A.D. and Gathercole, S.E. (2004) Can reading and comprehension be separated in the Neale Analysis of Reading Ability? *British Journal of Educational Psychology*, 74, pp. 187–204.

Sprenger-Charolles, L., Stegel, L.S., Bechennec, D. and Serniclaes, W. (2003) Development of phonological and orthographic processing in reading aloud, in silent reading, and in spelling: a four-year longitudinal study. *Journal of Experimental Child Psychology*, 84, pp. 194–217.

Stanovich, K.E. and Cunningham, A.E. (1991) 'Reading as constrained reasoning', in S. Sternberg and P. Frensch (Eds.) *Complex Problem Solving: Principles and Mechanisms*. Hillsdale, NJ: Erlbaum, pp. 3–60.

Stanovich, K.E., West, R.F. and Feeman, D.J. (1981) A longitudinal study of sentence context effects in second grade children: tests of an interactive-compensatory model. *Journal of Experimental Child Psychology*, 32, pp. 185–199.

Stothard, S.E. and Hulme, C. (1992) Reading comprehension difficulties in children: the role of language comprehension and working memory skills. *Reading and Writing*, 4, pp. 245–256.

Stuart, M. and Coltheart, M. (1988) Does reading develop in a sequence of stages? *Cognition*, 30, pp. 139–181.

Stuart, M., Masterson, J. and Dixon, M. (2000) Spongelike acquisition of sight vocabulary in beginning readers? *Journal of Research in Reading*, 23, pp. 12–27.

Stuart, M., Masterson, J., Dixon, M. and Quinlan, P. (1999) Inferring sublexical correspondences from sight vocabulary: evidence from 6- and 7-year-olds. *Quarterly Journal of Experimental Psychology*, 52A, pp. 353–366.

Thompson, G.B., Fletcher-Finn, C.M. and Cottrell, D.S. (1999) Learning correspondences between letters and phonemes without explicit instruction. *Applied Psycholinguistics*, 20, pp. 21–50.

Torgesen, J.K., Wagner, R.W., Rashotte, C.A., Burgess, S. and Hecht, S. (1997) Contributions of phonological awareness and rapid automatic naming ability to the growth of word reading skills in second- to fifth-grade chuldren. *Scientific Studies of Reading*, 1, pp. 161–185.

Wasik, B.A. and Bond, M.A. (2001) Beyond the pages of a book: interactive book reading and language development in preschool classrooms. *Journal of Educational Psychology*, 93, pp. 243–250.

Wasik, B.A., Bond, M.A. and Hindman, A. (2006) The effects of a language and literacy intervention on head start children and teachers. *Journal of Educational Psychology*, 98, pp. 63–74.

Whitehurst, G.J., Falco, F.L., Lonigan, C.J., Fischel, J.E., Debaryshe, B.D., Valdezmenchaca, M.C. and Caulfield, M. (1988) Accelerating language development through picture book reading. *Developmental Psychology*, 24, pp. 552–559.

Wimmer, H. and Hummer, P. (1990) How German speaking first graders read and spell: doubts on the importance of the logographic stage. *Applied Psycholinguistics*, 11, pp. 349–368.

Wright, D.M. and Ehri, L.C. (2007) Beginners remember orthography when they learn to read words: the case of doubled letters. *Applied Psycholinguistics*, 28, pp. 115–133.

5

The Irrelevancy – and Danger – of the 'Simple View' of Reading to Meaningful Standards

Victoria Purcell-Gates

Public and political pressure for high-stakes assessments linked to rigorous standards in the United States has unfortunately been accompanied in many arenas by a regressive move to conceptualise the construct to be assessed – reading – in a simplistic manner. This conceptualisation is referred to as the 'Simple View of Reading', and its re-emergence in educational and research circles in the United States is, in my view, disturbing, perplexing, and – ultimately – dangerous. The 'Simple View of Reading' posits that the process of reading involves only two components and that they are additive and linear: (1) decoding and (2) comprehension. This stance is disturbing because it is linked to political moves that appear to be power plays by special interest groups whose special interests do not include marginalised people, but rather those who have long held power and influence. It is perplexing because it represents several giant steps backwards, ignoring research and knowledge that has been accumulated over the past two decades of the ways sociocultural and cognitive factors interact and transact to influence academic success, including reading achievement. It is ultimately dangerous because it is not unlikely that the results of this simplistic view of learning to read, with its current link to high-stakes testing and new standards, will result in the reification – but this time under a 'scientific' mantle – of the academic marginalisation of underachievement of those groups of people who since time immemorial have represented the bottom quartile of achievement in our schools. It could very well lock non-mainstream students ever more solidly into categories of achievement that label them as 'not good enough', 'below average', 'not proficient', or whatever the norm-referenced or criterion-referenced term of choice is.

We need standards

Before I go further, though, let me briefly affirm the need for standards. This argument against a simplistic view of reading is not one against standards – by which I mean criteria or targets against which achievement is to be judged. If we do not have standards for achievement in

From: Fisher, R., Brooks, G. and Lewis, M. (eds) *Raising Standards in Literacy*, pp. 121–32 (London: Routledge Falmer, 2002).

education, we have no compass, no goal, nothing to guide or inform our teaching, nothing to promise our students, no real purpose for the institution of education.

Further, we need standards now because too many of our students appear to have invested valuable life time in the activity of schooling with very little payoff. It appears that, for many of our students, no promise was made or kept by the institutions of education. And with no promise or goal, it stands to reason that no organised effort will be invested in keeping the unmade promise. With rare exceptions, whole groups of students in the United States leave our schools with skills and abilities, and hopes and expectations for a 'good and prosperous' life, significantly lower than other whole groups of children.

We all know who these children are: they are, for the most part, the children of poor, marginalised, lower-class families. The achievement gap between the 'haves' and the 'have-nots' is an old, unwavering, solid fact of education. It has never been closed despite thousands of words of rhetoric paid to it, millions of dollars thrown at it and hundreds of legislative actions taken on its behalf. This virtually straight-line relationship holds across nations, in developed and developing countries across forms of government, across forms of education and teaching methods and across time (Kaestle *et al.,* 1991).

This unconscionable achievement gap is why we need standards – standards that are taken seriously for all children; standards that can guide and shape instruction as required by local contexts; promises that can be made and kept. I offer as an example of such standards those created jointly by the National Council of Teachers of English and the International Reading Association for Reading and Language Arts. The following sample exemplifies their tone and scope: 'Students read a wide range of print and nonprint texts to build an understanding of texts, of themselves, and of the cultures of the United States and the world; to acquire new information; to respond to the needs and demands of society and the workplace; and for personal fulfilment. Among these texts are fiction and nonfiction, classic and contemporary works' (NCTE/IRA, 1996: 27).

However, the nature of many of the state standards that have been imposed in the USA is troubling, as are the ways in which they have been put in place. Unlike the NCTE/IRA standards, state standards are being imposed by politically appointed bodies on schools and, thus, on colleges of education from without in the form of high-stakes achievement tests – the MEAP (Michigan Educational Assessment Program), the TAAS (Texas Assessment of Academic Skills), and so on. The 'high stakes' include promotion to the next grade, graduation from high school, and, in some cases, permission to drive a car!

The new moral panic

While some may argue that high stakes are needed for schools and school attendees to take standards seriously, I am disturbed by factors that have contextualised this new standards/assessment move. One of the more disturbing is the dubious claim that literacy levels are declining. The American public has been convinced, through an effective orchestration of public pronouncement, news releases, talk shows, commentaries, and so on, that a serious literacy crisis exists among the American people – not just children but adults as well! According to this theme, close to one half of the products of state schools do not possess literacy skills sufficient to function in the 'new information society'. Within this, the general opinion has been formed that children are failing to learn to read in school and that strong action must be taken by government to counteract the forces of sloth and poor teaching.

However, this claim is not backed by data. Berliner and Biddle in their award-winning critique of the myths of educational decline (1995) point out that (a) SAT scores have risen steadily since 1976, especially for students from minority homes; (b) since 1977, the National Assessment of Educational Progress (NAEP) scores indicate stable achievement combined with modest growth for students from minority groups and 'less advantaged' backgrounds. They suggest that 'some critics confuse what education has accomplished with what one might want it to accomplish' (Berliner and Biddle, 1995: 28), and that claims that stable or modestly growing achievement scores are not good enough 'cannot be substantiated because they are based on unanchored perceptions of national need and on predictions that are not necessarily sound' (ibid.: 27–8).

Arguably, the most famous case of falling scores in America, and the one that was widely used for the call for school reform, is that of the state of California, where in 1994 the NAEP scores placed California almost last among the fifty states in reading. This was immediately taken up by a vociferous group as an indictment of the reading instruction that had been very loosely in place in California for several years, termed Whole Language or Literature-Based Reading Instruction. What this group failed to acknowledge was the unprecedented influx of immigrants to this state, fleeing persecution and poverty, many of whom had received no education in their homelands and all of whom spoke a language different from English. They failed to document what reading instruction was like in those schools with the lowest scores. They failed to provide data as to how many classrooms in California actually *used* Whole Language and, for those that did, what form it took. They actually failed to document anything with actual data. Regardless, this fall in test-score status was somehow generalised to the entire country in the popular imagination and, before we knew it, we had a national literacy crisis on our hands, and Whole Language, Literature-Based, Meaning-Focused (whatever you want to call instruction that embeds phonics instruction within meaningful literacy activities) was dubbed the cause.

The above suggests to many an organised and orchestrated movement, opportunistically responding to public fears, to influence public belief. At the very least, it reflected a confluence of actions on the part of the federal government, state governments, special interest groups and the media. It all came together in a seeming second to form public belief and then to act on that with legislative mandates. Any attempts to moderate the discourse and to move the impending train onto a more informed track were quickly waylaid.

Another piece of the dubious nature of the high-stakes assessment/standards movement was the way in which influential panels were mandated, funded, shaped and used to document the supposed problem as well as its scientific answer. About the same time that the special interest groups in California and Texas were beginning to take control of the literacy instruction in their states, and that the popular press and media were inflaming the public with their sky-is-falling rhetoric, a panel was being formed by the National Research Council and the National Institute of Child Health and Development. The National Research Council is a policy advisory body to the federal government formed by the National Academy of Sciences and the National Academy of Engineering. The National Academy of Sciences describes itself as 'a private, nonprofit, self-perpetuating society of distinguished scholars engaged in scientific and engineering research, dedicated to the furtherance of science and technology and to their use for the general welfare' (Snow, Burns and Griffin, 1998: iv). The National Academy of Engineering 'was established in 1984, under the charter of the National Academy of Sciences, as a parallel organisation of outstanding engineers [and] shares with the National Academy of Sciences the responsibility for advising the federal government' *(ibid.)*. The appointed committee consisted of some literacy researchers with first-hand knowledge of children, schools and teaching, others from the neurological research field, and some policy people.

Despite a high level of mistrust from the literacy community, due in part to their sense of exclusion, the committee did a reasonable job in identifying and synthesising the research that would inform early reading and drew implications from this literature for instruction. They basically concluded what good teachers have always known: home language and literacy experiences dramatically affect the degree of success children will achieve in school literacy learning; children need to learn how to decode with accuracy early on in their format instruction; children need to read a lot as soon as they can from highly engaging texts. Drawing as they did from the dyslexia research, there was a great deal of focus placed on the need for beginning readers to possess 'phonemic awareness' (the knowledge that words can be reduced to theoretically isolable units or phonemes, and the ability to do this) before they could benefit from phonics instruction which teaches them to map letters to phonemes or phonemic units.

However, the troubling part of this is the way in which this report was used. While its basic conclusion implicated a 'balanced' approach to beginning literacy instruction, only its conclusions regarding phonemic awareness and direct, systematic teaching of phonics were highlighted by the press and the policy mavens. Rather than acknowledge the complexity of the learning to read process, which was reflected, implicitly at least, in the report, the powerful special interest groups used this report to 'document' again the need to replace Meaning-Based early reading instruction with direct, systematic teaching of phonemic awareness and phonics. This is also being used to justify the use of high-stakes assessments of this knowledge at state and local levels and the threat of them at the national level. Ready-to-go, expensive, code-based instructional programmes hit both the educational and the trade markets. The rest of the report is now almost completely lost in the public's mind. These manipulations of the public will are some of the troubling aspects of the procedures surrounding the high-stakes assessment and standards movements. Let me move on to the problems with the new-old simple view of reading.

Giant steps backwards

Within this disquieting sense of manipulation is the real question: why this move *back* to a simplistic notion of what is involved in learning to read and write – to a time when *literacy* was known as simply *reading*? What is missing from this simplistic picture is any notion of culture – of the ways that language and literacy are acquired and develop within sociocultural contexts, of the acknowledgement that academic and literacy achievement is highly correlated with sociocultural group membership. This perplexes me the most. Why act as if we have not explored and come to appreciate the deep and abiding ways that the sociocultural affects the cognitive (Gee, 1992; Heath, 1983; Purcell-Gates, 1995; Vygotsky, 1962)? Let me argue for a bit for why this stance results in irrelevant impacts of research on educational outcomes.

First of all, I challenge anyone to describe a scenario in which any mental process occurs outside a sociocultural context. From birth, we perceive objects, learn about them, think about them, act upon them, forget about them – *while we are in the world.* And the world is organised socially and culturally. It is not possible to truly think of the sociocultural and the cognitive as separable. The relationship between the two is not additive or linear. Rather, their relationship is nested and transactional, with the cognitive occurring always and forever within a sociocultural context. The obvious conclusion from this is that research into a cognitive process like reading, to have any veridical relationship to reality, to life, must reflect this contextualisation of the cognitive by the sociocultural.

But does this really apply to cognitive processes like word recognition? Do the basic cognitive processes like perception and recognition change, or look different, if their sociocultural contexts change? I know that at least some reading researchers deny that they do. Their assertion, therefore, is that the process of word recognition operates the same whether one is reading from a list of unrelated words, reading from a list of related words, reading words in the context of a single sentence, reading words in the context of a paragraph, reading words in the context of a novel, doing any one of these reading tasks in a lab in front of a computer screen as a subject in an experiment, within an fMRI machine with your head in a locked position reading from a reflected image, reading in a classroom during round-robin reading, reading in a classroom during free reading, reading at home from a recipe book during a cooking event, or reading in bed before drifting off to sleep. According to many researchers of the sub-components of reading, this process is unaffected by context, linguistic or situational. But, I have to ask, from the perspective of an unrepentant empiricist: how do we know? So far, the only data used to support the conclusion that the word recognition process is the same regardless of context is based on experiments conducted under carefully controlled conditions within the context of experimental labs. And I know of at least one study of first graders that discovered differential strategy use for word reading within the same children depending on whether they were reading independently, reading with a group, or reading with a peer – three different sociocultural contexts (McIntyre, 1992).

I would like to see more research done on the word recognition process as it operates under differing contextual conditions. There are enough indications from existing research to suggest that this process, if not fundamentally different, at least operates within a range of differences, as the context of the word changes. While work by Stanovich, West, Schwantes, and others (Schvaneveldt, Ackerman and Semlear, 1977; Schwantes, Boesl and Ritz, 1980; Stanovich and West, 1978, 1981) demonstrates convincingly that younger, less able readers rely on linguistic context to a greater degree than do readers for whom the word recognition process has become automatic, models of perception and recognition of real-world objects, including words, include the effects of context not as trivial but almost in a deterministic sense.

For perception of real-world objects, Palmer (1975) and others have demonstrated that objects will be recognised both faster and more accurately if they are encountered in congruent contexts. For example, when shown a picture of a living room, or a kitchen, complete with furnishings, subjects recognise a toaster faster and more accurately (that is, with fewer 'misses' or errors) in the picture of the kitchen as compared to the picture of the living room. Note that our conceptions, or schemas, of which objects more typically belong in a kitchen, a living room, a bedroom, and so on, come from our experiences living in our own specific, socioculturally organised worlds. When shown a picture of a cooking fire in different contexts, for example, I suspect that most of us here would recognise it faster and with fewer errors in the context of a campground than in the context of a 'kitchen'. But the people I worked with in the rural areas of El Salvador as I studied the workings of a women's literacy class, would,

I suspect, recognise it faster in the context of a kitchen than a campground since they cooked three times a day over a cooking fire placed on a raised platform and located inside their kitchens which were one-room structures built of sticks (Purcell-Gates and Waterman, 2000). I doubt if any of the women in the literacy class had ever even seen an electric toaster!

Regarding the recognition of letters and words, I point to Rumelhart's (1975) and McClelland and Rumelhart's (1982) interactive model of word recognition, a model that is still valid and is implicit, I believe, in much of the work that is still being done on word recognition. According to this model, as confirmed by a series of carefully designed and executed experiments, context aids the perception of letters as they are processed in the perceptual system. Context at the semantic level, the syntactic level, the lexical level, the letter cluster level, the letter level and the feature level significantly enables perception and recognition of letters and words. Note, again, that that which determines what constitutes congruent context – that is, context at all, at the semantic, the syntactic, the lexical, the letter cluster, the letter, and the feature levels – is determined by our experiences living in the world, in our own specific, socioculturally organised worlds.

Luria (1983) linked the written language encoding system to young children's grasp of the specific function of print as an aid for recalling messages. Dyson (1991) points out that Luria illustrated in detail how a functional and interactive context – a socioculturally organised context – might lead to the grasp of the function of print as an aid for recalling messages and the beginning of the child's search for ways of precisely differentiating meanings through letter graphics. In other words, experiencing the act of using print within an authentic, interactive, sociocultural context enabled the cognitive task involved in learning letter–sound encodings which enabled that print function – writing down messages.

Even within Schema Theory – that quintessentially cognitive, psycho-centred theory – the effect of context is at the forefront. It accounted for context effects, especially the context of expectation and background knowledge on all levels of cognition, from basic processes like letter recognition to more cognitive ones like comprehension and interpretation of text. And several researchers at the time went on to confirm the obvious conclusion from schema theory, that comprehension of text was affected by cultural perspectives.

The foregoing arguments were directed at those who view the world primarily through a cognitive lens. Other arguments against the Simple View of Reading, though, flow from the work of sociocultural researchers who have described the clear cognitive consequences of differing sociocultural ways of thinking about reading, writing and words (Heath, 1983), and of differing dialects and languages that do not share political and social power with the language of academic literacy (Purcell-Gates, 1995).

The danger of the Simple View of Reading

By denying the complexity of learning to read and write, we are missing critical research questions, and thus we run the very real risk of rendering our research results irrelevant – irrelevant to the actual problem, not the created problem described earlier. By assuming a purely cognitive lens and rejecting the sociocultural one, we cannot make any headway towards understanding why sociocultural group membership is the strongest predictor of academic achievement. Assuming only the cognitive lens, we have to pretend that sociocultural factors do not exist because we can't 'see' them through our lens. We are left with the conclusion that only teaching method is the operative factor (haven't we 'been there and done that'?), and, if the teaching method found to be the must beneficial to middle-class children does not work as well with low-SES children, then there must be something wrong with those children – back to the old, ethnocentric deficit theories!

Let me first list some of the flawed research conclusions that have led us, I believe, along this slippery slope – one destined to end, I fear, with the further academic alienation of traditionally educationally under-served sociocultural groups. First, there is the strong belief that research has documented that parents from low-SES groups (and many in the USA assume this means ethnic minorities) do not know how to talk to their children. This ranges from the belief that these parents do not talk to their children at all to the belief that, while they do say things, they don't say the 'right' things in the 'right' way – that is, as middle-class parents do.

Conclusions drawn from this type of research implicate poor children's vocabulary, syntax and phonemic awareness. And what data is this based on? This is primarily based on data that come from (a) small samples of middle-class children from disproportionately represented academic homes and (b) larger samples of poor children and their parents who are asked to engage in culturally obscure tasks for the sake of research.

These types of studies also assume that because reading is a language activity, one's oral language performance is the precursor and determiner of one's literacy ability. By assuming this 'language ability writ large' stance, this research strand totally ignores the sociolinguistic research that documents the deterministic role that such social factors as setting, purpose and speaker–listener relationships have on language production. Further, this research ignores the documented linguistic differences between speaking and writing – differences that reflect these sociolinguistic factors (Purcell-Gates, 2001). In other words, readers do not read their oral language, no matter what form that oral language may take, and certainly no one reads the oral language used in homes between parents and children. Blaming the oral language of poor families for the school failures of poor children misses the boat by more than a mile.

Another line of mistakenly applied research conclusions I wish to address is that which is currently driving reading policy in the USA. Few are aware that the 'solid body of research' on early reading touted by NICHD is research on the causes of dyslexia. Similar concerns about dyslexia helped to focus activists behind the California rush to impose a systematic direct instruction model of phonics teaching and to discredit meaning-based literacy instruction. I must ask, what is the neurological condition of dyslexia doing driving the general education agenda?

According to the federal definition of this learning disability, dyslexia is a relatively rare neurologically based condition that makes it unusually difficult to learn to read and write.[1] People who have this condition are born with it and it is not considered to be curable. Rather, dyslexics require a different type of reading instruction – one that involves very systematic and rule-governed instruction in letter–sound relationships.

Knowing that it is the research on the underlying causes of dyslexia that is driving the current early reading instruction reform movement helps to answer some of the questions regarding this movement, but not all. Because all learning disabilities, including dyslexia, are presumed to be neurologically based and not the result of cultural differences (National Joint Committee on Learning Disabilities, 1989 in Myers and Hammill, 1990), sociocultural factors are not included in the research lens used by researchers studying it. But how did we segue from a specific type of difficulty in learning to read to the entire population of learners who experience difficulties in learning to read and who thus experience problems, or slower development, with academic literacy throughout their schooling?

The impression I have gained from a reading of the public documents is that, while different 'causes' of reading disability exist (at least hypothetically), including biological ones (i.e. dyslexia), (a) it is still a matter of contention that learning disabilities have a neurological aetiology,[2] and (b) it is too hard to sort this out now. Therefore, the Preventing Reading Difficulties in Young Children committee stated that their recommendations extend to all children, regardless of their level of risk of experiencing difficulties in learning to read and regardless of the presumed cause of such difficulty (Snow, Burns and Griffin, 1998). From a group that touts the necessity of empirical data to back conclusions, this is problematic.

And this leads to some dangerous implications coming from this simple-view-of-reading, cognitive-only-lens movement that is driving school reform with its control over instruction, teacher education, and high-stakes assessment:

Danger 1:   We will put a type of instruction into place in all classrooms for all children that has been verified as effective only for a small percentage of children.

Danger 2:   We will fail to understand the sociocultural factors that contribute to the systematic failure of whole groups of children in our schools because the research lens being validated and funded does not include these factors.

Danger 3:   Because the possibility of an untested instructional programme and/or a simplistic educational programme applied to problems that are neither recognised nor understood will fail, high-stakes assessments will drive another nail in the coffin of academic underachievement for further generations of children from low-status social and cultural groups.

Danger 4:   This nail may prove to be the one made of steel due to the public's uninformed and non-critical understanding of 'science', and rules of implication.

An argument for complexity

I wish to end with an argument and call for embracing complexity. When we consider literacy development for different people in different contexts from different sociocultural worlds for different purposes, we are in a complex arena. To deny this is not only foolish, it is foolhardy and borders on the unethical. We cannot allow the politicians and their policy appointees to act as if a young learner from a low-literate family who speaks a mountain dialect will learn to read in the same classroom, with the same instruction, and in the same way to the same level as one from a highly literate family who speaks like those in power. We cannot allow them to insist, as they are now beginning to do in the United States, that all teachers accept this supposition and teach all children to read in the same way and then pay the consequences when it does not 'work'.

Rather, I believe that we must first insist that our existing knowledge of the complexity that results from sociocultural contexts of learning be integrated into policy decisions and, secondly, that this knowledge base be expanded with more research that can ultimately hone and sharpen policy for reading instruction. We need empirical data to answer crucial questions like: (a) How do beginning readers take from their instruction to learn to effortlessly and effectively process print for meaning? (b) Why do beginning readers from homes of poverty accomplish this more slowly and less well? Does it make a difference whether these children are taught by community insiders or outsiders? Why? (c) What exactly do learners from mainstream affluent homes know that allows them to accomplish this process faster and better in mainstream schools? How did they learn this? (d) How do you explain the almost straight-line relationship between family income and reading achievement around the world? (e) If successful learners go through different processes, or follow different paths toward literacy depending on the focus of their instruction, then how is it that they arrive at the same place, if they do?

We need studies that will tell us: (f) not only what cognitive and linguistic skills learners need to begin to read successfully, but how they learned those skills, in what contexts, under what conditions, within what types of interactions with whom; (g) what is the relationship, if any, between what I call the *actualisation* of literacy learning (i.e. literacy in practice outside school settings) and the ways in which literacy was taught and experienced by learners in school. We need to design a study that would accommodate and explain the work Shaywitz and Shaywitz (1996) are doing with the neurology of dyslexics, as well as the work done by Rosalie Fink on successful adult dyslexics (1998), who explain their success as professionals – and overcoming the debilitating effects of dyslexia – with the fact that at some point in their lives as students they became actual readers in response to personal intense motivations to read extensively on their own on a topic of personal interest.

Unless we reject the politically motivated calls and manipulations for simplistic solutions to created and misrepresented problems and instead embrace the world of learning and development in all of its complexity, we will continue to contribute to the real literacy problem: the under-representation of poor and marginalised people among the academically successful.

Notes

1   Best estimates put the incidence at between 2–6 per cent of the general population (Myers and Hammill, 1990).
2   The history of research into learning disabilities is a long and chequered one, plagued from the beginning by real problems of differentiating types and subtypes of LD. Its legacy is this notion that LD as a construct is questionable. However, most teachers who have ever worked with learners with diagnosed learning disabilities and researchers who study them in neurology labs agree that for some learning difficulties, no other explanation exists besides a neurologically based difference in processing information.

References

Berliner, D.C. and Biddle, B.J. (1995) *The Manufactured Crisis: Myths, Fraud, and the Attack on America's Public Schools*, New York: Addison-Wesley.

Dyson, A.H. (1991) 'Viewpoints: the word and the world – reconceptualizing written language development or do rainbows mean a lot to little girls', *Research in the Teaching of English* 25: 97–123.

Fink, R.P. (1998) 'Literacy development in successful men and women with dyslexia', *Annals of Dyslexia* 48: 311–47.

Gee, J.P. (1992) *The Social Mind: Language, Ideology and Social Practice*, New York: Bergin & Garvey.

Heath, S.B. (1983) *Ways With Words: Language, Life and Work in Communities and Classrooms*, Cambridge: Cambridge University Press.

Kaestle, C.F., Damon-Moore, H., Stedman, I.C., Tinsley, K. and Trollinger, W.V., Jr. (1991) *Literacy in the United States*, New Haven, CN: Yale University Press.

Luria, A. (1983) 'The development of writing in the child', in M. Martlew (ed.) *The Psychology of Written Language* (pp. 237–77), New York: John Wiley.

McClelland, J. and Rumelhart, D. (1982) 'An interactive activation model of context effects in letter perception: Part 2. The contextual enhancement effect and some tests and extensions of the model', *Psychological Review* 89: 60–94.

McIntyre, F. (1992) 'Young children's reading behaviors in various classroom contexts', *JRB: A Journal of Literacy* 24: 339–71.

Myers, P.I. and Hammill, D.D. (1990) *Learning Disabilities: Basic Concepts, Assessment Practices, and Instructional Strategies*, 4th edn, Austin, TX: Pro-Ed.

National Council of Teachers of English and International Reading Association (NCTE/IRA) (1996) *Standards for the English Language Arts*, Urbana, IL: National Council of Teachers of English.

Palmer, S. (1975) 'The effects of contextual scenes on the identification of objects', *Memory and Cognition* 3: 519–26.

Purcell-Gates, V. (1995) *Other People's Words: The Cycle of Low Literacy*, Cambridge, MA: Harvard University Press.

Purcell-Gates, V. (2001) 'Emergent literacy is emerging knowledge of written, not oral, language', in J. Brooks-Gunn and P.R. Britto (eds) *The Role of Family Literacy Environments in Promoting Young Children's Emerging Literacy Skills* (pp. 7–22), San Francisco, CA: Jossey-Bass.

Purcell-Gates, V. and Waterman, R. (2000) *Now We Read; We See; We Speak: A Portrait of a Freirean-based Adult Literacy Class*, Mahwah, NJ: Lawrence Erlbaum.

Rumelhart, D.E. (1975) *Toward an interactive model of reading*, Technical Report No. 56, Center for Human Information Processing, La Jolla, CA: University of California, San Diego.

Schvaneveldt, R., Ackerman, B. and Semlear, T. (1977) 'The effect of semantic context on children's word recognition', *Child Development* 48: 612–16.

Schwantes, G., Boesl, F. and Ritz, R. (1980) 'Children's use of context in word recognition: a psycholinguistic guessing game', *Child Development* 51 (Summer): 730–6.

Shaywitz, S.E. and Shaywitz, B.A. (1996) 'Unlocking learning disabilities: the neurological basis', in S.C. Cramer and W. Ellis (eds) *Learning Disabilities, Life-long Issues* (pp. 255–60), Baltimore, MD: Paul H. Brookes.

Snow, C.E., Burns, M.S. and Griffin, P. (eds) (1998) *Preventing Reading Difficulties in Young Children*, Washington, DC: National Academy Press.

Stanovich, K.E. and West, R. (1978) 'Automatic contextual facilitation in readers of three ages', *Child Development* 49: 99–118.

Stanovich, K.E. and West, R. (1981) 'The effect of sentence context on ongoing word recognition: tests of a two-process theory', *Journal of Experimental Psychology: Human Perception and Performance* 7: 658–72.

Vygotsky, L.S. (1962) *Thought and Language*, Cambridge, MA: Harvard University Press.

6

Ehri's Model of Phases of Learning to Read: A Brief Critique

John R. Beech

[...]

For some time in the reading literature, there has been considerable interest in the notion that children progress in reading according to defined stages of development. Such a conception not only has a potentially useful practical implication for teachers in that they can monitor and structure the stage of progress of the developing reader, but it also has important ramifications for any theory of reading development. In 1995, a short paper on the phases of such development was published by Linnea C. Ehri, which subsequently became one of the most cited papers so far in the *Journal of Research in Reading*. The present [chapter] provides a critique of this work, and as this is not the only paper that Ehri published on the topic (e.g. Ehri, 1994, 1998, 1999, 2002; Ehri & McCormick, 1998), some discussion will be included of these other sources as well.

In her *Journal of Research in Reading* paper, Ehri (1995) starts with the challenge of how to account for the development of word reading, within the context of full comprehension of written materials, up to the adult phase of automaticity. A précis of her arguments will suffice here. Ehri argues for four phases of development (illustrated schematically in Figure 6.1); but before examining this, she refers to Frith's (1985) influential stage model and explains that the Frith model labels need to be replaced. In labelling her phases in the way she does, she makes the concept of alphabetical processing pivotal to the definition of all four phases. These are Ehri's four phases:

Pre-alphabetic phase

This is so called because it occurs prior to any alphabetic knowledge, in other words, identification does not involve making any letter-to-sound connections. Instead connections are made between some visual features (called *cues* by Ehri) of the word and their pronunciation or semantic representation. She gives the example of words as part of advertising logos being identified purely by the surrounding context. If a letter were altered, it would not necessarily be noticed, as the child is using few salient letter features. The lack of an alphabetic connection is clearly indicated when children identify the word using context and no alphabet as when they

From: *Journal of Research in Reading*, 28 (1), 2005, pp. 50–8.

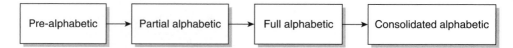

Figure 6.1   A schematic representation of Ehri's phases of reading

read CREST as 'brush teeth'. Frith called this phase the 'logographic' phase, and Ehri changed the label to 'pre-alphabetic' as she thought 'logographic' sounded as if beginning readers read words like mature readers. Unfortunately, giving it this label is akin to calling it 'not the alphabetic phase' and gives no indication of its functionality, except of course that whatever it is comes before the alphabetic phase. This does not mean that Ehri does not propose a particular form of processing. Later in her conclusion, she writes that children in this phase use 'nonalphabetic, visually salient features of words to remember how to read them …' (1995, p. 122). Perhaps it would have been more appropriate to have called this a 'salient visual feature' phase?

Partial alphabetic phase

In this phase, the reader uses a combination of reading some letters in the words and using these to attempt a pronunciation; the first and final letters are usually the most important within this phase. Ehri coined the term 'phonetic cue reading' to characterise the phase. These efforts at generating pronunciations in combination with the visual appearance of the word are stored in memory to be activated on the next encounter. Ehri and Wilce (1985) were able to distinguish readers who were in either of these phases by teaching them words that were either alphabetically similar or dissimilar to the original (e.g. LFT versus WcB for the word 'elephant'). ('WcB' in this example is not only alphabetically dissimilar but was designed also to be more visually distinctive compared to its alphabetically similar counterpart 'LFT'.) Those in the partial alphabetic phase found it easier to learn words with letters congruent to their pronunciation, whereas the pre-alphabetic readers had the same level of difficulty with both.

In subsequent experimental work (obviously not discussed here by Ehri), Stuart, Masterson and Dixon (2000) pre-screened 5-year-old beginning readers into those with or without phonological awareness and alphabetical knowledge and proceeded over the coming months to expose them to a set of words with feedback. The children were not different in age or in visual memory. The children with phonological knowledge were much better at remembering these words and I calculate the effect size between the two groups to be very large, at $d = 1.47$ after 36 exposures and $d = 1.02$ after a delayed recall of one month. Furthermore, there was a significant correlation of 0.79 between visual memory and performance after 36 exposures for the *non*-phonological group compared to [a] low negative correlation of -0.11 for the phonological group. Within the frame of these first two phases, this suggests a strong element of using visual features of words for the children still in the first phase, contrasting with greater reliance on phonological information for children within the second phase. Furthermore, phonological coding proved to be much more potent in helping children to remember the words (as shown by the large effect sizes) and concurs with previous work by Ehri and Wilce (1985) and by Mason (1980). Ehri explains this difference in memorability in terms of the alphabetic system assisting retrieving connections between written words and their pronunciations in contrast to a less systematic method based on visual connections.

Full alphabetic phase

The reader is now able to form alphabetic connections, but not just alphabetic ones. The developing reader can also map graphemes to phonemes of 'sight words'. Sight words are defined here in terms of words that have been read several times. Readers with this full alphabetic skill are able to achieve more accuracy in their recognition, as they are now processing the constituent letters. These readers are also able to read new words by blending the generated pronunciations. Ehri discusses the way that during this phase there is an integral development towards using 'sight word reading' over decoding individual letters. There is now a particular advantage for irregularly spelled words as there is more focus on their irregularities as an aide-mémoire. Children in this phase adopt strategies to handle such words, for example by noting silent letters (e.g. the *s* in 'island').

This is perhaps the most important phase; Ehri (1999) comments that the development of sight vocabulary is central to her theory, whereas in her view Frith emphasises development in more general terms. Another distinction with Frith is that Ehri regards the formation of connections between graphemes and phonemes to be essential, whereas (according to Ehri) Frith considers sight word reading to be non-phonological. (This does not mean that phonological processing is not in Frith's model – Frith's alphabetic phase involves this.) Indeed, Frith proposes an orthographic strategy (if Ehri is interpreting this as 'sight word' processing) that continues into adulthood; however, Frith does leave the way for an alphabetic strategy to be used, although it '... might be less accessible' (Frith, 1985, p. 307).

Consolidated alphabetic phase

This is equivalent to Frith's orthographic stage. With continuing practice at reading in this final phase, recurring letter patterns become consolidated or unitised. Ehri discusses the advantages of this process for reducing memory load, for example the word 'chest' might be processed only as two units 'ch' [and] '-est' in the consolidated phase compared with four *(ch, e, s, t)* in the full alphabetic phase. As an illustration of this, she cites the work of Ehri and Robbins (1992) of First Graders who had some decoding skills. These were subdivided and one group was taught a set of words followed by a second analogous set with the same rime spellings (e.g. 'need', 'feed'). The second group was given a second set that had the same letter–sound connections but not analogous rime patterns. The first group learned their analogous words faster than the second because the shared letter patterns helped this consolidation process. The inference is that the process of accumulating sight-word information is going to make acquiring new words increasingly easy.

Overview and Ehri's other papers on the topic

To summarise and perhaps over-simplify up to this point, in her 1995 paper, Ehri has redefined Frith's model of stages of reading by subdividing Frith's alphabetic phase into two parts – partial and full – and has relabelled the first and last stages of Frith's model (Frith's logographic and orthographic stages). In contrast to Frith, Ehri uses the word 'phase' rather [than] 'stage', implying that these processing stages are perhaps fuzzier at the edges and not so clearly defined.

It is interesting to note what she did *not* propose in this paper. She did not explicitly state that there was progression from one phase to the next, nor indeed whether a child could be in two or more phases in parallel. Perhaps her partial alphabetic phase is one such phase where this might happen. (On this same point, Ehri does begin by proposing that reading development is a progression up to the point of automaticity on the part of the mature reader and so there is perhaps an implication of such a progression.) She does not offer strict operational definitions of entry to each phase for researchers to use as criteria for classification. (This is not to say that these could not be developed.) There is no mention here of the teaching style that children might experience and how this would interact with the phases. Similarly, there is no mention of plasticity; in other words, whether there were any developing underlying cognitive structures related to the developing reading process. There do not appear to be any age norms related to these phases (but see later). On this point – perhaps confusingly – when discussing the final consolidated alphabetic phase, a study of First and Second Graders (Leslie & Thimke, 1986) is discussed. Is this final phase really reached by the equivalent of the US Second Grade? Furthermore, is this really the final phase? What about the way in which adults read – is this equivalent to being in the consolidated alphabetic phase?

Does Ehri in her other writings add anything to this basic theoretical framework? Although there are earlier writings on phases of reading than Ehri (1995), let us begin with her paper published three years earlier (Ehri, 1992), which starts with the dual route model of reading (e.g. Coltheart, 1978; Coltheart, Davelaar, Jonasson & Besner, 1977). This proposes dual processing by means of a grapheme-phoneme conversion (GPC) route or by means of direct lexical analysis. Ehri is critical of this model. For example, she dislikes the lexical route as proposed. Instead of a connection between a word's orthography and its semantic representation, she envisages a systematic connection between spellings and their pronunciations. It is not relevant here to look at her arguments too closely, only to note that in offering an alternative conceptualisation to the dual route model, we can see the embryo of her later phases model. In this paper, the first phase is, to give it its full circumlocutory title, the 'logographic phase of sight word reading: visual cue reading'. This is followed by the 'rudimentary alphabetic phase of sight word reading: phonetic cue reading'. Lastly, there is the 'mature alphabetic phase of sight word learning: cipher reading'. As in her later 1995 paper, she puts considerable emphasis on the concept of the way that 'sight words' are memorised. She emphasises that this is a not a rote memory process; instead it involves making systematic connections between the spelling of the words and their pronunciation.

The reason why she wanted to dissociate her model from the possibility of rote memorisation was partly because she attributed the proposed use of rote memory to dual route theorists; also, presumably, she implies a degree of active rather than passive coding during the reading process. In addition, Marsh, Friedman, Welch and Desberg (1981) proposed a four-stage theory of reading development in which rote learning played a significant part in the first linguistic guessing stage – very similar to Frith's logographic stage. In 1994, Ehri wrote a chapter in Ruddell, Ruddell and Singer's edited book that describes a phase model that is much closer to the 1995 paper. A useful summary description of the components is given by Ehri (reproduced in Table 6.1), which adds to the overall picture. It can be seen that the actual labels of the phases are still evolving at this point. The first two phases in the figure are self-explanatory. However, the 'amalgamated cipher reading' in the 'mature alphabetic' phase needs further explanation. Ehri is referring to the association of a word's spelling to its pronunciation. Here

Table 6.1   Ways to read words classified by developmental phase (reproduced from Ehri,1994)

Ways to read words	Phases of development			
	Logographic	Novice alphabetic	Mature alphabetic	Orthographic
Ways to read words familiar in print By sight	Visual cue reading	Phonetic cue reading	Amalgamated cipher reading	Amalgamated cipher reading (advanced)
Lexical access routes	Salient visual cues connected to meanings by rote learning; connections do not involve letter identities, sounds	Salient letters connected to pronunciation by letter-name or sound knowledge; spellings partially connected	Letters amalgamated to phonemes in pronunciation by grapheme-phoneme knowledge; spellings fully connected	Single- and multi-letter units amalgamated to phonemes and syllabic units in pronunciations by grapheme-phoneme, morphographic knowledge; spellings fully connected
Characteristics of sight-word lexicon	Context dependent: environmental print; variable pronunciations: isolated written words (few recognised, hard to remember, unstable); does not support text reading	Isolated written words can be recognised, remembered; partial letter-based representations; similar spelled words mistaken; text reading supported	Rapid, unitised word reading possible; complete letter based representations; spellings may influence phonemic analysis; word reading in text made effortless	Easier to store multisyllabic words; representation of word morphology; organised by orthographic neighbourhoods; similarly spelled words read easily
Ways to read words unfamiliar in print				
By guessing	Wild; constrained by context; constrained by memory for text (pretend-reading)	Constrained by context; constrained by initial letter	Constrained by context; constrained by spelling	Constrained by context; constrained by spelling
By mistaken lexical access	New word misread as sight word having same visual cues	New word misread as sight word having same letter cues	(Less likely to occur)	(Less likely to occur)
By phonological recoding	(Not possible)	(Not possible)	Sequential decoding	Sequential and hierarchical decoding
By orthographic recoding	(Not possible)	(Not possible)	Analogising to specific words	Analogising to specific words, word families, orthographic neighbourhoods

the term 'cipher' presumably refers to the sense of an uncracked code, perhaps as initially encountered by the mature alphabetic reader. It is a little unclear if the term 'amalgamation' used here is meant to be referring to the blending of the phonemes produced from the graphemes, or the connecting of letters to sounds or both.

In her 1994 chapter, Ehri connects these four phases to school ages. The logographic phase is pre-school; novice alphabetic reading begins normally at the start of schooling, but may be developed beforehand. Mature alphabetic reading happens in the first two years of school, while the orthographic phase begins during the second or third year of school. Ehri notes the similarities with Chall's (1983, 1996) theory. There is also some discussion of the reading processes in the mature reader, placing emphasis on those theorists who have advocated the involvement of phonetic codes in mature reading (e.g. Van Orden, 1987; Van Orden, Johnston and Hale, 1988). We have to make allowances for the era of writing, however; Van Orden's work on mature reading, although very useful, is not within the mainstream of current work on adult word recognition.

Moving to the period after the publication of the 1995 paper, there are further papers (e.g. Ehri, 1998, 1999, 2002) that go over similar ground, but do not add too much. In a chapter in a book she co-edited (1998), Ehri emphasises the importance of grapheme-phoneme knowledge and in the closing part re-describes her four-phase model. She then goes on to discuss how reading and spelling have an interactive reciprocal relationship with each other. Thus, the process of memorising words in order to read also helps children to spell. Similarly, having to spell out words while writing further helps the development of reading, as illustrated by the work of Ehri and Wilce (1987). In her 2002 paper, Ehri explains why she proposed a theory of phases rather than of stages. This was to introduce flexibility, and she also acknowledges that there is evidence that each stage is not a prerequisite for the following stage. The evidence she alludes to, but does not cite, is from researchers such as Stuart and Coltheart (1988), who demonstrated that beginning readers do not always pass through a logographic type of process. She also states that word reading in the pre-alphabetic phase does not actually make a contribution to later processing through the alphabetic phases. However, she also proposes an element of parallel processing of the alphabetic phases to give it a different form to that depicted in Figure 6.1.

Ehri (1998) draws implications of her theory of phases of reading development for teachers given here in summary form:

(1)   It is important for beginners to learn all the letters and to use this information to relate to their own speech processes. This will include learning graphemes such as 'ch', 'sh' and 'th'.

(2)   Children need to develop awareness of phonemes and relate this to their graphemic knowledge.

(3)   By the First Grade, teachers should help all children to achieve the full alphabetic phase. The major grapheme-phoneme connections, particularly those involving vowels, need to be learned.

(4)   Children need practice at learning unfamiliar words both by breaking down their graphemes to form sounds and by the use of analogy. This will be easier for students in the full alphabetic phase.

(5)   Learning to spell is an important part of reading development. The important initial phase is to be able to create appropriate graphemes from the constituent sounds.

Memorising word lists should not be started until this is mastered because this will make learning such lists easier.

(6)   Later work should expand to learning morphemes, affixes and families of related words.

Conclusion

The concept of phases of progression in the development of reading has become widely accepted among reading researchers and Linnea Ehri has made a considerable personal contribution to this process both within the academic community and within the teaching community. This is not just through her writings but from her work at national level; for example, from 1998 to 2000 she was one of the fourteen members of the National Reading Panel that had been commissioned by the US congress to sift through and assimilate the evidence concerning the most effective methods for teaching reading.

Her contribution to the work on phases of reading has been to introduce greater flexibility into these phases as well as to break down and define the alphabetic phases more clearly. Ehri is by no means the first researcher to suggest a progression of phases of reading (e.g. Chall, 1983; Frith, 1985; Gough & Juel, 1991; Marsh, Friedman, Welch & Desberg, 1981; Seymour & MacGregor, 1984) and she will not be the last (e.g. Adams, 1990; Jackson & Coltheart, 2001; Morris, Bloodgood & Lomax, 2003; Spear-Swerling & Sternberg, 1998). One aspect of the history of psychology is that successive theorists formulate similar theories dressed in new labels (e.g. 'stages', 'phases' and 'steps' in this instance – but labels within the area of 'short-term memory' perhaps represent the worst case of this in psychology). Theorists developing the concept of reading phases will surely be no different in the future. Amongst these contributors to phase theory, Linnea Ehri has been one of its most influential advocates; but her model has served more as a framework than as a set of falsifiable scientific hypotheses. Given the flexibility of the frame, the 'tent' of the theory is more likely to bend with the winds of evidence rather than be broken. Nevertheless, it should serve researchers well for some time to come.

   [...]

References

Adams, M.J. (1990). *Beginning to read: Thinking and learning about print.* Cambridge, Mass: MIT Press.

Chall, J. (1983). *Stages of reading development.* New York: McGraw-Hill.

Chall, J.S. (1996). *Stages of reading development* (2nd edn). Fort Worth, Tex: Harcourt-Brace.

Coltheart, M. (1978). Lexical access in simple reading tasks. In G. Underwood (Ed.), *Strategies of information processing.* (pp. 151–216). London: Academic Press.

Coltheart, M., Davelaar, E., Jonasson, J.T. & Besner, D. (1977). Access to the internal lexicon. In S. Domic (Ed.), *Attention & performance,* 6. (pp. 535–556). Hillsdale, NJ: Erlbaum.

Ehri, L.C. (1992). Reconceptualizing the development of sight word reading and its relationship to recoding. In P. Gough, L. Ehri & R. Treiman (Eds.), *Reading acquisition.* (pp. 107–143). Hillsdale, NJ: Erlbaum.

Ehri. L.C. (1994). Development of the ability to read words: Update. In R. Ruddell, M. Ruddell & H. Singer (Eds.), *Theoretical models and processes of reading*. (4th edn, pp. 323–358). Newark, Del: International Reading Association.

Ehri, L.C. (1995). Phases of development in learning to read by sight. *Journal of Research in Reading*, 18, 116–125.

Ehri, L.C. (1998). Grapheme-phoneme knowledge is essential for learning to read words in English. In J.L. Metsala & E.C. Ehri (Eds.), *Word recognition in beginning literacy*. (pp. 3–40). Mahwah, NJ: Erlbaum.

Ehri, L.C. (1999). Phases of development in learning to read words. In J. Oakhill & R. Beard (Eds.), *Reading development and the teaching of reading: A psychological perspective*. (pp. 79–108). Oxford: Blackwell Science.

Ehri, L.C. (2002). Phases of acquisition in learning to read words and implications for teaching. *British Journal of Educational Psychology: Monograph Series*, 1, 7–28.

Ehri, L.C. & McCormick, S. (1998). Phases of word learning: Implications for instruction with delayed and disabled readers. *Reading and Writing Quarterly*, 14, 135–163.

Ehri, L.C. & Robbins, C. (1992). Beginners need some decoding skill to read words by analogy. *Reading Research Quarterly*, 27, 12–26.

Ehri, L.C. & Wilce, L.S. (1985). Movement into reading: Is the first stage of printed word reading visual or phonetic? *Reading Research Quarterly*, 20, 163–179.

Ehri, L.C. & Wilce, L.S. (1987). Does learning to spell help beginners learn to read words? *Reading Research Quarterly*, 22, 47–65.

Frith, U. (1985). Beneath the surface of developmental dyslexia. In K. Patterson, J. Marshall & M. Coltheart (Eds.), *Surface dyslexia: Neuropsychological and cognitive studies of phonological reading*. (pp. 301–330). London: Erlbaum.

Gough, P.B. & Juel, C. (1991). The first stages of word recognition. In L. Rieben & C.A. Perfetti (Eds.), *Learning to read: Basic research and its implications*. (pp. 47–56). Hillsdale, NJ: Erlbaum.

Jackson, N.E. & Coltheart, M. (2001). *Routes to reading success and failure: Toward an integrated theory of atypical reading*. Philadelphia, PA: Psychology Press.

Leslie, L. & Thimke, B. (1986). The use of orthographic knowledge in beginning reading. *Journal of Reading Behavior*, 18, 229–241.

Marsh, G., Friedman, M., Welch, V. & Desberg, P. (1981). A cognitive-developmental theory of reading acquisition. In G.E. MacKinnon & T.G. Waller (Eds.), *Reading research: Advances in theory and practice*. Vol. 3 (pp. 199–221). New York: Academic Press.

Mason, K. (1980), When *do* children begin to read: An exploration of four-year-old children's letter and word reading competences. *Reading Research Quarterly*, 15, 203–227.

Morris, D., Bloodgood, J.W. & Lomax, R.G. (2003). Developmental steps in learning to read: A longitudinal study in kindergarten and first grade. *Reading Research Quarterly*, 38, 302–328.

Seymour, P.H.K. & MacGregor, C.J. (1984). Developmental dyslexia: A cognitive experimental analysis of phonological, morphemic and visual impairments. *Cognitive Neuropsychology*, 1, 43–83.

Spear-Swerling, L. & Sternberg, R.L. (1998). *Off track. When poor readers become 'learning disabled'*. Boulder, Colo: Westview Press.

Stuart, M. & Coltheart, M. (1988). Does reading develop in a sequence of stages? *Cognition*, 30, 139–181.

Stuart, M., Masterson, J. & Dixon, M. (2000). Spongelike acquisition of sight vocabulary in beginning readers? *Journal of Research in Reading*, 23, 12–27.

Van Orden, G.C. (1987). A rows is a rose: Spelling, sound, and reading. *Memory & Cognition*, 15, 181–198.

Van Orden, G.C., Johnston, J.C. & Hale, B.L. (1988). Word identification in reading proceeds from spelling to sound to meaning. *Journal of Experimental Psychology: Learning, Memory, and Cognition*, 14, 371–86.

7

Siblings Bridging Literacies in Multilingual Contexts

Ann Williams and Eve Gregory

[…]

Introduction

Eleven-year-old Wahida is at home playing school with her younger sister Sayeeda, aged eight. They have a blackboard and chalk and Sayeeda has an exercise book for her work. Wahida is the 'teacher' and they are practising spellings:

> Wahida: Now we're going to do a spelling test. Are you ready Sayeeda?
> Sayeeda: Yes Miss.
> Wahida: I'm going to give you at least 20 seconds for each of them. OK? The first one is tricycle …. tricycle. A tricycle has three wheels. Tricycle. The next one is commandment. I command you to do it Sayeeda, otherwise you're going to be in big trouble. Commandment. The next one is technology. Technology is a subject. Once you grow up Sayeeda, you're going to do hard technology. The next one is polydron. Polydron is something to play with or do maths with. Don't look at each others' work, Sayeeda especially …

Knowing that Wahida and Sayeeda spend almost as long in their combined Bengali and Qur'anic classes per week as in their London state school, we might begin to question the nature of the excerpt above. How far does their 'lesson' reflect activities from each domain? Undoubtedly, much of their play originates in their English classroom. Although both Wahida's and Sayeeda's first language is Sylheti, a dialect of Bengali, the activity takes place in English. Wahida adopts not only the lexis and language structures, but also the intonation patterns of her English teacher. The content of her 'teaching' is typical of that in British primary schools at the start of the twenty-first century. Yet Wahida's 'lesson' is not just a replica of her English school class. Although the language and approach to teaching may be English, the seriousness with which the children go about the task, Wahida's firm yet careful individual monitoring of her sister's work and Sayeeda's respectful attitude towards her older sister are reminiscent of much of the interaction in their Bengali and Qur'anic schools. In contrast with the literacy play between Anglo siblings outlined later in this [chapter], there is no 'messing about' in this playing school game.

From: *Journal of Research in Reading*, 24 (3), 2001, pp. 248–65.

It is commonly assumed that the home and community literacy practices of families from economically disadvantaged groups are very different from those taking place in school. But is this necessarily the case? [This chapter] questions this opposition and illustrates a reciprocity in both literacy beliefs and practices between two primary schools and their communities in East London. It also demonstrates the unique role played by siblings in 'bridging' both domains by bringing school literacies into their home play and syncretising these with their home and community games and practices.

Background: economic disadvantage and home/school dissonance

Since the 1960s, it has generally been believed in both Britain and the USA that dissonance will exist between what is expected at school and the home learning practices of children from economically disadvantaged families, and that this is likely to equate with school learning difficulties. Dissonance between language, literacy and learning practices has been widely documented in official government reports (CACE, 1967; DES, 1975) as well as in large-scale statistical studies (Wedge and Prosser, 1973). This dissonance, it is argued, may be even more pronounced between ethnic-minority children and their often white, monolingual teachers, with the result that parents can feel disempowered in the education system (DES, 1981; DES, 1985; Tomlinson, 1992; Gillborn and Gipps, 1996; Blackledge, 2000; Gillborn and Mirza, 2000).

Analyses of ways in which discontinuity between home and school manifests itself have appeared at various levels of representation. A number of studies relate to what might be seen as the social context, i.e. the wider belief systems of families and how they interpret their role in the schooling process. These 'belief systems' have been referred to in various ways. Bourdieu (1977) uses the notion of 'capital' (economic, social, cultural and symbolic) possessed by children upon entering school. Children whose families have little economic capital are more likely to enter school possessing different social and cultural capital from that expected by their teachers, resulting in difficulty in gaining access to the wider symbolic capital required. Bourdieu's notion of symbolic capital bears a strong similarity to the 'ethno-theories', essential beliefs or constructs held by individuals within different cultural or social groups. Reese et al (1996) and Volk (1997) outline the key ethno-theories held by Mexican-American and Puerto-Rican parents who see themselves primarily as teachers or guardians of moral and responsible behaviour. In Britain, similar findings are available from studies with the Bangladeshi British community in London (Gregory, 1994) and in Northampton (Brooker, 2000) and the Pakistani community in Watford (Drury, 1997). All the above studies contrast the ethno-theories held by parents with those of the school and children's teachers who, in contrast with the families, believe that the most important parental responsibility is that of fostering children's academic learning.

A further layer of analysis might unpick what symbolic capital or ethno-theories might comprise in terms of the linguistic knowledge of children from economically disadvantaged groups and their families. Gee (1996) uses the term 'discourse' to emphasise the link between ways of behaving, interacting and valuing and ways in which these are expressed through language. Dissonance between home and school and the ways in which this is expressed are again the subject of many studies of language and families from economically disadvantaged backgrounds. At an obvious level, it has been shown that parents who do not speak the language of the school tend to feel excluded and powerless (Tomlinson and Hutchinson, 1991; Blackledge, 2000). However, dissonance has also been suggested as a reason for learning problems where the family and the school do share the same first language. Majority group children from economically disadvantaged homes have been shown to experience difficulty in knowing when to switch to standard English and/or the format type of discourse required in school (Williams, 1989). School-valued discourse might comprise using certain question forms (Heath, 1983; Tizard and Hughes, 1984) or a particular approach to narrative during news-telling sessions (Michaels, 1986). Further studies detail the particular difficulties involved in learning these linguistic forms and discourse styles when pedagogies are of an implicit rather than explicit nature (Bernstein, 1971; Gregory, 1993).

A third layer of analysis, overlapping with and including language, details more fully the nature of cultural capital and how this might be expressed through access to particular cultural practices valued by the school. Studies have contrasted the bedtime story-reading practice expected by teachers and common in school-oriented homes with the Qur'anic or community classes[1] in the Pakistani or British Bangladeshi community (Robertson, 1997; Gregory and Williams, 1998) or with games, comics and newspapers in African-American, Anglo-British and urban Australian families of low socio-economic status (Anderson and Stokes, 1984; Freebody, Ludwig and Gunn, 1995; Williams, 1997). Others show precisely how these practices differ in terms of purpose (the seriousness of religious classes as opposed to the fun of games), materials (the Qur'an or Bible as opposed to comics) and behaviour or interaction patterns ('listen and repeat' as opposed to guessing and experimentation) (Baynham, 1995; Gregory and Williams, 2000). The common theme throughout all these studies, however, is that of discontinuity between home and school, which may give rise to learning difficulties in 'non school-oriented' children.

In contrast, consonance between home and school language and literacy practices has been shown to give children access to the appropriate symbolic capital favouring early school success. A number of studies reveal patterns of consonance between the school and different groups of parents, variously referred to as 'mainstream' (Heath, 1983), 'school-oriented' (Cochran-Smith, 1984) or 'middle-class' (Bernstein, 1996). Such parents share the same ethno-theories concerning child-rearing as the teachers (Cochran-Smith, 1984), the same language and literacy practices (Heath, 1983; Tizard and Hughes, 1984) and the same expectations of school (Bernstein, 1996). So the implications of economic disadvantage are clear: low socio-economic status is synonymous with dissonance and difficulty in the education system; high socio-economic status is synonymous with consonance and educational success.

Although some studies of innovative classroom practices in the USA avoid this polarisation by highlighting the benefits to children whose teachers manage to build upon the 'funds of knowledge' in their communities (Moll et al, 1992), most studies in Britain and the USA outline the successful nature of home/school links when families are encouraged to engage in *school-type* literacy and learning tasks at home (Dickinson, 1994; Hannon, 1995). While illustrating programmes that have immediate success, these studies do not provide evidence that such activities go on to be incorporated into parents' own life-long literacy repertoires.

The notion of reciprocity between schools and communities in economically disadvantaged areas, therefore, does not fit comfortably with existing assumptions. We do not see a reflection of the families' symbolic capital or of parental ethno-theories reflected in the school, nor do we detect community literacy practices or patterns of interaction incorporated into day-to-day school activities. One important factor in explaining the 'disadvantage = dissonance = failure' model might be that home/school relationships are ossified into relationships between *parents* and school, thus ignoring the wider family, and particularly the role played by siblings in mediating school and community practices. The present study reveals ways in which siblings may be invisible yet crucial sources for the reciprocity between schools and families we see taking place below.

Theoretical perspectives

The study synthesises and extends perspectives that originate in a range of disciplines and research traditions. The framework used draws from six perspectives. The first comes from what is now known as the New Literacy Studies. These studies challenge the notion of a 'great divide' between literacy and orality, arguing that there is no single, monolithic, autonomous literacy: rather, there are 'literacies' or 'literacy practices' whose character and consequences differ in each context (Baynham, 1995; Barton and Hamilton, 1998). Viewed in this way, school-sanctioned literacy, or 'Literacy' to which Street (1995, p. 14) refers, is just one of a multiplicity of literacies present in peoples' lives, in different languages, in different domains and with a range of purposes.

From the New Literacy Studies, we have taken and extended Baynham's (1995, p. 39) term 'mediator of literacy' to refer particularly to siblings. Baynham defines a mediator as 'a person who makes his or her skill available to others, on a formal or informal basis, for them to accomplish specific literacy purposes'. Siblings, however, play a more important role than simply offering literacy skills. They initiate younger members of the family into whole new discourses (Gee, 1996) comprising ways of behaving, valuing and expressing new opinions, beliefs and views. Through their care-giving, they open up new cultural worlds to their siblings who 'apprentice themselves' to their older role model. Thus childhood initiation into literacy might be viewed as a collaborative group activity rather than the dyadic activity typical of parent/child interactions.

The second perspective informing the study is drawn from cultural psychology which offers a 'cultural mediational model of reading' which stresses that 'successful adult efforts depend crucially upon their organising a "cultural medium for reading" which must use artefacts (most notably but not only) the text, must be proleptic, and … must organise social relations to co-ordinate the child with the to-be-acquired system of mediation in an effective way' (Cole, 1996, p. 273). By prolepsis, Cole refers to the way 'the cultural past greets the new-born as its cultural future' (ibid., p. 183). Bateson (1979, p. 13) personalises this relationship as follows: 'We come to every situation with stories, patterns of events that are built into us. Our learning happens within the experience of what important others did'. Siblings may be 'important others' bridging home and school experiences as well as past and future events for their younger siblings.

The next perspective draws upon the powerful metaphor of 'scaffolding' (Bruner, 1986) from early childhood studies. This metaphor describes how adults or older experts provide a 'scaffold' to assist the young child that is slowly dismantled as the child becomes competent in a task. This interpretation of the learning process complements that promoted earlier by Vygotsky (1978) who sees the adult as assisting the child across the 'zone of proximal development' (ZPD), which is the space between what the child is capable of alone today and, with adult assistance, what she or he will be capable of tomorrow. The nature of scaffolding is likely to differ from one cultural group to another. Thus, although all caregivers have been shown to provide their offspring with 'finely-tuned scaffolding', the nature of the 'curriculum' (Dunn, 1989) will vary. Rogoff (1990) provides examples of scaffolding in different cultures and also changes the term to 'guided participation' in order to emphasise the active part played by the infants themselves in structuring their own learning.

A final and important perspective informing the study is that of syncretism as used by cultural anthropologists. This view states that young people are not confined within any single early-childhood literacy practice. The families in this study reveal a complex heterogeneity of traditions, whereby the children blend literacy practices from different cultures, resulting in a form of reinterpretation which is both new and dynamic. Duranti and Ochs (1996) refer to this type of blending as syncretic literacy, which merges not simply linguistic codes or texts but different activities. They use the example of Samoan Americans doing homework to show how Samoan and American traditions, languages, teaching and child-rearing strategies combine. In this study, we see how school lessons are assimilated and transformed through games and play at home.

The study

The study discussed below was conducted with two groups of children, a Bangladeshi British group and an Anglo-British group, in two neighbouring primary schools in East London. School A, attended by the Bangladeshi British children had an intake that was 100% Bangladeshi British, while School B, attended by the Anglo group, took children from a range of backgrounds, including Bangladeshi, Korean, Chinese, African, African Caribbean and Anglo-British. Eight families from each school with an older child[2] in Years 4, 5 or 6 (i.e. aged 9–11) and a younger child in the Nursery or the Infants (i.e. aged 4–7) were invited to take part. The data consisted of interviews with the older siblings, conducted both individually and in group sessions throughout the project, and with the younger siblings at the end of the year. Parents, class teachers, the two mainstream school head teachers and community class teachers were also interviewed. School literacy lessons were observed on a weekly basis and community Bengali classes were visited. Day-to-day evidence of the children's out-of-school literacy practices was obtained in the form of diaries. In addition, the siblings were asked to audio-tape themselves at home engaging in some form of play that involved literacy such as reading, writing, reciting or playing games.

Playing with siblings

The project families lived in rented accommodation in tower blocks or small houses in an ethnically mixed neighbourhood that is one of the poorest in Britain. Family sizes ranged from eleven children to two. All the children spent most of their out-of-school time in the company of their siblings, and a good deal of that time playing. A wide range of games was recorded in the interviews and diaries, with children of both groups reporting playing house, playing school, cops and robbers, hide and seek, bikes, football and other ball games as well as indoor activities such as board games, computer games and watching TV:

A: What do you do after school?
N: Play out
A: What sort of games do you play?
N: Hide and seek
A: Do you play any Bangladeshi games?
N: Yes we play house. We wear saris and cook and stuff

Clear gender differences emerged, especially in the Anglo group, where the older girls spent a good deal of time playing with their younger siblings:

Sandra: I like cooking fairy cakes for my baby sister. I cook the cakes for her and then she puts … you know those little funny character things in icing … she puts them on … and hundreds and thousands … cos mum says she can't cook

Older brothers, in contrast, appeared to play with younger siblings only when obliged to by their mums:

AW: What about playing schools?
R: My sister (aged 7) does it with my brother (aged 3)
AW: Does she ever try to get you to play?
R: She did once and I told her I didn't want to
AW: What about playing schools?
J: Sometimes with Sally cos my mum tells me to. Sally normally be's [sic] the teacher and calls out the register and has to do everybody's name.

Literacy practices in the Anglo homes

When focusing specifically on literacy activities with their siblings, the Anglo children reported a range of games and practices which included reading stories, telling jokes, reading comics and magazines, writing cards and letters, entering competitions, writing to fan clubs, playing word games, playing cards, buying books from the supermarket and going to the cinema. Zarah (aged 11) played with Barney (aged 4):

We play this number … maths game … and we've got this abacus … and we have these little cards that we made out of paper … and we're making a new game with the dictionary … and it's got all pictures in it.

Two older sisters of similar age, who enjoyed teenage fiction, frequently read aloud together:

AW: How do you read together?
S: Like page to page
Z: Sometimes we read out lines together … the same things together … which gets on our nerves … so then we just read page to page.

The children read a wide variety of materials. Ronnie's inventory of 32 books read during the Christmas holidays included the following: *A Christmas Carol* by Charles Dickens,

Encyclopaedia, The Bash Street Kids (comic annual), *Shakespeare Stories (Modern), The Arsenal Supporters' Book, Flags of the World. The Angry Aztecs* by Terry Dreary, *Demons, Gods and Holy Men, Evolution, The Highly Dangerous Joke Book, Tom Thumb.*

Playing games: literacy at home

The home recordings of the Anglo children included reading to siblings, teaching them clapping songs or nursery rhymes, playing cards and word games and playing school. One family elected to play a word game. Players select a category such as musical instruments or animals, and then find one item for each letter of the alphabet. In the following extract, Ronnie (aged 10), Melanie (aged 7) and their mum are playing the game and Grandad, who is present in the room, occasionally offers a contribution:

1.	Mum:	Melanie, you're on J
2.	Melanie:	Erm …
3.	Grandad:	Juniper berry
4.	Melanie:	Juniper berry
5.	Mum:	Yes
6.	Ronnie:	Not!
7.	Melanie:	Ginger
8.	Mum:	Melanie, since when has ginger been J?
9.	Melanie:	Oh yeah it's G
10.	Mum:	Juniper berry then
11.	Ronnie:	Conferring!
12.	Mum:	K
13.	Melanie:	I know this
14.	Ronnie:	Kiwi
15.	Melanie:	Conferring!
16.	Mum:	Lemon
17.	Melanie:	What have I got? M?
18.	Mum:	Yeah. … easy
19.	Melanie:	Melon. I always say melon
20.	Mum:	N
21.	Ronnie:	(laughing) Oh no!
22.	Mum:	No, not allowed to say norange
23.	Ronnie:	Nana, banana
24.	Melanie:	Nincompoop, nincompoop!
25.	Mum:	Yeah, they've always been tasty them nincompoops. Is it a vegetable or a fruit?
26.	Mum:	Orange
27.	Ronnie:	Norange!
28.	Mum:	You've got P, Melanie … go on … pineapple
29.	Melanie:	Oh pineapple
30.	Ronnie:	Conferring!
31.	Melanie:	Yeah and I conferred you one!
32.	Ronnie:	Oh no! Not Q!
33.	Grandad:	I've got one for N. Nectarine.

Mrs A and her three children, who live in a two-bedroomed flat on the 13th floor of an East-End tower block, would doubtless be categorised as of 'low socio-economic status' and as such assumed to have little cultural capital in common with the school. The word game they are playing however, clearly a family favourite and a common literacy practice in this home, is 'educational' in that it enriches the children's vocabulary, improves their spelling and teaches the alphabet. Yet this is not formal literacy learning of the kind the children might experience during the Literacy Hour in school. There is scope for a good deal of fun and laughter, opportunities to create nonsense words, to make jokes, to challenge rivals, to express mock anguish at getting an impossible letter. There are allusions to popular TV quiz programmes (line 11) and to family in-jokes (line 22). The text provides evidence of a rich linguistic tradition in this East End home where children have ample opportunity to acquire and to display alternative discourse skills not often exploited in school but which have considerable currency in the community, namely the ability to *play* with language. The text thus provides an example of prolepsis, of three generations taking part in an activity that is not merely a family literacy practice but also part of a much wider cultural tradition. In this family then, where we might have expected to find dissonance between home and school, we find a blending or syncretism of home and school literacy practices.

Playing school

In a second household, the children chose to record themselves playing school. Lee (aged 9) is the teacher and his younger sisters, Lizzie (aged 5) and Cathy (aged 7) are the pupils:

1. Lee: First in your literacy diary, I want you to write what you've done today in literacy.
2. Lizzie: But we do da di dai dooh dah (singing)
3. Lee: Right in a minute it's time for football practice
4. Cathy: Sir, do we have to stay for football practice?
5. Lee: Only a penalty shoot out
6. Cathy: Sir, do we have to do a penalty shoot out?
7. Lee: Yeah. Right Lizzie take the penalty
8. Cathy: Sir that's what I brought you. That's for your girlfriend, Sir
9. Lee: Very nice
10. Cathy: (singing)
11. Lee: Right take the penalty Lizzie
12. Lizzie: Not yet
13. Lee: Right then Cathy it's time for your choir singing practice and Lizzie it's time for your football practice
14. Lizzie: Football practice
15. Lee: Oooooooooh what a goal!!
16. Cathy: (singing)
17. Lee: Second penalty! Oooh saved it
18. Lizzie: Sir sir
19. Lee   Lizzie, on your head! on your head! Yeah well done Lizzie! What a goal! Right get your book bags.

This short extract, from a much longer playing school session, ostensibly mirrors part of a real school day with pupils filling in their literacy diaries, going to choir practice, fetching their book bags and so on. There can be no question, however, that this is very much an imaginative play session, with the participants adopting roles and obeying the rules of socio-dramatic play, skilfully negotiating multiple perspectives as the script takes unexpected directions. Lee as teacher, for example, remains in the frame throughout, somehow managing to engineer football, his favourite activity, into the script, sorting out Cathy's reluctance to play football by suggesting she goes to choir practice and dealing with Cathy's impertinent mention of his girlfriend with a patient and teacherly 'Very nice'. The girls, who are in reality model pupils, use this opportunity to try out being naughty and disobedient, making references to a totally taboo subject, the teacher's private life. As with much socio-dramatic play, the resulting text is a blend of fantasy and reality. The children call upon selected images from their real-life experiences and their very real preoccupations and interests and weave them into a fantasy where anything is possible. Although there is no 'formal' teaching (except for football skills possibly), Lee and Cathy are initiating little Lizzie, still a Reception class pupil, into the routines and discourses of 'real school'.

Literacy practices in the Bangladeshi British homes

The Bangladeshi British children's experience of out-of-school literacy was very different from that of their Anglo colleagues. For the Muslim children, after-school play and literacy were sharply differentiated. Although they too played house and rode their bikes after school, they also spent several hours a week engaged in 'formal' literacy activities. Speakers of Sylheti, an as-yet unwritten dialect of Bengali, they all attended classes to learn to read and write Standard Bengali either in the local community centre or in neighbours' homes. As members of a deeply religious Muslim community, they also attended Qur'anic classes in the mosque or at home where they read the Qur'an and related books in Arabic (see Table 7.1). In addition, most of the children attended after-school clubs or homework clubs run by the school or the local community centre:

> We do Arabic at home now. A hafiz[3] comes to our home on Fridays and Saturdays from 5.30 to 7.30 or 8.30. I go to Bengali from 4.00 to 6.30, Monday to Friday and on Saturdays from 10.00 to 12.00 and 2.00 to 4.00. (Wahida, aged 11)

For these children, the time spent on such formal literacy outside school ranged from 10–18 hours per week and meant that the children were regularly operating in four language codes: Sylheti spoken at home and in the community; Standard Bengali which they learnt to speak, read and write in their community classes; English, the language of the mainstream school; and Arabic, the language of the Qur'an. In contrast with their Anglo peers, home literacy was not necessarily perceived as fun and enjoyment:

> A: Do you enjoy learning Bengali and Arabic and all these things?
> W: No. I don't like learning Bengali because I don't like going to Bengali school.

Table 7.1   Community class attendance: older Bangladeshi British siblings

Child	Mon	Tues	Wed	Thurs	Fri	Sat	Sun
P		A	A	B	B	A	A
N	A	A	A	A	B		
A	A + B	A + B	A	A + B	A		
J	A	A + B	A + B	A + B	A		
K	B	A + B	A + B	A + B	A + B		
F	A	A	B	B	B	A	
W	B	B	B	B	A + B	A + B	
R	A	A + B	A + B	A + B	A		

Key: A = Arabic/ Qur'anic class; B = Bengali class. Each session lasts two hours.

> A: So why do you think people insist that we learn Bengali?
>
> W: Because we have the Bengali language so we have to learn. It's necessary.

Playing school

Home literacy in the Bangladeshi British community was a serious and formal activity, a factor that was evident in the children's choice of home recording. Whereas the Anglo children chose to tape a range of play activities, the Bangladeshi children chose only two: playing school or reading to siblings. Moreover, playing school in the Bangladeshi British community was very different from that of Lee and his sisters. The following is a further extract from Wahida and Sayeeda playing school. The girls are in the family sitting room and it is the 'Literacy Hour':

> W: Now we're going to do homophones. Who knows what a homophone is? No one? OK. I'll tell you one and then you're going to do some by yourselves. Like watch: one watch is your time watch, like 'What's the time?' watch; and another watch is 'I'm watching you. I can see you …' OK? So, Sayeeda, you wrote some in your book haven't you? Can you tell me some please? Can you only give me three please?
>
> S: Oh I wanted to give five
>
> W: No Sayeeda, we haven't got enough time. We've only got five minutes to assembly
>
> S: Son is the opposite of daughter …
>
> W: Yes?
>
> S: And sun is … it shines on the sky so bright.
>
> W: Well done! That's one correct one! And the next one is?

Just as in all socio-dramatic play, the children assume roles – Sayeeda as pupil and Wahida as teacher, the rest of the class are present in the imagination only and the setting is the family sitting room rather than a school classroom. But that is where the imaginary ends. There is very little fantasy in this lesson. The content is real and accurate. The aim of this play is to teach and Wahida is a skilful teacher, carefully scaffolding her sister's learning by providing clear examples, encouraging, checking that answers are correct, giving praise where it is due, and adeptly moving the lesson on. The benefits to Sayeeda if she absorbs this lesson will be evident when she reaches the 'homophone lesson' in the National Curriculum. Wahida, like siblings in many Bangladeshi British families where the parents were educated in Bangladesh, is the mediator of schooled literacy in this household, passing on to her sibling useful cultural capital in terms of knowledge that has real educational value. In this household, school learning is brought home but it is not transformed into fantasy play. It is treated with the same seriousness as the other literacies in which Bangladeshi children engage in their after-school hours.

Why should approaches to home literacy be so different in the two communities? One element in socio-dramatic play is 'imitating the actions or verbalisation of a character other than self' (Smilansky, 1990). Wahida and Sayeeda are not playing school in their home language but in English,[4] their second language, and unlike the Anglo children who have a wealth of models for English in the shape of parents, siblings, extended families, playmates and the media, the Bangladeshi British children, living in this homogeneous, tightly knit community, have only their school teachers as models for English, as their head teacher readily acknowledges:

> This is an area where they don't have many peer models. They don't pick up language accidentally in the playground. They don't watch much ordinary TV. The only modelling they get is from their teachers. (Ms R)

Just how closely Wahida models herself on her teacher can be seen in the following extract taken from a class recording:

Jill   (teacher): Does anyone know what we call words that have different meanings but sound the same?
Child: Homophones
Jill: Homophones. And what's a homophone?
Child: Two words that sound the same but have different meanings
Jill: Two words that sound the same but have different meanings. If you look on line 4, see if you can pick out a homophone.
Child: Meet
Jill: Meet. Why is meet a homophone?
Child: There's a meat that you eat …
Jill: There's a meat that you eat. How do you spell that?

Like Lee and his sisters, Wahida incorporates real-life models into her play, but as an older sibling in a Bangladeshi community, she also has a responsibility for her sister's learning. Not only must these children become proficient in English if they are to be successful in the dominant culture, but as members of a minority community, they will ultimately be responsible for the survival of the language, religion and cultural values of the Bangladeshi community in Britain. In this community, therefore, childhood is not only a time for play but a time of serious preparation for future responsibilities, as the following section illustrates.

Ethno-theories and views of childhood

The Bangladeshi British families

The analysis of the social context revealed very different attitudes or ethno-theories about childhood and child-rearing practices in the two communities. In the Bangladeshi homes, for example, great emphasis was placed by both parents and children on good behaviour, obedience and respect:

A: What do your parents teach you?
J: (aged 11): Obedience and how to speak properly
A: What's the most important thing a family teaches its children?
P   (aged 10): Discipline
A: What?
P: You have to respect them
A: What about other things?
P: Prayer.

Indeed, it appeared that good behaviour and respect for elders were considered to be as crucial a part of a child's schooling as academic learning, as the following conversation between the researcher and a mother suggests:

A: What is the most important thing the school does for the children?
Mrs P: It gives them education, teaches them to behave properly ... how they should conduct themselves properly, talk courteously and sensibly with due consideration
A: The school teaches all this?
Mrs P: Yes it should.
A: What else?
Mrs P: If the children come out of school with some good certificates, it would help them in life.

Play and fun were not considered of primary importance:

I've no problems I tell you. They don't start watching TV if they need to do their schoolwork. They don't play about. They concentrate on doing their homework. I actually have to force them to come and eat sometimes. (Mrs B)

Family responsibilities were taken seriously. Older girls helped their parents with housework and all children had to help with younger siblings:

A: Who helps you with your homework?
K: (aged 10): My sister – both my big sisters.
A: Do you help Halima and Tasmin? (younger sisters)
K: I helped Halima yesterday and Mohammed (7th child) reads his book to us
A: Do you ever read to him?
K: No he reads his book to me.

The families were devout Muslims. Not only did the parent generation regularly go to the mosque and/or read the Qur'an, but serious commitments to the faith were expressed by some of the children:

A: Which is more important, Bengali or Arabic?
P   (aged 10): Arabic
A: Why?
P: Because we need to read the Qur'an, our Holy Book, before we die.

Thus, although they were growing up in a crowded, cosmopolitan capital city, the Bangladeshi British children expressed strong views about adherence to family values, respect for religion and serious attitudes to literacy that closely reflected those of their parents who grew up in villages in rural Sylhet. For most of the project families, ties with 'the homeland' were still strong. Many had land or property in Bangladesh and one father had moved back to Sylhet so that the seven-year-old son could attend a Madrassa[5] there. In many ways, the Bangladeshi British group fitted the stereotype of agrarian societies described by Levine and White (1986), who conformed to 'moral codes favouring filial piety and intergenerational reciprocity, gender-specific ideals, social and spiritual values rather than specialized intellectual ones, concepts of childhood that emphasise the acquisition of manners …'

The Anglo-British families

While family values were also important to the Anglo parents, their ethno-theories concerning childhood and child rearing were very different. In this community the 'western' view of childhood as predominantly a time for play, prevailed: children were seen very much as individuals and children's individual needs in terms of play and happiness appeared to be the parents' overriding concern. Mothers were anxious that living in cramped flats in inner London, play opportunities were curtailed. Mrs T lives on the 13th floor of a tower block:

It's terrible for the kids here because you can't play out without having your mum with you. But we've started to try and give them a bit of independence and they go swimming on Saturdays now …

Parents spent a good deal of time organising hobbies and activities.

They do something every night of the week. Seven days a week I do two or more activities – Beavers, tennis, swimming, football, Youth Club … you name it … (Mrs R, mother of three boys)

Wherever possible, parents compensated for the children's lack of physical freedom by providing a wide range of games, books, comics and electronic equipment to play with at home. Mothers themselves were very involved in their children's play and extremely knowledgeable about their children's preferences, hobbies and activities. In many cases, as we saw earlier, mothers themselves spent time playing with their children.

At the moment they are doing a millennium house the three of them, a mediaeval one from a thousand years ago and they're going to do a futuristic circle one. That's their new buzz in life. It was on Blue Peter.

Although the Anglo mothers were pleased that their children spent a good deal of time reading, they made no distinction between 'good' books that would be approved by school and other kinds of material (Gregory and Williams, 2000). While they encouraged siblings to play together, there was no expectation that older ones would help the young ones:

AW: How did you learn to read then?

Sam (aged 6): When I was four I knew some spellings and then I started to read good when I was five.

AW: Who taught you?

S: Teacher

AW: Not Leslie (brother aged 9), not Ricky (brother aged 8), not your mum?

S: Only my mum helps me

AW: Do you ever read with Leslie and Ricky?

S: Nah!

In these families, reading the school reading book was just one of many informal literacy practices in which the children and their families engaged after school. Although they were well aware of the necessity and benefits of reading and writing, the uses of literacy for the children at this stage of their lives were seen in terms of play and enjoyment, and permitting them to participate in a wider culture.

School cultures

The differences in attitudes to play and literacy between the Bangladeshi British and Anglo East End families clearly reflected differences between their respective cultures, and given that neither culture could be said to be consonant with mainstream school culture in Britain, it might be expected that both groups of children would be at a disadvantage in school. Interviews with the two head teachers, however, revealed a very different picture. Although all state schools are obliged to follow a tightly prescribed National Literacy Strategy, each head imposed her own individual interpretation on the teaching of literacy. Ms R (School A) had herself come to Britain as a young Muslim girl from East Africa and had had to overcome many obstacles to become a teacher. As a result, she was acutely aware of the need for 'outsiders' to work hard in order to succeed in the system. Her approach to literacy was a pragmatic one, stressing the importance of structure in education, of high academic standards and clear boundaries. Since there were so few opportunities for her pupils to practise their English out of school, for example, she maintained an English-only policy in school:

We have to create situations where children can practise their English. We are always ramming it down their throats that they need to speak English because English is the key to success. They have to do their SATs in English and that's what's going to take them to secondary school, to university and on to a good job – we are forever telling them that here. English is the language to learn and to speak if they want to succeed in their studies. English is what they come here to learn and that is our job and we'll get them to succeed.

In spite of following the same curriculum, the approach to literacy was quite different in School B, attended by the Anglo children. Mrs H, mindful of the physical and economic limitations on families who lived in high-rise flats, was determined to extend the horizons of her pupils by introducing them to a wide variety of new experiences. She and her staff felt strongly that literacy should be interpreted in its broadest sense and should be enjoyable:

My expectations are that we give the children a really broad and balanced curriculum … and that we expect them to do what they *can* do. Now they (the government) want all children to be at level 2 or above at Key Stage 1, and all children to be level 4 or above at Key Stage 2. That isn't my expectation. My expectation is that we make sure the children move on and learn and move on and achieve, and that we also look at other areas besides the academic which sometimes children never get an opportunity to do in an area like ours … music and dance and art. I expect to give them good experiences that they can build on and learn from. If children haven't had experiences how can you expect them to learn? They've done drama, presentations, singing, puppet shows, assemblies …

(Enjoying reading) is to do with books, interesting literature, what you can do with books … a culture of reading. And we don't use reading schemes, we use good children's literature … you show them that words are magic.

In contrast with the findings of earlier research studies then, we found in these two particular schools a reciprocity between the school culture and that of the community they served. The views of the two heads actively reflected the ethno-theories of their respective communities: for Mrs H, literacy and reading were not just part of the daily literacy hour, nor even the sole responsibility and prerogative of the school, but embedded in a much wider, all-embracing culture. Mrs H and her teachers were not the sole transmitters of English literacy for their pupils. Family, friends, the media and the society around them all played a role in shaping the younger generation's attitudes and literacy practices and the reading, singing and play that were part of the children's home lives were appreciated in school. There was no such shared responsibility for English literacy in the lives of the Bangladeshi British children. Ms R and her staff saw themselves as the sole intermediaries in their pupils' struggle to gain a toehold in an unfamiliar culture. The serious nature of the enterprise was impressed upon pupils such as Wahida, who carried the message and methods of her school into the home, where they fitted in alongside the other formal literacy practices of their community. In both groups, however, it was the older siblings who were the intermediaries, interpreting the discourses, values and practices of the school and bringing them into their living rooms, where they were combined with the home and community practices to make up the rich repertoire of sources on which the children could draw in their play activities.

[…]

Notes

1   Community classes might only teach the language and literacy of the heritage language, but might also teach numeracy and/or the whole curriculum in the mother tongue.

2   In some cases where there was more than one sibling in the top Juniors, both children were
    included in the project.
3   A hafiz teacher who knows the Qur'an by heart.
4   We know that the children played role games in Sylheti:

>   A: Do you play any Bengali games?
>   K: Yes, cooking. Cooking with toys.

5   A Muslim college where boys train to become hafiz.

References

Anderson, A. B. and Stokes, S. J. (1984). Social and institutional influences on the development and
    practice of literacy. In H. Goelman, A. Oberg, and F. Smith (Eds) *Awakening to literacy*. London:
    Heinemann Educational.
Barton, D. and Hamilton, M. (1998). *Local literacies: Reading and writing in one community*. London:
    Routledge.
Bateson, G. (1979). *Mind and nature*. London: Wildwood House.
Baynham, M. (1995). *Literacy practices. Investigating literacy in social contexts*. London: Longman.
Bernstein, B. (1971). A sociolinguistic approach to socialisation: With some reference to educability.
    In D. Hymes and J. Gumperz (Eds) *Directions in sociolinguistics*. New York: Holt, Rinehart and
    Winston.
Bernstein, B. (1996). *Pedagogy, symbolic control and identity: Theory, research and critique*. London:
    Routledge.
Blackledge, A. (2000). *Literacy, power and social justice*. London: Trentham Books.
Bourdieu, P. (1977). *Outline of a theory of practice*. Cambridge: Cambridge University Press.
Brooker, L. (2000). *Learning how to learn: parental ethno-theories and young children's preparation
    for school*. Unpublished paper presented at the *Education and Ethnography Conference*, Oxford:
    11–12 September 2000.
Bruner, J. (1986). *Actual minds, possible worlds*. Cambridge, MA: Harvard University Press.
Central Advisory Council for Education (England) (1967). *Children and their primary schools* (Plowden
    Report). London: HMSO.
Cochran-Smith, M. (1984). *The making of a reader*. Norwood, NJ: Ablex.
Cole, M. (1996). *Cultural psychology: A once and future discipline*. Cambridge, MA: Harvard University
    Press.
Department of Education and Science (1975). *A language for life* (The Bullock Report). London: HMSO.
Department of Education and Science (1981). *West Indian children in our schools* (The Rampton
    Report). London: HMSO.
Department of Education and Science (1985). *An education for all: The report of the Committee of
    Inquiry into education for children of minority groups* (The Swann Report). London: HMSO.
Dickinson, D. K. (Ed.) (1994). *Bridges to literacy: Children, families and schools*. Cambridge, MA:
    Blackwell.
Drury, R. (1997). Two sisters at school: issues for educators of young bilingual children. In E. Gregory
    (Ed.) *One child, many worlds: Early learning in multicultural communities*. London: Fulton.
Dunn, J. (1989). Siblings and the development of social understanding in early childhood. In P. G. Zukow
    (Ed.) *Sibling interaction across cultures: Theoretical and methodological issues*. New York:
    Springer Verlag.
Duranti, A. and Ochs. E. (1996). *Syncretic literacy: Multiculturalism in Samoan American families*.
    University of California: National Center for Cultural Diversity and Second Language Learning.

Freebody, P., Ludwig. C. and Gunn, S. (1995). *Everyday literacy practices in and out of school in low socioeconomic status urban communities: A descriptive and interpretive research program*. Unpublished draft report.

Gee, J. (1996). *Social linguistics and literacies: Ideology in discourse*. London: Routledge/Falmer.

Gillborn, D. and Gipps, C. (1996). *A review of recent research of achievement by minority ethnic pupils*. London: OFSTED (Office for Standards in Education).

Gillborn, D. and Mirza, H. S. (2000). *Educational inequality. Mapping race, class and gender*. London: OFSTED.

Gregory, E. (1993). What counts as reading in the early years classroom? *British Journal of Educational Psychology*, 63, 214–230.

Gregory, E. (1994). Cultural assumptions and early years pedagogy: The effect of the home culture on minority children's interpretation of reading in school. *Language, Culture and Curriculum*, 7(2), 111–124.

Gregory, E. and Williams, A. (1998). Family literacy history and children's learning strategies at home and at school: perspectives from ethnography and ethnomethodology. In G. Walford and A. Massey (Eds) *Children learning in context: Studies in educational ethnography, Vol. 1*. Stanford, CT: JAI Press.

Gregory, E. and Williams, A. (2000). *City literacies: Learning to read across generations and cultures*. London: Routledge.

Hannon, P. (1995). *Literacy, home and school: Research and practice in teaching literacy with parents*. London: Falmer Press.

Heath, S. B. (1983). *Ways with words: Language, life and work in communities and classrooms*. Cambridge: Cambridge University Press.

Levine, R. and White, M. (1986). *Human conditions: The cultural basis of educational development*. New York: Routledge and Kegan Paul.

Michaels, S. (1986). Narrative presentations: An oral preparation for literacy with first graders. In J. Cook-Gumperz (Ed.) *The social construction of literacy*. Cambridge: Cambridge University Press.

Moll, L., Amanti, C., Neff, D. and Gonzales, N. (1992). Funds of knowledge for teaching: Using a qualitative approach to connect homes and classrooms. *Theory into Practice*, 31(2), 132–141.

Reese, L., Balzano, S., Gallimore, R. and Goldenberg. C (1996). The concept of 'educacion': Latino family values and American schooling. *International Journal of Educational Research*, 23(1), 57–80.

Robertson, L. (1997). From Karelia to Kashmir: A journey into bilingual children's story-reading experiences within school and community literacy practice. In E. Gregory (Ed.) *One child, many worlds: Early learning in multicultural communities*. London: Fulton.

Rogoff, B. (1990). *Apprenticeship in thinking: Cognitive development in social contexts*. Oxford: Oxford University Press.

Smilansky, S. (1990). Sociodramatic play: Its relevance to behaviour and achievement in school. In E. Klugman and S. Smilansky (Eds) *Children's play and learning: Perspectives and policy implications*. New York: Teachers' College Press.

Street, B. V. (1995). *Social literacies*. London: Longman.

Tizard. B. and Hughes, M. (1984). *Young children learning: Talking and thinking at home and at school*. London: Fontana.

Tomlinson, S. (1992). Disadvantaging the disadvantaged: Bangladeshis and education in Tower Hamlets. *British Journal of Sociology of Education*, 13(2), 437–446.

Tomlinson, S. and Hutchinson, S. (1991). *Bangladeshi parents and education in Tower Hamlets*. Research Report, Advisory Centre for Education, University of Lancaster.

Volk, D. (1997). Continuities and discontinuities: Teaching and learning in the home and school of a young Puerto-Rican five year old. In E. Gregory (Ed.) *One child, many worlds: Early learning in multicultural communities*. London: Fulton.

Vygotsky, L. (1978). *Mind in society: The development of higher psychological processes*. Cambridge, MA: Harvard University Press.

Wedge. P. and Prosser, H. (1973). *Born to fail?* London: Arrow Books in association with the National Children's Bureau.

Williams, A. (1989). Dialect in school written work. In J. Cheshire, V. Edwards, H. Munstermann and B. Weltens (Eds) *Dialect and education*. Clevedon: Multilingual Matters.

Williams, A. (1997). Investigating literacy in London: three generations of readers in an East End family. In E. Gregory (Ed.) *One child, many worlds: Early learning in multicultural communities*. London: Fulton.

8

Boys' Underachievement: Issues, Challenges and Possible Ways Forward

Joe Burns and Paul Bracey

[…]

The primary focus for this research attempts to identify recent patterns of boys' achievement at age 16 at one of the authors' own school, an 11–18 comprehensive (all ability) school in the Midlands area of England. Specific comparisons are made with two similar-sized schools elsewhere in the Midlands and the differing approaches adopted within those institutions. In addition, the authors try to evaluate the effectiveness of strategies employed by these focus schools to address perceived underachievement in boys at 16.

The underachievement of boys of all ages has been raised as an issue of national and international concern. Lyn Yates, Associate Professor of Education at La Trobe University, Australia, writing in the *British Journal of Education* in 1997, comments on how the degree of concern expressed in Australia and elsewhere over boys' achievement had led to 'policies on gender equity being hastily rewritten to give more prominence to the needs of boys' (Yates, 1997, p. 337). However, this article will consider boys' underachievement within the context of the UK. It will attempt to analyse this problem through a detailed evaluation of the issue at age 16 and, by considering the approaches used, to respond to this challenge through case study research of three schools. One of the authors has responsibility for raising achievement in his school and this study reflects his professional interest in the study of this area. Although we recognise that underachievement is an issue across all stages, its significance is perhaps at its greatest when boys are 16 because of the impact of school league tables (the measure by which secondary schools in England are judged each year) and the influence of examination grades at 16 on educational prospects post-16.

> If we want to improve significantly the overall national level of achievement for the 21st century, then it is the under-achievement of boys which must be tackled vigorously. (Wragg, 1997, p. 1)

Underachievement of boys needs to be set in the context of concern about British educational achievement compared with its global competitors. Pressure to meet this challenge has been at the forefront of government policy, as is reflected in the number of documents issued directing schools towards raising their overall levels of achievement through target-setting,

From: *Westminster Studies in Education*, 24 (2), 2001, pp. 155–66.

for example. The joint Department for Education and Employment (DfEE) and the Office for Standards in Education (OFSTED) report, *Setting Targets to Raise Standards*, in 1996, the DfEE *Excellence in Schools: The White Paper* in 1997(a); *From Targets to Action* in 1997(b) and *Setting Targets for Pupil Achievement* in 1997(c) all stress the need for schools to address the issue of underachievement in general and boys' achievement in particular.

Boys' underachievement has been a concern in the UK for some time. Alun Evans, writing in 1996, for example, commented how 'cultural, structural and pedagogic issues of considerable significance ... relate to the serious underachievement of boys' (Evans, 1996, p. 20).

Concern over the achievement of boys has been particularly prominent when looking at examination performance. This is shown as a changing trend where the relative performance of boys and girls has been reversed:

> Until the late 1980s, the major concern was with the underachievement of girls ... However, in the early 1990s girls began to out perform boys in all areas and at all levels of the education system. The main problem today is the under-achievement of boys. (Browne & Mitsos, 1998, p. 1)

Underachievement of girls was formerly attributed to the belief that boys were intrinsically cleverer on average than girls. Dale Spender's (1982) work in schools seemed to support this theory.

> Teachers of both sexes are inclined to believe that boys are brighter, boys are inclined to believe that boys are brighter, and girls are inclined to believe that boys are brighter – regardless of the performance of boys in the classroom. (p. 77)

Spender conducted experiments in three other countries where teachers were asked to assess pieces of work, which were sometimes identified as being produced by girls and sometimes by boys. The overwhelming response was that teachers rated and marked the work more highly when they believed it had been produced by boys, confirming their view that boys were more intelligent than girls. So familiar and potent was this argument that it seemed to be accepted by both sexes; as Spender comments:

> Girls – and boys – consistently underestimate the abilities and performance of girls and overestimate the abilities and performances of boys. (p. 80)

Many feminists believed that the educational system, particularly pre-comprehensive, was biased in favour of boys to prevent selective schools being dominated by girls (Epstein *et al.,* 1998, p. 5) and the current success of girls owes more to greater equity in education, rather than any shift of bias in favour of girls (Boaler, 1998).

This situation was addressed by the Sex Discrimination Act 1975 (Her Majesty's Stationery Office [HMSO], 1975), which provided a clear, legal framework for the equal treatment of boys and girls in schools. Subsequent Education Acts reinforced this approach. The Education Reform Act (HMSO, 1988), for example, had wide-reaching implications for so many areas of school life, not least the launch of the National Curriculum.

Some pundits identify the introduction of (the General Certificate of Secondary Education) (GCSE) as the pivotal moment. All mainstream secondary school students must take public examinations at ages 14 and 16. The examinations at age 16 (GCSE) are, by far, the most important as they can affect, quite markedly, the future options open to each student. GCSE replaced the previous examination system at 16, which was almost entirely terminal examination-based, and encouraged the development and increased significance of coursework, which girls – being more mature and more careful in their approach than boys – were able to excel at. One suggestion put forward to explain boys' underachievement was that girls attached a greater degree of importance to schoolwork and to examinations:

> girls are more likely to view exams in a far more responsible way, recognising their seriousness and the importance of the academic and career choices that lie ahead of them. (Browne & Mitsos, 1998)

An opposing argument is that education has been 'hijacked' by a feminist, anti-male agenda which has, in effect, discriminated against boys by making them work in an 'unnatural' way (Biddulph, 1994). Changes in the structure of examination courses, with a shift in weighting from terminal examinations to coursework, were also perceived in some quarters as being detrimental to boys, who performed better 'under pressure'; certainly, this was the view of School B's headteacher (see later) when questioned about factors affecting boys' performance at 16.

Whatever the view, official evidence clearly indicates that boys are doing significantly less well than girls are at 16. A joint publication by the Equal Opportunities Commission and OFSTED (OFSTED & EOC, 1996), *The Gender Divide: performance differences between boys and girls*, confirms that girls are outperforming boys at 16 to an unprecedented degree. Perhaps it is boys' influence on other boys which is to blame. Boys who succeed at school often have to run the gamut of their peers' disapproval. It's not 'cool' to be seen as an academic success, so many boys try to avoid placing themselves in this situation by deliberately underachieving in class.

> Boys' identification with macho values and relations, where school learning is seen as unmanly, often leads to significant, academic underachievement in some groups of boys (particularly working class and some black groups). (Jackson & Salisbury, 1996, p. 105; their brackets)

There has been much comment on this 'new laddishness' in boys' attitude to doing well at school, although how 'new' this attitude is remains a moot point. In the USA, Kleinfeld (1997, p. 2) writes about the development among male students of 'an anti-intellectual subculture where doing well at school is not cool'.

In a similar vein, David Jackson (1998) comments on the way in which boys straddle the gap between appearing 'cool' and, at the same time, being successful in their studies by 'carefully avoiding an open commitment to work', thereby deflecting the criticism of their peers. This strategy may work effectively for a boy who was academically able but the less academic student might well find himself falling further behind his peers who *are* working but only give an *impression* of not doing so.

The pejorative labelling of boys who work hard in school is yet another dimension of the debate. Boys who work hard are labelled as 'swots' or 'keano' (a 'keen', enthusiastic student) (Jackson, 1998), whilst schoolwork is dismissed as being beneath boys' contempt:

'The work you do here is girls' work. It's not real work. It's just for kids' (Mac an Ghaill, 1994, p. 69). Boys may deliberately cultivate an air of indifference so as to avoid the jibes of their peers, placing much greater importance on being accepted than on achieving academic success. Schoolwork is often viewed as a 'girly' under-taking, wholly inappropriate for 'men' to spend their time on. Mac an Ghaill's research at 'Parnell School' in 1994 identified different groups of students within a school's own culture. Mac an Ghaill (1994) comments on the ridicule 'Academic Achievers' experienced because of their academic success;

> Macho Lads at Parnell School made … association of academic work with an inferior effeminacy, referring to those who conformed as 'dickhead achievers'. Consequently, they overtly rejected much schoolwork as inappropriate for them as men. (p. 59)

The view that working at school was irrelevant and should be avoided was one that one of the authors had become familiar with when working in the south-east of England in the 1980s. At that time, 16-year-olds could readily obtain a relatively well-paid job in London without needing a high level of academic qualification. As earning a wage equated with success, what need was there for boys to work hard at school? Boys could drift through school and still be almost guaranteed a well-paid job. Why bother with working hard at school to scrape together a handful of indifferent paper qualifications when you can walk into a good job and make a decent wage without them? This belief seems to be particularly prevalent in some working-class areas where fathers may actively encourage their sons to look on school and academic achievement as 'unimportant' compared to the 'real world' of having a wage-earning job to call your own.

Research indicates that fathers may have, perhaps, a greater influence on their children's behaviour and, ultimately, their academic achievement than mothers do, even though fathers are generally likely to spend less time in the company of their children. Writing in 1983, Michael Marland observes that it would appear that it is those fathers who spend least time with their children who are most likely to reinforce sex-stereotyped play. Angela Phillips (1993) examines the way in which boys learn from their fathers that certain types of behaviour are appropriate for males, and between males, but that other behaviour is not:

> A boy who greets his father with a playful punch in the stomach, and is rewarded by being hoisted in the air, will get a very different reaction if he tries similar tactics with his mother … He is learning that some things are OK only with Dad. Some forms of behaviour are labelled masculine. (Phillips, 1993, p. 162)

The influence of such enforced stereotyping of behaviour in a child's formative years might reasonably be construed as a factor in boys' rejection of 'feminine' qualities, such as academic achievement, later on in life. Phillips (1993) argues that the 'stuff of masculinity' is passed on from father to son in the first three years of the boy's life, thus helping to shape his subsequent attitudes and behaviours. So, whilst recent concern is with boys' achievement, the influence of fathers on boys' behaviour and attitude has been well documented and must be considered a significant factor, even when they (the fathers) are largely absent. Other factors will come to light as we consider the responses of the case study schools to the issue of boys' underachievement.

Case study project

The researchers have used three case studies for this study; one researcher's own school and two similar-sized schools, all in the Midlands. The authors attempt to identify recent patterns of achievement at 16, for both boys and girls, at each school. They also consider the perceptions held by senior staff as to why boys' performance lags behind the girls' at their own institution. Data have been gathered from interviews and from the school's own records of examination performance between 1996 and 1998. In addition, the researchers consider the approaches employed to address perceived underachievement in boys at 16.

The three focus schools have factors in common, which allows the researchers to make comparisons between them, not least the fact that their respective headteachers were prepared for them to participate in the research. They are all 11–18 comprehensive (all ability) schools with between 1050 and 1700 students on roll. The schools may be described as urban comprehensive, though none are specifically inner-city, and they are located in different areas of the Midlands. It was felt that having the three focus schools in different areas would reduce the likelihood of local factors inadvertently skewing any resulting data. This may be seen as providing purposive sampling, as described by Blaxter *et al.* (1997). Research of this nature is small in scale and clearly this needs appreciating when analysing the data (Bassey, 1995). However, the research is intended to suggest a hypothesis, which could be tested by repeating it with further case studies.

The researchers conducted interviews at each school with a key member of staff on the subject of boys' underachievement. (Two staff were headteachers and the third was the senior teacher responsible for raising student achievement.) The interviews were semi-structured, with the use of broad questions to allow comparison, with opportunities to probe and encourage interviewees to elaborate on their original responses. In all cases, staff interviewed had a clear appreciation of the issue and gave frank, honest responses to the questions. The researchers also examined data related to GCSE examination performance at each school for the years 1996–98 and, in one case, with the school's Performance and Assessment (PANDA) report (OFSTED, 1998a). This is an annual report produced by OFSTED on each school's performance set against other schools, using the information that OFSTED holds on its databases (e.g. the number of students on roll, examination performance, the number of students eligible for free school meals, etc.)

School A is an 11–18 Roman Catholic comprehensive school with approximately 1050 students on roll. Its catchment spreads over a wide area and over half of its students travel more than three miles to attend. The pupil intake is 'comprehensive' in that there is a full ability range and the school draws its members from across a wide cross-section of the population.

School B is an 11–18 comprehensive school in the Midlands, with 1200 students on roll. Until 1978, it was a secondary modern (a school for students who had 'failed' the selection examination taken at age 11 for the local selective grammar school); over the last 20 years, the school has doubled in size. It still serves the same area, however [it is] a mix of rural, semi-rural and urban with very low unemployment figures locally, compared to the national average. Although its population includes a significant number of children from professional, middle-class backgrounds, most are from working-class homes.

School C is an urban 11–18 comprehensive school in the West Midlands with 1700 students on roll. The majority of students live within walking distance of the school and most are

Table 8.1   Average GCSE examination performance scores at each focus school compared with national figures: 1996–98 (rounded to the nearest whole number)

	1996	1997	1998
School A Boys	30	36	34
School A Girls	41	38	45
School B Boys	42	38	41
School B Girls	42	45	41
School C Boys	31	28	29
School C Girls	30	31	32
National Figures Boys	33	33	34
National Figures Girls	37	38	39

Figures taken from School A's PANDA report, 1998, published by OFSTED.

GCSE grades A* (referred to as 'A star'), A, B, C, D, E, F and G are officially recognised as 'pass' grades, with A* as the highest. However, Grade C is generally seen as the minimum level of qualification in a specific subject when applying for employment or further/higher education.

Table 8.1 shows the average GCSE points score total for boys and girls and is calculated using the scale: A* = 8, A = 7, B = 6, C = 5, D = 4, E = 3, F = 2, G = 1. Although the reliability of student attainment indicators is clearly dependent on the size of year groups, it is felt that the numbers of students in all three schools (between 180 and 300 students) was large enough to provide meaningful data that could be used for comparison.

from predominantly white, working-class homes, unlike either School A or School B. Parents of School C students have traditionally enjoyed full employment at the many factories and manufacturing plants in the area.

The fact that School A is a Church school may have a significant bearing on its population when compared with the two other focus schools, i.e. students travel from well beyond the local area to attend. In contrast, students at School B and School C mostly live locally. One might well consider that, of the three focus schools, School A is the most 'comprehensive' in its intake, which may have an effect on the performance of its boys.

To gain an impression of how the three schools compare at GCSE, we need to look at Table 8.1 which displays the differences between boys' and girls' GCSE performance at the three schools for the period 1996–98. Students are awarded grades in each subject examined ranging from A* (the very highest level) to U (Unclassified). What Table 8.1 shows is that girls are doing considerably better than boys at GCSE. The average points score for girls at each school (with only one exception) is greater than that achieved by their male peers. National figures show similar differences. The gap between the genders could not be more evident: girls do appear to be outperforming boys at age 16. The school league tables referred to earlier compare percentages of students achieving higher grades (A*–C) at 16 and rank schools by their performances. These tables are then published nationally and serve to fuel the debate on boys' achievement, as all-girls schools almost invariably seem to achieve the 'best' results.

Examination results only provide part of the picture, however. The headteacher of School A was in no doubt that boys were being outperformed at GCSE by girls but that this gap in achievement was already evident when students joined the school in Year 7.[1] The trend thereafter was for boys' performance to continue to slip below that of the girls during Years 7–10. By the time that students were in Year 11, and taking their GCSE examinations, the gap was much too wide for the boys to bridge.

School A's headteacher considered that this was a generalisation; certain groups of boys have flourished and continue to achieve as highly as their female counterparts. One factor was the introduction of significant coursework elements into examination courses, which he perceived as being of greatest benefit to girls. The most significant difference, however, was in the performance of average and below-average boys and girls. He felt that the boys would lose heart and give up on the work. Girls, on the other hand, would keep on trying.

Literacy levels were also perceived by the headteacher as being a key factor in boys' under-achievement, particularly with less able students. Boys were much less willing to read than girls, in his view, and were more likely to struggle with written tasks. Linked to this, in his opinion, was the way in which boys regard school and schooling as being of little worth when compared with other, more important, areas of their lives, such as their friends. School A's headteacher was of the opinion that a lot of boys tend to 'back off from schoolwork because it was not one of their priorities and they did not see it as 'cool' or manly to work. This attitude is clearly discernible elsewhere; Tony Sewell (1997) describes how black boys in 'Township' school (the comprehensive school which formed the basis for much of his research) see academic success as 'anti-masculine' (p. 104). The OFSTED Review of Research (OFSTED, 1998b), which produces a distillation of numerous pieces of research from the UK and elsewhere, highlights the influence of peers on achievement and behaviour at school:

> Peer group cultures and their definitions of masculinity and femininity play an important role in disaffection and underachievement. (p.77)

Boys may feel insecure about challenging the expectations of their peer groups and becoming isolated and vulnerable. The easier and safer option is to be seen to conform to the group's norm and to avoid working at school. This does not appear to be a factor for girls, who seem to be much more open about recognising and applauding others' success.

Boys' underachievement is a concern at School B also. There is an additional factor, however, in that whilst girls at School B may not seem to be outperforming boys at GCSE, this may be because there are fewer more able girls at the school than there are boys. Local competition from two high-profile selective schools (schools which may select students by dint of their academic prowess or religious affiliation) sharing the same catchment area attracts the equivalent of one class of (30) girls each year from feeder primary schools who are generally more able students. The resulting ability imbalance is added to by the presence of an all-girls' secondary school in the area, which also attracts a number of more able girls each year. Despite this, School B does have some high-achieving boys, but the spread of ability is much less than at School A. School C experiences a similar gender imbalance to that of School B, for many of the same reasons, but the students at School B generally come from a higher socio-economic group than those at School C.

As was the case with School A and the findings of the research carried out by Browne and Mitsos (1998), School B's headteacher puts some of the girls' success down to changes in the structure of examinations and in the nature of assessment:

> The nature of exams is an important factor. Girls complete coursework to a higher standard. Even though coursework counts for less overall it is still very important, particularly in subjects such as design.

Despite the fact that coursework may account for a slightly lower overall percentage in some subjects than it did previously, girls are still doing better than boys at 16 in School B, so there needs to be other factors contributing to their success. School B's headteacher identifies girls' 'greater affinity' with language as an aid to success, which is comparable to comments on literacy made by School A's headteacher. This concurs with research carried out by those concerned with issues of language and gender. Janet Holmes (1994) talks about girls being 'supportive speakers', actively collaborating with their classmates in discussion while boys are described as being 'dominant' in classroom debate, using 'talk inhibition' strategies to put their views across whilst, at the same time, refusing to listen to others.

Another key factor which the staff at School B see as contributing to boys' under-achievement there is the traditional, working-class nature of the area and its culture, which does not promote boys' academic attainment. Work has always been plentiful in the local area and there has been no perceived need for boys to exert themselves at school as they have been virtually guaranteed jobs following their fathers into local factories. Not all of School B's students are from the same socio-economic group; many students come from more middle-class backgrounds whose parents have opted to send their children to School B as a matter of political principle, rather than to the selective alternatives. The headteacher believes that in year groups which have more boys from this background than any other background, boys enjoy much greater academic success overall, providing they outnum-ber the proportion of girls from the same background.

School C differs from School A and School B in that its catchment is predominantly white and working class. It has little or none of the ethnic mix of School A. Nor does it have students from higher socio-economic groups, as is the case at both School A and School B. As regular, fairly well-paid employment has historically been easy to obtain, the consequent attitude displayed by many of the fathers of boys at the school is that educa-tion is not very important – they did not work hard at school and they have done well enough, so why bother? As with School B, however, this traditional source of employment for unskilled and semi-skilled workers is fast disappearing.

The presence of a girls' comprehensive school within two miles of School C and two girls' selective schools locally, without a local equivalent for the boys, has led to a gender imbalance at the school, as is the case at School B. Two-thirds of School C's students are male (approxi-mately 200 boys to 100 girls per year group from Years 7 to 11). Additionally, the academic ability of the girls is generally lower when compared with the boys on intake. Despite this apparent disadvantage, girls *still* manage to outperform the boys.

Work done by a senior teacher at School C charged with raising achievement and atten-dance, indicates the group of students who are most likely to underachieve at 16. At pri-mary school, these students were able to score quite highly in the SATS (Standard Assessment Tasks – government prescribed testing in English, mathematics and science for all state school students at ages 7, 11 and 14) through their innate ability and oral skills. The more demanding processes involved in secondary schools, particularly in Years 9, 10 and 11, prove to be beyond boys and they will begin to fail. It is this senior teacher's view that the result of this failure will be an increasing tendency for boys to truant, either as a way of avoiding 'difficult' lessons or of abandoning their efforts altogether. The identifi-cation of such male students in Year 7 may yet prove to be a key element in raising achieve-ment at 16 as they can be provided with extra support to help them cope with these increased academic demands and experience success rather than failure.

In all three schools, therefore, we see evidence of boys being outperformed by girls at GCSE. Boys seem to cope less well with coursework and are more readily influenced by their peers to attach little importance to their studies. The parents of boys, particularly fathers, may seem to be compounding the matter by placing greater emphasis on the importance of employment and regarding academic success as less significant and, in some cases, almost an effeminate trait. We shall now consider how the three focus schools have responded to the issue of boys' underachievement.

Raising boys' attainment: the three schools' responses

School A's headteacher believes his school had already begun to address the issue through its development plan. One way in which this was done is via a policy of looking closely at the balance of boys and girls in each group and keeping apart those boys who might feel inclined to misbehave and underperform. In addition, a policy of 'positive discrimination' with regard to boys in Years 9, 10 and 11 was pursued in some subject departments. It was felt that placing these boys in an environment where it was 'cool' to work, and to succeed, would encourage them to raise their own levels of performance.

Another strategy employed at School A is target-setting. Targets are negotiated on a half-termly basis with each student for each subject. These targets have to be 'SMART', (Specific, Manageable, Achievable, Realistic, Temporal), and are recorded by the students in their work folders. The practice continues throughout Years 7–9 inclusive and is supplemented by the use of Writing Frames (a structure to support extended writing) in some subjects as a way of enabling boys to produce longer pieces of writing by breaking the task up into smaller, more manageable 'chunks'.

School A has a well-established structure for GCSE examination revision. Also established is the practice of mentoring Year 11 students prior to their GCSE examinations. The mentoring of students at 16 has developed into a fundamental element of the academic programme at School A. Likely candidates for mentoring are identified towards the end of Year 10 and are mentored by staff from across the school during Year 11 (the criterion for selection has been to identify those students who might, with additional support, achieve five GCSE passes at grades A*–C). The scheme has recently been developed further, with trained mentors from the local community working with students in Year 11, but it is too early yet to gauge the impact of this increased provision.

At School B, form tutors act as mentors. Testing of the Year 7 intake is later linked with SAT scores al 14 to make GCSE prediction of student performance. Staff comments and assessments contribute to the process. This information is shared with the students and mentoring begins at the end of Year 10 and carries on through Year 11. This system of mentoring provides form tutors with the information they need to set practical, helpful and achievable targets. Parents and students have responded very positively to mentoring at School B. Teaching staff also view this approach favourably, seeing it as fitting in with their underlying philosophy of attempting to treat each student as an individual.

A more sophisticated system of mentoring in place at School C, designed to meet the changing needs of students from Year 7 to Year 11, takes place throughout the school year. On Tuesday, school finishes for the majority of students at 3 pm but one year group per week (boys and girls) remains for a small group mentoring session of 25 minutes. Mentors and their mentees meet regularly throughout the year but the students in Year 10 and 11 meet most regularly with their tutors. Teaching staff will mentor the same students from Year 7 to the end of Year 11. In Year 11, mentors focus on four main criteria with their groups: predictor grade, attendance, effort and behaviour. The predictor grade is set by the local education authority and is shared with all staff whilst mentors set targets for students. Year 11 students see this mentoring as an effective way to raise achievement and are very positive about it, as, increasingly, are their parents.

School C has a Raising Achievement action group, containing key members of each subject department, which aims to address the issue of boys' underachievement. The strategy developed has focused on raising the achievement of *all* students by improving literacy skills. Improving literacy should, the school believes, enable students to access the curriculum more readily. School C also uses baseline assessment (an assessment of students' academic level on entry to the school) to identify those students who are likely to underachieve at 16. The results are then mapped to identify those students (mainly boys) who have a deficiency in learning skills (especially literacy) which will inhibit their access to the curriculum. Staff are then able to target these students early and work on improving the deficits in their learning skills.

Boys' performance cannot improve unless they are in school and prepared to learn. School C invests a great deal of time and resources in working to improve attendance. There is an electronic register system used by all teachers: A4-size 'pads' on which attendance at each lesson is recorded and monitored and which helps to reduce internal truancy, i.e. students avoiding specific lessons during the school day. Running alongside this is a behaviour management policy, which delivers strategies for the school, and individual teachers, to cope with boys' disaffection and poor behaviour in class. Classroom and behaviour management training plays an important role by equipping staff with the resources and strategies necessary to remain in control of the situation. Whole-school training also helps develop and maintain a consistency of approach that establishes clear parameters for students, especially boys, to work by.

What are the implications for the case study schools of the evidence presented here?

Clearly, the organisational response of all schools has suggested that raising literacy levels is a key element in all three schools; strategies and practice which encourage and develop this aim should form a core element of a school's response to the challenge of boys' underachievement. Evidence from the schools used in this study suggests that they have developed strategies and approaches by which boys' achievement may be raised. Early identification of potential underachievers, as at School C, and a programme of literacy support and development may well prove to be as effective a way as any of raising boys' achievement. Given the success of the Literacy Hour (a government-prescribed strategy addressing perceived literacy needs) in primary schools, it is generally anticipated that similar success will ensue when this strategy is adopted by secondary schools in the very near future.

Empowering boys to make appropriate decisions about themselves and their lives is a further element in helping to raise their overall level of achievement, something all three schools have done by mentoring students. Boys' attitudes towards achievement in each school may need to change, however. Both School B and School C felt that first altering the attitudes of parents, principally some fathers, increased the chances of such a development being successful.

The fact is that boys now leaving these schools, unlike their fathers, encounter the situation where there are no jobs for life. By raising boys' awareness of the situation that faces them, the schools may well help boys to recognise the importance of their education and give them added motivation to succeed. Careers education provision within School A, for example, actively promotes well-informed, realistic decision-making, with the intention of enabling boys to make appropriate choices for their futures. In this vein, the schools are encouraging boys to work towards the acquisition of appropriate skills and qualifications for future employment. By making adequate provision for vocational courses and qualifications, the schools try to persuade boys that the work they do is not 'unmanly' (Jackson & Salisbury, 1996). While there is a range of socio-economic factors which are likely to affect achievement (e.g. levels of employment, deprivation and parental attitudes) and potentially inhibit the impact of schools' efforts, it is to be hoped that the measures adopted by the schools are enough to turn the tide.

However, the vexing question of boys' underachievement is a long way yet from being resolved. In future, we will see what the impact of literacy initiatives at both primary and secondary phases of schooling have on achievement levels of boys and girls. Improving literacy, target-setting, and career planning and the provision of appropriate vocational courses are but some of the strategies which might be considered for raising the level of boys' success at school. Mentoring schemes, such as the one currently under development in School A or the well-established model at School C, may yet prove to be crucial in enabling boys to exceed present levels of achievement, although further research into these is necessary before their impact can be accurately assessed.

Clearly, the emphasis and practice of achievement-raising strategies will vary according to the circumstances in different schools. However, the approaches used by the three schools within this research will, it is hoped, contribute to the debate in this area. It was Ted Wragg who wrote in 1997 of the bleak future facing our society if boys' underachievement was not addressed promptly and thoroughly. [...] The situation is clearly being addressed, which raises hopes that Wragg's later assertion may yet become a reality: 'Good news: boys will be boffs' (Wragg, 1999, p. 1).

Note

1   Students aged 11–12 are in Year 7; those aged 12–13 are in Year 8; and so on.

References

Bassey, M. (1995) *Creating education through research: a global perspective of educational research for the 21st century* (Newark, Kirklington Moor Press in conjunction with the British Educational Research Association).

Biddulph, S. (1994) *Manhood: a book about setting men free* (Sydney, Finch Publishing), cited in: D. Epstein, J. Elwood, V. Hey & J. Maw (Eds) (1998) *Failing Boys? Issues in Gender and Achievement* (Buckingham, Open University Press).

Blaxter, L., Hughes, C. & Tight, M. (1997) *How to Research* (Buckingham, Open University Press).

Boaler, J. (1998) Mathematical equity – underachieving boys or sacrificial girls? In: D. Epstein, J. Maw, J. Elwood & V. Hey (Eds) *International Journal of Inclusive Education,* Special Issue on Boys' 'Underachievement', 2(2), pp. 19–134.

Browne, K. and Mitsos, E. (1998) Gender differences in education: the underachievement of boys. *Sociology Review*, September.

Department for Education and Employment (DfEE) (1996) *Setting Targets to Raise Standards: a survey of good practice* (London, HMSO).

Department for Education and Employment (DfEE) (1997a) *Excellence in Schools: The White Paper* (London, HMSO).

Department for Education and Employment (DfEE) (1997b) *From Targets to Action* (London, HMSO).

Department for Education and Employment (DfEE) (1997c) *Setting Targets for Pupil Achievement* (London, HMSO).

Epstein, D., Elwood, J., Hey, V. and Maw, J. (Eds) (1998) *Failing Boys? Issues in Gender and Achievement.* (Buckingham, Open University Press).

Evans, A. (I996) Perils of ignoring our lost boys. *Times Educational Supplement,* 28 June, p. 20.

Her Majesty's Stationery Office (HMSO) (1975) *Sex Discrimination Act* (London, HMSO).

Her Majesty's Stationery Office (HMSO) (1988) *Education Reform Act 1988,* chapter 40 (London, HMSO).

Holmes, J. (1994) Improving the lot of female language learners, in: J. Sunderland (Ed.), *Exploring Gender questions and implications for English language education* (London, Prentice-Hall).

Jackson, D. (1998) Breaking out of the binary trap: boys' underachievement, schooling and gender relations, in: D. Epstein, J. Elwood, V. Hey and J. Maw (Eds) *Failing Boys; Issues in Gender and Achievement* (Buckingham, Open University Press).

Jackson, D. and Salisbury, L. (1996) Why should secondary schools take working with boys seriously? *Gender & Education,* 8, pp. 103–115.

Kleinfeld, J. (1997) None dare call it a problem: male underachievement, *The Women's Freedom Network Newsletter.* Winter, 4; available from: http:www.womensfreedom.org/artic414.htm

Mac an Ghaill, M. (1994) *The Making of Men: masculinities, sexualities and schooling* (Buckingham, Open University Press).

Marland, M. (Ed.) (1983) *Sex Differentiation and Schooling* (London, Heinemann).

Office for Standards in Education (OFSTED) (1998a) *PANDA reports,* various (London, HMSO).

Office for Standards in Education (OFSTED) (1998b) *Recent Research on Gender and Educational Performance* (London, HMSO).

Office for Standards in Education & Equal Opportunities Commission (OFSTED & EOC) (1996) *The Gender Divide: performance differences between boys and girls at school* (London, HMSO).

Phillips, A. (1993) *The Trouble with Boys: parenting the men of the future* (London, Pandora).

Sewell, T. (1997) *Black Masculinity and Schooling: how black boys survive modern schooling* (Stoke-on-Trent, Trentham Books).

Spender, D. (1982) *Invisible Women. The Schooling Scandal* (London, Co-operative Society Ltd in association with Chameleon Editorial Group).

Wragg, E.C. (1997) Oh boy! *Times Educational Supplement,* 10 May, pp. 4–5.

Wragg, E.C. (1999) Good news: boys will be boffs. *Times Educational Supplement,* 12 November.

Yates, L. (1997) Gender equity and the boys debate: what sort of challenge is it? *British Journal of Sociology of Education,* 18, pp. 337–346.

9

Re-counting 'Illiteracy': Literacy Skills in the Sociology of Social Inequality

Geoff Payne

[…]

One of the more dramatic educational statistics about contemporary Britain is that seven million adults – 20 per cent of the population – are illiterate.[1] Some of the rhetorical power of this statistic comes from the stigmatizing word 'illiterate', but it is the figure of 'seven million' that signifies an undesirably high rate of skills deficiency, inviting us to see this as a serious social problem. The media should in fact use the term 'functionally illiterate' which, as we shall see, has a technical meaning, but to a non-specialist audience *functional* illiteracy sounds at least as bad as illiteracy per se, and possibly even worse.

As individuals, people with poor literacy and numeracy skills suffer personal embarrassment and dysfunction in social situations: recent television advertisements for adult education depict 'gremlins' living off the inability of the 'victims' to fill in forms, help their children with homework, read aloud to other people, or join leisure classes. Poor literacy limits restricts life-chances [sic] and excludes from the 'good life'. At a structural level (the main concern of this [chapter]), educational skills are necessary to achieve success in present-day society: skills deficits are associated with low-skilled work or unemployment, while damage to the national economy is attributed to skills shortages (DfEE 1999: 8, 25; Bynner and Parsons 1997; Parsons and Bynner 2002a, 2002b). Lack of literacy wastes human potential, which is both individually damaging and socially inefficient.

It might therefore be a reasonable expectation that the sociology of literacy would be an integral, even if perhaps not a dominant, feature of four areas of discourse: the sociology of structural social inequality; the measurement of national rates of literacy, particularly with respect to definitional issues and the social construction of a 'national problem' in terms of social exclusion; the sociology of work and employment, with regard for workplace skills and labour market capacities; and the sociology of education (not least with respect to educational inequalities and their relationship to social mobility through the credentialism thesis). However, while some important work has been carried out in each area, employing a generally 'social' perspective, the output is still small compared with other fields of the discipline, and its influence on mainstream, and particularly quantitative, sociology has been relatively slight.

This generalization should be qualified with respect to certain more recent developments within the specialist field of literacy studies. Here the impact of post-modernism has led to a more sophisticated 'cultural' or 'social' perspective, in which issues of discourse, textual

From: *The British Journal of Sociology*, 57 (2), 2006, pp. 219–40.

analysis, non-verbal communication, ideology and power have come to the fore (e.g. Maybin 1993; Street 1993, 1995; Barton and Hamilton 1998; Wagner, Venezky and Street 1999; Barton, Hamilton and Ivanic 2000). In particular, the 'New Literacy Studies' approaches (Collins and Blot 2003; Street 2003) and reactions to them (e.g. Brandt and Clinton 2002) have made a significant contribution, not least through deployment of ethnographic accounts (Green and Bloome 1997; Finnegan 1999; Street 2001). We do not wish to denigrate these advances: however, despite some signs to the contrary (e.g. Robinson 2003), our view is that they too have yet to make a major influence on the 'national surveys movement' or on traditional sociology (although they have made more impact in social anthropology). The key point is not that sociology has totally ignored literacy, but that literacy studies have yet to fulfil their potential for mainstream and quantitative sociology's concerns with structural social inequality, and that sociology in turn has not been sufficiently involved in the social construction of literacy as a contemporary public problem.

We can sustain this generalization in two ways. First, none of the four main British sociology journals, *British Journal of Sociology, Sociological Research Online, Sociological Review, and Sociology*, have carried even a single article with the words literacy or illiteracy in their title or keywords (Google search, February 2005). In the academic year 2004–5, no British department of sociology offered literacy as a core component of its Honours Degree in Sociology, or Sociology 'Major' Degree. Almost none offers literacy as an 'elective', although such modules can be found in some degrees in Cultural Studies or Education. The British Sociological Association's *Non-Disablist Language Guidelines* (2005) shows appropriate sensitivity to many forms of disability: however, at the time of writing, it includes no reference to illiteracy (a condition which we are told afflicts seven million adults), thus suggesting that the members of the BSA have been relatively unaware of, or unconcerned with, literacy as either a social or sociological problem.

Second, sociology had little influence on the research behind the major national surveys which have dominated public thinking about rates of literacy. A review of their bibliographical references (e.g. Bynner and Parsons 1997; Carey, Low and Hansbro 1997; DfEE 1999; Williams 2003; see also OECD 1997; Basic Skills Agency 1989) shows a virtual absence of sociological sources. The moral panic over literacy rates in this country has escalated without any significant contribution from sociologists.

These two sets of evidence of sociology's relative neglect of literacy in this country are all the more surprising given the existence of intellectual frameworks which might easily have embraced literacy. Whereas *formal* educational qualifications have received considerable attention dating from the early LSE studies by, inter alia, Marshall (1965 [1950]); Halsey, Floud and Anderson (1961); Little and Westergaard (1964); Halsey, Heath and Ridge (1980), this has focused on class differentials in educational access, and how formal *qualifications* have increasingly determined entry to mainly middle-class occupations. The debate on meritocracy stimulated by Saunders (1996) [...] makes no reference to seven million people with literacy deficits. The distinctive features of low literacy skills for life chances and social mobility have received much less discussion, even in the sociology of education, other than at an ethnographic level.

More generally, the sociology of social inequality provides ample scope for modelling differences between groups of people, where one group is more advantaged than another. The disadvantages of not being literate are fundamentally similar to other forms of disadvantage, such as being disabled, a member of a minority ethnic group, female, or the child of unskilled manual workers. Lack of literacy is not such an alien phenomenon that we have had no conceptual frameworks that would have allowed us to tackle it. To give a simple example, because literacy is a socially valued skill, in Weberian class terms, it allocates a differential location in the labour market for those who possess it, and hence an advantaged social class situation. On the other hand, while literacy may not be a social division of the same order as class, gender, or ethnicity (Payne 2006), it cannot be entirely subsumed under other structural features. This [chapter] is therefore intended to provide a step towards raising awareness of literacy among sociologists who still seem to regard it with the same discomfort that they viewed visual, aural and other physical impairments until the 1990s.

However, while the comparatively recent 're-discovery of illiteracy' (Aluluf 1992: 12–13) points to the need to treat it seriously as a social condition, an economic problem, and a sociological concept, the more basic point that there may be *seven million* people in this country lacking reading and counting skills is mind-boggling. One in every five adults is a very large proportion, and on a common sense basis, seems implausible. Scepticism is likely to increase when one notes that the data on which the claim is based were not collected by sociologists, i.e. by that branch of social science claiming particularly sensitivity to the social construction of categories and official statistics. A re-examination of the methods used to identify the 'seven million' is clearly necessary.

It follows that we wish to address two issues: most directly we question the *amount* of low literacy in contemporary Britain, and in the process, advocate the need to see literacy as a *theorized* component of social inequality *structures* (obviously, completion of this second, larger task is beyond the scope of a single article). We acknowledge that this is to hold what at first may seem a somewhat paradoxical position. This article argues that literacy is an important sociological phenomenon, but one largely under-researched in British sociology. At the same time, we demonstrate that the *number* of people with low literacy skills has been over-estimated, thus reducing the scale of the problem. However, these are not in fact incompatible arguments, as we hope to show by examining how some literacy specialists and the media generated a false impression of large numbers of people with low literacy, in parallel with indicating a more sociological perspective of literacy as a facet of social inequality. We seek to achieve this by combining original work with relatively unrecognized contributions, both in Britain and elsewhere, which have begun (sometimes perhaps less directly) to address these issues (e.g. Freebody 1998; Wagner, Venezky and Street 1999; Barton, Hamilton and Ivanic 2000; Brandt and Clinton 2002).

The new illiteracy: 'there seems to be a lot of it about'

A few years ago, reports began to appear in the British media that at least seven million of the nation's adults, about one in five, were either 'illiterate' or very nearly so. Other estimates followed, giving different numbers, but all similarly alarming. These remarkably high figures seemed doubly problematic. First, to have large numbers of people (regardless of the exact magnitude) so disadvantaged was intrinsically unwelcome news. Second, given varying estimates, precisely how many people (with what sorts of social characteristics and in what social situations) were involved?

In Spring 1999, *The Guardian* forecast that Government-sponsored research would shortly show 'one in four hardly able to read a broadsheet newspaper … [O]ne in six adults, around 8 million, are unable to read at a level to enable them to cope with everyday life simple tasks

Table 9.1   Media coverage *(The Guardian/Observer)*

Date	Illiteracy reference	Event/Policy
16.03.99	Moser Report	New HMG plan for ITV illiteracy show
24.03.99	8 m. illiterates	Publication of Moser Report
12.07.99	22% UK popn. illiterate	Publication of UNESCO Report
19.01.00	1 in 4 illiterate	Guardian Launch Campaign v. Illiteracy
30.01.00	[HMG Illiteracy Campaign]	[Typo in new anti-illiteracy posters]
16.05.00	1.2 m. Scots can't read	Scottish Exec. plan to count illiterates
16.05.00	7 m. illiterate	New BSA research report
30.05.00	7 m. illiterate	FE Colleges report training successes
16.07.00	1.3 m. with reading age of 7	Leak of extra HMG funding for education
03.09.00	7 m. illiterate	New adult education spending
05.09.00	Moser Report	Male Wicks: 1st yr. as Education Minister
17.10.00	Moser Report	Appointment of literacy 'tsarina'
19.10.00	1 in 5 illiterate	HMG launch leaflet for literacy teachers
05.12.00	7 m. illiterate	Follow-up of new literacy 'tsarina' story
29.03.01	1 in 3 inadequate literacy	LSC Launch/4th yr. Stage 4 programme
12.06.01	7 m. or 1 m. illiterate debate	Wells' challenge to Moser
19.08.01	7 m./15 per cent illiterate	New research report from Univ. of Ulster
09.10.01	15 percent illiterate	Follow-up: worse than 1912 says Ulster
29.02.02	Moser Report	Pubn. of Schlink's The Reader in UK
10.03.02	7 m./I in 5 illiterate	PM Statement on Edn/BSA funding/etc.
02.06.02	20 per cent illiterate	Pubn. of ESRC World of Work study
06.11.02	6 m. illiterate	Apt. of new Minister of Education
24.11.02	['Big problems of illiteracy']	[general edn. piece/top up fees: no event]
01.12.02	7 m. illiterate	Pre-Budget Report: education spending
07.01.03	1 in 3 no/low qualifications	Launch of Employer Training pilots.

Source: *Guardian Unlimited* (2003a).

such as reading a bus timetable or a menu' (*The Guardian* 24 March 1999). In July, a UNESCO publication was reported as showing '22 per cent of the UK population illiterate' (12 July 1999). If we consider the coverage of the 'responsible press' during the four years from March 1999, *The Guardian's* online Archive (accessed mid-March 2003) listed 25 such references in the paper and its sister publication, The *Observer* (see Table 9.1).

In addition, Government-sponsored websites, such as those of the Learning Skills Council and the Basic Skills Agency (confusingly for sociologists, the 'BSA'), have carried factual statements that there were seven million adults in England and Wales with 'serious basic skills needs in literacy, numeracy and basic IT', and that 'as many as 1 in 5 adults in the UK has poor basic skills' (Learning Skills Council 2001; Basic Skills Agency 2002). It might be an over-statement to describe this as a 'moral panic', but there has certainly been a strong media reaction; at the least, a 'moral anxiety attack'.

Table 9.1 also shows how versions of these findings became re-cycled each time new basic skills initiatives, policy documents and government appointments were announced. There have been ample opportunities for this. Even allowing for New Labour's tendency to re-announce its programmes and 'new' spending, the array of initiatives is impressive. Schemes like Employer Training, FE College provision for Adult Learners (although this is often aimed at those with low knowledge of English), Individual Learning Accounts, the University of Industry, the Learning and Skills Councils, and the funding of the Basic Skills Agency were mainly addressed at those who have already left school. Setting the 80 per cent Key Stage 4 literacy targets, the literacy hour, advice for teachers of literacy, the Quality Initiative for staff training, and the Connexions programme for young people have been aimed at improving the output of qualified young people from schools. Over £100 million per annum is now being directed towards improving literacy skills. The announcement of each initiative has been accompanied by repetition of low literacy levels. Even a recent claim of improvement (see below) was based on the starting point of seven million, and appeared in the press under headlines stressing how far there was still to go (*Guardian Unlimited* 2003b).

Apart from within the neglected specialist field of literacy studies (e.g. Freebody 1998), there appears to have been only one significant dissenting public comment. Alan Wells, Director of the Basic Skills Agency, has objected:

I'm a firm supporter of the strategy to improve the basic skills of all too many adults and I'm not arguing that we don't have a very urgent problem with under-education in this country. But we won't get anywhere if we keep going on about seven million illiterates and innumerates (sic) or one in five adults who can't read or write or use numbers. … It's not true that one in five adults cannot read or write or use numbers. … What is true is that in an international study in 1997, one in five adults in the UK came in the bottom group in literacy and numeracy. (Reported in *The Guardian* 12 June 2001)

The article continues:

Wells's verdict on the seven million statistic was instantly rebutted by Sir Claus Moser … 'There's absolutely no question – and it's been internationally accepted and by all authorities here – that between six and seven million adults have problems with functional illiteracy and innumeracy,' Sir Claus says. 'I would go to the stake as a statistician for that being correct.' (*The Guardian* 12 June 2001)

To those of us raised on Moser and Kalton's (or indeed, Moser's) *Survey Methods in Social Investigation* (1958 et seq.), this is endorsement indeed. Moser does, however, acknowledge different levels of literacy skills. There is also no escaping the variation in estimates, from *one in three* (OECD 1997) to *one in six* (1999 *Guardian* story) of *'adults'* in *'Britain'*, the *'UK'* or *'England and Wales'*. We need to clarify how literacy has been measured, and to check on the numbers reported.

Unfortunately, literacy has not been a significant research topic in British sociology. In following up these reports of the seven million adults trapped in a 'vicious circle of disadvantage and marginalisation' (Bynner and Parsons 1997: 10), the near-silence of British sociology was striking. The bibliographies of the literacy studies (see Carey, Low and Hansbro (1997); OECD (1997); DfEE (1999); and the several publications by Bynner and Parsons in the References below) contain almost no sociological references, with a few exceptions such as Levine (1986). This is not to deny that there have been a number of specialist sociological studies, mainly ethnographic in method: what the evidence clearly shows is that these have been inadequately incorporated into the public debate about literacy, as distinct from academic and practitioner discourse. Surveys of literacy rates are dominated by social psychologists, educationalists, and to a lesser extent, economists.

From the outset, it was clear that many standard sociological questions had not been explored by those who dominate in this field. For example, despite technical debate about operationalization, there has been only limited discussion of the approach taken by the IALS survey (e.g. Street 1996; Barton and Hamilton 1998) and what is actually meant by the terms 'literacy' or 'numeracy'. *Who* uses the label, in what circumstances, and with what consequences? In which social environments do literacy problems occur; and what are their key social correlates, like gender, ethnicity or class background? The issue is not whether a few studies have addressed these questions, but the failure of such studies to make a wider impact on the national surveys (see also Hamilton and Hillier 2004). A necessary prior step in establishing how many people in Britain today lack literacy skills is to investigate how this has been measured.

Defining 'literacy': conceptual problems with 'functional literacy'

While the research exercise of operationalizing literacy inevitably elaborated taken-for-granted, common sense ideas of being 'illiterate', the extent of operational re-definition would not be obvious to a lay person. Moser's 'functionally illiterate' (quoted above) is not simply a turn of phrase, but a technical expression, meaning those having *low* levels of literacy and/or numeracy skills for tackling *specific social tasks*. The seven million 'illiterates' were not in fact illiterate, i.e. unable to read and write in a strict sense. Instead they were 'functionally illiterate'. Media accounts have largely omitted the word 'functional' despite it being part of a specific technical term.

This idea of functional literacy, being able to 'function' in society, emerged in the 1950s. Leaving aside negative vernacular connotations (i.e. ignorance, lack of education and stupidity), prior studies treated literacy and illiteracy as dichotomous, absolute conditions. People either could read and write, or they could not. In specialist academic circles, this view was then increasingly replaced by a more flexible approach, recognizing that across societies, and at different times, there is a range of literacy *expectations.*

In Britain, the 1996 Adult Literacy Survey ('ALS': Carey, Low and Hansbro 1997) shared the basic approach of the OECD International Adult Literacy Survey ('IALS': OECD 1997), identifying literacy and numeracy as the capacity to use 'printed and written information to function in society, to achieve one's goals and to develop one's knowledge and potential' (Carey, Low and Hansbro 1997: 8). The 1999 DfEE ('Moser') report, *A Fresh Start,* broadly follows this but concentrates on technical definitions expressed as performance levels on (mainly BSA) literacy and numeracy tests. The literacy studies use slightly different systems of measurement and classification, but share a common approach, testing for skills in several 'domains' (prose, document usage, numeracy) by using material drawn from real-life situations (reading newspapers, understanding advertisements, using bus timetables, etc.). While there are individual differences, performance across the domains of functional literacy are 'highly correlated' (Carey, Low and Hansbro 1997: 14): for convenience, this article refers mainly to rates of literacy, not numeracy. The studies allocate informants to four or five functional literacy 'Levels': see Figure 9.1.

Although a functional literacy definition grounded in actual social conditions is attractive, it has its own problems. If the unit of analysis is to be *individual* dysfunctionality (due to lack of 'ability', or 'incorrect attitudes' to schooling), this inhibits discussion of social processes as causes. How is the *individual* level to be linked to the *social* level: how far do individuals, and groups of individuals (genders, classes, ethnicities) *share* the social 'goals' referred to by Carey and others?

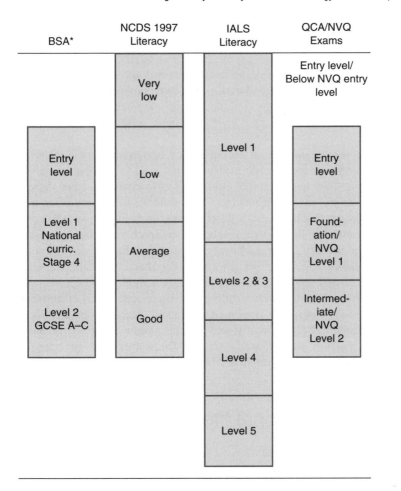

Figure 9.1   A comparison of literacy levels and formal qualifications (to approximate scale)

Source: Author's adaptation from Bynner and Parsons 1997; Carey, Low and Hansbro 1997; DfEE 1999; OECD 1997).

Note: *equivalent to school qualifications.

Alternatively, and given that the debate about literacy is embedded in education policies designed to modify *systems* of provision, the definition can be treated as an essentially *social* one. The focus then becomes not the aims of the individual, but the expectations of the individual's group or community. How are such standards established, how can they be identified, how are they to be represented in the measurement of literacy, and by whom?

A second definitional problem is that in accepting the IALS view that 'there is no generally agreed interpretation of the minimum skills threshold for functioning in modem society' (Carey, Low and Hansbro 1997: 20), one does not thereby escape from the necessity to measure literacy. Instead, measurements have to be justified as best they can, knowing that they are inherently contestable, and that despite the work of OECD in seeking comparability in the IALS, other researchers (e.g. the BSA) may be using different measurement devices. As Slavenburg observes, the generic definition means that each member state:

> must operationalize it according to its own context and situation. After all, 'his (sic) group' and 'his community' will make their own demands; concepts such as 'for his own development' and 'for the community's development' can also produce different interpretations. (1992: 3)

A third problem is the logical inconsistency between the cultural relativism of the generic definition, and the specific measurements used in the operationalization process. Function literacy assumes *relativist, context-specific definitions,* but these only succeed when the *operational measurements* have face validity. To put it another way, the general definition promises flexibility, with its core concept being apparently constructed from personal experience in social situations, but the researchers' actual measurements of literacy may still be just as rigid and arbitrary an operationalization as 'absolute' literacy. All that is really happening is that the threshold for literacy is being raised, the domains extended, and several levels recognized, to replace a single fixed cut-off point.

Functional literacy in fact draws on normative conceptions of citizenship, community activism, and work. Literacy is presented as the skill needed to be a *concerned* citizen, a *responsible* member of a community, and a *useful* employee (see particularly Bynner and Parsons 1997; Parsons and Bynner 2002a, 2002b). Rather than 'functional literacy', this view could be better called *'normative literacy'.*

Measuring functional literacy

Literacy researchers, despite their context-oriented generic definitions of functional literacy, actually impose a series of arbitrary cut-off points, based on what they think acceptable functioning in society must be. In the assessment interviews, respondents were presented with extracts from newspapers, adverts or diagrams as concrete representations of abstract performance criteria. The published reports are not entirely clear whether the researchers saw these representations as requiring *real-life literacy performances* per se, or as *symbols of underlying literacy skills.* The media headline accounts quoted earlier quite reasonably take the concrete tasks at face value, and not as indicators of a more abstract skill level:

> all the stimuli in the assessment were real items drawn from the countries taking part ... (Items) reflect the diversity, reality and challenge of everyday life. (Carey, Low and Hansbro 1997: 14)

This suggests that being able to read a newspaper, for example, can be seen as an actual direct test of literacy, rather than just a signifier in an abstract criterion test. In this interpretation, reading a broadsheet newspaper becomes a test which is actually based on a normative view of social behaviour, drawing on the researchers' own middle-class, literacy-based culture. The problem is not that there should be such a prescription – how else could research or social policy operate? – but that it should be confused with the culturally relativistic definition derived from UNESCO, quoted above.

This is not just a technical matter of measurement philosophy. The heart of the problem here is the extent to which one believes that the printed word is the only way to function in society. Even avid news freaks (like the present author) sometimes watch television news instead of reading the *Guardian*. If reading a broadsheet newspaper were a genuine requirement for citizenship (and added to the new 'citizenship test'?), each copy sold would need to be read by 14 different people to cover every citizen in the labour force (see MediaGuardian.co.uk 2003).

Similarly, normative literacy treats an ability to understand bus timetables as an essential skill (but like most urban dwellers, when I travel by bus, I simply wait at the stop until the next bus [comes] along – who seriously believes bus services are related to the published timetables?). Understanding written dosage instructions for medicine is another test (however, my GPs always insist on *telling* me the amounts to take, while writing the prescription in the surgery). When I last needed a plumber, I asked neighbours and colleagues for a reliable name, rather than looking up the Yellow Pages. Advocates of normative literacy may themselves operate in a written-word culture, but substantial parts of the rest of society have found other ways to lead their lives.

Despite these objections, we find ourselves trapped, as in all secondary analysis, within the definitions of the original sources. Without a fresh approach, further discussion here – such as attempts to re-formulate the way literacy relates to social inequality, or even to improve calculation of how many people have severe literacy deficits – can only proceed on the basis of available data. Although the tests of literacy have been unduly normative, so exaggerating how many people have severe problems, the remainder of this [chapter] addresses the core definitional terms of 'functional literacy' as used in the earlier research.

Who lacks literacy skills? Gender, ethnicity and literacy

The constraints of this normative aspect of functional literacy become obvious as soon as one addresses the various counts of the literacy rate. The discussion so far has talked of 'adults' or 'individuals'. However, one of the first results of trying to clarify the range of estimates was the discovery that the term 'adult' had, in *all* the national surveys identified above, been quietly transmuted from its normal meaning (people over 16) to mean only those aged 16–65. Functional literacy is so inextricably linked to conventional ideas about employability and economy that the term 'adult' has been taken to mean only persons of working age (e.g. Carey, Low and Hansbro 1997: 8; DfEE 1999: 16). The surveys do not see this as an issue. The only explanation offered is that the sample was restricted:

> because of *the relevance of the skills being measured to the labour market* as well as known difficulties associated with administering such assessment to older people. (Carey, Low and Hansbro 1997: 158, emphasis added)

More than 18 per cent of the population, those over male retirement age, were excluded. While we acknowledge the technical constraints of data-collection among older people, the literacy studies' concentration on the *labour force* is remarkably congruent with their other justifications for literacy research as contributing towards improvement in national economic performance (e.g. Carey, Low and Hansbro 1997: 18–19; DfEE 1999: 8, 25; Parsons and Bynner 2002b: 8).

Readers will have noted the use of the male retirement age as the sample's upper cut-off. The survey reports themselves do not comment on the different retirement age for women, and indeed have little to say about gender elsewhere. Nor do they pay much attention to ethnicity, while their treatment of educational qualifications and occupational class is not much more informative. More attention to these other social divisions would not only have yielded a more rounded picture of those with literacy problems than the gender-neutral non-ethnic 'adults' they do report, but would have enabled a more accurate measurement of literacy rates. There can be little justification for ignoring the work of more socially oriented researchers, and indeed, some more recent debates have recognized this.

It should be pointed out these criticisms are based on normal academic reading, photocopying, and note-taking, rather than on a careful key word, line by line content analysis search of the documents. However, the very limited information presented about gender and ethnicity was striking. In fairness, the BSA does pay more attention to gender (e.g. Bynner and Parsons 1997). It has also carried out some specialist research on language skills among minority ethnic groups (BSA 1989; Carr-Hill et al. 1996), but their technical methods make it even harder to compare them with the main literacy studies than comparing the latter with each other.

The major surveys did not *ignore* these key social divisions. Literacy data were gathered from women and (in some cases) members of minority ethnic groups, and these are at least briefly mentioned. However, even allowing that later researchers could have followed up such issues by accessing the raw data – although these were not initially readily available for all of the studies discussed here – this was not done. The result is that the 'message' of the surveys remains in its original homogenized gender-neutral non-ethnic form.

It might be unfair to say that these 'neutral' persons ('7 million adults illiterate' (see Table 9.1)) are implicitly white and male, but just as normative literacy tests are based on implicit class assumptions about the written culture, so too do the statements about 'adults' make most sense if they are read as if they referred to white males. The extensive reports contain literally only a few handfuls of pages dealing with differences in literacy between genders and ethnic groups, and even less about the distinctive social milieus in which they lead their lives. For example, gendered schooling experiences as causes of poor numeracy, or the distinctive labour market consequences of poor literacy for each gender, go virtually un-mentioned in the main reports.

Where they are discussed, gender differences fall under three main headings. The first is that men and women score differently on the literacy tests. The general conclusion is that their scores are broadly similar, although women do less well in the numeracy domain, and perform better with prose than document tests. At the lower ALS Level, there are no statistically significant differences in prose or documentary performance, but whereas 18 per cent of men are at this level for numeracy, 29 per cent of women are assessed as in this category (Carey, Low and Hansbro 1997: 21). Bynner and Parsons (1997) report very similar figures. The main information used in this [chapter] has been prose domain scores, particularly at the lower level.

Much of the (small) difference is most obvious in the upper levels of accomplishment. The OECD study, discussing gender very briefly, suggests that this is consistent across industrialized countries. Girls out-perform boys in school reading assessments, but this does not carry through to adult performance, largely because more men go on to post-secondary education, and the scores of this latter group influence gender distributions at lower levels (1997: 32–3).

However, the OECD and ALS stress similarities rather than differences (whereas the DfEE report offers almost nothing on gender). In one regression analysis of 10 factors associated with low literacy scores, gender had a small and not significant effect; much less than ethnicity, age, education, achieved class or income (Carey, Low and Hansbro 1997: 53, 55, 60). Most of the overall differences are attributed to sampling variation.

Bynner and Parsons (1997) do however frequently use the term 'men and women' rather than 'adults' or 'people', reporting gender differences in literacy levels in greater detail: e.g. Chapter Two on basic differences and Chapter Three on education and paid employment. They also address experiences such as family life and health, showing how women with low literacy scores enter motherhood earlier and are more prone to depression. Men with low scores are more likely to remain unmarried. Of those squeezed out of paid employment in the past, women tended to describe themselves as 'at home', whereas men described themselves as 'unemployed'.

Despite this better recognition of gender, Bynner and Parsons do not develop their discussion. Like the other studies, there is little attempt to make connections with prior experiences that might lead men and women to score on the tests in particular ways. Nor is there any discussion of whether the tests themselves might be gendered. Although we are told a little about occupational and class outcomes, there is no consideration of the way the demand side of a gendered labour market influences what jobs are available. The real possibility that having low literacy might mean something different for women and men seems to have passed the authors by. For instance, data on TV watching, and reading, are presented as if the domestic division of labour debate had never happened.

Whereas the studies seem to have under-utilized their data on gender, they lack good data on ethnic differences. It is a generally recognized problem that relatively small groups are poorly covered in national samples. While it is clearly inadequate to discuss minority ethnic groups without allowing for at least the major cultural traditions, each of these is only a few percentage points of the total population. When gender is also included in the analysis, typical sample numbers become too few to use as a basis for confident generalization. Thus key groups, such as young Afro-Caribbean males in urban areas, who are known to experience distinctively poor levels of qualification and employment, are invisible in most national studies (Iganski, Payne and Roberts 2001). The best that can be said of the literacy studies is that with budgets sufficient for samples of only, say, 3811 achieved interviews (ALS), there may have been insufficient funding to include special 'over-samples' of the minority ethnic groups. Most of the main BSA reports cannot address ethnicity directly, because they are based on an analysis of a 10 per cent sample from the National Child Development Study, which originated from an historical point when ethnicity was seen as less important. Even Hamilton's (2004) efforts to confront ethnicity and gender are based on small sub-samples that cannot sustain tests of generalizability (Payne and Williams 2005).

This is all the more disappointing, given Aluluf's point about the stimulus that immigrant workers gave to literacy awareness (1992: 12–13). Seven per cent of the ALS sample was 'born outside of the UK' and 6 per cent 'reported that the language they had first spoken as a child was not English'. The latter were twice as likely to be classified into Level 1 as UK born or English first-speakers, but the confidence intervals are rather wide, and the commentary is very cautious, describing its estimates as 'rather imprecise' (Carey, Low and

Hansbro 1997: 28). Only two other pages (56 and 60) refer to birth country and language, offering similar but even briefer comments about proportions in higher Levels.

The Moser Report (DfEE 1999: 19–20) devotes perhaps 1 per cent of its pages to ethnic differences, drawing on the two specialist BSA studies (BSA 1989; Carr-Hill et al. 1996). Like the ALS, it suggests that while literacy in other languages may be greater, in English there are severe deficits.

> Nearly three-quarters of the total (Carr-Hill) sample scored below 'survival level' … a significant number of people from linguistic minority communities have very little knowledge or understanding of English; and a rather higher number have only limited English language skills. (DfEE 1999: 19)

Among the respondents in the BSA study, the older members were noticeably less familiar with English.

There is simply nothing else in these main literacy surveys that throws further light on ethnicity and literacy. They were not studies of gender, ethnicity and literacy as most sociologists would recognize them. The result is a gap in our knowledge which can only be filled if sociologists become more involved in research on literacy.

Who lacks literacy skills? Age, education, work and literacy

The literacy studies also pay insufficient attention to age, and even to educational qualifications, and employment. Again, the problem is not that these factors are totally ignored but that their sociological significance (and therefore the way they are used in analysing the raw data) is not recognized. The ALS, in coming closest to recognizing the significance of age effects, notes that literacy levels vary:

> because of changes in the participation rates in education over the years younger people are more likely to have … higher levels. As the older age-groups move out of the available labour market, the overall distribution of literacy skills in the population of working age should improve. (Carey, Low and Hansbro 1997: 22)

Here the age differences are attributed to historical factors, and not to ageing effects: 'there is no skill loss among those in the lower age ranges with advancing years' (Carey, Low and Hansbro 1997: 22). In reporting the same data, the DfEE ('DfES' since 2001; the government department responsible for the schooling systems as experienced by the older members of the current workforce) claimed without citing any evidence or sources that:

> people's literacy skills do alter after they leave school, improving into early middle age, remaining steady for some time, before declining again in later years. (DfEE 1999: 19–20)

The same report continues that there can be short-term fluctuations if skills are not used in employment, and that 'skills problems tend to rise with people over 45', which can be read as favouring an explanation based on such individual changes, rather than on the consequences of previous structural disadvantage attributable to the schooling policies of DfEE and its predecessors.

The weakness of the DfEE model is its failure to explain the step changes found in low levels of literacy. Respondents aged between 16 and 45 have fairly consistent 'lowest literacy' rates of between 17 and 18 per cent. In the group aged from 46 to 55, the rate increases by nearly 30 per cent. Those aged over 56 have rates *130* per cent higher (Carey, Low and Hansbro 1997: 22, Table 2.1). It is improbable that these older people started with the same rates as their current younger counterparts, and then experienced such an acute loss of literacy in the course of a decade upon reaching their mid-50s. A much stronger case can be made for an explanation based on structural changes in education.

The very oldest respondents passed through education before the 1944 Education Act reforms. The raising of the minimum school leaving age first to 15 and then to 16, and the introduction of comprehensive education in the 1960s, by-passed all of the older respondents and a slice of the next oldest age group. A decade later, almost all of the original 55–65 year olds in the 1996 sample have already left the labour force. Given the literacy studies' concern with the labour force, low functional literacy *today* is therefore already running at about the level ALS found among 16–45 year olds, namely 17 per cent, and not 22 per cent, the headline figure originally proposed.

While a parallel argument can be made about age and formal educational qualifications, a more important point is that *all* of the age cohorts contain remarkably high proportions of less literate people who none the less have acquired educational qualifications. Among those having the 'lowest' literacy skills, 40 per cent in fact obtained exam passes at GCSE or equivalent, or better (Carey, Low and Hansbro 1997: 24). Indeed, 7 per cent of these 'functionally illiterate' people actually had A-levels or better, including a few with degrees! While literate people do sometimes fail to acquire credentials, it is harder to see how those lacking literacy skills could pass school exams. This makes nonsense of the literacy measurements as currently presented. A better estimate would include only those with the lowest literacy scores *and* no formal qualifications i.e. about two-thirds of the original 22 per cent.

It has already been proposed that this 22 per cent figure should be reduced to 17 per cent because of the age effect. There is a risk that, if both age and qualifications are factored in, their effects may be exaggerated, but taken together, the original 22 per cent becomes about *10* per cent.

A similar argument for reduction can be applied to the literacy studies' data on occupations. Despite repeated but unsubstantiated assertions, their own evidence on literacy and employment fails to show that low literacy skills trap people in unskilled work. The ALS table showing literacy level by occupation – one of the few exceptions where the literacy reports actually do present literacy cross-tabulated with occupations (1997: 36) – shows that fewer than two-thirds of the 22 per cent at Level 1 are doing low-skilled jobs. Over a quarter are in 'medium skilled' level jobs, and one in seven of the 22 per cent are in professional, managerial, and technical occupations. It is true that, as the reports say, a *bigger* proportion of those with lower literacy skills fall into unskilled work, but by no means are *all* of them constrained to less skilled jobs and economic marginality.

It is reasonable to assume that the individuals comprising the 60 per cent of the lowest literacy group with no qualifications are not the exact same 60 per cent working in low-skilled jobs, but there is likely to be a very high degree of overlap. Therefore, we do not wish to argue for a further decrease in our new figure of 10 per cent in the lowest level. However, any adjustment would be a further reduction. This adds confidence to our basic position that the original 22 per cent figure is much too large.

Re-estimating literacy rates

Although we have concentrated on the original ALS figure of 22 per cent, it is important to remember the variability of previous estimates over four years of media coverage. The 'one in five' headline figure is 20 per cent. The BSA's 10 per cent re-survey of the National Child Development Study cohort talks about 19 per cent of adults (not 22 per cent) having poor literacy skills. Of these, 6 per cent had 'very low' and 13 per cent 'low' level scores on the normative literacy tests (DfEE 1999: 16; Bynner and Parsons 1997: 22). The 6 per cent receive very little discussion as a separate group in the reports' subsequent analyses.

The confusing testimonies of Wells and Moser can be added to the reports' use of 22 per cent, 20 per cent and 19 per cent. Wells (*The Guardian,* 12 June 2001) has gone on record as saying that one million might be a better estimate of those with severe literacy deficits (i.e. about 3 per cent of the approximately 35 million people of working age). Even Moser distinguishes between the 1.5 to two million adults 'who have extreme problems' (i.e. between 4 per cent and 6 per cent) and another two or three million (another 6 per cent to 9 per cent) who 'have what are quite inhibiting problems' (*The Guardian,* 12 June 2001). Moser's two upper range figures put functional illiteracy at around five million, not seven million. However, by linking the two, Moser shifts attention away from the 1.5 to two million that brackets his lower estimate with those of Wells and the BSA, and back towards the headline figures.

We are now in a better position to reconsider numbers at different levels of literacy skill, in particular how many people are in the lowest categories. We recognize that even improving such estimates is still to work within the limitation of broad 'levels' of ability, much like the original studies, and so to use a blunt instrument (although of course better than a simplistic dichotomy). However, our approach is pragmatic and not intended to foreclose on other approaches (e.g. Wagner 1988, 1993; Kirsch et al. 1993).

Re-connecting literacy to age, school qualifications and occupational class not only demonstrates that the lowest Level estimate of 22 per cent is too high but also enables us to separate those with low skills into three categories or 'bands' (to distinguish them from the original 'Levels'). Literacy Band 1 draws on Wells' estimate of one million, and Moser's lower estimate of 1.5 million [sic], to identify those who have severe literacy skills deficits, together with no qualifications, and poor or no paid employment. Given other estimates for the distribution of physiological intellectual impairments (e.g. Barton and Tomlinson 1984), the approximately 3 per cent of people (just over one million) falling into this band probably have a limited scope for improving their literacy skills. This band is closest to the old-fashioned commonsense view of illiteracy. Their needs are probably not so much for literacy skills acquisition as for interventions directly to improve their quality of life.

In contrast, Band 2 represents those who also lack qualifications and good employment, but whose literacy skills are 'poor' rather than 'very poor', and could be improved. The size of this band is calculated by subtracting the 3 per cent in Band 1 from our working estimate of 10 per cent for those who should only be called functionally illiterate after allowing for the age, qualifications and employment data previously ignored by the literacy studies. This gives a Band 2 figure of around 7 per cent, or 2.5 million. That leaves Band 3 as the remainder of those who were originally classified at the lowest Level but who, in contrast to Bands 1 and 2, have obtained employment in occupations ranked above unskilled and semi-skilled manual work in the Registrar-General's classification. People here, amounting to about 5.25 million or 12 per cent of the labour force, are also more likely to have obtained school qualifications. While the needs of Bands 2 and 3 are different, both stand to benefit from programmes aimed at literacy skills enhancement. The remainder of the population fall outside of these low-level categories.

Thus, instead of *one in five*, we have *one in 35* who have severe problems, and *less than one in 15* who might be deemed 'educational victims'. This is still a substantial number, worth further investigation, but it is a long way off the media's shock-horror headlines. Indeed it shows that Government policy is based on false assumptions, because of the way the lowest levels of literacy were defined and counted. Whereas those in the lowest band need a very basic kind of assistance, but are unlikely to make dramatic improvements, the other bands consists of those who were probably the worst served by the educational system. They might potentially have become (or could still become) more productive members of a knowledge-based economy. In other words, the argument conventionally used to justify literacy policy, that there is a potential economic benefit in up-grading skills, in practice only applies to Bands 2 and 3, and to others at higher but still limited levels of literacy.

The central point here is that the 'problems' of the three bands, and any policy solutions, should not be run together. Concentrating headlines on those with the worst literacy misrepresents the different interests of the three groups. Education policy needs to maintain the distinctions so that interventions can be properly targeted. Of course, major changes to literacy levels are likely to take a long time, as Paterson's admirable analysis of secondary education reforms demonstrates (2001). Standards will go on changing, and not every single individual can become 'expertly literate'. None the less, the lower rates of functional literacy currently found in other countries suggest that major improvements can be made.

Some concluding remarks

This [chapter] identifies the mistaken consensus about the prevalence of literacy problems constructed by media coverage of the major literacy reports since 1997 and the use of suspect evidence by political figures seeking to publicize new educational policies. Despite showing some welcome signs of slightly more sophisticated analysis in later research reports (Williams 2003), the DfES's press notice announcing, it claims, that *due to its educational policies*, illiteracy 'has fallen from the 7 million estimated in 1997 to 5.2 million adults now' (DfES 2003). In other words, the original seven million benchmark is used to measure the reduction. The reduction is attributed solely to the policies, not to the different birth cohorts being sampled (or indeed, changes in the methods used to measure literacy).

Even allowing for the new figure of 5.2 million (which is close to our estimate of 17 per cent calculated above by allowing for the retirement of the oldest respondents), the main government literacy studies have over-estimated the number of people with serious functional literacy deficits. At the same time, there are many people whose life-chances and quality of life are constrained by lack of skills, and whose skills could be enhanced. The question is how to strike a balance between the two perspectives.

While agreeing with Wells that Moser's seven million figure 'is an absolute myth' (*The Guardian,* 12 June 2001), concerns remain about the quality of life of the one million or so with the lowest ranges of literacy skills. A parallel concern extends to the 2.5 million who are poor readers, having particularly suffered at the hands of the school and employment systems, and also for the non-literate among the older population omitted from the national surveys, who by the same standards would add another 0.5 and 1.25 million people to the revised disadvantaged bands. International comparisons, despite their flawed methodology, suggest that unless national populations have different 'ability' levels, there must be many British people with the intellectual potential to be more literate than they presently are.

Although these victims of structural processes are genuinely handicapped by lack of skills, some of them seem to be functioning relatively well. It may be that those who are in higher levels of employment are those whose equivalents in other countries are already gaining higher levels of literacy skill. If so, the label of 'functionally illiterate' may be an inappropriate indicator of economic and social exclusion.

OECD research suggests the prospect of higher rates of literacy, as already achieved by other countries, and that there is a body of people who could benefit from policy interventions. More children are already leaving school with better qualifications. We therefore should consider the social consequences of a period of substantial up-grading of literacy skills, not only for the newly empowered, *but for the rest of us*. The literacy studies assume, again with little evidence or detailed discussion, that a better trained workforce will neatly fill skill shortages, so absorbing all those who would otherwise become unemployable (as unskilled work shrinks) or are currently under-employed (in work where skills are increasingly required). It is unclear how far this view is justified.

An upgrading of literacy skills resulting in greater economic efficiency might equally destabilize the current occupational class regime. Adults who do acquire new skills (at some personal costs) may either create upward social mobility pressures, or fail to receive financial rewards from better employment. Lloyd and Payne (2003) have pointed out that despite government rhetoric about a literate high skills society, employers can still exploit low wages and insecure work. Labour market forces do not neatly link skills and rewards, least of all in the short term. Education policy could be successful in a narrow sense, but still not achieve its wider social objectives of less waste of human potential and greater social justice.

How we see that depends as much on our assumptions about social justice, as on how we measure literacy and numeracy. It is here that sociological analysis has much to offer. By comprehending people as social entities with social identities in terms of gender, ethnicity, age, education and employment, we can make more sense of what literacy actually means. It is all the more striking that mainstream sociology, so confident in dealing with other social divisions, has yet been so slow to incorporate literacy into its theoretical treatments of social inequality, or to contribute to substantive national surveys which influence public policy.

Note

1 'Illiterate' is a pejorative term, often implying low intelligence and a lack of culture: it is therefore better avoided. However, given its familiarity in common usage, this is sometimes difficult to achieve. In this [chapter], the use of 'illiterate' and 'illiteracy' are intended to carry no negative connotations.

References

Aluluf, M. 1992 *The Unemployment Trap,* Strasbourg: Council of Europe Press.
Barton, D. and Hamilton, M. 1998 *Local Literacies,* London: Routledge.
Barton, D., Hamilton, M. and Ivanic, R. (eds) 2000 *Situated Literacies: Reading and Writing in Context,* London: Routledge.

Barton, L. and Tomlinson, S. 1984 'The Politics of Integration in England', in L. Barton and S. Tomlinson (eds) *Special Education and Social Interests,* London: Croom Helm.

Basic Skills Agency 1989 *A Nation's Neglect,* London: The Basic Skills Agency.

Basic Skills Agency 2002 *Research FAQ.* www.basic-skills.co.uk [The original link to this page is no longer available but several studies are available by following the link to 'Observatory' and then 'Adult'.]

Brandt, D. and Clinton, K. 2002 'Limits of the Local: Expanding Perspectives on Literacy as a Social Practice', *Journal of Literacy Research* 34(3): 337–56.

British Sociological Association 2005 *Non-Disablist Language Guidelines.* Durham: BSA. www.britsoc.co.uk [Follow link to 'Equality and Ethics' and then 'Diversity Resources'.]

Bynner, J. and Parsons, S. 1997 *It Doesn't Get Any Better,* London: Basic Skills Agency.

Carey, S., Low, S. and Hansbro, J. 1997 *Adult Literacy in Britain,* London: Stationery Office.

Carr-Hill, R., Passingham, S., Wolf, A. with Kent, N. 1996 *Lost Opportunities,* London: The Basic Skills Agency.

Collins, J. and Blot, R. (eds) 2003 *Literacy and Literacies,* Cambridge: Cambridge University Press.

DfEE 1999 *Improving Literacy and Numeracy: A Fresh Start,* London: Department for Education and Employment, CMBS 1.

DfES 2003 Improving Adult Basic Skills. DfES Press Notice 2003 0219. www.dfes.gov [Follow link to 'Press Notices'; select 'October 2003'; search 'adult'.]

Finnegan, R. 1999 'Sociology/Anthropology: Theoretical Issues in Literacy', in D. Wagner, L. Venezky and B. Street (eds) *International Handbook of Literacy,* New York: Garland.

Freebody, P. 1998 *Assessment as Communal Versus Punitive Practice: Six New Literacy Crises* (with replies by B. Street and C. Kell). AILA Special Commission on Literacy Virtual Seminar Series: www.education.Uts. Au/AILA

Green, J. and Bloome, D. 1997 'Ethnography and Ethnographers of and in Education', in J. Flood, S. Heath and D. Lapp (eds) *A Handbook of Research in Teaching Literacy Through Communication and Visual Arts,* New York: Simon Schuster.

Guardian Unlimited 2003a www.guardian.co.uk/Archive.

Guardian Unlimited 2003b www.education.guardian.co.uk [Search 'skirting'; select '2003', 'November', 'John Crace'; open 'Skirting the issue on skills'.]

Halsey, A., Floud, J. and Anderson, L. (eds) 1961 *Education, Economy and Society,* London: Collier-Macmillan.

Halsey, A., Heath, A. and Ridge, J. 1980 *Origins and Destinations,* Oxford: Oxford University Press.

Hamilton, M. 2004 *Changing Faces Project.* www.lancs.ac.uk/fss/projects/edres/changingfaces/work.htm

Hamilton, M. and Hillier, Y. 2004 *Adult Basic Education to Basic Skills.* Paper presented to the Learning and Skills Research Network Annual Conference, Coventry: University of Warwick.

Iganski, P., Payne, G. and Roberts, J. 2001 'Inclusion or Exclusion? Reflections on the Evidence of Declining Racial Disadvantage in the British Labour Market', *International Journal of Sociology and Social Policy* 21(4/ 5/6): 184–211.

Kirsch, I., Jungeblut, A., Jenkins, L. and Kolstad, A. 1993 *Adult Literacy in America,* Washington, DC: National Centre for Educational Statistics; US Department of Education.

Learning Skills Council 2001 www.lsc.gov.uk/nationalaims.cfm

Levine, K. 1986 *The Social Context of Literacy,* London: Routledge and Kegan Paul.

Little, A. and Westergaard, J. 1964 'The Trends of Class Differentials in Educational Opportunity in England and Wales', *British Journal of Sociology* 15(4): 301–15.

Lloyd, C. and Payne, J. 2003 'What is the "High Skills" Society?', *Policy Studies* 24(2/3): 115–33.

Marshall, T. 1965 [1950] *Class, Citizenship and Social Development,* New York: Double-day Anchor Press.

Maybin, J. 1993 *Language and Literature in Social Practice,* Buckingham: Open University Press.

MediaGuardian.co.uk 2003 London: Guardian Newspapers Limited. http://media.guardian.co.uk [Go to 'Guardian Unlimited'; select 'Archive search'; search 'Circulation'; filter search by selecting 'Media','2003', 'January', 'Roy Greenslade', and open 'Reading Problems'.]

Moser, C. 1958 et seq. *Survey Methods in Social Investigation,* London; Heinemann.

OECD 1997 *Literacy Skills for the Knowledge Society,* Paris: Organisation for Economic Co-operation and Development.

Parsons, S. and Bynner, J. 2002a *Basic Skills and Social Exclusion,* London: Basic Skills Agency.

Parsons, S. and Bynner, J. 2002b *Basic Skills and Political and Community Participation,* London: Basic Skills Agency.

Paterson, L. 2001 *Education and Inequality in Britain.* Paper presented at the British Association for the Advancement of Science Conference, Glasgow.

Payne, G. (ed.) 2006 *Social Divisions,* second edition. Basingstoke: Palgrave.

Payne, G. and Williams, M. 2005 'Generalization in Qualitative Research', *Sociology* 39(2): 295–314.

Robinson, C. 2003 *Literacies – the New Meanings of Literacy,* UNESCO; UNESCO Position Paper.

Saunders, P. 1996 *Unequal But Fair?* London: Institute of Economic Affairs.

Slavenburg, J. 1992 'Illiteracy in the European Community', in W. Fase, W. Kreft, P. Leseman and J. Slavenburg (eds) *Illiteracy in the European Community: Research Problems and Research Findings,* De Lier: Academisch Boeken Centrum.

Street, B. 1993 *Cross-Cultural Approaches to Literacy,* Cambridge: Cambridge University Press.

Street, B. 1995 *Social Literacies,* Harlow: Longmans.

Street, B. 1996 'Review of International Adult Literacy Survey' (with comments by H. Gaffand and S. Jones), *Literacy Across the Curriculum* 12(3): 8–15. (Montreal: Centre for Literacy.)

Street, B. 2001 *Literacy and Development; Ethnographic Perspectives,* London: Routledge.

Street, B. 2003 'What's "New" in New Literacy Studies? Critical Approaches to Literacy in Theory and Practice', *Current Issues in Comparative Education* 5(2): 1523–615. http://www.tc.columbia.edu/cice/

Wagner, D. (ed.) 1988 *The Future of Literacy in a Changing World,* Oxford: Pergamon.

Wagner, D. 1993 *Literacy, Culture and Development,* Cambridge: Cambridge University Press.

Wagner, D., Venezky, L. and Street, B. (eds) 1999 *International Handbook of Literacy,* New York: Garland.

Williams, J. 2003 *The Skills for Life Survey,* DfES Research Brief RB490. London: HMSO for DfES.

Part 3

Literacy Curriculum Policy Contexts

10

Research and the National Literacy Strategy

Roger Beard

[...]

What is the National Literacy Strategy?

The National Literacy Strategy (NLS) was established in 1997 by the incoming UK government to raise standards of literacy in English primary schools over a five to ten year period. (Scotland, Wales and Northern Ireland have their own curricula and Education Departments and are not formally affected by the NLS.) The Strategy was the result of the work of a Literacy Task Force which had been set up by the Shadow Secretary of State for Education and Employment, David Blunkett, in May 1996. The Task Force published a preliminary consultation report in February 1997 (LTF, 1997a) and a final report in August 1997. In its final report (LTF, 1997b), the Task Force set out the details of a 'steady, consistent strategy' for raising standards of literacy which could be sustained over a long period of time and be made a central priority for the education service as a whole.

What are the main strands of the National Literacy Strategy?

The main strands of the Strategy include the following:

1. A national target that, by 2002, 80% of 11-year-olds should reach the standard expected for their age in English (Level 4). (The proportion reaching this standard in 1996 was 57%.)
2. A *Framework for Teaching* (DfEE, 1998a) which (i) sets out termly teaching objectives for the 5–11 age range and (ii) provides a practical structure of time and class

From: *Oxford Review of Education*, 26 (3 & 4), 2000, pp. 421–36.

management for a daily Literacy Hour. The *Framework* notes that further literacy work should be productively linked to other curriculum areas and that additional rime may also be needed for:

- reading to the class (e.g. in end of day sessions);
- pupils' own independent reading (for interest and pleasure);
- extended writing (especially for older pupils).

3. A programme of professional development for all primary teachers, centred on a *Literacy Training Pack* (DfEE, 1998b). This *Pack* is made up of course booklets, overhead transparencies and audio- and video-tapes to support three in-service training days in 1998–99 and further training in after-school sessions.

4. Other community-based elements of the Strategy include a media campaign and a series of events in a National Year of Reading (1998–99), Summer Literacy Schools and a range of recommendations for other agencies and institutions.

How did the National Literacy Strategy come about?

There were a number of influences that shaped the nature and structure of the National Literacy Strategy. It may be helpful to see some as 'predisposing' influences, implying that literacy teaching in England was in need of radical change. Over the previous thirty years, standards in literacy in England had not increased in line with the hopes and expectations of policy makers. The teaching of early literacy had become largely individualised and appeared to be out of line with the practices suggested by school effectiveness research. The teaching of early reading often largely comprised hearing children read books in an order suggested by commercial publishers. Accumulating inspection evidence suggested that there was often relatively little 'teaching' per se. Furthermore, England (and Wales, according to Brooks *et al.,* 1996) appeared to have a long tail of under-achievement, which seemed to call for the kinds of direct interactive teaching approaches which had been successful with 'at risk' pupils in the USA and Australia.

If these were the influences that predisposed the Literacy Task Force towards the possible structure of a National Literacy Strategy, then the 'precipitating' influence was the early success of the National Literacy Project (NLP) which had been set up by the previous government in its final year of office. The NLP reflected many of the implications of the school effectiveness research and shared several of the priorities of the overseas literacy research with at risk pupils. The NLP was also led by a senior member of Her Majesty's Inspectorate, John Stannard. He was not only very familiar with the inspection evidence of recent years but also with the findings from the school effectiveness and overseas literacy research. He saw these influences as having major implications for school improvement and for changing the way that literacy was taught in English primary schools (Stannard, 1997). All these influences are set out below to show the timescales involved.

Circa 1988–97
'Predisposing Influences':
International comparisons of reading standards
School effectiveness research
Accumulating inspection evidence
Literacy research evidence

1996
'Precipitating Influence':
The National Literacy Project
- Literacy Hour in 15 LEAs
- Draft *Framework for Teaching*
(Termly objectives at 'text level', 'sentence level' and 'word level')

1996–7
Literacy Task Force
- National targets
- NLP appraisal
- National Professional Development Strategy
- National Year of Reading (1998–9)

National Literacy Strategy for 1997–2007
National targets
Literacy Hour encouraged in all primary schools
Framework for Teaching sent to all primary schools
NLS *Training Pack* sent to all primary schools
National Year of Reading (1998–9) etc.

Some of the main features of each of these influences will now be briefly discussed in turn.

International comparison of reading standards

Standards in literacy among English primary school children remained largely stable [in] 1948–1996 (Brooks, 1998). Compared with other countries, English reading standards are similar to those in a 'middle' group of countries. In the middle and upper parts of the range of scores, children from England performed as well as those in countries much higher in the rank order. However, England has a long 'tail' of under-achievement (Brooks *et al.*, 1996).

The comparison of literacy standards between countries raises various issues about cultural and linguistic biases (see Elley, 1994, and Purves, 1992, for a discussion of these issues). The study of literacy standards within countries, but between different points in time, raises additional issues. The National Curriculum assessments (SATs) are criterion-referenced and can accommodate shifts in the distributions of performance without re-standardisation being necessary (TGAT, 1988). At the same time, the specific level descriptions have annually to be translated into different test formats to avoid the difficulties created by excessive 'teaching to the test'. This re-writing raises further questions about year on year comparisons. As Level 4 in English is being used as a national target for 80% of 11-year-olds by 2002, there is a concomitant need for the body which oversees the national testing, the Qualifications and Curriculum Authority (QCA), to be rigorous in ensuring the consistency of Level 4 requirements (LTF, 1997a, p. 7; Sainsbury & Twist, 1999).

School effectiveness research

The NLS reflects the implications of school effectiveness research. School effectiveness is generally gauged by the further progress which pupils make than might be expected from consideration of the school's intake. The measures are normally in basic subjects, especially reading and numeracy, and examinations. The most valid research of this kind is longitudinal, so that cohorts can be followed over time. Leading researchers in the field stress that the outcomes from their work are not appropriate for the production of 'blue-print' schools (e.g. Mortimore, 1991).

A meta-analysis by Jaap Scheerens has identified two characteristics of school effectiveness which are found in multiple studies (Scheerens, 1992):

(i)   structured teaching: making clear what has to be learnt
                                  dividing material into manageable units
                                  teaching in a well-considered sequence
                                  encouraging pupils to use hunches and prompts
                                  regular testing for progress
                                  immediate feedback.

(ii) effective learning time: whole class teaching can often be superior to individualised teaching because, in the latter, the teacher has to divide attention and the net result per pupil is lower.

Similar factors are found in a meta-analysis of the effective classroom (Creemers, 1994; see also Reynolds, 1998 and Teddlie & Reynolds, 1999).

An earlier British study is generally seen as a landmark in school effectiveness research (Mortimore *et al.*, 1988). Subsequent investigations have confirmed the importance of primary school provision:

- once pupils begin school, the school itself can have a greater influence than background; and
- this variance may be greater in primary schools than in secondary schools (Sammons, Hillman & Mortimore, 1995);
- positive primary school factors affect examination attainment at the age of 16 + (the end of compulsory schooling) (Sammons, Nuttall, Cuttance & Thomas, 1995).

The NLS takes up the implications of Scheerens' analysis in several ways, Firstly, it stresses the importance of direct teaching by the use of whole class teaching in the first half of the Literacy Hour and the maintenance of direct teaching with groups, and then with the class again, in the second half. Secondly, it maximises effective learning time by ensuring that there is a dedicated Literacy Hour during each school day, with further suggestions on providing for additional literacy learning time during the rest of the day (DfEE, 1998a, p. 14), Thirdly, it draws directly on the National Curriculum in the content of the *Framework* and assists the related 'opportunities to learn' by adopting a clear objectives-based approach for each primary school term.

Accumulating inspection evidence

Important issues for the teaching of literacy are raised in the annual reports on the teaching of English which are produced from school inspections by Her Majesty's Inspectorate (HMI) and the Office for Standards in Education (Ofsted). Since it was set up in 1992, Ofsted has inspected all government-maintained schools in England every four years; more often if schools are deemed by Ofsted to be 'failing' overall. The inspection reports provide broad indications of how different aspects of the National Curriculum for English are being taught. Taking 1989 as a starting point (the first year of the National Curriculum), there has been a pattern of findings which provides strong support for many elements of the NLS.

The reports and commentaries contain comments which indicate the need for (i) many schools to strengthen the ways in which some aspects of literacy are taught and for (ii) substantial in-service support to be given to develop teachers' professional knowledge related to these aspects. In particular, there are recurrent comments on the need for the following to be strengthened in many schools:

(i)   the use of direct teaching, related to clear objectives and including skilful questioning;
(ii)   the provision of effective learning time;
(iii)   the appropriate balance of teaching methods and range of tasks provided;
(iv)   the use of systematic phonics;
(v)   the teaching of writing, including provision for a range of writing tasks and the diagnosis of pupils' weaknesses and related learning needs;
(vi)   the extension of reading skills beyond the initial stages;
(vii)   teachers' subject knowledge in literacy teaching.

The National Literacy Strategy incorporates a variety of features to accommodate these:

(i)   *Teaching Approach.* There is provision for extensive and consistent direct teaching of literacy, related to an objectives-based curriculum *Framework* and which also delineates the range of questioning that teachers can use when working with children in this way. There is detailed guidance on training pupils [in] how to work on their own so that the teacher can focus on a group at a time.
(ii)   *Effective Learning Time* is provided for through a dedicated Literacy Hour, together with indicators of how at least three more aspects of literacy development can be fostered at other points in the day: individual reading, reading to the class and extended writing.
(iii)   *Balance and Extension* are major features of the National Literacy Strategy *Framework for Teaching.* There is provision for consistent attention to the different

levels of language and literacy learning by the systematic use of the text-sentence-word level sub-sections in the *Framework*. The sub-sections provide for a comprehensive mapping of each part of the National Curriculum, 'Knowledge, Skills and Understanding' and 'Breadth of Study'. Illustrative details are included, particularly to encourage attention to the role of different skills and types of text in assisting the extension of literacy throughout the primary years.

(iv) *Phonics*. Similarly, there is provision for consistent and systematic attention to the teaching of the English alphabetic writing system, in both reading and writing. The specific phonics and spelling work in Years R to 2 is also set out in an appendix (DfEE, 1998a, pp. 64–65). This emphasis reflects the intention of the incoming government in 1997 that it would 'encourage the use of the most effective teaching methods, including phonics for reading ...' (Labour Party, 1997, p. 8).

(v) *Writing*. There is detailed attention to the compositional and presentational aspects of writing through the 'text level' work in composition; the 'sentence level' work in grammatical awareness, sentence construction and punctuation and revision; and the 'word level' work in spelling, vocabulary and handwriting The *Framework* (p. 14) also notes that extended writing may need to be tackled in independent work outside the Literacy Hour, thus recognising the central role of reading and writing in many subjects across the curriculum.

(vi) *Teachers' Professional Knowledge*. The National Literacy Strategy supports staff development opportunities on an unprecedented scale, in that three full days of training (plus after-school sessions) are provided for the staff in every primary school. The *Training Pack* and its audio-visual components structure this training through carefully timed activities, discussion opportunities and source material. The *Framework* includes a Glossary of terms used. The NLS appears to reflect the belief that 'there is a link between the investment in staff development and the learning of children' (Joyce & Showers, 1995, p. 17).

Literacy research evidence

The NLS has clearly been influenced by the work of Bob Slavin and his colleagues in the USA. Slavin presented a paper at the launch of the Literacy Task Force Consultation Report (Slavin, 1997). His work at the Center for Research on the Education of Students Placed at Risk in Baltimore has consistently supported several features of educational provision now adopted by the NLS:

- a fast-paced, structured curriculum;
- direct, interactive teaching;
- systematic phonics in the context of interesting text;
- a combination of shared and paired reading and writing;
- early interventions for pupils who have not made expected progress after one year at school.

These are very similar to the approaches adopted by the NLS, with the exception of the last one. The evaluation of the National Literacy Strategy may indicate whether it needs to be extended to provide additional systematic intervention for children at risk after one year of schooling.

A similar strategy especially to address the needs of disadvantaged pupils is being implemented in Melbourne, Australia, in the Early Literacy Research Project (ELRP) led by Carmel Crévola and Peter Hill (1998). The project is in part a response to the evidence cited in the Commission on Reading of the USA National Academy of Education: that a country receives highest returns on investment in education from the early years of schooling when children are first learning to read and write (see Adams, 1990). Crévola and Hill draw on evidence that schools only have a narrow 'window of opportunity' to make a difference in helping pupils with difficulties in literacy learning. Very little evidence exists for the success of programmes designed to correct reading problems beyond the second year of schooling. However, they draw upon a range of evidence, including Slavin's (e.g. Wasik & Slavin, 1993), that dramatic improvements are achievable within the context of a fully implemented, comprehensive strategy that involves both system- and school-wide commitment and coordination.

Crévola and Hill emphasise that the starting point of all comprehensive early literacy prevention and intervention strategies is attitudinal: high expectations; a belief in the capacity of all students to make progress, given sufficient time and support; and a relentless determination to persist with those who are not experiencing success.

The National Literacy Project

The National Literacy Project (NLP) was set up in the Spring of 1996 in 15 local Education Authorities. It had the following aims:

- to improve standards of literacy in participating primary schools in line with national expectations;
- to provide detailed support to schools and teachers through a structured programme and consultancy support;
- through the national network, to develop detailed, practical guidance on teaching methods and activities, and to disseminate these to the project schools;
- to disseminate the work of the NLP to other, non-participating LEAs and institutions;
- to evaluate the effectiveness of the programme.

Participating schools implemented two key structures, a *Framework for Teaching* and the Literacy Hour. These were earlier versions of what were subsequently to be included in the NLS. The *Framework* provided schools with a means of shifting the emphasis in planning for the revised National Curriculum for English (DfE, 1995) from 'what' to 'how'. This was done by using three strands (text level, sentence level and word level) to provide coverage, balance and progression in literacy teaching. The purpose of this *Framework* was to present teachers not with increased prescription but with a wide range of new and challenging decisions about tasks, activities and methods (Stannard, 1997).

Teaching objectives

Teachers were given further assistance in this by the use of objectives for each of the three levels of teaching for each term of the seven primary school years. In Years 1–6, there were separate, sometimes overlapping, objectives for each of the 18 terms. For the Reception age range (4-year-olds, to whom the National Curriculum does not formally apply until they reach the age of five), there were objectives for the whole year. This yearly provision helps to cater for variations in local admissions policies: some pupils begin school at the beginning of the school year when they are to become five; others at the beginning of the respective school term.

The use of objectives for curriculum planning draws on the tradition of educational thinking going back to the work of Ralph Tyler. Tyler (1949, p. 3) acknowledges that excellent educational work can be done by teachers who do not have a clear conception of goals but who have an intuitive sense of what is good teaching. He adds, however, that, if an educational programme is to be planned and if efforts for continued improvement are to be made, it is very necessary to have some conception of the goals that are being pursued. These educational objectives become the criteria by which materials are selected, content outlined, teaching approaches developed and assessment procedures prepared.

The NLS extends the use of objectives in innovative ways beyond the programmes of study set out in the National Curriculum. For example, its structured and routinised approach allows teachers to share and explain the objectives with their pupils. This sharing can develop a common sense of purpose in the classroom. It can increase a sense of responsibility in independent working. The recursive features in the objectives can extend the sense of purpose across yearly transitions. Shared objectives, translated into appropriate language, can also help to focus on key points in plenary sessions.

The literacy hour

The daily amount of time allocated to dedicated literacy teaching was derived from the Final Report of the review of the National Curriculum and its Assessment by Sir Ron Dearing. Assuming a 36-week teaching year, to allow a margin for the induction of new pupils, assessment work, school events and educational visits (Dearing, 1994, p. 30), the Dearing Report recommended that 180 hours of English be taught directly in Key Stage 1 (5–7-year-olds), an hour a day in the 36 weeks referred to above. A related recommendation was that another 36 hours were to be taught through other subjects. In Key Stage 2 (7–11-year-olds), the figures were 162 and 18 respectively.

The general model of reading and writing in the Framework for Teaching

The model of reading and writing used in the *Framework* uses a consistent sub-division between 'word level', 'sentence level' and 'text level' work. These distinctions are common in linguistic description:

- The word is the smallest free-standing unit of linguistic description. (Morphemes are the smallest units of meaning but may not be independent e.g. 'un-' or '-ness'; words can also be single morphemes e.g. 'book'.)
- The sentence is the largest linguistic unit within which grammatical rules systematically operate.
- A text (sometimes referred to as 'discourse') is a collection of one or more sentences that display a coherent theme and appropriate grammatical cohesion.

Other more detailed distinctions can be built on these. For instance, phonemes, the smallest sound units which contrast with each other (e.g. /b/ or /r/), exist below word level. Clauses are part of sentence level. Phrases exist between sentence/clause level and word level. The word/sentence/text level distinctions are a convenient way of referring to the visual features of what we read and write and are helpful in providing consistent points of reference for teachers and pupils when talking about the processes and products of literacy learning.

In recent years, there have been two substantial changes in how fluent reading is under-stood: firstly, in relation to how the relationships between word recognition and the use of con-text are viewed and secondly, in relation to the role of phonological processing (see the section below on Phonics and Spelling). For some years, several influential writers argued that fluent reading was characterised by increasing use of contextual cues and minimal use of visual cues. In the last 20 years, a great deal of evidence has been put forward in support of the opposite view: that it is less-skilled readers who are more dependent on context in word recognition. The word recognition processes of skilled readers are so rapid and automatic that they gener-ally do not need to rely on contextual information – except to decide between homonyms. These changing views of the nature of fluent reading and their influences on educational prac-tice have been discussed by researchers such as Marilyn Jager Adams (1990, 1991); Jessic Reid (1993); Keith & Paula Stanovich (1995) and Charles Perfetti (1995).

It should be noted that, although the skills of the fluent reader are distinguished by fast, context-free, word recognition, where the effective reader does use context extensively is in comprehension. Indeed, Perfetti (1995) concludes that the hallmark of skilled reading is fast context-free word identification and rich context-dependent text understanding.

The evaluation of the National Literacy Project

The NLP was evaluated by Ofsted and the National Foundation for Educational Research using data from 250 schools. The latter's test results revealed a significant and substantial improvement over the 18-month period. Final test scores had improved by approximately six standardised score points for Year 3/4 and Year 5/6 pupils, equivalent to 8 to 12 months progress over and above what is expected in these ages. Girls had higher average scores than boys and made more progress during the project. Children eligible for free school meals, those with special educational needs and those learning English as an additional language had lower scores, but all these groups also made statistically significant progress. All ethnic groups benefited equally (Sainsbury *et al.*, 1998).

Some key sources in the field

A range of research evidence has been drawn upon to inform recent developments in liter-acy education in England. The range includes sources that have psychological, sociological, linguistic and literary perspectives, as well as work in curriculum development. The following table includes some extracts from the associated *Review of Research and Related Evidence* (Beard, 1999) which further illustrate the range of the sources that support current policy and practice in English primary schools.

THE RECEPTION AGE RANGE

Reception practice is likely to be assisted by some form of collaboration between homes and schools to promote early literacy development (e.g. Hannon, 1995; Weinberger, 1996).

Researchers have associated phonological development with early success in learning to read for some years (Goswami, 1999) There is a significant connection between children's phonological development and their later reading success, linking oracy and literary in highly specific ways. Children's phonological development follows a clear pattern, from being aware of syllables, to being aware of onsets and rimes within syllables, to being aware of phonemes (Treiman & Zukowski, 1996).

Children's ability to write their name without a model has been found to be correlated with a number of aspects of writing at 7 years (Blatchford, 1991). In addition, there is a strong link between children's early letter-name knowledge and their subsequent reading development (Blatchford *et al.*, 1987; Blatchford & Plewis, 1990). However, the results on later attainment from the direct teaching of letter names have been largely inconclusive (Riley, 1996).

The Reception age range warranted a separate section in the Review because its teachers have to strike a balance between promoting early progress and avoiding an inappropriate emphasis on academic provision for children so young.

Concerns about inappropriate provision are valid but they have also to be related to the findings of a three-year study of 33 schools by Barbara Tizard *et al.* (1988). Children made relatively more progress in literacy learning between beginning school and the end of the Reception year than they did in any of the following three school years (see also Ofsted, 1998).

SHARED READING

Shared reading, in which teacher and pupils simultaneously read aloud a large format text, has been especially promoted in the writing of Don Holdaway (1979, 1982). He was particularly interested in developing methods which resembled the visual intimacy with print which characterises the pre-school book experience of parents reading with their children. Interestingly, Holdaway's early work did not involve commercially produced big books. Instead it involved the teacher transcribing popular texts in bold print onto large 'newsprint' paper or overhead transparencies (Holdaway, 1979, p. 66).

In subsequent publications, Holdaway elaborates further on some of the key principles in successful shared book experience:

- the texts used need to be those which children enjoy;
- the teacher needs to present new material with wholehearted enjoyment;
- the ancient satisfactions of chant and song can be used to sustain the feelings of involvement among pupils;
- teaching-learning sequences can be developed to revisit favourite poems, jingles, songs and stories; to attend to words, letters and sounds; to use a new story to model and explain word-solving strategies; to link shared reading to independent and group reading and writing (Holdaway, 1982).

GUIDED READING 'Guided reading' is an approach in which the teacher works with a small group of pupils who use similar reading processes and are able to read similar levels of text with support (Fountas & Pinnell, 1996). The teacher (i) introduces a text to the group; (ii) works briefly with individuals as they simultaneously read their own copy at their own individual pace; and (iii) may select one or two points for the whole group to consolidate or extend their reading experience. The ultimate goal of guided reading is to help children learn how to use independent reading strategies successfully. It has several advantages over hearing children read on an entirely individual basis. It substantially increases the time which children actually spend reading. It creates a helpful social context for reading and responding to texts. It allows the teacher to make considered decisions in drawing the children's attention to significant points of interest.

SHARED WRITING Shared writing, the joint construction of a text by teacher and pupils, has attracted increasing attention in educational publications. It has built upon research which has revealed the complexity of the writing process (Hayes & Flower, 1980; Hayes, 1996) and the recognition of the value of teachers modelling what is involved.

After over a hundred experiments into the psychological aspects of writing, Carl Bereiter and Mariene Scardamalia (1987, pp. 362–3) make a number of recommendations:

- pupils (and teachers) need to be made aware of the full extent of the composing process;
- the thinking that goes on in composition needs to be modelled by the teacher;
- pupils will benefit from reviewing their own writing strategies and knowledge;
- pupils need a supportive and congenial writing environment, but will also benefit from experiencing the struggles that are an integral part of developing writing skill;
- pupils may also benefit from using various 'facilitating' techniques to help them through the initial stages of acquiring more complex processes e.g. listing words which may be used, points which may be made or the wording of final sentences etc., in advance of tackling the full text.

GUIDED WRITING

Guided writing is a pragmatic aspect of managing children's independent writing in the Literacy Hour. It allows the teacher to support and encourage pupils who are tackling a similar task and to monitor their use of the range of skills and processes in writing (Hayes & Flower, 1980; Hayes, 1996). Close observation of pupils gives teachers information on the way pupils are composing a text, the fluency of their transcription skills (grammatical order, hand-writing and spelling) and how far they are re-reading and revising. As in guided reading, the sense of shared context assists the teacher in exploiting common concerns and to draw upon the key links between reading and writing.

Meta-analyses of research evidence suggest that provision for writing development is most effective if writing is undertaken when teachers and pupils discuss and tackle targeted writing tasks in a spirit of inquiry and problem-solving (Hillocks, 1986, 1995). The potential of guided writing is further explored in Beard (2000).

PHONICS AND SPELLING

The National Literacy Strategy *Framework* follows the recommendations of such reviews of research evidence as that in *Beginning to Read* by Marilyn Jager Adams which was commissioned by the USA Congress (Adams, 1990). Adams' conclusions were that teaching approaches in which systematic code instruction is included along with the reading and writing of meaningful text results in superior reading achievement overall, both for low readiness and better prepared pupils (Adams, 1993, p. 213).

There is now much more interest in the nature of the English alphabetic writing system: 26 alphabetic letters are used as graphemes, singly and as digraphs (e.g. <sh>) and trigraphs (e.g. <igh>) to represent approximately 44 speech sounds (phonemes). As a recent major survey of English spelling shows (Carney, 1994), the correspondences between phonemes and graphemes are in some cases highly consistent: the phoneme /b/ is represented by the letter <b> 98% of the time. Such research is an important reminder that phonics teaching needs to be well-informed and undertaken with a sense of proportion regarding the patterns and inconsistencies of the English orthography.

One of the most influential publications on spelling in recent years has been a paper by Richard Gentry (1982). Gentry outlines a five-stage model of spelling development, using data from a case study by Glenda Bissex (1980) of her own son's early writing. The NLS *Framework* brings phonics and spelling together in the word level strand, and by providing different objectives under 'spelling strategies' which allow for the visual and aural aspects of learning to support each other.

These strategies also reflect how success in spelling involves understanding other kinds of links between language and literacy. This understanding needs to include vocabulary connections between words which are pronounced differently (e.g medicine/medical). It also needs to include grammatical influences on words which are pronounced differently (e.g. the use of -ed in kissed, purred and booted). John Mountford (1998) explores these different influences on the spelling system.

LITERATURE AND POETRY

For many years, children's literature has been an area of substantial strength in British education (e.g. Meek *et al.*, 1977; Tucker, 1993; Fox, 1995; Styles, 1998).

Provision of literature for children also needs to be informed by what they choose to read in their leisure time (Hall & Coles, 1999).

The conspicuous structures and forms of poetry arouse interest and invite investigation. Teachers can also explain what to expect from particular poems and help children to understand the techniques from which poetry is constructed (Morse, 1995).

READING AND WRITING FOR INFORMATION

The EXEL project at Exeter University has been an important influence on the NLS *Framework*. The project has drawn together a range of skills and strategies to form the EXIT model ('Extending Interactions With Text'). The model maps ten process stages and related questions from activation of previous knowledge, through establishing purposes and locating information, to interacting with a text and communicating the information to others (Wray & Lewis, 1997). To assist children in the writing of non-fiction, the project has used a number of 'frames', skeleton outlines of starters, connectives and sentence modifiers, to help to 'scaffold' early attempts to write in particular genres (Lewis & Wray, 1995).

GRAMMER AND PUNCTUATION

Contemporary approaches to grammar tend to be concerned with the ways in which different words and phrases add interest to texts and reflect particular genre features (Halliday, 1985; Perera, 1998). Recent investigations by Nigel Hall and Anne Robinson (1996) have highlighted how little is known about how punctuation is taught and learned. It is salutary to note that the use of punctuation marks in books for children is often inconsistent from one author to another. Katharine Perera's research has shown very different approaches in authors' practices and how these variations are accompanied by marked differences in how several grammatical structures are presented, including the use of pronouns and reduced forms ('I'll' etc.) (Perera, 1993; 1996).

Conclusion

The National Literacy Strategy is underpinned by evidence from survey, experimental and observational research; analyses and discussions from literary scholarship; and reports from curriculum development projects and school inspections. The relationship between research and practice, in this as in other areas of education, is not a perfect one. It is a relationship which is mediated by many other factors (see Beard, 1999, pp. 11–15).

Overall, however, there is substantial evidence to support the case for raising literacy standards in the UK and considerable support for modifying the ways in which reading and writing are taught in many primary schools. The success of the NLS will be influenced by a widespread professional recognition of the need for the modification referred to above and a willingness to accommodate the challenges to knowledge and practice which it will bring. The complementary nature of much of the evidence is a clear indicator that, if it is widely and sensitively implemented, the National Literacy Strategy offers a major promise of significantly raising standards and of improving the life-chances of thousands of children.

References

Adams, M.J. (1990) *Beginning to Read: thinking and learning about print* (Cambridge, Mass., MIT Press).

Adams, M.J. (1991) Why not phonics and whole language? in: W. Ellis (Ed.) *All Language and the Creation of Literacy* (Baltimore, Maryland, The Orton Dyslexia Society).

Adams, M.J. (1993) Beginning to read: an overview, in: R. Beard (Ed.) *Teaching Literacy: balancing perspectives* (London, Hodder & Stoughton).

Beard, R. (1999) *The National Literacy Strategy: review of research and other related evidence* (London, Department for Education and Employment).

Beard, R. (2000) *Developing Writing* 3–13 (London, Hodder & Stoughton).

Bereiter, C. & Scardamalia, M. (1987) *The Psychology of Written Composition* (Hillsdale, N.J., Lawrence Erlbaum).

Bissex, G. (1980) *GNYS AT WRK: a child learns to write and read* (Cambridge, Mass., Harvard University Press).

Blatchford, P. (1991) Children's handwriting at 7 years: associations with handwriting on school entry and pre-school factors, *British Journal of Educational Psychology*, 61, pp. 73–84.

Blatchford, P. & Plewis, I. (1990) Pre-school reading-related skills and later reading achievement: further evidence, *British Educational Research Journal*, 16, 4, pp. 425–428.

Blatchford, P., Burke, J., Farquhar, C., Plewis, I. & Tizard, B. (1987) Associations between pre-school reading related skills and later reading achievement, *British Educational Research Journal*, 13, 1, pp. 15–23.

Brooks, G. (1998) Trends in standards of literacy in the United Kingdom, 1948–1996, *Topic*, 19, pp. 1–10.

Brooks, G., Pugh, A.K. & Schagen, J. (1996) *Reading Performance at Nine* (Slough, National Foundation for Educational Research).

Carney, E. (1994) *A Survey of English Spelling* (London, Routledge).

Creemers, B.P.M. (1994) *The Effective Classroom* (London, Cassell).

Crévola, C. & Hill, P.W. (1998) Evaluation of a whole-school approach to prevention and intervention in early literacy, *Journal of Education for Students Placed At Risk*, 3, 2, pp. 133–157.

Dearing, R. (1994) *The National Curriculum and its Assessment: final report* (London, School Curriculum and Assessment Authority).

Department for Education (1995) *English in the National Curriculum* (London, Her Majesty's Stationery Office).

Department for Education and Employment (1998a) *The National Literacy Strategy: framework for teaching* (London, DfEE).

Department for Education and Employment (1998b) *The National Literacy Strategy: literacy training pack* (London, DfEE).

Elley, W.B. (Ed.) (1994) *The IEA Study of Reading Literacy: achievement and instruction in thirty-two school systems* (Oxford, Pergamon).

Fountas, I.C. & Pinnell, G.S. (1996) *Guided Reading: good first teaching for all children* (Portsmouth, N.H., Heinemann).

Fox, G. (Ed.) (1995) *Celebrating Children's Literature in Education* (London, Hodder & Stoughton).

Gentry, J.R. (1982) An analysis of developmental spelling in *GNYS AT WRK, The Reading Teacher*, 36, pp. 192–200.

Goswami, U. (1999) Phonological development and reading by analogy: epilinguistic and metalinguistic issues, in: J. Oakhill & R. Beard (Eds) *Reading Development and the Teaching of Reading: a psychological perspective* (Oxford, Blackwell).

Hall, C. & Coles, M. (1999) *Children's Reading Choices* (London, Routledge).

Hall, N. & Robinson, A. (Eds) (1996) *Learning About Punctuation* (Clevedon, Multilingual Matters).

Halliday, M.A.K. (1985) *An Introduction to Functional Grammar* (London, Edward Arnold).

Hannon, P. (1995) *Literacy, Home and School: research and practice in teaching literacy with parents* (London, Falmer Press).

Hayes, J.R. (1996) A new framework for understanding cognition and affect in writing, in: C.M. Levy & S. Ransdell (Eds) *The Science of Writing: theories, methods, individual differences, and applications* (Mahwah, N.J., Lawrence Erlbaum Associates).

Hayes, J.R. and Flower, L.S. (1980) Identifying the organisation of writing processes, in: L. Gregg & E.R. Steinberg (Eds) *Cognitive Processes in Writing* (Hillsdale, N.J., Lawrence Erlbaum Associates).

Hillocks, G. (1986) *Research on Written Composition* (Urbana, Il., National Conference on Research in English/ERIC Clearinghouse on Reading and Communication Skills).

Hillocks, G. (1995) *Teaching Writing as Reflective Practice* (New York, Teachers College Press).

Holdaway, D. (1979) *The Foundations of Literacy* (Sydney, Ashton Scholastic).

Holdaway, D. (1982) Shared book experience: teaching reading using favourite books, *Theory into Practice*, 21, 4, pp. 293–300.

Joyce, B. and Showers, B. (1995) *Student Achievement Through Staff Development: fundamentals of school renewed* (2E) (New York, Longman).

Labour Party (1997) *New Labour: because Britain deserves better* (*Election Manifesto*) (London, Labour Party).

Lewis, M. & Wray, D. (1995) *Developing Children's Non-Fiction Writing: working with writing frames* (Leamington Spa, Scholastic).

Literacy Task Force (1997a) *A Reading Revolution: how we can teach every child to read well* (London, The Literacy Task Force c/o University of London Institute of Education).

Literacy Task Force (1997b) *The Implementation of the National Literacy Strategy* (London, Department for Education and Employment).

Meek, M., Warlow, A. & Barton, G. (Eds) (1977) *The Cool Web: the pattern of children's reading* (London, The Bodley Head).

Morse, B. (1995) Rhyming poetry for children, in: R. Beard (Ed.) *Rhyme, Reading and Writing* (London, Hodder & Stoughton).

Mortimore, P. (1991) The nature and findings of school effectiveness research in the primary sector, in: S. Riddell & S. Brown (Eds) *School Effectiveness Research: its messages for school improvement* (London, Her Majesty's Stationery Office).

Mortimore, P., Sammons, P., Stoll, L., Lewis, D. & Ecob, R. (1988) *School Matters: the junior years* (Wells, Open Books).

Mountford, J. (1998) *An Insight into English Spelling* (London, Hodder & Stoughton).

Office for Standards in Education (1998) *Standards in Primary English* (London, Ofsted).

Perera, K. (1998) Understanding language, in: N. Mercer (Ed.) *Language and Literacy from an Educational Perspective* (Milton Keynes, Open University Press).

Perera, K. (1993) The 'Good Book': linguistic aspects, in: R. Beard (Ed.) *Teaching Literacy: balancing perspectives* (London, Hodder & Stoughton).

Perera, K. (1996) Who says what? Learning to 'read' the punctuation of direct speech, in: N. Hall & A. Robinson (Eds) *Learning About Punctuation* (Clevedon, Multilingual Matters).

Perfetti, C. (1995) Cognitive research can inform reading education, *Journal of Research in Reading,* 18, 2, pp. 106–115. Reprinted in: J. Oakhill & R. Beard (Eds) (1999) *Reading Development and the Teaching of Reading: a psychological perspective* (Oxford, Blackwell).

Purves, A.C. (Ed.) (1992) *The IEA Study of Written Composition II: education and performance in fourteen countries* (Oxford, Pergamon).

Reid, J. (1993) Reading and spoken language: the nature of the links, in: R. Beard (Ed.) *Teaching Literacy: balancing perspectives* (London, Hodder & Stoughton).

Reynolds, D. (1998) Schooling for literacy: a review of research on teacher effectiveness and school effectiveness and its implications for contemporary educational policies, *Educational Review,* 50, 2, pp. 147–162.

Riley, J. (1996) *The Teaching of Reading: the development of literacy in the early years of school* (London, Paul Chapman).

Sainsbury, M., Schagen, I., Whetton, G., with Hagues, N. & Minnis, M. (1998) *Evaluation of the National Literacy Project: Cohort I, 1996–98* (Slough, National Foundation for Educational Research).

Sainsbury, M. and Twist, E. (1999) *The Key Stage 2 English Tests.* Paper presented at the United Kingdom Reading Association International Conference, Chester, July.

Sammons, P., Hillman, J. & Mortimore, P. (1995) *Key Characteristics of Effective Schools: a review of school effectiveness research* (London, Ofsted).

Sammons, P., Nuttall, D., Cuttance, P. & Thomas, S. (1995) Continuity of school effects: a longitudinal analysis of primary and secondary school effects on GCSE performance, *School Effectiveness and School Improvement,* 6, 4, pp. 285–307.

Scheerens, J. (1992) *Effective Schooling: research, theory and practice* (London, Cassell).

Slavin, R.E. (1997) *Success for All: policy implications for British education.* Paper presented at the Literacy Task Force Conference, London, February.

Stannard, J. (1997) *Raising Standards Through the National Literacy Project.* Paper presented at the Literacy Task Force Conference, London, February.

Stanovich, K.E. and P.J. (1995) How research might inform the debate about early reading acquisition, *Journal of Research in Reading,* 18, 2, pp. 87–105. Reprinted in: J. Oakhill & R. Beard (Eds) (1999) *Reading Development and the Teaching of Reading: a psychological perspective* (Oxford, Blackwell).

Styles, M. (1998) *From the Garden to the Street: three hundred years of poetry for children* (London, Cassell).

Task Group on Assessment and Testing (1988) *National Curriculum Task Group on Assessment and Testing: a report* (London, Department of Education and Science).

Teddlie, C. and Reynolds, D. (Eds) (1999) *The International Handbook of School Effectiveness Research* (Lewes, Falmer Press).

Tizard, B., Blatchford, P., Burke, J., Farquhar, C. & Plewis, I. (1988) *Young Children at School in the Inner City* (London, Lawrence Eribaum).

Treiman, R. and Zukowski, A. (1996) Children's sensitivity to syllables, onsets, rimes and phonemes, *Journal of Experimental Child Psychology,* 61, pp. 193–215.

Tucker, N. (1993) The 'Good Book': literary aspects, in: R. Beard (Ed.) *Teaching Literacy: balancing perspectives* (London, Hodder and Stoughton).

Tyler, R.W. (1949) *Basic Principles of Curriculum and Instruction* (Chicago, University of Chicago Press).

Wasik, B.A. & Slavin, R.E. (1993) Preventing reading failure with one-to-one tutoring: a review of five programmes, *Reading Research Quarterly,* 28, pp. 178–200.

Weinberger, J. (1996) *Literacy Goes to School: the parents' role in young children's literacy development* (London, Paul Chapman).

Wray, D. & Lewis, M. (1997) *Extending Literacy: children reading and writing non-fiction* (London, Routledge).

11

Literacy Policy and Policy Literacy: A Tale of Phonics in Early Reading in England

Kathy Hall

Introduction and background

A major literacy theme currently exercising educators, policymakers, researchers, media people, and publishers in the United Kingdom is the beginning reader and the role of phonics. How best to teach reading is a perennial hot topic in education, but the current debate is much narrower in focus than this: it concerns how best to teach the necessary phonic knowledge that underpins word recognition. This chapter examines the current controversy in England about how to teach reading. It is in two parts. The first part overviews the evidence for the most recent official recommendation to Government that an approach known as synthetic phonics should be adopted as an exclusive pedagogical model for developing children's knowledge of the alphabetic principle. The second and longer part examines possible explanations for this recommendation, a recommendation that constitutes a more prescriptive shift in literacy policy in England. Here my analysis also shifts from literacy policy to policy literacy.

In December 2005, an Interim report of a government-commissioned review of early reading was published (Rose, 2005). This was followed in March 2006 with a Final Report (Rose, 2006), which confirmed the recommendations of the earlier one. The first question in the remit of the review was, what best practice should be expected in the teaching of early reading and synthetic phonics? (Rose, 2005, 2006, para 1). Under the chairmanship of Mr. Jim Rose, the committee prioritized this aspect in the Interim Report, noting that the Final Report would attend more fully to other aspects of early reading, thus implying the expectation at that stage that the decision taken on this question would not be significantly attended in the Final Report and thus was the case. From the point of view of this chapter, the Interim Report therefore is of more interest. The Interim Report recommends to government that pupils 'should be taught to use the knowledge and skills that define synthetic phonic work as their first strategy in decoding and encoding print' (para 72). Teachers of 5-year-olds are being urged to adopt synthetic phonics as *the* method of teaching the relationship between letters and sounds. The report also advocates that, once a programme of systematic synthetic phonic work is begun, it 'should be followed faithfully' (para 43). There are references to 'fidelity to the programme' (para 43) and how it would be 'unwise to "pick and mix" elements from several different programmes because such an approach

From: Openshaw, R. and Soler, J. (eds) *Reading Across International Boundaries: History, Policy, and Politics*, pp. 55–67 (Charlotte, NC: Information Age Publishing, 2007).

would disrupt "planned progression"' (para 43). There are also claims made about evidence from 'successful programmes' and whole class teaching (para 44) and how within one such programme used in Scotland, teachers 'are able to intervene promptly because the explicit structure of the programme sets out exactly what needs to be learnt' (para 48). There are references to commercial phonics programmes (although of course no particular commercial programme is actually named) and to how teaching assistants can be trained to use programmes based on synthetic phonics (para 48). The Final Report repeated the earlier recommendations on synthetic phonics (Rose, 2006, para 30–88). The (then) Secretary of State for Education, Ruth Kelly, commented on and endorsed the recommendations in both Reports. The views of the present Secretary of State for Education, Alan Johnson, are entirely consistent with his predecessor's 'Teaching of "Three R's"' (*The Times*, 8 September 2006).

What is the problem? The problem is the lack of evidence to support the position taken on synthetic phonics in these Reports despite existing evidence that supports an alternative position (see Hall, 2006, for a more detailed review of this evidence). The concern is that the Rose Reports are set to influence national and local policy decisions about the teaching of reading, about initial teacher education, about staff development and curriculum materials and published programmes, decisions on which state funds may be spent. Their position therefore merits constructively critical scrutiny and analysis, which is the basis on which flaws in policy recommendations can be identified and hopefully corrected. As other researchers have noted (Taylor, Anderson, Au, & Raphael, 2000), one would expect that at a minimum research cited to justify policy should reflect a broad definition of the subject, that such research should be rigorous and robust in relation to evidence, and that it would have the potential to improve learning. Since this is far from the case here, this chapter explores why. What factors might explain the current stance on phonics in these reports? Before addressing this question, I explain the pedagogical debate in a little more detail.

Analytic and synthetic phonics and the pedagogical debate

In essence, the controversy about phonics centers on the relative effectiveness of two different teaching methods: synthetic and analytic phonics (Cook, 2002; Hall, 2003; Lewis & Ellis, 2006; Torgerson, Brooks, & Hall, 2006). Crudely put, synthetic phonics is about sounding out and blending, whereas analytic phonics is characterized by perceiving patterns and drawing inferences. A synthetic approach emphasizes letter-by-letter phonological decoding (e.g., in the case of the word *cat*, the sounds *kuh*, a, and *luh* are separately sounded out and blended to make *cat*). What is emphasized is the phoneme – the smallest unit of sound in a word. An analytic approach places emphasis on inferring sound–symbol relations. In this approach, learners are taught key words that contain common spelling patterns, the thinking being if you know the letter pattern *at*, this helps you to build up your knowledge of other words with this letter pattern, so you make lists of words with the same pattern (e.g., *hat, sat, mat*, etc.). Analytic phonics is sometimes called analogy phonics (White, 2005).

Synthetic phonics has come to be associated with small phonological units (phonemes), and analytic phonics has come to be associated with large phonological units (onsets and rimes). Phonological awareness refers to the insight that speech can be broken down into smaller units (syllables, onset-rimes, phonemes). In practice, phonemic awareness refers to phonological awareness linked to letters. The alignment of synthetic phonics with small phonological units and of analytic with large phonological units stems from the claims in some psychological research that knowledge of small phonological units, more specifically phonemic knowledge, is a better predictor of success in reading than knowledge of large phonological units, more specifically onsets and rimes (Hulme et al., 2002; Muter, Hulme, Stevenson, & Snowling, 2004). This finding, which in itself is problematic, has led, unhelpfully, to a corresponding polarization of teaching methods.

Scottish research in Clackmannanshire (Johnston & Watson, 2005), which was set up to assess the relative merits of synthetic and analytic teaching approaches, highlights the value of explicit phoneme-level training linked to letters. Other research makes similar claims about the relative effectiveness of synthetic phonics over analytic phonics (Lupker, 2005). So it would seem that an emphasis on small phonological units, specifically phoneme, is important and this is in line with synthetic phonics. However, two recent systematic reviews of evidence on the relative effectiveness of both approaches (National Reading Panel, 2000; Torgerson et al., 2006) agreed that the approaches were statistically indistinguishable in their effects.

I have argued elsewhere that since large and small phonological units are necessary for reading, it is not helpful to seek to compare the effectiveness of analytic and synthetic phonics methods of teaching and it is certainly not appropriate to suggest that teachers should privilege one method of developing the necessary phonic knowledge in beginner readers. The important point is that synthetic and analytic phonics are linked – they are not dichotomous, 'either–or' teaching approaches. This claim is justified by several sources of evidence that I note but do not develop in detail here (see Hall, 2006, for full discussion).

First, there is evidence of a developmental sequence that suggests that phonological sensitivity proceeds from early awareness of large units (syllables, onset-rimes) to later awareness of small units (phonemes). Second, the capacity of the human brain for pattern recognition suggests that word-sorting activities, a key feature of analytic phonics, encourages learners to notice patterns and to think flexibly about letter–sound correspondences. By virtue of the human brain's pattern detection abilities, a teacher may not need to work through all of the 40-plus phonemes of English, which in turn suggests that it is not sensible to prescribe one programme or method that all children should experience. Third, phonological knowledge, phonemic knowledge, and letter name knowledge are all interconnected such that phonemic knowledge is both a cause and a consequence of learning to recognize printed words. Advocates of a synthetic phonics-only approach do not recognize this fact, emphasizing instead that learners should be taught the sound of letters and common letter blends *before* they move on to reading books. Fourth, the deep orthography of the English language, showing considerable inconsistency in mappings of letters and sounds, makes learning to read English much harder than learning to read many other languages. Some words in English, for example, *people*, *yacht* and *chair* represent no pattern in the language in that there are no other words with similar sound–letter mappings and so have to be learned as distinct units (Goswami, 2002). A whole-word approach therefore is relevant for such words, highlighting the inadequacy of just one teaching method. However, while vowels are especially inconsistent in their letter–sound mappings, their consistency increases when one considers the entire rime – in other words, the phoneme for a given vowel is more predictable when the time itself is taken into account – a point that is pivotal for the teaching of phonics as shown by Usha Goswami's work (Goswami, 2002, 2005; Ziegler & Goswami, 2005). This research shows that orthographic consistency and pedagogical methods are linked: a consistent orthography (e.g., German) lends itself to a more systematic teaching by a synthetic phonics method, whereas an inconsistent orthography like English demands more varied and complex methods of teaching. These briefly summarized points indicate that more than one method of teaching decoding will be helpful in the classroom. Whole-word, analytic, and synthetic pedagogical approaches, research suggests, would be useful.

Seduced by the solo method mentality

Although the idea is attractive, there are many reasons why a single method is an inadequate basis for improving practice. If one examines the method, the package or the fixed curriculum in action, it is probably about 'as fixed as the clouds in the sky,' to quote Bruner (Olson, in press). The problem with mandating schemes and programmes, as we know from sociocultural learning theory, is that they can't take into account the contexts of their implementation and thus they can't place learners at the center of the learning enterprise. This is not to suggest they haven't their uses, merely to point out that they shouldn't be mandatory or assumed to be teacher-proof.

An input–output model of learning whereby a programme is specified and teachers are urged to implement it faithfully, as is being suggested in the Rose Review, is to assume that you can treat teachers and learners in a detached way much like 'an entomologist regards a colony of ants or a beekeeper a colony of bees' (Olson, 2008). As Olson, drawing on Bruner, observes: 'the beekeeper's problem is to extract the maximum amount of honey from the hive. While you have to know something about bees there is no need to fuss about the beliefs and desires of the bees or think about whether they share your goals – there is little room for negotiation or inter-subjectivity.' This assumption is implicit and sometimes explicit in the Rose Reports, as exemplified by the language used to urge a systematic approach to the teaching of letter–sound relationships: 'children are highly unlikely to work out this relationship for themselves … it cannot be left … for children to *level out*, on their own' (Rose, 2005, para 27, emphasis added). Not recognized here is the fact that it is the learner who makes the knowledge: learners must do their own learning.

There is an assumption throughout the reports that we can ignore the vicissitudes of the learner's mind, the learner's knowledge, identity, and goals and we can't do that no matter how elegantly packaged the programme or the method. Also, there is the teacher's mind. From the perspective of teachers and teaching, the more we dictate moves and script their lines, the more we're likely to alienate good teachers, something we can ill afford to do at a time in this country when recruitment to and retention in the profession remain a challenge (see Hall, 2004).

Framing the debate

Would those on the Rose Review not have been aware of all this: how is it that the emphasis on one type of programme and on one teaching method is so strong and so plainly out of line with what I have reasoned is the evidence? To answer this, I suggest we need to examine the political context more closely, for the political and the policy processes are ever close when it comes to reading pedagogy, as this book so powerfully demonstrates. The Rose Report in this sense can be read as a policy text that, like all policy texts, is rhetorical and persuasive, seeking not merely to describe a reality but to do so in a way that legitimates a particular course of action. Given the way the problem of reading was constructed for and by the Rose Committee, the public can be persuaded that the solution is obvious and logical, based on a version of sound science and clearly intended for the common good. What really framed the debate? In what way was the policy environment of the Rose Review tinged? I suggest there are many interrelated factors at work here, each of them acting to shape public opinion and to constrain any committee embarking on a review of the teaching of early reading. Among them are the child project, literacy linked to the economy and a surveillance project, the review remit and committee composition, lobbying, and a Scottish study showing the merits of synthetic phonics.

In an increasingly complex, uncertain, and unstable world, the child assumes enormous significance. The child is malleable, is in the process of becoming, is unfinished and as such is a prime project for shaping the future, for intervening to temper that uncomfortable uncertainty and instability of our age. Government attention to children's education convinces the public that it cares about quality education and is willing to intervene to improve the current situation. And intervening early to prevent reading failure is especially appealing. A strongly framed and classified curriculum of the kind recommended in the Rose Report fits nicely into this child project.

All political parties in the United Kingdom and in other advanced economies speak of literacy in terms of the economy. Literacy, more than any other area of the curriculum, has been subsumed into a human capital discourse (Hall, 2004) making politicization all the more likely. The problem for government is how to measure human capital. Invisible capital, as Jo Lo Bianco (2001) says, must be rendered visible to the gaze of accountants and economists. And literacy, defined unidimensionally, that is, in terms of print literacy only, and, in the case of the first year of school, in terms of word recognition only, offers a proxy and becomes a code for educational achievement that can be communicated to the public in the form of league tables. Prestige for many people is enhanced by the neighborhoods in which they live and where their children go to school. Estate agents in England typically comment on the quality of the schools in their descriptions of houses in order to sell homes for higher prices in higher-performing areas. The very first year of formal schooling has, to date, escaped the kind of literacy surveillance now characterizing all other years of primary education in England. The prescriptive approach being recommended in the Rose Review is guaranteed to bring all 5-year-olds and their teachers more securely into the surveillance net.

I already mentioned the narrow focus of the Rose Review at the beginning of the chapter – a remit that circumscribed what could be discussed. Notice that reading was not located in the broader sociocultural context of family and community literacies, or the new literacies associated with the new technologies. It did not even include comprehension or writing. The fact is that any literacy curriculum exists within this broader social context. To concentrate in our teaching or in our policymaking on only one aspect, like the alphabetic principle, is to ignore this larger system, any element of which can influence achievement negatively or positively (Taylor et al., 2000). Moreover, the narrow view of the remit gives the false impression that the way to enhance the teaching of reading is simple and straightforward. The key point is that the remit was framed in a way that fitted neatly into the surveillance project: the aim is to render literacy measurable and the early years teacher-accountable. The recommendations in the Rose Review mean the door to this is now wide open to such measurement and accountability.

In addition to the narrow remit, the composition of the committee itself is significant. Though undoubtedly eminent scholars in their different fields, most of the chosen members were like-minded in their views about what constitutes 'scientific evidence' in reading and they were not people, in the main, whose research orientation could be described as sociocultural, all of this making it more likely that within the review committee a consensus document could be produced.

The course of action recommended by the Rose Review had been hinted at and had already obtained a measure of consensus through previous policy moves, especially through the House of Commons Education and Skills Committee (2005), which reported on the teaching of reading just a month or so before the Rose Review was initiated. And the people who gave evidence to this particular committee were heavily oriented toward synthetic phonics and some of those who offered opinions, referred to as evidence in the report, have commercial interests in synthetic phonics materials. Despite its tide, *Teaching Children to Read*, the overwhelming emphasis in that report was on synthetic phonics and whether or not the National Literacy Strategy had got the status of synthetic phonics right.

Phonics is 'big business' with financial rewards awaiting anyone who invents the best scheme of programme for teaching it. Nowhere is this more evident than in the United States where lobbying is often counter-productive, stimulating practice, policy, and research in artificially narrow domains without encouraging consideration of the broader picture. In addition, lobbyists almost always distort policy and research by introducing a political and an adversarial dimension where polarities and simplifications win out over the realities and complexities. Such policy entrepreneurs (Kingdon, 2002) energetically shape the policy process from within and without – through their vocal presence on committees, especially government committees, in schools, with publishers, in the media, and so on. They get to know influential people in politics and in the media, as well as at the 'chalk face' of practice, and lobby them tirelessly. Six years ago, Colin Harrison (1999) reported in the UKLA journal *Literary* that whenever you get a situation where there isn't agreement among members of the research community, like we have currently about the teaching of phonics, rhetoric and lobbying often become the basis on which decisions about teaching come to be made. While debate continues, it is my view that the theory of reading pedagogy has progressed and we now have much clearer implications for practice than were available six years ago, as I was trying to explain earlier. Nevertheless, rhetoric and lobbying remain features of the literacy policy process, as evidenced in the Report of the House of Commons Committee where opinion and evidence were indistinguishable, and where the views of those with commercial interests appear to hold the same weight and status as the views of others.

The tipping point

Who is really interested in reading research? In the past, just other reading researchers might have been the answer. But now policymakers and the public in general are centrally involved in debates about teaching reading. This can only be good for democracy but it is not helpful if research is not subjected to critical review or if research and opinion are conflated. The

Scottish research (Johnston & Watson, 2005) claiming to show the merits of synthetic phonics received an unprecedented amount of attention before it went through the conventional peer review process and, to my knowledge, it still hasn't been published in a refereed source. This study, conducted in Clackmannanshire, a small local authority in Scotland with about 20 primary schools and some special schools, was the tipping point in the policy process in that that study propelled the question of how to teach reading right into the public consciousness. This is what finally made the issue of reading pedagogy salient for the British public. 'Greater than the tread of mighty armies is an idea whose time has come,' said Victor Hugo (cited in Kingdon, 2002) and the idea whose time had come now was not reading, or phonics even, but synthetic phonics.

In the Rose Reports and in the House of Commons Report, which immediately preceded them, this study received a noncritical summary. Because of its unusual and extensive media coverage, including uptake by politicians from more than one political party, the study is now set to exert inordinate influence. The leader of the Conservative Party, David Cameron, put synthetic phonics in his four-point manifesto before the Interim Rose Review was even published. He wants 'concrete action to enforce synthetic phonics' and promoted synthetic phonics long before Labour politicians even knew the word existed! And speaking for his party in June 2005, Cameron stated that 'based on evidence, we believe synthetic phonics is a far more effective teaching method than the combination of methods currently advocated' (Blair, 2005). As already noted, Ruth Kelly, the then Minister of State for Education, endorsed the Report's recommendations on synthetic phonics. Intriguingly, she had endorsed this same recommendation when she commissioned the review in June 2005, as indicated by the following quotation: 'Synthetic phonics, properly taught, can and does play an important part in teaching reading skills' (Blair, 2005). Synthetic phonics would appear to be a bandwagon onto which politicians of all persuasions can now climb.

It is a mistake to assume that problems are always the focus of policy, that is, that problems necessarily precede policy. Problems are not independent of the policy process itself, as several policy theorists have already demonstrated (Kingdon, 2002; Lo Bianco, 2001; Luke, Lingard, Green, & Comber, 1999; Taylor et al., 2000). The assumption that they are distances policy from politics. Policymaking is at least as much about the construction and foregrounding of problems in a way that captivates the public imagination so that the public is unaware of other problems or that other problems, if identified, are less urgent ones and do not merit prominence at the level of the state (Kingdon, 2002: Lo Bianco, 2001). Chronologically, the solution may come first and then the problem follows – the Clackmannanshire study offered a simple solution and a problem was quickly constructed to fit it. Of course, the public has to be prepared for the problem and the solution – and here lies the discursive role of policy, and, in turn, the need for all of us who are interested in shaping literacy policy and practice to be, increasingly, policy-literate.

Persuading practitioners

What is the reaction of the professional community to this report? This is a key question as without the compliance, if not the support, of enough of the teaching profession, it is likely that implementation will be problematic for Government. It is noteworthy in this regard that the United Kingdom Literacy Association's special interest group on reading prepared and published a substantial response for the Review Committee (UKLA, 2005) and members of the SIG, including myself, met personally with Mr. Rose to discuss our report and his review before the Interim Report was published. In addition, several other scholarly organizations, including particularly early years' associations and university education departments, cautioned against such a prescriptive stance.

So how are teachers brought 'on side'? After all, teachers will have to make the policy happen. Where is the 'thin silver of agitational space' (Lo Bianco, 2001, p. 218) to ensure that the divergence between policy and practice is not so geat as to deny compliance in due course? Again, taking the Rose Reports as rhetorical and persuasive texts that seek to shape opinion, I would suggest that teachers this time are positioned as part of the solution (unusually). No longer part of the problem but rather positioned as a group of people doing the best they can, they are nevertheless positioned as needing to be rescued in order to be truly part of the solution. This time, the villain of the piece is the research community. By positioning researchers, academics, and research itself as troublesome, the Reports seek to empower teachers and, in this way, persuade them to comply. The conventional practices of academic – namely, debate, dialogue, argument, critique, and investigation – are now perceived as negative, frustrating, irritating, unhelpful, and inconsistent.

Unreasonable researchers seemingly refuse to provide a solution about how best to teach the beginner reader; they are unwilling to give clear, simple answers. To illustrate this negative language, the first page of the summary of the Interim Report claims that 'there is a *futile* debate that risks *distracting* attention from the important goals of understanding how beginners learn to read and write,' while paragraph 29 says, 'a prime *irritant* for practitioners and teachers is what they see as a *wrangle* in which advocates of phonics work are *unable* to agree definitions. Furthermore these *disputes* often occur *within their own camps*' (emphasis added). Teachers need to be rescued from such self-serving and out-of-touch academics, as revealed in paragraph 30: 'Discussion with practitioners and teachers revealed an understandable sense of frustration with this debate. As they engaged in the daily teaching of phonic work in settings and schools, some felt they were "at the mercy of rows of back seat drivers pointing in different directions." The call is for consistent guidance that offers them "structure, simplicity and some flexibility."' Clearly, Government will come to the rescue and solve the problem that academics won't or can't solve. The upshot is that academics can't be trusted as they are too tentative, too cautious about evidence, and perhaps are too ready to point to the complexity of the reading process. Only governments can be really trusted to provide simple, straightforward answers. Finally, although the 'sliver of agitational space' remains 'thin' indeed, I would suggest that it is widened just slightly by the Report's contradictions, exemplified in the reference to 'structure, simplicity and some flexibility' (Rose, 2005, para 30).

Conclusion

Is policymaking an end in itself such that the real goal of policymakers is to make their mark on the policy process, to have done something, particularly something that public opinion polls support? If this is the case then we can expect a continued flow of literacy policies that would suggest busyness rather than vision. In sum, any coherent vision of how literacy pedagogy might improve is likely to be absent. Although it is unlikely that how to teach reading can ever be depoliticized completely (Allington, 1999: Pressley, Duke, & Bolling, 2004; Soler & Openshaw, 2006), it is nevertheless important that government recommendations and mandates about teaching reading are debated and closely examined. The citizenry needs to become more policy literate. While Government is always likely to make decisions about education on a political basis, academics and professionals individually and collectively within their learned societies and with the voting public have to do their utmost to at least temper what they see as misguided decisions and, if possible, change them.

A first step toward such an approach would be to recognize the complexity and nonlinearity of the policy process, and specifically recognize that a society's problems are not always or necessarily the initial focus of policymaking. This requires closer attention to the discursive function of policy texts as I have sought to do in this chapter. It requires some sense of the (different) pressures on and agendas of all those involved in shaping policy in a democracy and an awareness of the influences different interest groups are able to exert on decisions. Such an approach, therefore, invites those interested in informing debates about reading pedagogy to have a critical understanding, not just of the research evidence about the teaching and learning of early reading but also to have a critical understanding of the ways of policy decision making – to be policy literate.

References

Allington, R.L. (1999). Crafting state educational policy: the slippery role of research and researchers. *Journal of Literacy Research*, 51, 457–482.

Blair, A. (2005, June 3). Schools told to go back to basics for reading, *The Times*.

Cook, M. (Ed.) (2002). *Perspectives on the Teaching and Learning of Phonics*. Royston: United Kingdom Literacy Association.

Goswami, U. (2002). Rhymes, phonemes and learning to read: interpreting recent research. In M. Cook (Ed.), *Perspectives on the Teaching and Learning of Phonics* (pp. 41–60). Royston: United Kingdom Literacy Association.

Goswami, U. (2005). Synthetic phonics and learning to read: a cross language perspective. *Educational Psychology in Practice*, 21(4), 273–282.

Hall, K. (2003*). Listening to Stephen Read: Multiple Perspectives on Literacy*. Maidenhead, UK: Open University Press.

Hall, K. (2004). *Literacy and Schooling: Towards Renewal in Primary Education Policy*. Aldershot, UK: Ashgate.

Hall, K. (2006). How children learn to read and how phonics helps. In M. Lewis & S. Ellis (Eds.), *Phonics: Practice, Research and Policy*. London: Sage.

Harrison, C. (1999). When scientists don't agree: the case for balanced phonics. *Reading*, 33(2), 59–63.

House of Commons, Education and Skills Committee (2005). *Teaching Children to Read, Eighth Report of Session (2004–05)*. London: The Stationery Office.

Hulme, C., Hatcher, P., Nation, K., Brown, A., Adams, J., and Stuart, G. (2002). Phoneme awareness is a better predictor of early reading skill than onset-rime awareness. *Journal of Experimental Child Psychology*, 82(2), 1–28.

Johnston, R., and Watson, J. (2005). *The Effects of Synthetic Phonics Teaching on Reading and Spelling Attainment*. Edinburgh, UK: Scottish Executive Education Department.

Kingdon, J.W. (2002). *Agendas, Alternatives and Public Policies* (2nd ed.). New York: Longman.

Lewis, M., and Ellis, S. (Eds.) (2006). *Phonics: Practice, Research and Policy*. London: Sage.

Lo Bianco, J. (2001). Policy literacy. *Language and Education*, 15(2 & 3), 212–227.

Luke, A., Lingard, L., Green, B., and Comber, B. (1999). The abuses of literacy: educational policy and the construction of crisis. In J. Marshall & M. Peters (Eds), *Educational Policy* (pp. 1–25). London: Edward Elgar.

Lupker, S.J. (2005). Visual word recognition: theories and findings. In M.J. Snowling & C. Hulme (Eds.), *The Science of Reading: A Handbook* (pp. 39–60). Oxford, UK: Blackwell.

Muter, V., Hulme, C., Stevenson. J., & Snowling, M. (2004). Phonemes, rimes, vocabulary and grammatical skills as foundations of early reading development: evidence from a longitudinal study. *Developmental Psychology,* 40(5), 1–7.

National Reading Panel (2000). *Teaching Children to Read: An Evidenced-based Assessment of the Scientific Research Literature on Reading and its Implications for Reading Instruction.* Washington, DC: National Institute for Child Health and Human Development.

Olson, D. (2008). *Jerome Bruner: The Cognitive Revolution in Educational Theory.* New York: Continuum International.

Pressley, M., Duke, N.K., and Bolling, E.C. (2004). The educational science and scientifically-based instruction we need: lessons from reading research and policy-making. *Harvard Education Review,* 74(1), 30–61.

Rose, J. (2005). *Independent Review of the Teaching of Early Reading: Interim Report.* London: DfES.

Rose, J. (2006). *Independent Review of the Teaching of Early Reading: Final Report.* London: DfES.

Soler, J., and Openshaw, R. (2006). *Literacy Crises and Reading Policy: Our Children Still Can't Read.* London: Routledge.

Taylor, B., Anderson, R.C., Au, K.H., and Raphael, T.E. (2000). Discretion in the translation of research to policy: a case from beginning reading. *Educational Researcher,* 29(6), 16–26.

The Times (2006, September 8). Teaching of 'Three R's' is overhauled as pupils fail to progress.

Torgerson, C.J., Brooks, G., & Hall, J. (2006). *A Systematic Review of the Research Literature on the Use of Phonics in the Teaching of Reading and Spelling* (Research Report 711). London: Department for Education and Skills. Available at http:// www.dfes.gov.uk/research/dara/ uploadfiles/RR711_pdf.

United Kingdom Literacy Association (UKLA) (2005). Submission to the Review of Best Practice in the Teaching of Early Reading. Royston, Herts.: UKLA.

White, T.G. (2005). Effects of systematic and strategic analogy-based phonics on grade 2 students' word reading and reading comprehension. *Reading Research Quarterly,* 40(2), 234–255.

Ziegler, J.C., & Goswami, U. (2005) Reading acquisition, developmental dyslexia, skilled reading across languages: a psycholinguistic grain-size theory. *Psychological Bulletin,* 131(1), 3–29.

12

'To Be or Not to Be?': The Politics of Teaching Phonics in England and New Zealand

Janet Soler and Roger Openshaw

[…]

Introduction: the politics of early literacy instruction

Debates over the place of phonics in early reading instruction currently rage in most English-speaking countries and nowhere more than in England and New Zealand where, wide geographical separation notwithstanding, there is a shared tradition in literacy policy and pedagogy. In order to provide insight into the specific contexts that have surrounded the debates over teaching of phonics in both countries, we have drawn upon the work of critical literacy theorists such as Luke, Freebody and Muspratt, which illustrates how the teaching of reading arises from social activity that, in turn, is shaped by historical, social and political concerns (see, for example, Luke, 1991, 1993; Muspratt et al., 1997). Our focus upon the reception accorded to phonics teaching within specific socio-historical, political and national contexts in this [chapter] arises from our earlier co-authored and edited work (Soler and Openshaw, 2006; Openshaw and Soler, 2007). This work focused on specific periods since 1945 where intense debates over phonics and whole language had emerged in both England and New Zealand. We demonstrated clearly that these debates received the most public attention where there were periods of increasing nationwide concern over literacy standards. These periods, known as 'literacy crises', drive curriculum practice and initiatives at a level far beyond the classroom and have a direct impact on government policy (Welch and Freebody, 2002). This, in turn, has profound implications for the teaching of phonics versus whole language.

A key theme in our work has been: what role did public debates over reading standards in England play in bringing about a political environment highly receptive to the introduction of a centralized and prescriptive approach to the teaching of phonics? In turn, this raises further questions such as whose interests are being pursued under the guise of particular literacy programmes and policies; and how particular methods of reading come to

From: *Journal of Early Childhood Literacy*, 7 (3), 2007, pp. 333–52.

predominate over others. When we looked in depth at particular individuals and specific instances that sparked these debates, we found that underpinning the highly politicized public debates were complex interactions and viewpoints with layers of interaction.

Our investigations into the debates over how to teach reading in England and New Zealand have shown that all initiatives related to teaching reading and early literacy arise from pressures, tensions and crises embedded in the particular national and regional political contexts. In both countries, a significant development over the past decade has been the increasing interest and involvement of national governments in specific decisions regarding both the curriculum and teaching of early literacy in order to raise literacy standards. Yet despite these similarities, the specific debates, politics and policies related to instructional approaches to early reading in both countries are markedly different.

The road to the dominance of phonics in England

At the beginning of the 1990s, England did not have an established national reading programme that could support claims that there was a consistent and successful philosophy of teaching early reading that could maintain high literacy standards. This helped fuel a high profile public debate over the teaching of reading and the adherence to whole language/real book approaches to teaching reading. This debate was initiated by a group of educational psychologists who released data based on reading tests on seven-year-olds in nine LEAs that appeared to indicate a decline in reading standards since 1985 (Education, Science and Arts Committee [ESAC], 1991: 261–8). The initial media attention was followed by one of the psychologists, Martin Turner, publishing a report entitled *Sponsored Reading Failure: An Object Lesson* (Turner, 1990).

This report, based on reading test results from nine LEAs, argued that reading standards had suffered a serious decline across the southern half of England and perhaps throughout Britain by the early 1990s (Turner, 1990: 4). Turner argued that this was due to the introduction of a whole language/real book 'new methods' based approach to teaching reading. Frank Smith and Kenneth Goodman were seen to be the main instigators of this approach and were characterized as anti-formal reading instruction, anti-phonics teaching, anti-dyslexia, anti-testing and anti-formalism (Turner, 1990: 7).

The concern generated by the crisis generated attacks on the advocates of the whole language/phonics approach and progressive educational ideals in general. Frank Smith was reported by John O'Leary writing in *The Times* as occupying 'a place in the demonology of child development once reserved for Dr Spock' and was reportedly accused of 'triggering a national decline in reading standards with so-called "real books" theory of learning'. He was also described as having 'been dubbed the Billy Graham of the reading world, a guru of the left and a crank'. Moreover he was 'an opponent of the national curriculum, testing and the separation of pupils by identity'. O'Leary also noted that Tim Eggar, the Education Minister, had now taken sides against the whole language/real book approach and attacked these beliefs. Eggar was quoted as stating that Mr Smith had a long way to go to prove his case. The Education Minister also felt that the real books campaign was a serious attack on standards in schools (O'Leary, 1991: 1).

Report on 'standards of reading in primary schools'

In submitting its report in May 1991, the ESAC, commenting on teaching methods, noted Turner's claim that the apparent decline in reading standards could be attributed to the growth of 'real books' methods of teaching reading and the abandonment of the systematic teaching of phonics, but rejected it on the evidence from the HM Inspectorate (HMI) survey that found only five per cent of teachers described their approach as 'real books'. The HMI report, however, found a clear link between higher standards and systematic phonics teaching, although it was acknowledged that the questions of how to teach phonics, and with what frequency, were still controversial. Accordingly, the ESAC Report recommended that '... the various methods of teaching phonics should be evaluated in order to establish the most effective way of using phonics in the teaching of reading' (ESAC, 1991: xii).

The high degree of public and professional interest in the reading standards issue resulted in the Government coming under immediate pressure to act on its recommendations. A Commons Select Committee was meeting at the same time to investigate Turner's claims that standards of reading were falling because of faulty teaching methods in primary schools. This committee dismissed his claims that phonics was at fault, but supported the need for the national testing of seven-year olds as the tests would provide the 'first solid basis for judging standards' (MacLeod, 1991: 10).

During this period, the debate over phonics versus real books/whole language featured strongly both in House of Commons exchanges and in the press. During the debate, the Opposition argued that only Labour enjoyed the confidence of the public because it was the only party that had clearly articulated policies for improving standards across the entire system. Fatchett observed that Labour would '... improve education performance school by school, local authority by local authority, through its powerful, independent, much-acclaimed and non-political education standards commission' (Hansard, 1991: 683). In response, the Conservative politician Rhodes Boyson reiterated his longstanding view that intellectual 'trendies' within the inspectorate and teacher training colleges had forced the discovery methods of learning on teachers that had largely been responsible for the decline in educational standards they were now witnessing. Boyson observed that:

> At the same time there was a move to the 'look and say' method and 'real books' and away from phonics, which is the method by which most children learn to read. He argued that ten per cent of teachers could teach by any method if they were left alone; 10 per cent could not and should therefore be dismissed; but the remaining 80 per cent required the phonics method. (Hansard, 1991: 684–5)

Impact of national testing for seven-year-olds

In the press, commentators such as Roger Beard, who was at the time a senior lecturer in Primary Education at the University of Leeds, advocated caution and a 'mixed-method' approach that utilized phonics to help children with 'reading fluency and the need to decode unfamiliar words – on which the meaning of the texts often disproportionately depends' (Beard, 1991: 17). The release of the results of national testing of seven-year-olds in November 1991, however, led to a renewed press condemnation of teaching methods. The results were interpreted as showing that '28 per cent of our children cannot read'. The apparent decline in reading standards was contrasted with the success of reading in other countries such as France, Germany and Japan. The *Daily Telegraph* also renewed its general condemnation of primary teaching methods and once again launched into a derisory rhetoric against progressive approaches (*Daily Telegraph*, 1991: 20).

The Government's response took the form of a DES memorandum later appended to the Report itself, outlining the Government's position on the various issues raised in the Report. The recommendations regarding the teaching of phonics in this report endorsed the HMI position that exclusive reliance on any single method of teaching reading hindered progress. It also stopped short of recommending any particular method, and went on to endorse investigating the 'most successful ways of combining a range of teaching methods, including phonics' (ESAC, 1991: vii).

The publishing of league table results and their perceived support for 'falling reading standards' served to provide further support for an anti-progressive stance and the resulting setting up of a government inquiry into 'primary school teaching methods' (Judd and Wilby, 1991: 4). The Secretary for Education, Kenneth Clarke, announced the inquiry in early December, in language 'which could not disguise his preference for over-turning teaching methods that have prevailed for 30 years' (Judd and Wilby, 1991: 4).

The 'Three Wise Men Report'

The inquiry into primary education resulted in a report on primary school teaching methods that was published in late January 1992. The Education Secretary appointed 'three wise men' to produce the report: Robin Alexander of Leeds University; Jim Rose, Chief Primary Inspector in the Schools Inspectorate; and Chris Woodhead, Chief Executive of the National Curriculum Council (Tytler, 1992: 4). This Report was seen to endorse a change to traditional teaching methods and cautioned against too much diversity in teaching methods (Bates, 1992: 3).

Press coverage of the report on *Curriculum Organisation and Classroom Practice in Primary Schools* (Alexander et al., 1992), which came to be known as the 'Three Wise Men Report', highlighted the increasing emphasis upon regulating primary pedagogy and the construction of a 'normal pupil' defined by quantifiable norms through national assessment. This stress upon attainment with its associated requirements that teachers diagnose and judge ability, was seen to be linked to whole-class skills-based teaching of the basics in particular subject areas (*Daily Telegraph*, 1992: 16).

The public debate and political contexts surrounding literacy standards and subsequent how to teach reading prescriptions in the early 1990s had initiated a discursive shift away from the progressive vision of literacy teaching as an 'art', which envisaged teachers working 'intuitively' and being 'sensitive' to the 'imaginative needs of their children' (Plowden Report, 1967: 10, para. 550). This ideal was being replaced with a vision of literacy teaching as 'best practice' through regulation, performance, and technical skill in the 'basics'. This discursive shift would ensure that it would be the latter vision that would become the dominant discourse underpinning the development of subsequent literacy policies and pedagogical initiatives.

The Literacy Task Force report and the National Literacy Strategy

In May 1996, the debate over the teaching of early reading again achieved prominence when the Labour Party announced a back-to-basics drive to improve literacy standards if it became the Government in the election to be held the following year. David Blunkett, the shadow education secretary, stated that teachers were to 'use teaching methods which work and are not just the latest fashion'. The Labour Party dissatisfaction with the quality of newly trained teachers also resulted in a pledge to place greater emphasis on basic skills, classroom discipline and whole-class teaching. Blunkett also stressed the use of phonics. He argued that phonics is a crucial tool for teaching children reading in the early stages of literacy acquisition (Rafferty, 1996). This emphasis was also evident in the incoming Labour Government's statement in 1997 that it would 'encourage the use of the most effective teaching methods, including phonics for reading' (Labour Party, 1997: 8).

In their report, the Literacy Task Force indicated that they recognized that both the decoding of phonics and reading for meaning strategies are necessary (Literacy Task Force, 1997: 132). The task force, however, tended to emphasize phonics as they indicated that 'systematically teaching phonics' had a 'sound basis' in evidence of what works. Their report therefore placed an emphasis upon the recognition of the critical importance of phonics:

> There have been few more vigorous educational controversies in the last decade than the one over how reading should be taught. Opposing sides in a vigorous national debate took to the barricades with banners proclaiming their loyalty to 'phonics' or 'real books'. But while this debate has raged, research and the understanding of 'best practice' have moved on. We now know a great deal about the best technologies for the teaching of reading and that they include a recognition of the critical importance of phonics in the early years. (Literacy Task Force, 1997: 129)

This viewpoint was carried through to the National Literacy Strategy (NLS), which advocated a range of strategies that could be 'depicted as a series of searchlights, each of which sheds light upon the text' (DfEE, 1998: 3). This model emphasized both a 'knowledge of context', and 'word recognition and graphic knowledge' as well as 'phonic sounds and spelling' and 'grammatical knowledge' (DfEE, 1998: 4). The Framework noted that while teachers may 'know all about these', they have 'often been over cautious about the teaching of phonics-sounds and spelling' and cautioned against expecting pupils to distinguish the 'different sounds of words simply by being exposed to books':

> Research evidence shows that pupils do not learn to distinguish between the different sounds of words simply by being exposed to books. They need to be taught to do this. When they begin to read, most pupils tend to see words as images, with a particular shape and pattern. They tend not to understand that words are made up of letters used in particular combinations that correspond with spoken sounds. It is essential that pupils are taught these basic decoding and spelling skills from the outset. (DfEE, 1998: 4)

In the media, the adoption of this 'searchlight' model of reading and the particular emphasis on phonics was attributed to John Stannard, the Director of the NLS in the media (see, for example, Palmer, 1999). Roger Beard in his analysis of the influences that shaped the NLS also acknowledged John Stannard's role in putting 'together some pedagogical principles derived from international research' to develop the approach adopted in the NLS and in particular 'the development of a strategy to obtain a more "balanced" approach, using greater direct teaching of reading, including systematic phonics and the use of an appropriate range of texts' (Beard, 2000: 248).

The adoption of the searchlight method, however, proved to be an uneasy compromise between an emphasis upon 'teaching phonics systematically and separately' with the need to 'give children good books to read to supplement phonic decoding', as Stannard himself was to recognize in later reflections upon future directions for the searchlight method within the NLS (Stannard, 2005: 21). From 2003 onwards, the searchlight method came under public attack as an increased emphasis upon analytic and synthetic phonics led to proclamations that the 'searchlight method' gave too little emphasis to phonics (see, for example, Hofkins, 2003).

After the implementation of the National Literacy Strategy, there was an even greater push from agencies such as the Office for Standards in Education and the Department of Education and Skills for 'more systematic' and 'rigorous' teaching of phonics in both primary and pre-school settings, as it became clear that targets set to raise literacy standards were going to be increasingly difficult to achieve. In 2002, the Office for Standards in Education praised reception teachers for their teaching of phonics, stated that the approach of their Year 1 and 2 colleagues was not systematic enough for pupils who are falling behind, and said that the problem gets worse in Year 3. It was argued that the teaching of phonics 'was good in only one in four schools in 2000/1' (Ward, 2002: 9). At the same time, David Hopkins, the director of the government's Standards Unit, which was responsible for overseeing the literacy strategy, pledged to look at the teaching of phonics in the early years (Ward, 2002).

It was also noted that OFSTED still identified phonics as a weak area and that schools needed to receive consultant and other support to strengthen phonics teaching, including the provision of Progression in Phonics materials. The advocates of synthetic phonics, which included OFSTED and the Reading Reform Foundation, argued that the Literacy Strategy was now out of date. Synthetic phonics was seen to be 'the key to success in literacy in this country' as the 'National Literacy Strategy has got it wrong all these years' (Ward, 2002).

The Rose Report

In December 2004, Chris Woodhead, the ex-chief inspector of schools in England and Wales during the initial years of the NLS, criticized the current chief inspector of schools David Bell, for supporting the searchlight method and a range of approaches to the teaching of reading. Woodhead was against the range of approaches implicit in the searchlight method, arguing that 'In the crucial early years of a child's education we need phonics and only phonics' (Woodhead, 2004). The attacks on the searchlight method continued on through 2005 with the release of the research related to synthetic phonics by Rhona Johnston and Joyce Watson, which prompted further arguments that phonics teaching needed to be improved in the NLS (see, for example, Bald, 2005).

In March 2005, the support for phonics-based approaches and condemnation of the searchlight method resulted in an investigation into the success of the NLS and the publication of the House of Commons Education and Skills Committee (HCESC) Eighth Report, *Teaching Children to Read*, which focused specifically on the methods used in schools to teach children to read (HCESC, 2005: 3). In July 2005, the HCESC published the 'Government's Responses to "Teaching Children to Read"', which stated that the emphasis would be about 'phonics fast and first' approaches (HCESC, 2005: 13).

The Interim Rose Report was published in December 2005 with a clear emphasis upon phonics, and in particular synthetic phonics. This was reflected in the key issue initially set out in the Interim Report: 'what best practice should be expected in the teaching of early reading and synthetic phonics'? Both the Interim and Final Reports adopted synthetic phonics as the key method of teaching relationships between letters and sounds. They also advocated that a programme of systematic synthetic phonics should be 'followed faithfully', and warned that it would be unwise to 'pick and mix' elements from several different programmes in order to avoid disrupting progression through the programme (Rose, 2005: 18).

The Final version of the Rose Report argues that from 1980 to 1998 there was very 'little impact made on raising standards of reading' (Rose, 2006: 3) even though The National Curriculum had made phonic work a statutory part of the curriculum. This was seen to have changed 'markedly' with the introduction of the NLS with its 'structured teaching programme of literacy that included not only what phonic content should be taught but also how to teach with a subsequent rise in standards' (Rose, 2006: 3). It also reiterated the Interim Rose Report's support for synthetic phonics as the 'best route' to teaching reading skills in the introduction (Rose, 2006: 4).

The recommendations section of the Final Report strongly stressed the role of phonics and synthetic phonics in the teaching of early reading as is evident in examples from the recommendations section headed, 'What best practice should be expected in the teaching of early reading and synthetic phonics':

> High quality, systematic phonic work as defined by the review should be taught discretely. The knowledge, skills and understanding that constitute high quality phonic work should be taught as the prime approach in learning to decode (to read) and encode (to write/spell) print. (Rose, 2006: 70)

The period from 1990 to the publishing of the Rose Report in 2006 marks an era where firstly phonics, and then synthetic phonics, have become increasingly emphasized as the key to success in achieving and maintaining literacy standards. The decade of the 1990s saw public debate and changes in the educational structures and assessment. This resulted in an increasing emphasis upon phonics within an increasingly centralized curriculum policy. From 2002, the push for teaching phonics in the early years accelerated and became focused on the teaching of synthetic phonics as problems emerged with teaching predetermined government targets to raise literacy standards. In 2006, the Rose Report embedded phonics and synthetic phonics even more firmly in curriculum policy, through its emphasis upon the role of phonics and synthetic phonics in the teaching of early reading.

The road to whole language/real books dominance in New Zealand

In contrast to the present situation in England, the position of phonics in New Zealand currently remains rather marginal in the face of a continuing official endorsement of whole language/real books approaches to the teaching of reading. Moreover, especially since 2002, the whole language versus phonics debate has increasingly melded with other ongoing educational, social and political debates. These include debates over the extent to which teachers and schools can be held directly responsible for the academic progress of their students, and the ongoing controversy over the origins, nature and causes of educational inequality.

The road to whole language dominance

During the early 1990s, both in England and North America, New Zealand was often regarded as an outstanding example of how high reading standards could be maintained through the consensual implementation of a scientifically based early intervention programme based on a whole language approach (whole language/real book in the UK), and marketed worldwide under the trademark, *Reading Recovery* (RR). The RR programme had its immediate origins in New Zealand during the late 1960s and early 1970s. During the first half of this era, educational progressivism as interpreted by a new series of departmentally produced curriculum handbooks, and by influential books such as Richardson's *In the Early World* (1964), made considerable inroads in primary schools. This was accompanied by a growing pride in indigenously developed educational programmes such as the Arvidson approach to spelling and the introduction of the whole language-based *Ready to Read* series, the latter claiming to better address the learning styles of Maori children (Openshaw, 2006). By the mid-1970s, however, there was growing public and educational concern over the nation's high youth unemployment rate and a sharpening perception of racial tensions exacerbated by continuing Maori educational under-achievement (Openshaw, 2007).

It was in response to this contradictory mixture of optimism and pessimism that Auckland University psychologist, Marie Clay, was able to successfully promote RR as an all-embracing early intervention strategy that extended existing whole language/real book approaches to the individual tuition of young children identified as having difficulties with reading (Clay, 1967). Given the highly centralized nature of the New Zealand education system, however, the expansion of RR nationwide was to be largely dependent on Department of Education endorsement and resourcing. Especially from 1976 on, the Department was to have considerable involvement in RR (Wellington, 1984). As a result, by the mid-1980s, RR had come to enjoy a monopoly underwritten by both the Department and by successive governments, who routinely pointed to the apparent success of the programme and to New Zealand's growing international reputation as a world leader in the teaching of reading as evidence of their own commitment to quality education. Thus, the Department, replying on behalf of the then Minister of Education, the Rt Hon. David Lange, to a correspondent wishing to do research into New Zealand reading programmes, asserted that it was generally accepted that the standard of literacy in the country was very high. The Department also noted that New Zealand schools made use of a threefold strategy to teach reading comprehensively: the whole language-based 'Ready to Read' texts, the RR programme, and the use of Resource Teachers of Reading. Taken together, this package provided a complete philosophy of learning to read, developed in New Zealand, which had proved very successful (Foster, 1989; Foster, for Director General, 1989).

A contemporary paper by Ro Griffiths, the Department of Education's Officer for Language and Reading, related in glowing terms the uniqueness of New Zealand's reading programmes, including the now revised *Ready to Read* series, RR and the then still extant ERJC/LARIC in-service courses (Griffiths, 1989; Slane, 1978); all of which were whole language/real books based. Griffiths also cited University of Arizona Professor of Education,

Ken Goodman's assertion that New Zealand was, as a result, the most literate country in the world (Griffiths, 1989). Few, least of all those in New Zealand's government or educational bureaucracy, would have been willing at the time to disagree with this verdict.

A major administrative reorganization of the New Zealand education system in 1989 saw the Department of Education, education boards and local school committees disappear. A new two-tier system was established consisting of a new Ministry of Education, and the learning institutions themselves (centres, schools, colleges, tertiary institutions). As a result, all RR tutors were upon completion of their training shifted over to the administrative control of the nation's teachers' colleges. The effect was to further tighten centralized control of the programme with the colleges becoming strongholds of the whole language philosophy. This location within teachers' colleges, however, also helped to make RR increasingly resistant to research that questioned its efficacy, particularly if this research emanated from the country's universities.

Reading recovery comes under critical scrutiny

When an OFSTED delegation from England visited New Zealand in the early 1990s to examine RR in action, its subsequent report singled out the programme's high degree of centralization and virtual monopoly for praise (Soler and Openshaw, 2006). However, despite continuing official endorsement of the programme's success, RR, together with its underlying whole language philosophy, was now to come under increasing academic and public scrutiny. Professor William Tunmer and Professor James W. Chapman of Massey University, together with Associate Professor Tom Nicholson at the University of Auckland, played a key role in questioning some of RR's underlying assumptions. Tunmer and Chapman claimed to be in general agreement with 90–95 per cent of what New Zealand teachers currently did to facilitate the acquisition of reading skills in young children. Nevertheless, they argued that predicting words from context was 'a highly ineffective and inappropriate learning strategy,' warning that encouraging children to rely primarily on context to identify unfamiliar words counteracted many of the good things teachers did. Instead, they argued that beginning readers 'should be encouraged to look for familiar spelling patterns first and to use context to confirm hypotheses about what unfamiliar words might be, based on available word-level information' (Tunmer and Chapman, 1996: 1–2).

Although this was a well-researched and measured critique of RR, the early 1990s were to also witness the growing popularity of mass-circulation magazines in New Zealand such as *North and South* and *Metro* expressly catering for a clientele seeking independent political, social and educational commentary. An article in the popular magazine *North and South* by staff writer Jenny Chamberlain was one of several that brought a hitherto largely academic controversy into national prominence. Chamberlain alleged that 'Government, teachers and those good-news merchants book publishers constantly block[ed] the literacy debate' (Chamberlain, 1993: 68). Reading, she observed, was big business in New Zealand. Local publisher, Wendy Pye, exported 40m school readers to 12 countries in the last 12 years. International visitors flocked in to see the New Zealand approach to reading in action. Yet, despite the emphasis placed on reading in primary schools, in the early 1990s, it was '… almost as though we've made a national pact with each other to ignore our illiteracy' (Chamberlain, 1993: 68). One in four six-year-olds required remedial assistance after one year at school; 47 per cent of unemployed 14–19 year-olds had no formal qualifications; one third of school leavers went straight from school onto the unemployment benefit with no post-secondary education, while polytechnics and universities struggled to provide basic literacy skills for their clients (Chamberlain, 1993). Subsequent MOE analyses based on the New Zealand data from the International Adult Literacy Survey of March 1996 were to confirm these depressing statistics (Ministry of Education, 1997).

An article by Noel O'Hare, in the popular magazine *New Zealand Listener*, elaborated on this theme but also added the long-standing concerns of those who supported a return to phonics-based approaches that had supposedly been at the centre of reading teaching prior to the 1970s. O'Hare alleged that the powerful proponents of whole language had a vested interest in maintaining the status quo, silencing those who supported the teaching of phonics both inside and outside the teaching profession through fear, ridicule and even stand-over tactics (O'Hare, 1995). When O'Hare cited Nicholson's view that whole language supporters were often 'anti-scientific' and anti-research in their educational views, he touched upon a controversy soon to be sharpened by a spate of government-mandated mergers between tertiary institutions responsible for teacher education. This controversy increasingly pitted university-based academics who emphasized the central place of research and detached scientific objectivity in the study of education, against teacher educators within colleges of education who espoused cultural relativism and stressed the practical experience of classroom teachers.

The increasing bitterness of the reading debate and the apparently widening gap between key university researchers and some teaching profession commentators can be clearly discerned in the response of a regularly produced professional newsletter for teachers that enjoyed wide distribution at the time. One particular issue lambasted the O'Hare article as 'a new low in education reporting and academic behaviour'. Promising a series of articles in response to the issues it raised, the newsletter labelled the use of the numbers of children in RR to demonstrate the failure of New Zealand approaches to reading by Nicholson and Tunmer as 'either an example of academic stupidity, waywardness, or perversity' (Developmental Network Newsletter, 1995). It questioned the appropriateness of their continued access to schools and suggested that in future any access should be rigorously supervised. It advocated that someone with a leadership role in whole language and RR be appointed to guide future research. Finally, it called upon teachers to write to Nicholson, Tunmer, Chapman, the *New Zealand Listener* and the Ministry to protest 'this shameful episode', which was another example of 'The media, Business Roundtable and academics at it again' (Developmental Network Newsletter, 1995).

Seemingly alarmed by the apparently growing public and academic concern over reading standards in schools, the New Zealand Labour Government by the end of 1998 had set up both a National Literacy Task Force and a separate Literacy Experts group. Both bodies subsequently produced reports recommending varying degrees of movement away from whole language strategies in reading and English teaching (Literacy Task Force, 1997). The Minister of Education, the Hon. Trevor Mallard, however, subsequently chose to disregard these recommendations on the grounds that the government was not legally bound to accept them. The Minister's reluctance to intervene was largely governed by political considerations. By 2001, although there were indications that RR was under serious review by the New Zealand Ministry of Education, the vexed issue of who actually owned the RR franchise was once again current. Sue Douglas, the Ministry's literacy and numeracy strategy manager, was thus compelled to warn that since Clay had a trademark on the name Reading Recovery to protect the programme's integrity, any changes made would be confined to its administration only, or 'they would risk being in breach of the programme's trademark' (Rivers, 2001: 1).

The debate widens

RR's seeming resistance to suggestions for even relatively minor modifications helped to ensure that, following the return of Labour to the Treasury benches in the July 2002 General Election, the 'Reading Wars' would continue. Somewhat ironically, a further reason for their prolongation was that the debate over methods soon became intertwined once again with ongoing concerns over the relatively poor levels of literacy and numeracy achieved by Maori and Pasifika students, arguably the most intractable problem confronting New Zealand's educational policy makers during the post-war years. As we have noted, whole-language-based literacy programmes came into favour during the late 1960s and early 1970s, in part because they were seen as providing an answer to this problem. Thirty years later, however, the problem remains. Indeed, the current Labour Government frequently employs the slogan 'closing the gaps' to signify its continuing commitment to equity through equalizing educational opportunity.

Given the prevailing political climate in New Zealand, any research suggesting that more effective teaching methods will effectively close existing gaps inevitably holds a strong attraction for politicians and educators alike. *Picking up the Pace* is an apt example of such research. Developed in the late 1990s, *Pace* is a professional development programme contracted by the Ministry of Education to University of Auckland academics and associated professional staff. Intended to improve the reading levels of children in low decile schools, where parents tend to be in lower socio-economic groupings, and implemented in metropolitan south Auckland, *Pace* was designed to provide teachers with a course of in-service professional development that would support current Ministry policy initiatives (Harker, 2003; Nash, 2003).

A major contention of the *Pace* research has been that teacher expectations are largely responsible for the disparities in reading attainment between Maori and Pasifika students on one hand, and Pakeha (European) students on the other. Despite its claims to success, however, a number of university-based researchers have remained unconvinced. Reading researchers Tunmer and Chapman have argued that while whole-language experiences may be suitable for children with an abundance of cultural capital, phonologically related knowledge skills and strategies are particularly important for some beginning readers who may not possess such advantages (Tunmer et al., 2004). At the same time, critical sociologists such as Nash (2003) have observed that teacher expectations, while a legitimate area for research, are responsible for but a small percentage of achievement variations. The answer, therefore, lies in accepting a more complex theory of inequality/difference. Such a theory, however, especially when it is linked to phonetic reading strategies, remains politically unpalatable to whole-language supporters and their allies within the New Zealand Ministry of Education, as well as to those who embrace culturalist theories to explain educational disparity. Thus, as part of the newly emergent middle-class capitalist neo-tribal elite, many Maori academics and Pakeha biculturalists have come to embrace identity politics (Openshaw, 2006; Rata, 2003). This entails emphatically rejecting what they regard as deficit theory, along with any suggestion that there are social class factors that might militate against the unity of Maori culture, thereby challenging their leadership (Nash, 2006).

Nash and Prochnow clearly illustrated the embracing nature of literacy alliances when they recently highlighted a Ministerial press release asserting that 'research indicates that effective classroom teaching can explain up to half of a child's educational achievements' as well as to an editorial in the mass-circulation weekly *Sunday Star Times* entitled: 'It's the teachers, stupid' (Nash and Prochnow, 2004). Nash and Prochnow also note the current dominance of Professor John Hattie's research, the key assumptions of which substantially inform the New Zealand Ministry of Education's own position (Nash and Prochnow, 2004: 177). Hattie contends that a perceived inability in academic performance by Maori and Pasifika pupils can be attributed to a lack of expectations on the part of teachers rather than to social or economic disadvantage. The recent Progress in International Reading Literacy Study (PIRLS) revelations of a significant gap in reading attainment between ethnic groups in New Zealand is therefore to be attributed to teachers treating students markedly differently (Nash and Prochnow, 2004: 177–82). In turn, this provides justification, not only for the maintenance and extension of whole-language-based reading programmes, but also for further tightening the regime of surveillance of teachers on the grounds that they are clearly not implementing the government's policy objective of 'closing the gaps'.

The fate of phonics: comparing national contexts

In England and in New Zealand, there have been national policy initiatives that have placed the drive to raise standards at the heart of the early literacy curriculum. This has led more recently to striking similarities and exchanges in policy rhetoric evidenced in the development of National Literacy Strategies in both countries. Both countries have had National Literacy Task Forces who have produced reports designed to influence the teaching of early literacy though phonics and/or whole-language approaches. There are, however, significant differences in the reception recorded to phonics and whole language in these reports and in subsequent developments after the release of both countries' national literacy strategies in the late 1990s.

In England, the public debate over literacy in the early 1990s can be seen to have helped facilitate a commonsense consensus that literacy standards were low and the notion that the purposes of schooling were changing. This in turn led to the child-centred vision of primary teachers, which focused upon the individual child, learning through play, child development, and readiness for learning, being replaced by a technicist view, which stressed basic skills of literacy and numeracy controlled by market mechanisms and specific and prescribed methods and approaches to teaching early literacy.

These debates marked the emergence of a new dominant narrative in literacy curriculum and pedagogy, whose impact reaches down through the 1992 Report on Primary School Teaching Methods to the 1998 National Literacy Strategy, and the recently released Rose Report. In the context of these developments, the emphasis in the Rose Report upon a faithful adherence to a specific method and explicit structure of 'systematic phonic work' can be seen as the latest stage in an evolving, politically driven process that has led to the domination of phonics-based approaches to early reading in English primary schools.

In New Zealand, the relatively new realignment between the Ministry of Education, teacher effectiveness researchers, whole-language supporters and prominent Maori academics on one hand, and university-based reading specialists and critical sociologists on the other, clearly illustrates how literacy debates often transcend reading, to encompass wider political, social and educational social issues. In turn, this helps polarize the debate because so many vested interests are involved that any significant change would inevitably have major political implications. Hence, in New Zealand, a complex mosaic of shifting alliances that are in turn rooted in a distinctive local politics means that continued support for what is a simplistic 'one size fits all' whole language/real books remedy for reading failure remains securely in place, while phonics remains in many quarters a 'dirty word'.

This [chapter] argues that the political and public debates and contestation surrounding the teaching of phonics and the subsequent implementation of methodological initiatives have resulted in a significant difference between the ways in which phonics teaching has been adopted in England and New Zealand. While phonics and synthetic phonics have been wholeheartedly adopted into curriculum policy and implemented in England, they do not have this recognition and uptake in New Zealand. This has in turn resulted in significant differences in the relative fates of phonics and whole-language-related programmes in each country.

While both countries had a different history of developing early reading programmes at the beginning of the 1990s, during the late 1990s they were driven at the government level by similar pressures to raise literacy standards through developing national literacy strategies. Both of these literacy strategies embodied moves away from the previous dominance of whole-language teaching; however, despite this, England and New Zealand have continued to develop extremely different national positions in curriculum debates and policy in relation to the teaching of phonics. In England, phonics teaching has become dominant in policy and practice with the release of the Rose Report in 2006, whereas in New Zealand phonics-based approaches have been unable to gain a prominent position due to the continued influence and implementation of whole-language-based programmes such as RR. This is a clear indication of the extent to which local politics and cultural contexts can impact upon curriculum policy and attempts to raise literacy standards through the implementation of particular approaches to the teaching of reading.

This [chapter] provides a comparative insight into how the highly politicized public debates over the teaching of phonetic knowledge are linked to specific contexts, complex interactions, differing viewpoints and multiple layers of interaction between politicians, policy makers, academics and educators. It demonstrates how these dynamics can generate different conflicts between phonics and whole-language approaches in different national contexts. This can in turn result in different stances on phonic knowledge in policies and pedagogies related to the teaching of early reading.

References

Alexander, R., Rose, J. and Woodhead, C. (1992) *Curriculum Organisation and Classroom Practice in Primary Schools*. London: HMSO.

Bald, J. (2005) 'Without Improved Phonics Teaching We Are Not Giving Children a Full Range of Tools to Tackle Reading, Says John Bald', *Guardian* (5 April): 4.

Bates, S. (1992) 'Teachers Told to Rethink Methods', *Guardian* (23 January): 3.

Beard, R. (1991) 'Letter: Balance Required in the Reading Debate', *Independent* (30 November): 17.

Beard, R. (2000) 'Long Overdue?: Another Look at the National Literacy Strategy', *Journal of Research in Reading* 23(3): 245–55.

Chamberlain, J. (1993) 'Our Illiteracy: Reading the Writing On The Wall', *North and South*: 66–76.

Clay, M.M. (1967) 'The Reading Behaviour of Five Year Old Children: A Research Report', *New Zealand Journal of Educational Studies* 2(1): 11–31.

Daily Telegraph (1991) 'Facing Primary Facts' (7 November): 20.

Daily Telegraph (1992) 'Primary Concerns' (24 January): 16.

Department for Education and Employment (DfEE) (1998) *The National Literacy Strategy: Framework for Teaching*. London: DfEE.

Developmental Network Newsletter (1995) 'A New Low In Education Reporting and Academic Behaviour', The O'Hare Article, *New Zealand Listener* (15 July): 2–3.

Education, Science and Arts Committee (ESAC) (1991) *Standards of Reading in Primary Schools*, Third Report, Vol. 1 (May).

Foster, K. (1989) 'Reading Recovery in Context: A Response', Comments to Director, Research and Statistics Division. Department of Education (4 pp.), 5 April. ABEP. W4262.Box3783.NSSS/1/32-RR miscellaneous.

Foster, K. for Director General (1989) Letter to P. Maxwell, 3 March. ABEP. W4262. Box 3783. NS55/1/32-RR miscellaneous.

Griffiths, R. (1989) 'Background Paper on Reading for Harvey Mcqueen', c. February 1989. ABEP. W4262. Box 3783. NS55/1/32-RR miscellaneous.

Hansard (1991) *Schools*, Vol. 195, sixth series, 15–25 July 1990–91, 19 July 1991.

Harker, R. (2003) 'Research Note: External Validity and the Pace Research', *New Zealand Journal of Educational Studies* 38(2): 245.

Hofkins, D. (2003) 'Reading the Riot Act to Both Sides in Phonic Dispute', *Times Educational Supplement* (14 February): 19.

House of Commons Education and Skills Committee (HCESC) (2005) *Teaching Children to Read*. London: The Stationery Office.

Judd, J. and Wilby, P. (1991) 'Major Rings the Bell on Playtime: The Prime Minister Wants More Sitting on the Old School Bench', *Independent* (8 December): 4.

Labour Party (1997) *New Labour: Because Britain Deserves Better*, Election Manifesto. London: Labour Party.

Literacy Task Force (1997) *A Reading Revolution: How We Can Teach Every Child to Read Well. The Preliminary Report of the Literacy Task Force*. London: University of London, Institute of Education.

Luke, A. (1991) 'The Political Economy of Reading Instruction', in C.D. Baker and A. Luke (eds) *Towards a Critical Sociology of Reading Pedagogy*, pp. 3–26. Amsterdam and Philadelphia, PA: John Benjamins.

Luke, A. (1993) 'The Social Construction of Literacy in the Primary School', in L. Unsworth (ed.) *Literacy, Learning and Teaching: Language as Social Practice in the Primary School*, pp. 1–54. Melbourne: Macmillan Education.

MacLeod, D. (1991) 'MPs Dismiss Claims of Reading Crisis in Primary Schools', *Independent* (17 May): 10.

Ministry of Education (1997) *Adult Literacy in New Zealand: Results from the International Adult Literacy Survey*. Wellington: New Zealand Ministry of Education.

Muspratt, S., Luke, A. and Freebody, P. (1997) *Constructing Critical Literacies: Teaching and Learning Textual Practice*. Cresskill, NJ: Hampton Press.

Nash, R. (2003) 'Commentary: One Pace Forward Two Steps Backwards?', *New Zealand Journal of Educational Studies* 38(2): 249.

Nash, R. (2006) 'Challenging Ethnic Explanations for Educational Failure', in E. Rata and R. Openshaw (eds) *Public Policy and Ethnicity: The Politics of Ethnic Boundary-Making*, pp. 156–69. London: Palgrave Macmillan.

Nash, R. and Prochnow, J.E. (2004) 'Is it Really the Teachers?: An Analysis of the Discourse of Teacher Effects on New Zealand Educational Policy', *New Zealand Journal of Educational Studies* 39(2): 175–92.

O'Hare, N. (1995) 'What's Wrong With Reading?', *New Zealand Listener* (15–21 July): 18–22.

O'Leary, J. (1991) 'Reading Guru Wins Real Notoriety', *The Times* (22 April): 1.

Openshaw, R. (2006) 'Putting Ethnicity Into Policy: A New Zealand Case Study', in E. Rata and R. Openshaw (eds) *Public Policy and Ethnicity: The Politics of Ethnic Boundary-Making*, pp. 113–27. London: Palgrave Macmillan.

Openshaw, R. (2007) 'What Can the International Literacy Community Learn from the New Zealand Experience with Reading?', in R. Openshaw and J. Soler (eds) *Reading Across International Boundaries: History, Policy and Politics*, pp. 3–17. Greenwhich, CT: Information Age Publishing.

Openshaw, R. and Soler, J. eds (2007) *Reading Across International Boundaries: History, Policy and Politics*. Greenwich, CT: Information Age Publishing.

Palmer, S. (1999) 'Between the Lines of Debate: Literacy Interview: Marilyn Jager Adams', *Times Educational Supplement*, Friday Features (17 December): 20.

Plowden Report (1967) *Children and Their Primary Schools*. London: HMSO.

Rafferty, F. (1996) 'Labour Gets Back to Basics', *Times Educational Supplement* (31 May). URL (consulted November 2006): http://web.lexis.com/executive/

Rata, E. (2003) 'Leadership Ideology in Neotribal Capitalism', *Political Power and Social Theory* 16: 43–71.

Report of the Literacy Task Force (1999) Wellington: New Zealand Ministry of Education.

Richardson, E.S. (1964) *In the Early World*. Wellington: New Zealand Council of Educational Research.

Rivers, J. (2001) 'Reading Recovery Review', *New Zealand Education Review* (16 February): 1.

Rose, J. (2005) *Independent Review of the Teaching of Early Reading*, interim report. London: Department for Education and Skills (DFES).

Rose, J. (2006) *Independent Review of the Teaching of Early Reading*, final report. London: Department for Education and Skills (DFES).

Slane, J. (1978) 'Eric: A New Concept for In-Service Education of Teachers', *Education* 27(2): 7–11.

Soler, J. and Openshaw, R. (2006) *Literacy Crises and Reading Policy: Children Still Can't Read*. London and New York: Routledge.

Stannard, J. (2005) 'Give Them Literacy with All the Lights On', *The Times Educational Supplement* (9 December): 21.

Tunmer, W.E. and Chapman, J.W. (1996) 'Beginning Readers Self-Reports on Strategies Used for Identifying Unfamiliar Words in Text', paper presented at the annual meeting of the New Zealand Association for Research in Education, Nelson, December.

Tunmer, W.E., Chapman, J.W. and Prochnow, J.E. (2004) 'Why the Reading Achievement Gap in New Zealand Won't Go Away: Evidence From the Pirls 2001 International Study of Reading Achievement', *New Zealand Journal of Educational Studies* 39(1): 127–46.

Turner, M. (1990) *Sponsored Reading Failure. An Object Lesson*. Warlingham: Education Unit. Warlingham Park School.

Tytler, D. (1992) 'Let Common Sense Take Over', *The Times*, Features Section (27 January), URL (consulted November 2006): http://web.lexis.com/executive/

Ward, H. (2002) 'Inspectors Spell Out Bigger Role for Phonics', *The Times Educational Supplement* (15 November): 9.

Welch, A.R. and Freebody, P. (2002) 'Explanations of the Current International "Literacy Crises"', in J. Soler, J. Wearmouth and G. Reid (eds) *Contextualising Difficulties in Literacy Development: Exploring Politics, Culture, Ethnicity and Ethics*, pp. 61–72. London: Routledge Falmer.

Wellington, M.I., the Hon., Minister of Education (1984) Letter to M.K. Andrews, Secretary, Belmont School Committee dated 7 May, ABEP W4262, Box 1574. 30/2/10/5 reading

Woodhead, C. (2004) 'Some Sound Advice on Learning To Read', *Sunday Times* (19 December), URL (consulted August 2007): http://www.timesonline.co.uk/tol/news/article.403973.ece

13

Powerful Literacies: The Policy Context

Mary Hamilton, Catherine Macrae and Lyn Tett

Introduction

This chapter offers an overview of the policy context within which the developments described in the rest of this book need to be understood. It focuses on the four countries of the UK and Ireland, but also comments on the wider international scene. It aims to describe briefly the recent history of Adult Basic Education (ABE) in the UK, to compare and contrast developments in the different countries and to identity the main influences that are shaping the field. In 1998 and 1999, new education initiatives in all of these countries raised the profile of, reasserted, or shifted the agenda for literacy programmes. These initiatives, framed with reference to lifelong learning, the knowledge economy and the knowledge society, are set to have a significant influence on practitioners and learners here and may shape future developments elsewhere: in this sense, the literacies they define and promote are powerful literacies. This chapter focuses on the nature of these shifts and their apparent potential to expand or diminish the scope and purpose of literacy programmes.

Some influences on recent ABE policy in the UK and Ireland are international and suggest links with developments in other countries represented in this book as well (for example, South Africa and Australia). The European Union is of obvious importance regionally. A further key influence is the activities of the Organisation for Economic Co-operation and Development (the OECD) and in particular the International Adult Literacy Survey (IALS) which is now routinely cited in government and media publications about adult literacy (OECD, 2000). The OECD has worked with the national governments of its member states to produce a 'league table' of adult literacy standards in each country. The statisticians who have developed the test used in the IALS work with a model of literacy that treats it as a set of unproblematic, information-processing cognitive skills that are independent of the context in which they are used. The test deals primarily with reading and it identifies three dimensions of literacy (prose, document and quantitative literacy). Despite a number of serious critiques of the methodology and validity of the IALS findings (summarised in Hamilton and Barton, 2000), this powerful piece of research has become central to policy discussions. It has framed the terms of the debate, defined the scope and content of 'literacy need', who

From: Hamilton, M., Tett, L. and Crowther, J. (eds) *Powerful Literacies*, pp. 23–42 (Leicester: National Institute of Adult Continuing Education, 2001).

is deficient in literacy and why, and denied the central role of culture and relationships of power in determining literacy needs and aspirations. [...]

In this chapter, we begin with brief pen sketches of the history and current situation in each country. The second part is more critical and evaluative. In organising the information about variations in policy, we have been guided by four main questions with the aim of getting to the values embodied by a set of practices in ABE which for the most part are only implicitly stated in government documents:

- What concept of literacy underpins recent policies?
- How are learners and teachers positioned by the policies?
- What kinds of learning activities/processes are programmes or initiatives expected to engage in?
- What outcomes are literacy programmes and learners expected to achieve?

Adult basic education in the countries of the UK and Ireland

We use the term United Kingdom here as the generic name for the union of England, Scotland, Wales and Northern Ireland. Each of these countries is currently moving toward greater autonomy, and there are distinctive differences among them in the history and organisation of their educational provision[1] which may well become more pronounced in the near future.

England and Wales

The Right to Read literacy campaign in the early 1970s was the first time that adult literacy was identified as a national policy issue in the United Kingdom. The public awareness campaign was initiated by volunteer activists and supported by politicians and the broadcasting services, especially the BBC. Community, adult and further education throughout the country began to offer 1:1 and small group tuition. (For overviews, see Withnall, 1994; Hamilton, 1996; Street, 1997.) A central resource agency for adult literacy (now known as the Basic Skills Agency) was set up by the central government in 1975 with a remit covering both England and Wales. The central resource agency produced materials for students and tutors, organised training events, supported new developments and disseminated good practice.

Now, as in the 1970s and 1980s, the majority of those working in ABE do so in part-time or voluntary posts. There has been, however, growth in the number of paid staff and an increasing emphasis on professionalism.

In the late 1980s, an accreditation framework for ABE (*Wordpower and Numberpower*) was introduced. This established a set of basic skills standards and assessments that continue to be developed. The framework is related to a unified system of national vocational qualifications (NVQs) that are tied to a set of national training targets and quality assurances. This system is designed to provide a means of determining equivalence amid the maze of different vocational qualifications and to bridge the divide between academic and vocational qualifications. Teacher credentials have also been linked with the NVQ system.

The Further and Higher Education Act of 1992 made ABE part of the system of further education in England and Wales which is mainly concerned with providing accredited vocational qualifications. As a result of these developments, ABE has become more firmly established, increasingly formalised and less rooted in the interests and experiences of people in communities. About two-thirds of the approximately 320,000 ABE students in England and Wales (Further Education Funding Council, 1998) now study within further education colleges, and less than a quarter in local authority adult and community-based programmes. This reverses the proportions at the start of the 1990s (BSA, 1997). This reorganisation of practice has been part of a policy focus that seeks to link education more closely with initial education and the economy and to provide clearer measures for evaluation and achievement.

Under the previous Conservative government, the arguments used to justify the need for ABE were framed in terms of global economic competitiveness: creating a skilled workforce rather than an informed citizenry. The European experience counters this to some degree with the concept of social exclusion, arguing that society is threatened by a dispossessed minority who are systematically excluded not only from the good jobs but also from participation in their community. In England, long years of isolation and conflict with its European partners prevented this concept from entering the policy discourse. The 1997 change of government brought the UK more in line with other European countries.

The present New Labour government strongly supports the concept of lifelong learning (Department for Education and Employment, 1998) and concerns about the effects of social exclusion are increasing, as highlighted in a series of important reports (Tomlinson, 1996; Fryer, 1997; Kennedy, 1997). In 1999, the government carried out a major review of Adult Basic Education as part of a National Literacy Strategy addressing the needs of both children and adults (Moser, 1999). The vision behind Moser is of a much tighter, quality controlled system of provision with a core curriculum, new national qualifications, a baseline national literacy test and better teaching training. It uses the language of entitlement (alongside 'functional illiteracy') – but this seems to mean first and foremost an 'entitlement to be assessed', for example through the New Deal Gateway for unemployed people. The plans for the new strategy include national targets for a vastly expanded service with a heavy reliance on computer-based learning technologies for both teacher training and learner provision and the use of local partnerships between different agencies (DfEE, 1999). Better quality and inspection system are also promised and provision will link with other initiatives to increase adult participation in lifelong learning, such as the University for industry, all under the control of the new funding agency, the Learning and Skills Council. This integrated approach is designed to avoid the marginalisation of ABE that has limited it – but possibly enabled it to occupy a creative space – so much in the past. Moser's final recommendation is on research, but no link is proposed between research and professional development in the field so there are no mechanisms proposed for this development.

Adult literacy in Wales has been patterned on that in England and is under the remit of the BSA. The main difference has been the inclusion of Welsh as an official language for educational provision, resulting in bilingual materials and tuition. A new National Strategy for Basic Skills in Wales (BSA, 2000) has been written in consultation with Welsh colleagues, and it directly parallels the English literacy and numeracy strategies. Although there are no detectable differences in this document, there are differences in the way the education system operates in Wales that may affect the future shape of ABE, allowing the development of a distinctively Welsh model. Control of education has recently been delegated from the Welsh Office to the new Welsh Assembly. There is a separate Welsh Inspectorate (OHMCI) run on the same lines as the English Ofsted. There is more flexibility and local discretion in school-based literacy teaching strategies and there are no primary school league tables or compulsory literacy hour. A separate curriculum accommodates Welsh language teaching into secondary schools.

Scotland

Adult literacy emerged as a field of work in Scotland as a result of the BBC's 'On the Move' campaign in the early 1970s. Although there was much scepticism that the initiative was as pertinent to Scotland (where educational standards were thought to be superior to the rest of the UK), large numbers of viewers responded, even after programmes went off the air. The Scottish Adult Literacy Agency worked to secure what they describe as 'well established and thriving adult literacy schemes' in virtually all regions. By 1983, there were 17,850 literacy students in Scotland, mainly learning 1:1 with a volunteer tutor in the home or a local centre in programmes organised by local authorities' community education services. Programme organisers found that many learners were more interested in developing writing or numeracy than reading. Programmes began to broaden out from their original focus on reading in response to this and tutors and organisers began to develop more adult learning material. Some Regional Councils developed an English as a Second Language provision.

The Scottish Adult Literacy Agency was succeeded by another government-funded body, the Scottish Adult Literacy Unit, and then in the early 1980s by the Scottish Adult Basic Education Unit (SABEU). SABEU encouraged providers to move away from the individualised, remedial model of the early literacy campaign and introduced the term EAL (essential adult learning) alongside the term ABE. These terms were not (as elsewhere) euphemisms for literacy and numeracy but an attempt to encourage councils to develop broader 'positive action' type adult learning programmes covering a range of skills such as life management, confidence building, learning about health issues and learning for democratic participation.

At a time of increasing local government funding cuts, the regional councils generally ignored the advice and continued to provide literacy provision but often as a 'remedial' and temporary adjunct to mainstream community education. Other councils understood the advice as providing a rationale for incorporating their literacy staff and budget into mainstream community education and reversing their commitment to literacy. A small minority of councils continued to expand and develop literacy and numeracy programmes alongside other adult learning within community education.

In the mid-1980s, SABEU was absorbed into the Scottish Community Education Council (SCEC) with accompanying staff losses. Since then, Scotland has not had a national agency responsible for promoting adult literacy. By the end of the 1980s, there were wide disparities in the nature and extent of literacy and numeracy provision across different areas of the country and generally programmes continued to rely heavily on volunteer tutors working with individual students, although increasingly these met in centres rather than at home.

By the early 1990s, education providers looked to the government for clearer guidance on their role and several developments guided their thinking. New guidance to college principals stated that a poor match between students' literacy skills and course demands should be avoided via better guidance and admission systems, but where these were not fully effective, subject teachers could offer help and if necessary refer the learner to ABE classes. While colleges were being discouraged from taking on a role in literacy, local authorities were allowed to deliver programmes although their duty to provide remained very general. The Further & Higher Education (Scotland) Act laid a new duty on colleges to provide ESOL. At the committee stage of this new Bill, the Secretary of State for Scotland issued a statement to authorities that 'extensive provision of basic skills education and provision for other special groups currently made through the community education services can continue'. Around the same time, the Scottish Adult Basic Education Forum (1989–1992) continued to encourage a broad definition of ABE as referring to 'literacy, numeracy *and the other basic skills* necessary for life in a modern society'.

The HMl Report on ABE in all post-school education sectors (SOED, 1993) evaluated a range of provision operating under the title of ABE Programmes varied form access/return to learn courses to computing, sewing or driving courses. The Report argued that whilst the number of adults with literacy and numeracy difficulties was unclear, it was clear that the majority 'had come to terms with their handicap' and therefore recommended that literacy and numeracy provision become 'an integral and inseparable strand of a much wider educational provision'. Many local authorities responded to the Report by further withdrawing funding from dedicated literacy programmes, reducing staffing levels and prioritising ICT and other 'more attractive' basic skills programmes under the heading of 'Essential Skills'. These changes were also responses to the impending Local Government Reorganisation and the funding constraints it was expected to bring.

By 1998, research quoted in the Convention of Scottish Local Authorities (COSLA) Report (COSLA, 1998) suggested that the numbers of students participating in ABE across all sectors had fallen by at least 40 per cent compared with 1992 figures. Recent research (carried out by the National Development Project referred to below) suggests that there may now be only around 6,000 adult students, the majority in local council organised community education programmes and the remainder in FE colleges and voluntary organisations. The National Development Project's Survey of Programmes (NDP, 2000) suggests that the quality of programmes is as much a matter of concern as their limited capacity. The Project has emphasised that poor capacity and quality need to be understood as an outcome of several factors. These are: the structural variety of adult literacy provision in Scotland over the last 25 years, the lack of specific guidance from the national agencies or government and the uneasy relationship between literacy provision and under-funded local authority services.

The low priority placed on adult literacy and numeracy in Scotland is now being addressed in recent policy developments, with a new visibility within the wider agendas of lifelong learning, social inclusion and active citizenship. A number of recent government documents have referred to adult literacy and basic skills. These include: the review of community education (SOEID, 1998a) and subsequent written guidance to local authorities, the Green Paper on lifelong learning, *Opportunity Scotland* (SOEID, 1998b), the Strategic Framework for Further Education (Scottish Executive, 1999a) and the Skills Strategy *Skills for Scotland* (Scottish Executive, 1999b). Although these documents have little to say on strategy and policy, local authorities are now expected to produce Community Learning Strategies along with all the relevant partners in their areas (from colleges and voluntary organisations to health agencies and enterprise bodies) incorporating explicit targets for adult literacy and numeracy. A National Development Project, 'Adult Literacies in Scotland', has produced a pack of resources for programme managers and practitioners, *Literacies in the Community* (Macrae, 2000). This pack includes a quality framework with good practice guidelines, as well as guidelines on tutoring and guidance in literacy programmes and on staff development and training. In a policy context which has previously been silent or hostile to adult literacy and numeracy provision, the newly devolved government has just announced a task group, 'Literacy 2000', to provide a focus for the development of national policy and strategy on adult literacy and numeracy.

Northern Ireland

In Northern Ireland, provision developed in Further Education Colleges, with each college appointing an adult literacy organiser and group tutors. Volunteer tutors were recruited to provide 1:1 tuition in the college or at home if necessary. ABE provision is still mainly located in the Further Education sector, although since 1990 basic skills support has been offered as part of vocational courses run by recognised training organisations through the Training and Employment Agency (T&EA). Voluntary and community groups together meet a growing need for literacy and ABE provision in the non-formal community sector and ABE is offered in all four prisons in Northern Ireland.

The Adult Literacy Liaison Group (ALLG) was formed by the Northern Ireland Department of Education in 1975 to provide a discussion forum for representatives of agencies and groups involved in adult literacy work such as the library service, broadcasters, prison service, referral agencies. The ALLG and its successor organisation, the Adult Literacy and Basic Education Committee (ALBEC), have supported provision through publishing tutor guides and teaching materials, arranging training courses and promoting the BSA's quality standards for tutors and programmes. In 1999, a Basic Skills Unit for Northern Ireland was established to promote and develop quality provision in basic skills education among adults but to date has established little independent leadership.

Northern Ireland's general approach to education is similar to that followed by the DfEE, the major exception being that Northern Ireland retained the 11+ with the related grammar school system (40 per cent of children having grammar school places). The other schools are known as secondary highs though recently many have renamed themselves as colleges. Most of the schools are denominational and many are single sex. The political context of Northern Ireland, involving long-term conflict between the two religious communities (Catholic and Protestant) and the military involvement of the British State, has prevented much organic change within education.

As in Scotland, Northern Ireland has not in the past had a separate agency responsible for promoting adult literacy. Such policy as has been explicitly developed follows that of England and Wales quite closely. Two main policy documents have been published recently: Sweeney *et al.* (1998) report on the findings of the IALS for Northern Ireland and the government Green Paper, *The Learning Age* (DENI, 1998), outlines a strategy for Lifelong Learning. Both parallel the equivalent documents in England. There is an economistic emphasis in the government documents with references to 'basic skills' rather than literacy.

The IALS research report includes an especially commissioned chapter on the literacy skills in the Catholic and Protestant communities showing that 'on all three literacy scales, Protestants had higher mean scores than Catholics'. It also suggests, however, that the gap is declining, with differences less pronounced within the youngest age groups and a mean score among youth in Northern Ireland that is higher than the international average. This literacy differential in the two communities, which has been known for some time, has enabled funding to be sought under the European Union Special Programme for Peace and Reconciliation (EGSA) for a number of community development projects. The sectoral partners mainly concerned with the distribution of this funding for adult literacy support have been the Educational Guidance Service for adults who have always provided the ABE referral service. This funding has often been distributed directly to community development organisations to put together their own forms of support within communities. The focus of the projects funded through this route has been very different from that provided through the FE colleges where the emphasis has been on delivering a pre-set curriculum focused on 'skills' requirements determined mainly by the providers.

Ireland

Ireland has a long history of voluntary literacy schemes. It was not until 1980, however, that a National Adult Literacy Agency (NALA) responsible for developing policy and good practice in adult literacy was created. NALA received government funding in 1985 when the Adult Literacy and Community Education (ALCE) budget was introduced. Subsequently, paid literacy organisers were appointed throughout the country by the Vocational Education Committees (VECs) and funding was made available for group tutoring hours.

The vast majority of literacy tuition still takes place in the locally based VEC schemes and literacy is integrated in other adult education and training programmes. Throughout the 1990s, NALA has co-ordinated a programme for training and development for literacy schemes and carried out a national research project on participation and access. In 1999, it hosted an EU project to consult on and develop a quality framework for adult literacy and to address the inconsistencies of provision around the country. The project on quality standards 'revealed a wide interest but lack of consistency in the development and monitoring of standards of ABE. Only the vocational programmes had developed a consistent approach to quality assurance, and approach that encourages self-evaluation' (NALA, 1999). Since 1997, student numbers have risen from 5,000 to 13,000.

Key recent government policy documents are 'Adult Education in an Era of Lifelong Learning' (DES, 1998), the first-ever Green Paper on adult education, and the subsequent White Paper *Learning for Life* published in July 2000; the National Development Plan, 2000–6 and the National Anti-Poverty Strategy, 1999. All give a high priority to adult literacy. The Green Paper argues that 'the most urgent task is that of confronting the literacy problem in Ireland' (p. 8) and suggests that 'education and skill deficiencies must not pose a barrier to any person in accessing a livelihood' (p. 7). This response has been partly a reaction to the IALS survey that pointed to 'Ireland lagging significantly behind other countries (except Poland) in terms of literacy performance' (p. 32). The concept of literacy underpinning these documents has been described by NALA as 'more than functional literacy, trying to embrace the holistic approach but falling short of the critical reflection aspect'. Currently, Ireland has low participation rates. The main influences apart from the IALS have been OECD policy and the skilled labour shortages cause [sic] by Ireland's booming economy. The White Paper is underpinned by three principles: a systemic approach to lifelong learning, equality and inter-culturalism that recognises the diversity of the population to be served. It also develops the notion of 'lifewide' as well as 'lifelong' learning to emphasis the broad, multidimensional approach that is necessary to support learning in the many situations in which it occurs (DES, 2000).

A comparison of policies addressing four key questions

What concept of literacy underpins recent policies?

In England (and by implication in NI and Wales as well), an earlier discourse of individual rights and welfare in educational and social policy had coexisted with a narrow functional definition of literacy. However, the discourse of human resource development now dominates the literacy agenda with managerial, technicist and corporate notions (see Gee *et al.,* 1996; Hamilton, 1996, 1997; Hamilton and Merrifield, 1999). This has resulted in an increasingly standardised definition of literacy that is linked to formal educational structures and methods of assessment at both initial and post-school levels. The new Labour government has overlaid this approach with a rhetoric that draws on concepts of lifelong learning and social exclusion. This reflects an increased sensitivity to European and other international thinking in the field. The vocational rationale is still powerful, however, and the Basic Skills Agency works with a functional definition: *'the ability to read, write and speak in English and use mathematics at a level necessary to function and progress at work and in society in general'.*

The policy emphasis in Northern Ireland generally follows England and Wales, but there is a special concern with community development resulting from civil and religious conflict.

In Scotland, policy and practice have largely been influenced by the same forces as above. However, the concept underpinning literacy may be more open at the moment. The best signals we have of future developments are found in the papers produced by the NDP which acknowledges the value of a socio-cultural approach to literacy and identifies three aspects of community learning: lifelong learning, social inclusion and active citizenship (see *Communities: Change through Learning* (SOEID, 1998a). These may provide a basis for a model of literacy provision that seeks to raise literacy levels through dedicated tuition and community development and recognises both individual and collective gains.

Government documents from Ireland recognise that there are different ways of conceiving of 'literacy' and are careful to avoid the narrowly economistic definitions, arguing for a broader view. Literacy learning is viewed as being not only the acquisition of a technical competence but also the development of the learner in many other ways. NALA, in their response to the Green Paper (Department of Education and Science, 1998), state that 'all good adult literacy work starts with the needs of individuals. Literacy involves the integration of listening, speaking, reading, writing and numeracy. It also encompasses aspects of personal development – social, economic, emotional, cultural, political – and it is concerned with improving self-esteem and building self-confidence. It goes far beyond the mere technical skills of communication. The underlying aim of good adult literacy practice is to enable people to understand and reflect critically on their life circumstances with a view to exploring new possibilities and initiating constructive change'.

In its explicit commitments to equality and inter-culturalism (diversity), the Irish strategy is most distanced from the market-driven rhetoric that is otherwise dominant. Ireland currently has the least formally developed state provision of all the countries considered here (still relying largely on voluntary provision) but is arguably the furthest on in defining its future policy strategy for literacy. It is therefore making an interesting leap from a situation that has stayed close to the adult literacy of the 1970s to a contemporary vision that responds to current national and international agendas but avoids the narrowness that has characterised notions of ABE over the past two decades in the UK.

How are learners and teachers positioned by the policies?

The influence of the IALS can be seen in how adult learners are constructed by policy in the different countries. In the IALS, adults are treated as one undifferentiated mass of people whose basic skills needs have been defined by experts and who may or may not recognise the difficulties that they face. The assumption made is that people with literacy problems have a deficit that needs to be rectified – primarily because of the needs of the economy. There is a strong tendency for this approach to be reflected in the policy statements that draw upon the IALS findings. The emphasis is on the huge scale of the 'problem' rather than a fine appreciation of its many dimensions in terms of diverse cultural groups and more nuanced understandings of literacies [...]. Despite reference to particular target groups and some specific commitment to cultural diversity (e.g. Ireland), the overall impact is an homogenising one that projects an inadequate mass in need of help.

The English documents most strongly follow the IALS in characterising learners as reluctant and deficient recipients who must be lured into programmes designed to address needs they may not yet be aware of. The Moser report (1999: 1.8) states that 'people with difficulties are often understandably reluctant to acknowledge, or are unaware, that they have a problem' and suggests that 'persuasive publicity' will be needed to encourage people into ABE programmes. Ireland is distinctive in that it promotes a student-centred model, reminiscent of England in the 1970s, which emphasises individual student input and negotiation. Students are construed as willing, voluntary participants with rights to determine what they get within an ABE programme and views of what they need. In Scotland, too, the Good Practice Framework produced by the National Development Project (2000) is underpinned by a principle of learner participation in the curriculum.

Teachers are unevenly present in the policy documents. Their role is defined very much in terms of how the learners are seen (joint partners in the learning process or receivers of knowledge). In the English policy documents, the teacher is positioned as technician, rather than as a professional who is to be 'upskilled' through short, prescriptive training programmes; there is sporadic consultation, but no rights to be involved in the process or representative bodies able to put forward the perspectives of practitioners. In Scotland, the NDP consulted extensively but was also hampered by the lack of bodies representing practitioners. Only in Ireland are tutors' needs for professional development and accreditation given top priority and this is in a situation where 85 per cent of tutoring is currently by volunteer staff.

Nowhere do tutors appear as powerful actors shaping ABE provision. The dominant assumption is that a strong, pre-formed framework for delivery is needed to ensure systematic and effective learning, rather than relying on the judgements of securely funded, high-level professional staff.

What kinds of learning activities/processes are programmes or initiatives expected to engage in?

There are big differences between the institutional framworks of the different countries reviewed here. The institutional possibilities are very wide for ABE. This is unlike almost any other kind of education of training, where there are usually clear-cut institutional affiliations and bases (e.g. school is the only widespread institutional setting available for children's initial education). This is extremely important for understanding the shape of ABE provision and how it might develop (see Hamilton, 1997) and is one of the focal points for policy debate and strategy. The constraints and possibilities for an ABE situated within a formal Further Education college are different from that taking place in a prison setting, a workplace or a community project. The relationships of co-operation and competition between these different agencies are also crucial. In England, Wales and Northern Ireland, provision is mainly in the formal FE College sector. In Scotland, it is mainly in the LEA-run community education sector staffed by paid tutors and volunteers, whilst in Ireland informal volunteer-run programmes are the norm. However, despite these different starting points, there is rhetoric common to all the policy documents referring to partnerships between institutions, with local learning plans being formulated by consortia of organisations.

Institutional structures also affect the learning processes that are possible or easy to support. In England, Wales and Northern Ireland, most learners are taught in a college setting, either in groups or in open learning centres. There is an increasing reliance on on-line resources, closely structured by the accreditation and curriculum frameworks. In Scotland, tuition is currently mainly 1:1 or in small groups. New guidance to local authorities on community learning strategies and plans emphasises literacy and numeracy in the context of core skills and it is unclear to what extent formal accreditation will be available through the Core Skills Units introduced in the new 'Higher Still' initiative.

In Ireland, tuition is also 1:1 and in small groups, supported mainly by volunteer tutors. Control of programmes is still very light and de-centred. Tutors are seen as being in partnership with students and are encouraged to carry out self-assessments, and there is a concern to develop robust consultation processes. A learner-centred approach is advocated with built-in progression opportunities, including accreditation. Participation for learners is voluntary and there is an emphasis on the importance of guidance and flexibility of learning opportunities. Future plans include family literacy programmes, an adult ICT Basic Skills programme, and use of TV and radio for both awareness raising and tuition.

All countries are under pressure to develop on-line learning rather than face-to-face contact with tutors and other students. This trend, plus decisions about formal versus community-based informal learning provision are key issues in determining the nature of the learning process that will be common in the ABE of the future. What may at first glance seem to be simple technical decisions, made for reasons of efficiency and easy dissemination and monitoring of programmes, have important consequences also for the kinds of learning activities that adults can engage in. In particular, the content and curriculum of literacy learning and the motivational and social aspects of learning will be influenced by a greater reliance on the use of information technologies. There is presently little evidence that governments are considering these consequences of their decisions. Neither is there much discussion of other measures that can be taken to develop and support a literate culture, for example through a more comprehensive language policy (see Lo Bianco and Freebody, 1997) or through supporting local resources for informal learning, rather than concentrating solely on expanding formally structured learning opportunities to develop literacy (see Hamilton, 2000).

What outcomes are literacy programmes and learners expected to achieve?

In all countries, the IALS is used to justify the need for increased participation rates in education and training with the ultimate aim of achieving increased levels of literacy/ numeracy in the population. In England and Wales, these aims are realised with target numbers to be met by specific dates.

In England and Wales, there is a very strong emphasis on standardised rests and learner qualifications that fit with the National Vocational Qualification system and will follow seamlessly from the Key Skills now embedded within initial education. Quality standards and accountability to funders are also important outcomes. In addition to these outcomes, in Northern Ireland, conflict reduction and mutual understanding are goals of the European Union Peace and Reconciliation funding. Whilst the placement of ABE in the formal, Further Education sector results in an emphasis on vocational outcomes, there is currently no real consistency or close monitoring of outcomes and a reliance on self-assessment on the part of providers.

In Scotland, a number of different outcomes are signalled as being important for the future. As well as targets for increased participation rates and increased levels of literacy/numeracy in the population, the value placed on social inclusion and active citizenship may well lead to important outcomes that are collective and social rather than primarily individual and vocational. The policy also refers to targets for participation and literacy and numeracy as core stills, implying that programmes should be accredited.

In Ireland, empowerment and critical reflection and the fulfilment of individual needs are at the forefront of NALA's strategic vision. The new adult education strategy foregrounds equal opportunities and cultural diversity and a systemic approach to lifelong learning, and collective as well as personal advancement. There is a concern for progression, and flexible learning and accreditation opportunities, quality and greater consistency of learning opportunities.

Discussion

It is possible from the detail offered above to draw out some main themes that will determine the shape of the ABE of the future.

A renewed policy interest in ABE prompted by international influences

As a service mandated by legislation, ABE now has a secure funding and institutional base in England and Wales. Scotland, NI and Ireland have yet to achieve this security but in all the countries there is currently a renewed policy interest in and commitment to ABE and priority is being given to improving the quality, extent and coherence of provision. Things are changing swiftly in all four countries and it is important to understand where the impetus for this change is coming from and who is involved in shaping the future of ABE in these countries. The publication of the International Adult Literacy Survey 'league tables' for international literacy and numeracy rates has played a major role in the drive to increase participation rates in the adult population with a corresponding deficit view of people's existing capabilities. The IALS survey has to be seen as part of broader OECD and EU influences which are also reshaping the larger schooling and training system as part of an agenda of human resource development (Hamilton and Barton, 2000). This agenda emphasises both literacy and lifelong learning for their assumed contribution to economic prosperity and aims to integrate basic skills provision across all educational and training sectors. The result is the strongly controlled and narrowly focused approach to literacy and numeracy evident in all the countries reviewed here.

The marketisation of literacy: standardising frameworks

One consequence of the renewed interest in literacy is a common concern with the quality, consistency and coherence of provision and accountability to public funders. In England and Wales, a substantial part of the new funding so far released is being used to put in place a standardised national curriculum and tests for adult literacy, underpinned by a limited and limiting standards framework. Despite the new rhetoric of social inclusion and citizen participation, this system is driven by a market ideology and a vision of the needs of global economic competitiveness. The imperative is to create a skilled workforce and an active consumer, rather than an informed citizen. It is based on a top-down definition of literacy where need is defined for learners rather than negotiated with them on the basis of their perceived needs. However subtle and flexibly designed the curriculum is, it cannot transcend this fundamental feature: it is designed for learners rather than with them or by them. To this extent, the more open and humanistic possibilities of a lifelong (and lifewide) system of learning opportunities for literacy are weakened and obscured.

Ideological and structural dominance of the English system

Despite the histories of each country which reveal diverse approaches to literacy and the organisation of ABE, the dominance of the English educational and policy frameworks both structurally and ideologically are evident across the UK. ABE in England is still the most systematised and narrowly defined first and foremost as part of education or training (rather than a social or community development issue). This vision also drives mainstream developments in Northern Ireland and Wales and is in contrast to the community development approach which has figured most strongly in Scotland and the EU-funded projects in Northern Ireland targeted at improved conditions within the religious communities.

The discourse of the national adult literacy agency in Ireland is still reminiscent of that prevalent in the 1970–80s with a strong emphasis on individual rights to literacy and an emancipatory goal, though with less emphasis on mutual learning and support or collective outcomes. As the present international pressures come to bear on the field more strongly, the impulse toward conformity will increase. The contrary trend of devolution of political power to individual countries and regions is the main assurance against this happening and the future shape of ABE will be one test of the robustness of the autonomy that has been achieved.

The role of the ABE professional

In none of these settings does there appear to be a strong professional voice moderating the official policy agendas. This is in contrast to what has happened in school-based reforms over the past 10 years, where teachers have influenced the development of new assessments and curricula. The reasons for this are clear: a fragmented and low status workforce, including many volunteers and part-time workers, lack of training and no representative professional associations or stable networks that could develop such bodies. This means that ABE practitioners are ill equipped to move into more powerful positions in the expanded provision that is currently envisaged. They are used to working creatively 'in the cracks' with inadequate funding or formal structures that do not support the understandings that they have gained from their experience about what good practice entails. However, they are not used to being involved in the wider processes of policy formation of designing structures that can work, to arguing their case in public or systematically documenting their achievements.

There also appears to be little influence from educational or organisational research about learning and literacy. This means that the imperatives of the economic arguments advanced by both national and international bodies tend to claim undisputed sway over policy rationales in the field of ABE. Recent research by Thomas Sticht (2000) suggests the dangers and insecurities of this situation. He argues that new evidence in the USA suggests that developed industrial nations may be facing a 'literacy surplus' rather than a deficit in terms of work-related skills and that this undermines arguments for the expansion of adult literacy on the grounds of human resource development needs. He suggests that the implications of this are that policies must argue on the basis of the wider benefits and rights of the population to literacy and play down the employment connection. For such alternative arguments to have persuasive force in policy circles, they need to be well articulated and based on a coherent model of literacy such as that advanced by the research work of the New Literacy Studies [...].

The role of national agencies

A key issue is the role of the national agencies in the policy development process. In Ireland, NALA sees itself as operating by carrying out consultations with learners and students and feeding these back to government, in order to help develop high quality literacy programmes including tutor training and the provision of a referral service. The role of the Basic Skills Agency in England and Wales, however, is seen as being much more top-down and there is a very real danger that the corporatist vision of ABE promoted by international bodies like the OECD will come to dominate the UK at the expense of more locally defined and appropriate responses. It will be particularly interesting to see what kind of infrastructure Scotland adopts in its new policy and how far it can preserve local autonomy in this process.

Models of the consultation process

Models for consultation are available from the NALA project on quality (see Bailey, 2000) and from the Equipped for the Future project in the USA (Merrifield, 1998). The pace of change is such that it is difficult to engage in a proper consultation process, even where respect for the rights of students and teachers to be involved is a strong core value. This difficulty is exacerbated where there are no, or only weak, mechanisms for consultation and few opportunities for collective voicing of opinion. Consortial partnerships are not the same as a democratic consultation process, as democratically accountable bodies like the LEAs have only a marginal role to play in them and there are no existing organisations that can represent either staff or learner views.

Conclusion

In Scotland and Ireland especially, and in community-based literacy in all countries, there is evidence of attempts to build in respect for some of the core values of ABE within transparent, consistent frameworks for improving access and quality in the context of a consultative and empowering policy process. How powerfully these values will be represented in the ABE of the future depends on the larger social policy context in each country and the possibilities for democratic control of the policy process. As always, there are competing policy discourses that may pull adult literacy in different directions. In this case, the lifelong learning, active citizenship and social inclusion agendas, if they are creatively and critically understood, offer possibilities for more open definitions of literacy than the human resources development model still dominant within initial education.

This is a moment of opportunity for ABE in the UK and in Ireland in which we can build on our history of participatory approaches to adult learning, the strong tradition of voluntary associations, and new research which can underpin and justify a broadly based and sustainable approach to practice (see Street, 1995; Barton and Hamilton, 1998). It remains to be seen how the different perspectives of potential learners, students, providers and policy makers will be heard about what adult literacy and numeracy are, where they stand in relation to other aspects of lifelong learning and in what ways they will contribute to the vision of the countries of the UK and Ireland as dynamic learning societies.

In developing the field of ABE, individual countries can exert a strong national steer, but this will inevitably be within a wider framework of interconnected social polices and international agendas. As practitioners and researchers, we need to understand this complexity and how it shapes day-to-day practice and funding opportunities. We need to be clear about where our commitments and underpinning values and assumptions about literacy lie, and skilful in articulating these within the policy arena.

[...]

Note

1 As the National Literacy Trust has pointed out, the national press tends to write as if every utterance of the English DfEE were statutory throughout the UK. But the Department for Education and Employment only deals with education in England; in Wales, its equivalent is the Education Department within the Welsh Office; in Scotland, it is The Scottish Office Education and Industry Department; and in Northern Ireland, it is the Department of Education for Northern

Ireland (DENI). Each of these departments has a different approach to education and therefore may use some different terminology to describe the various policy initiatives, programmes and sectors; this is particularly so in Scotland (see www.literacytrust.org.uk/Update; Cantor and Roberts, 1995; Clark and Munn, 1997).

References

Bailey, I. (2000) 'Ireland's evolving quality framework for ABE: an account of NALA's piloting process'. *RaPAL* Bulletin, 41, Special Issue on Quality, pp. 17–22.

Barton, D. and Hamilton, M. (1998) *Local Literacies: A Study of Reading and Writing in One Community*. London: Routledge.

Basic Skills Agency (1997) *Annual Report 1996/7*. London: BSA.

Basic Skills Agency (2000) *Improving Standards of Literacy and Numeracy in Wales: A National Strategy*. London: BSA.

Cantor, L.M. and Roberts, I.F. (1995) *Further Education Today: a Critical Review,* 3rd edn. London: Routledge and Kegan Paul.

Clark, M.M. and Munn, P. (eds) (1997) *Education in Scotland: Policy and Practice from Pre-School to Secondary*. London: Routledge.

COSLA (1998) *Promoting Learning – Developing Communities*. Edinburgh: COSLA.

Department for Education and Employment (1998) *The Learning Age, a Renaissance for a New Britain*. London: The Stationery Office.

Department for Education and Employment (1999) *Better Basic Skills*. London: The Stationery Office.

Department of Education and Science (1998) 'Adult education in an era of lifelong learning', Green Paper on *Adult Education*. Dublin: Stationery Office.

Department of Education and Science (2000) White Paper on Adult Education, *Learning For Life*. Dublin Stationery Office.

Department of Education for Northern Ireland (1998) Green Paper on *The Learning Age*. Belfast: DENI.

Fryer, R. (1997) *Learning for the Twenty-First Century: First Report of the National Advisory Group for Continuing Eduction and Lifelong Learning* (NAGCELL1. PP62/3111634/1297/33). London: Government Stationery Office.

Further Education Funding Council (1998) *Basic Skill Curriculum Area Survey Report*. London: Government Stationery Office.

Gee, J., Hull, G. and Lankshear, C. (1996) *The New Work Order: Behind the Language of the New Capitalism*. Sydney and Boulder, CO: Allen & Unwin and Westview Press.

Hamilton, M. (1996) 'Adult literacy and basic education' in Fieldbouse, R. (ed.), *A History of Modern British Adult Education*. Leicester: National Institute of Adult Continuing Education.

Hamilton, M. (1997) 'Keeping alive alternative visions' in Hautecoeur, J.P. (ed.), *ALPHA 97. Basic Education and Institutional Environments*. Hamburg, FRG: UNESCO Institute for Education, and Toronto, Canada: Culture Concepts.

Hamilton, M. (2000) *Sustainable Literacies and the Ecology of Lifelong Learning,* paper presented at the Global Colloquium for Lifelong Learning, www.ou.lifelonglearning

Hamilton, M. and Barton, D. (2000) 'The International Literacy Survey: what does it measure?'. *International Journal of Education,* UNESCO, Hamburg.

Hamilton, M. and Merrifield, J. (1999) 'Adult basic education in the UK. Lessons for the US', Commissioned Review Article in *National Review of Adult Learning and Literacy*, 1(1), National Center for the Study of Adult Language and Literacy, San Francisco: Jossey-Bass.

Kennedy, H. (1997) *Learning Works: Widening Participation in Further Education*. Coventry: Further Education Funding Council.

Lo Bianco, J. and Freebody, F. (1997) *Australian Literacies: Informing National Policy on Literacy Education*. Melbourne: National Languages and Literacy Institute of Australia.

Macrae, C. (2000) *Literacies in the Community: Resources for Practitioners and Managers*. Edinburgh: Scottish Executive, Enterprise and Lifelong Learning.

Merrifield, J. (1998) *Contested Ground: Performance Accountability in Adult Basic Education, NCSALL Report No. 1*. Cambridge, Mass: National Center for the Study of Adult Learning and Literacy.

Moser, C. (1999) *A Fresh Start: Improving Literacy and Numeracy*. London: Department for Education and Employment.

National Adult Literacy Association (1999) *NALA-SOCRATES Project Evolving Quality Framework for Adult Basic Education*. Dublin: NALA.

National Development Project (2000) *Good Practice Guidelines*. Edinburgh: Scottish Executive, Enterprise and Lifelong Learning.

Organisation for Economic Cooperation and Development (2000) *Literacy in the Information Age*. Paris: OECD.

SOED (1993) *Alive to Learning*. Edinburgh: HMSO.

SOEID (1998a) *Communities Change Through Learning*. Edinburgh: Scottish Office.

SOEID (1998b) *Opportunity Scotland. A Paper on Lifelong Learning*. Edinburgh: Stationery Office.

Scottish Executive (1999a) *Strategic Framework for Further Education*. Edinburgh: Scottish Office.

Scottish Executive (1999b) *Skills for Scotland. A Skills Strategy for a Competitive Scotland*. Edinburgh: Scottish Office.

Sticht, T. (2000) *Are We Facing a Literacy 'Surplus' in the Workforces of the United States and Canada?*, Research Note 3/21/00, e-mail 10 August 2000.

Street, B. (1995) *Social Literacies: Critical Approaches to Literacy in Development, Ethnography and Education*. London: Longman.

Street, B. (1997) *Adult Literacy in the U.K.: A History of Research and Practice*, National Center for Adult Literacy Policy Paper Series. Philadelphia: University of Pennsylvania.

Sweeney, K., Morgan, B. and Donnelly, D. (1998) *Adult Literacy in Northern Ireland*. Belfast: Northern Ireland Statistics and Research Agency.

Tomlinson, S. (1996) *Inclusive Learning: Report of the Learning Difficulties and/or Disabilities Committee*. London: The Stationery Office.

Withnall, A. (1994) 'Literacy on the agenda: the origins of the adult literacy campaign in the United Kingdom', *Studies in the Education of Adults*, 26 (1), pp. 67–85.

Part 4

Community, Family, Society and Individual Identity

14

The Self-concept and its Relationship to Educational Achievement

Robert Burden

One of the most important questions with which each of us is faced at various times in our lives is, 'Who am I?' As young children develop, they gradually become more and more aware that whilst there are many ways in which they are similar to other boys and girls, there are at least as many ways in which they differ. This realization, which is largely shaped by the social and cultural context into which they are born and the nature of their interactions with significant others in their lives, leads to the construction of each person's unique sense of identity. It has been suggested by the psychologist Eric Erikson that during the period of adolescence one of the most vital tasks for every individual is to establish a sense of 'ego integrity', a firm grasp of who we are and what we want to become. For Erikson, the resolution of the adolescence identity crisis is essential to enable a person to continue to mature and lead a satisfying and fulfilling life. At the same time, he considers that whether or not such a resolution is reached will depend upon how well the individual has passed through a series of earlier developmental stages. Thus, our early childhood experiences are considered to play a significant part in our attitudes towards ourselves and our place in the world (Erikson, 1959).

This shaping of a sense of identity is referred to by others as the construction of the self-concept, which has been defined by another psychologist, Carl Rogers, as: 'composed of such elements as the perceptions of one's characteristics and abilities: the percepts and concepts of the self in relation to others and to the environments; the value qualities which are perceived as associated with experiences and objects; and the goals and ideas which are perceived as having positive or negative valence' (Rogers, 1951, p. 138). A more succinct definition offered by Robert Burns (1982, p. 7) is that 'self-concept is best regarded as a dynamic complex of attitudes held towards themselves by each person'.

Jerome Bruner (1996) has suggested that sense of self is more or less equal to the individual's 'conception of their own powers'. This has been interpreted elsewhere as meaning that 'to know one's self is to appreciate one's capacities in different circumstances – to evaluate one's stream of thought and action as they fit into surrounding realities' (Reed, 2001, p. 121). One implication of such a definition is that education is less likely to lead to some kind of permanent change in the private self, as to an adaptation of the self within and to a variety of contexts. The two key properties of self-identification by Bruner are those of *agency* and *evaluation,* with

From: Burden, R., *Dyslexia and Self-concept: Seeking a Dyslexic Identity*, pp. 5–14 (London and Philadelphia: Whurr, 2005).

agency referring to the guidance of action by external, often shared, meanings and values, and evaluation used to refer to how well one's agency meshes with others' actions.

In his seminal work, *Self-concept Development and Education,* Burns (1982) put forward the suggestion that self-concept can be identified as a compound of two elements, self-image and self-evaluation. By looking at it in this way, we can see that it has many of the attributes of an attitude that people develop about themselves. Attitudes are usually considered to consist of three key elements: the cognitive, the connative and the behavioural, or, in more basic terms, the beliefs that we hold about something or someone, the strengths of our feelings towards or against that object or person, and our predisposition to act in certain ways.

It can be seen, therefore, that our self-image *is* the set of beliefs that we hold about various aspects of ourselves, how we look, how we get on with others, how good we are at various aspects of schoolwork and so on. Our evaluation of these beliefs, how strongly they matter to us, is what we usually mean when we refer to self-esteem.

The third major aspect of an attitude is the predisposition that it gives us to act in certain ways. If I believe something to be true and it matters a great deal to me, then I will be inclined to act accordingly when faced with an issue of this nature. As far as our self-concept is concerned, the images that we construct about certain significant aspects of ourselves and the strength of feeling that we have about those aspects will be likely to affect our behaviour in circumstances where such thoughts and feelings are pertinent. If I believe that I am a skilful games player and games playing is an important activity for me, I am likely to enter into games with some confidence of a successful outcome and will do my best to succeed.

A problem that immediately arises here is that there are practically limitless numbers of ways in which we can perceive ourselves. Psychologists have tended to focus upon six or eight major categories, but then disagree as to whether our self-image/self-esteem in each of these categories is cumulative, thereby producing an overall sense of global self-concept (GSC), or whether our thoughts and feelings about each of these individual aspects of ourselves exist relatively independently of each other. Does how I see myself as a parent or a friend necessarily have any connection with how I see myself as a musician or an academic? This is an important point because much of the research into the relationship between self-concept and other attributes such as achievement has been bedevilled by confusion as to exactly what is being measured. As Hansford and Hattie (1982) point out in their meta-analysis of research studies into the relationship between people's self-perceptions and their academic achievements, terms such as self-concept, self-image and self-esteem are often used interchangeably without adequate definition, and applied without valid and reliable measurement techniques. We therefore need to be clear as to exactly what aspect of self-concept we are particularly interested in and exactly how we intend to measure this. At the same time, we need to try to assess how specific aspects of our self-concept are shaped and whether there is a more general spreading effect to other areas of our developing sense of identity. In this book, for reasons which will become clear later, we shall be focusing on dyslexic young people's conceptions of themselves as learners and problem-solvers and the effect this can have upon their approach to learning and their eventual success or failure in their learning endeavours.

As Burns makes clear, the self-concept is a set of subjectively constructed attributes and feelings, which take on their meanings for an individual through the general evaluation of that quality or attribute in their particular society. It therefore follows that those of us who possess characteristics considered to be socially undesirable will begin to perceive ourselves as undesirable or in some way wanting. Since literacy is considered to be a highly desirable characteristic in our society, those who have difficulty in becoming literate will automatically find it difficult to develop positive academic self-concepts, particularly if we accept the premise that our self-evaluations are determined by our beliefs about how others see us. This is usually referred to as 'the looking glass self', a term that was first constructed in the early years of the twentieth century (Cooley, 1912).

Burns suggests further that the self-concept appears to have a threefold role: maintaining a sense of inner consistency, determining how experiences are interpreted, and providing a set of expectancies. The first role relates to what has sometimes been termed 'the principle of homeostasis'. It has been argued by many psychologists that, in order to survive, human beings need to establish a sense of inner harmony and equilibrium. This will be closely associated with what individuals think and feel about themselves and they will act in ways which are consistent with this. If we find again and again that we have difficulties in coping successfully with a culturally valued activity such as reading or spelling, we are likely to explain this to ourselves in terms of some enduring trait such as 'stupidity' and to begin to act in other situations in ways which confirm this. Burns argues that the maintenance of the self-concept, positive or negative, appears to be a prime motivator in all normal behaviour. In this he differs in some important ways from symbolic interactionists, who hold the view that our self-concept can and does shift as a result of our experiences in interacting with significant others (Pollard, 1996). As we shall see, belief in the consistency of one's self-concept is of particular significance to children struggling to overcome learning difficulties of a dyslexic nature.

The second important role performed by the self-concept is the way in which it shapes our interpretation of experiences, i.e. *it* plays an important part in helping us to make sense of and give meaning to what happens to us. If I have a negative academic self-concept, I am more likely to interpret my failure on a learning task, such as a spelling test, in global terms rather than as a one-off experience. Burns makes the important point that there is no action that a teacher can take that a child with a negative self-concept cannot interpret in a negative way. For this reason, merely providing praise or other forms of positive reinforcement will not be sufficient to change that child's view of him-/herself. It takes much more deep-rooted action to bring about positive change in how we see ourselves.

Expectancy theory suggests that we all carry with us a set of expectations about the world which determine how we are most likely to act. If we expect to have positive experiences, we will act in ways that will bring them about. If we expect negative experiences, we will similarly act in ways to make these happen. Thus, if a dyslexic child's academic self-concept is one that leads the child to expect failure in learning to read and/or spell, then he or she is likely to act in ways that will make this a self-fulfilling prophecy.

It is not difficult to see, therefore, how important a positive academic self-concept is likely to be in affecting the behaviour and expectancies of dyslexic children with regard to becoming literate, and how difficult it can be to change negative self-perceptions once they have been formed. Burns (1982) reports a number of research studies which show that underachievers see themselves as less adequate and less acceptable to others. He also makes the point (p. 214) that 'Most experienced teachers can recite a great many examples in which a student's concept of his abilities severely restricts his achievement, even though his real abilities may be superior to those which he demonstrates'. So a particular self-perception can easily become self-validating such that a child who avoids reading thereby bypasses the very experience which might change their concept of self. Thus, these notions of inability to learn become self-fulfilling prophecies. Burns is compelled to conclude (p. 226) that 'Children whose self-concepts do not include the view that they can achieve academically tend to fulfil that prediction.'

It is here that we need to be clear about the distinction between self-concept and self-esteem. If children who are performing poorly at their schoolwork respond honestly to questions about their academic self-concept, their responses will inevitably be negative. This does not necessarily mean, however, that their academic self-esteem need be negative, although this is highly likely to be the case if doing well at school is important to them. Positive self-esteem is not merely a matter of feeling good about oneself. It consists of a much more deep-rooted belief in one's capability to overcome the problems with which one is faced, the confidence to deal with negative issues as they arise and a realistic sense of agency, i.e. that one has the skills and strategies to act in an effective manner when called upon to do so. Only by building up such attributes to overcome feelings of poor self-esteem and drawing upon them in one's approach to learning will a negative academic self-concept be changed into a realistically positive one. This is no easy task, but it is by no means impossible, as we shall see.

What do we know about the self-concepts of people with dyslexia?

Surprisingly, there appears to have been comparatively little research into how dyslexic children and adults make sense of their disability or how this affects their perceptions of themselves as learners or as (prospective) citizens of the world. This is even more surprising in view of what we know about the importance of self-perceptions in contributing to academic and more general success in life. We also know that continuing feelings of failure whilst at school can have lifelong debilitating effects on individuals' ability to cope with stress (Lewandowski and Arcangelo, 1994).

In one adult study, Riddick and her co-workers found by comparing the past and present educational histories of 16 dyslexic university students with matched controls, that the dyslexic group displayed significantly lower self-esteem than the controls (Riddick et al., 1999). The dyslexics also reported themselves as feeling more anxious and less competent in their written work whilst at school than their contemporaries and as carrying these feelings of incompetence with them into university. This finding endorsed that of previous researchers (e.g. Gerber et al., 1990).

Research has also shown us that adolescent poor readers tend to have low self-esteem and to feel themselves less valued members of their classes (Fairhurst and Pumfrey, 1992). This finding has been confirmed in a variety of different countries such as Norway, where a study of 3000 schoolchildren found that those with specific learning difficulties had lower self-esteem and self-confidence than their contemporaries (Gjessing and Karlsen, 1989), and, the USA, where similar findings were obtained by Chapman (1988a). An important early study by Zimmerman and Allegrand (1965) compared the personality characteristics and attitudes towards achievement of two groups of poor ($n = 71$) and good ($n = 82$) readers equated as nearly as possible for age, sex, ethnic background and intelligence. Good readers were found to describe themselves as better adjusted, motivated and striving for success whilst the poor readers displayed feelings of discouragement, inadequacy and anxiety, and tended to set themselves ephemeral and short-term goals. More recently, Lerner (2000) has noted that as well as displaying underachievement during the elementary school years, children in the USA diagnosed as suffering from learning disabilities typically experience social-emotional problems such as low self-esteem and often struggle to make and maintain friendships. These problems are carried forward into adolescence where they can develop into learned helplessness, a significant drop in their confidence to learn and succeed, low motivation to achieve, attention problems and maladaptive behaviour.

Further confirmation of the potential negative consequences on the feelings of dyslexic children has been provided in a number of more personal accounts, mainly of a retrospective nature (e.g. Osmond, 1993: Edwards, 1994). Often such accounts are of an impassioned nature, describing the slights, the injustices, the emotional pain and unbearable stress suffered by individual or small groups of dyslexics as a result of unfortunate childhood experiences and/or the ignorance of significant others. Whilst such accounts should never be ignored or devalued, their very lack of objectivity means that they cannot necessarily be taken as representative of the experiences of all or even the majority of dyslexic children. We need more carefully controlled investigations before we can begin to reach such conclusions, but the fact that these are representative accounts of the feelings of some dyslexic children should not be overlooked.

As was indicated earlier, controlled studies of the emotional effects of dyslexia on children or adults have been relatively rare compared with research into other aspects of dyslexia. In the USA, studies by Saracoglu et al. (1989) and Lewandowski and Arcangelo (1994) both reported low self-concepts/self-esteem in adults with learning disabilities and accompanying difficulties with emotional adjustment. Data from the British birth cohort longitudinal studies reported by Bynner and Ekynsmith (1994) showed a relationship between continuing literacy difficulties, or, more correctly, *perceived* literacy difficulties, and feelings of depression.

Frederickson and Jacobs (2001) compared the academic self-perceptions and attributions for success and failure of 20 children with dyslexia with 20 matched controls with no learning difficulties. They found that the dyslexic children displayed significantly lower academic self-concepts than their matched peers, but their global self-worth was not significantly lower. They also found that children with a strong internal locus of control tended to have higher academic self-concepts than those who saw their success and failure as outside their control, even when actual reading attainment was taken into account.

These findings confirm previous research findings, mainly carried out in the USA with children with learning disabilities (Chapman, 1988b; Resnick and Harter, 1989), especially when such children were educated in mainstream classrooms rather than in special classes. However, when Kistner et al. (1988) monitored the progress of children with specific learning difficulties over a period of two years, they found that those who attributed failure to factors within their control (e.g. effort) made the greater achievement gains. At the same time, Jacobson et al. (1986) found that children with learning disabilities were more likely than normally achieving children to see both success and failure as due to factors outside their control.

The importance of focusing on domain-specific self-perceptions rather than on global self-esteem has been further emphasized by Carr et al. (1991). This point was supported by the findings of a study of the relationship between academic self-concept and achievement of 600 Norwegian primary school children (Skaalvik and Hagvet, 1990). The conclusion of these researchers was that academic self-concept acts as a mediating variable between academic performance and global self-esteem as well as providing a causal influence on academic achievement.

Attempts to measure dyslexic children's feelings about themselves have been fraught with difficulties, not least because of the lack of appropriate measurement techniques allied to meaningful psychological theories about dyslexic children's psychosocial development. Two studies (Thomson and Hartley, 1980; Humphrey, 2002) drew upon Kelly's Repertory Grid Technique in this endeavour with not altogether satisfactory results. A further study by Thomson reported in his book *Developmental Dyslexia* (1990), however, describes the use of a self-esteem inventory to compare the self-esteem of children who had spent a differential amount of time at a specialist school for dyslexics. He found that the social and academic self-esteem of the pupils increased considerably in accordance with the time spent at the school, whilst the initially high level of parental esteem remained constant.

Humphrey and Mullins (2002), in a more recent paper, emphasize the need to ground investigations in this area in sound psychological theory. They pinpoint, in particular, attribution theory, incorporating aspects of locus of control and learned helplessness. Briefly, attribution theory is concerned with the reasons to which individuals attribute their successes and failures in life, while locus of control relates to whether these reasons are perceived as *internal* and within the individual's own control, or *external* and in the control of more powerful other people or forces.

Learned helplessness is generally considered to be the state that people fall into when, usually as a result of constant failure, they feel that there is no point in making the effort to attempt tasks because of what they perceive as the inevitability of failure (Bar-Tal and Darom, 1979; Joiner and Wagner, 1995). As Seligman (1991, p. 5) puts it, 'Helplessness is the state of affairs in which nothing you choose to do affects what happens to you'.

From the results of their own study, Humphrey and Mullins conclude that the experience of dyslexia has clear and demonstrable negative effects on the self-concept and self-esteem of children, adding that 'the parallels between learned helplessness and children with reading difficulties are striking' (2002, p. 197). In one of the very few published studies attempting to apply these ideas, Butkowsky and Willows (1980) claim to have found that good and poor readers display different attributional styles, with poor readers being more likely to blame themselves for failure and to attribute success to luck. Poor readers also appeared to have lower expectations of success and to respond more negatively to failure.

We can conclude with some confidence from this review of the somewhat limited research literature that:

- there is a clear negative association between early and continuing literacy difficulties and self-concept/self-esteem;
- these negative feelings are likely to be long-lasting;
- the ways in which they may manifest themselves are likely to be complex, taking the form of vulnerability to stress, feelings of learned helplessness and depression.

What we do not as yet know with any confidence is whether such effects are inevitable in the long or short term, or whether they can be alleviated and even overcome by particular kinds of intervention programmes. Reports on the outcomes of intervention programmes implemented with dyslexic children and adults have tended almost exclusively to focus upon measured gains in academic achievement without reporting the broader psychological effects on the participants in either the short or long term. As Riddick et al. (1999, p. 244) state in concluding their study, 'we need to identify those dyslexic students who are low in self-esteem and/or high in anxiety and evaluate what forms of environmental changes and support will be most effective in raising their self-esteem and lowering their anxiety ... (therefore) ... consideration could be given to using measures such as these as part of a student's overall assessment'. They add that measures of these psychological aspects could also be used to help monitor the effectiveness of various forms of intervention or support. Even more radically, Herrington and Hunter-Carsch make the point that 'there does not appear to be a broad-based attempt to integrate models of dyslexia with either radical perspectives of literacy or social models of disabilities' (Herrington and Hunter-Carsch, 2001, p. 114).

[...]

References

Bar-Tal D, Darom E (1979) Pupils' attributions of success and failure. Child Development 50: 264–267.

Bruner J (1996) The Culture of Education. Cambridge, MA: Harvard University Press.

Burns RB (1982) Self-concept Development and Education. London: Holt, Rinehart and Winston.

Butkowsky TS, Willows DM (1980) Cognitive motivation and characteristics of children varying in reading ability: evidence of learned helplessness in poor readers. Journal of Educational Psychology 72: 408–422.

Bynner J, Ekynsmith C (1994) Young Adults' Literacy and Numeracy Problems: Some evidence from the British Cohort Study. London: ALBSU.

Carr M, Borkowski JG, Maxwell SE (1991) Motivational components of under-achievement. Developmental Psychology 27: 108–118.

Chapman JW (1988a) Learning disabled children's self-concepts. Review of Educational Research 58: 347–371.

Chapman JW (1988b) Cognitive-motivational characteristics and academic achievement of learning disabled children: a longitudinal study. Journal of Educational Psychology 80: 357–365.

Cooley CH (1912) Human Nature and the Social Order. New York: Scribners.

Edwards J (1994) The Scars of Dyslexia. London: Cassell.

Erikson E (1959) Identity and the Life Cycle. New York: IVP.

Fairhurst P, Pumfrey PD (1992) Secondary school organisation and the self-concepts of pupils with relative reading difficulties. Research in Education 47: 17–27.

Frederickson N, Jacobs S (2001) Controllability attributions for academic performance and the perceived scholastic competence, global self-worth and achievement of children with dyslexia. School Psychology International 22(4): 401–416.

Gerber PJ, Schneiders CA, Paradise LV et al. (1990) Persisting problems of adults with learning disabilities: self-reported comparisons from their school age and adult years. Journal of Learning Disabilities 23: 570–573.

Gjessing HJ, Karlsen B (1989) A Longitudinal Study of Dyslexia. New York: Springer.

Hansford BL, Hattie JA (1982) The relationship between self and achievement/performance measures. Review of Educational Research 52: 123–142.

Herrington M, Hunter-Carsch M (2001) A social interactive model of specific learning difficulties, e.g. dyslexia. In: Hunter-Carsch M (ed.) Dyslexia: A Psychosocial Perspective. London: Whurr.

Humphrey N (2002) Teacher and pupil ratings of self-esteem in developmental dyslexia. British Journal of Special Education 29(1): 29–36.

Humphrey N, Mullins PM (2002) Personal constructs and attribution for academic success and failure in dyslexia. British Journal of Special Education 29(4): 196–203.

Jacobson B, Lowery P, Du Cette J (1986) Attributions of learning disabled children. Journal of Educational Psychology 78: 59–64.

Joiner TE, Wagner KD (1995) Attribution style and depression in children and adolescents: a meta-analytic review. Clinical Psychology Review 15(8): 777–798.

Kistner JA, Osbourne M, Le Verrier L (1988) Causal attributions of learning disabled progress. Journal of Educational Psychology 80: 82–89.

Lerner JW (2000) Learning Disabilities: Theories, Diagnosis and Teaching Strategies, 8th edn. Boston: Houghton Mifflin.

Lewandowski L, Arcangelo K (1994) The social adjustment and self-concept of adults with learning disabilities. Journal of Learning Disabilities 27: 598–605.

Osmond J (1993) The Reality of Dyslexia. London: Cassell.

Reed ES (2001) Towards a cultural ecology of instruction. In: Bakhurst D, Skanker SG (eds) Jerome Bruner: Language, Culture, Self. London: Sage, pp. 116–126.

Resnick MJ, Harter S (1989) Impact of social comparisons on the developing self-perceptions of learning disabled students. Journal of Educational Psychology 81: 631–638.

Riddick B, Sterling C, Farmer M, Morgan S (1999) Self-esteem and anxiety in the educational histories of adult dyslexic students. Dyslexia 5: 227–248.

Rogers CR (1951) Client-Centred Therapy. Boston: Houghton Mifflin.

Saracoglu B, Minden H, Wilchesky M (1989) The adjustment of students with learning disabilities to university and its relationship to self-esteem and self-efficacy. Journal of Learning Disabilities 22: 590–592.

Seligman MEP (1991) Learned Optimism. New York: Knopf.

Skaalvik EM, Hagvet KA (1990) Academic achievement and self-concept: an analysis of causal predominance in a developmental perspective. Journal of Personality and Social Psychology 58: 292–307.

Thomson M (1990) Developmental Dyslexia. London: Whurr.

Thomson M, Hartley GM (1980) Self-esteem in dyslexic children. Academic Therapy 16: 19–36.

Zimmerman IL, Allegrand GN (1965) Personality characteristics and attitudes forward achievement of good and poor readers. Journal of Educational Research 59: 28–30.

15

The Self-concept and Dyslexia

David Pollak

Introduction

This chapter examines the constituent parts of the self-concept and relates them to dyslexia. It explores the socio-emotional aspects of dyslexia and discusses emotional support in higher education. First, some thoughts about discourse.

The concept of discourse in the context of dyslexia

The tensions between identity and self-hood […] may be resolved by examining the term 'discourse' in the context of dyslexia and identity. Ivanic (1998: 17) has examined 'discourse' in relation to identity and literacy, defining it as 'producing and receiving culturally recognised, ideologically shaped representations of reality'. She holds that people take on particular identities through discourse – this is the social construction of identity. Ivanic is analysing the discoursal construction of writer identity, specifically the identity of HE students as academic writers. Her work is pertinent to the present theme, because the concept of dyslexia may be said to be a 'culturally recognised, ideologically shaped representation of reality', and also because, like Ivanic's co-researchers, students labelled dyslexic are expected to express themselves through academic writing, which they usually find it hard to master (Benson et al, 1994; Clark and Ivanic, 1997; Singleton, 1999).

Fairclough (1989) points to a relationship between language and power. He also writes (Fairclough, 1992) about discourse and identity, proposing that discourse contributes to the construction of three elements: social identities and types of self, social relationships between people, and systems of knowledge and belief. As Ivanic (1998: 44) points out, Fairclough 'places the construction of identity in the context of fluctuating cultural and institutional values'. In the context of the present study, examining as it does the discourse of dyslexia in the context of higher education, this statement by Fairclough, even though it refers to spoken discourse, is apposite:

From: Pollak, D., *Dyslexia, the Self and Higher Education: Learning Life Histories of Studies Identified as Dyslexic*, pp. 31–42 (Stoke on Trent and Sterling: Trentham Books, 2005).

… discourse contributes to processes of cultural change, in which the social identities or 'selves' associated with specific domains and institutions are redefined and reconstituted. (Fairclough, 1992: 137)

He adds:

Most if not all analytically separable dimensions of discourse have some implications, direct or indirect, for the construction of the self. (*ibid*, 167)

This is supported by Gee (1990: 143), who defines a discourse as:

… a socially accepted association among ways of using language, of thinking, feeling, believing, valuing, and of acting that can be used to identify oneself as a member of a socially meaningful group.

Wilson (1999) claims that life span stories are the narrative sites of identity production. Linde (1993: 3) makes a similar point when she states that 'an individual needs to have a coherent, acceptable and constantly revised life story'. In order to achieve this, a 'coherence system' is required: Linde names Freudian psychology and astrology as examples of such coherence systems. Students identified as dyslexic may use discourses of dyslexia as coherence systems.

How can people conceptualise their identity? When we focus on self-knowledge in relation to a person's goals (Gerber *et al*, 1992; Gerber *et al*, 1996), we are adopting a cognitive approach to the self. As Markus and Nurius (1987: 158) put it, 'the self-concept is not a unitary or monolithic entity, but rather a system of salient identities or self-schemas that lend structure and meaning to one's self-relevant experiences'. Craib (1998) asserts that while identity is a process rather than a 'thing', the process also involves 'internal negotiation': we have a variety of social identities which may change over time, but membership of these – such as uncle, Councillor, nurse – takes place within our overall identity. Such a process is operating when students talk about whether or not to join a group for dyslexic people; they may be a daughter, a student, an ice hockey player, but are they 'a dyslexic' in the sense of belonging to a club? Craib links this dilemma with anxiety:

One of the ways in which we try to protect ourselves from the anxiety of living is by trying to identify ourselves with something, by trying to make our social identity into our identity. (*op cit*, 170)

This 'narcissistic' process may offer 'reassurance and relief' from social isolation. Markus and Nurius (1987) hold that the self-concept is not constant or static. Rather, there exists a 'working self-concept' (*op cit*, 162): 'that set of self-conceptions that are presently accessible in thought and memory'. They point to the variability of the self-concept: one can feel mature and confident in a work setting, very young in a family setting when being compared with a favoured sibling, and very old when in the company of much younger people. Once again, identity is located in contrasts with others, rather than 'sameness'.

Self-concept

Markus and Nurius (1987: 163) refer to a 'total repertoire of self-conceptions', some of which may be 'domain-specific'. Coopersmith (1967), whose self-esteem inventory is useful in work with school students (Pollak, 1993), believes that self-esteem is developmental: early in life it is relatively undifferentiated, but it gradually becomes more complex and hierarchical. This view is confirmed by Battle (1990), a more recent inventory deviser. Marsh (1992) gives the following outline of such a hierarchical model:

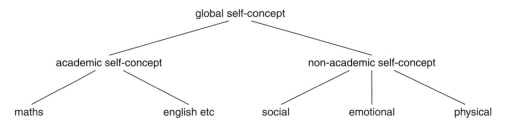

Figure 15.1   Marsh's hierarchical model of the self-concept

Here the items in the lowest row are specific to the domains in which they become salient (see also Schunk, 1990) According to this hierarchical view, whether or not poor self-esteem leads to poor academic performance or vice versa becomes irrelevant: it is seen as an interactional process, with separate components.

Self-esteem

Coopersmith (1967) adopted a similar theoretical approach to devise his self-esteem inventory. He allowed for the estimation of self-esteem in relation to social life (self/peers), home/parents and school/academic aspects, as well as what he called the 'general self' and the 'total self'. If self-concept is the umbrella term involving cognitive, affective and behavioural evaluation of the self (Burns, 1979; Riddick, 1996), then self-esteem is a measure of how far self-image matches the ideal self (Lawrence, 1996). This is Lawrence's diagram of the relationships between them:

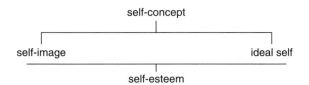

Figure 15.2   Lawrence's model of the self-concept

Lawrence comments on the central role of reading and writing at primary school in this regard, adding that it may not be failure to achieve which produces low self-esteem, but the way significant others react to it.

The notion of an 'ideal self' often develops from the remarks of such significant others: for example, parents and teachers often express expectations of 'good' behaviour, and young children often compare themselves with peers. Kelly usually included 'myself-as-I-would-like-to-be' as an 'element' in his repertory grid work, eliciting constructs by including this figure in triads with other elements such as 'best friend' and 'older sibling' (Kelly, 1955; Winter, 1992).

Among the 'core conditions' for successful psychotherapy, Rogers (1951) includes empathy and positive regard, adding that these principles apply equally to education (Kirschenbaum and Henderson, 1990). Riddick (1996: 34) adds that 'a sense of acceptance, competence and worth' is necessary for a positive self-concept, and that after the family, the school plays a significant role. Teachers are therefore central to developing pupils' self-esteem.

But teachers are as likely to reduce children's self-esteem as they are to enhance it (Lawrence, 1996; Humphrey, 2002). I brought Kelly's personal construct psychology to my investigation of teachers' perceptions of the students at a special school for dyslexic teenagers, and the students' perceptions of themselves (Pollak, 1993). The project confirmed Lawrence's view, which I summarised as the social construction of self-esteem. As one teacher told me, 'we are always looking at pupils, but we don't always get the time to reflect on our own part in this dynamic' (Pollak, 1993). Lawrence added a chapter on 'The teacher's self-esteem' to the second edition of his book on self-esteem in the classroom (Lawrence, 1996); and in my study, another teacher commented that 'teachers have self-esteem needs too' (Pollak, 1993). About the labelling of children with special needs. Salzberger-Wittenberg et al. (1983) point out:

> One way of easing everybody's distress has been by labelling the child as ESN, dyslexic, retarded or maladjusted and so on … Such labels can be used to write children off, as well as, more appropriately, to relieve a self-critical teacher. (Salzberger-Wittenberg et al., 1983: 132)

This view is contradicted by Humphrey (2002), who holds that identification as dyslexic should be carried out as early as possible, so as to enhance children's self-esteem.

There has long been a pecking order in education in the UK. Primary school teaching is seen as of lower status than secondary, FE lower than HE and so on. In the 1970s, it was difficult to find a PGCE course focusing on primary education, as it was assumed that graduates would wish to teach their subjects, ideally to A Level. Similarly, Adult Basic Education is regarded as low status work like what was known as 'remedial' teaching in compulsory education. This is where the desire of some parents to achieve special status for their children as dyslexic may coincide with the wishes of special needs teachers to be regarded as specialists. Much early literature on teaching dyslexic children emphasised this distinction between 'remedial' work and 'dyslexia specialist' teaching (Franklin and Naidoo, 1970; Naidoo, 1972; Newton and Thomson, 1974; Hickey, 1977).

Teachers and the self-concept

Teacher and tutor comments and reports are seen by students as sources of information about the self. Andersen (1987) notes that what others actually say in this 'social feedback' is less important than how these opinions are perceived. For example, students identified as dyslexic commonly contest the marks they have been given (Gilroy, 1995). However, as Riddick (1996) points out, feedback from teachers is only effective for a students if s/he sees the teacher as a significant other and if the teacher's and the student's perceptions of ability are congruent.

A key element in the reception of feedback from teachers is students' sense of their own intelligence. Stuart (Stuart and Thomson, 1995) points out that identity involves gender, cultural heritage and family background; that our perception of our intelligence intersects with all these aspects; and that a professional educator's assessment has particular weight. She quotes Mead (1934) as defining the 'significant other', whose ideas about us are highly likely to be internalised, and the 'generalised other': society as a whole. This theory of the self as generated through symbolic interactions was taken up by Goffman (1959), who described the way in which embarrassment is seen in relation to a contrast between shame and esteem: each time we experience embarrassment, we internalise shame and our self-image is confirmed. This process operates in the education system, and can powerfully affect undergraduates (Peelo, 2000a).

Self-representation

Social feedback is part of the overall process of social interaction. If we are to receive feedback, we must first present ourselves to others. What Ivanic (1998: 21) calls 'the emotionally fraught, usually subconscious nature of self-representation', Goffman (1959) describes in theatrical terms. Goffman differentiates between a person as 'character' and a person as 'performer'. This can apply to the investigation of dyslexia, with people seen as 'putting on' or reproducing socio-culturally constructed identities. Goffman sees identity as 'a status, a position, a social place' (*op cit*, 31).

Interviews of any kind, but particularly those which invite the respondent to remember the past, as in a learning life history, involve the representation of the self to the interviewer. Summerfield (1998) is a valuable source on the nature of self-representation. She refers to what she terms the 'inter-subjectivity' involved in the production of memory: 'the relationship between the narrator and his or her audience' (*ibid*, 23). In terms of the research process, an interviewer may be constructing an identity for him- or herself in each interview, and so may an informant.

Inter-subjectivity encompasses the 'assumption of consciousness, understanding and self in others' (Stevens, 1996: 169). It is thus part of the experiential perspective on the self. On the other hand, object relations theorists such as Klein propose that being attached to and confirmed by others is essential to the determination of the self, and this places inter-subjectivity in the psychodynamic realm (Klein, 1993). Psychotherapists Salzberger-Wittenberg *et al* (1983) believe that psychodynamic theory has a great deal to offer the study of learning and teaching situations. They list the expectations students might have of a teacher. They might see her as: the source of knowledge and wisdom; a provider and comforter; an object of admiration and envy; a judge; an authority figure. Conversely, the teacher might have fears of criticism, hostility or losing control. Either way, say Salzberger-Wittenberg and her colleagues, the teacher–student relationship is loaded with opportunities for transference (*ibid*, Chapters 2 and 3), but they do tend to pathologise this agenda.

In her interview study of the experiences of women during the Second World War, Summerfield (1998) attached labels to the types of attitude adopted by her informants ('heroes' and 'stoics'), seeing these as the images of women prevalent at the time. Summerfield's informants are talking about a relatively short period in British history and looking at their roles within it, whereas obtaining dyslexic students' learning life histories involves them in looking back over their whole lives, educationally speaking. Nevertheless, similar processes can be seen to be taking place.

Summerfield is using personal testimony for the purposes of historical study. 'Women speaking for themselves through personal testimony', she says (1998: 11), 'are using language and so deploying cultural constructions'. So such personal testimony cannot represent a truth which is independent of discourse. This is because, explains Summerfield quoting Scott: 'we are dependent on language for understanding who we are and what we are doing' (*ibid*, 11).

Summerfield proposes that the processes which affect people's memories of the past, far from having the negative effect of distorting the truth in historical terms, create layers of meaning which are worthy of study. Students' words about their experiences of dyslexia can similarly be examined for evidence of the discourses which they represent, since:

> cultural constructions form the discursive context not only within which people express and understand what happens to them, but also within which they actually have those experiences. (Summerfield, 1998: 12)

Hence, the task of the historian working with personal testimony is akin to that of the researcher into the learning life stories of dyslexic students: 'to untangle the relationships between discourses and experiences' (*ibid*).

Summerfield observes that 'there is not likely to be a single discourse at any one time which directly determines consciousness' (*ibid*, 15), and this is also true of students' use of discourses. She refers to 'the discursive formulations from which understandings are selected and within which accounts are made' in oral history. Her interviews showed women using multiple discourses concerning their wartime lives to 'constitute themselves'. Their testimony is inter-subjective in that it draws on 'the generalised subject available in discourse to construct the particular personal subject' (*ibid*, 15). Both these aspects apply equally to learning life history interviews.

However, Summerfield identifies another way in which the process is inter-subjective: the narrator or interviewee is aware of an audience. That audience has two parts: the immediate audience of the interviewer and the public or imagined audience for the research:

> Inter-subjectivity, understood as the relationship between the narrator and his or her audience, is a necessary and inescapable part of the production of memory. (*ibid*, 23)

The socio-emotional aspects of the dyslexia concept

Salzberger-Wittenberg *et al* write about dyslexia, describing the label as a 'psychiatric' one. One of their studies concerns a child whom they call Maurice who was failing to learn to read. His mother had taken him to a clinic and 'obtained a certificate of dyslexia':

> The diagnosis had been carefully made but later discussion with Maurice showed that he had interpreted the word to mean that he had a nasty, infectious illness and that his

brain did not work properly. The sad effect was to make him feel at the mercy of his handicap, reduce his own feeling of control, and, as his teachers reported, seemed quite destructive of his efforts to learn to read. (Salzberger-Wittenberg *et al*, 1983: 133)

Ravenette (1979) found that the label dyslexic led families to see children as disabled. Miles, on the other hand, has written at least once per decade (Miles, 1970, 1988, 1993) of the value of the label in giving children and their families a way of making sense of what is happening and a route out of self-blame.

A report on a British national inquiry into responses to dyslexia was carried out with a working group of EPs, and included contributions from Local Education Authorities and statutory and voluntary bodies (Pumfrey and Reason, 1991). It was one of the first studies on dyslexia that had a chapter on social and emotional factors. The chapter concluded that:

labels, limited to within-child variables, can detract attention from policies and organisation that take account of the full social and interpersonal context in which the learning difficulties arise. (Pumfrey and Reason, 1991: 73)

The report noted 'the need to take account of the sense the child is making of the situation and the perceptions of family members' (*ibid*). Importantly, Pumfrey and Reason recommended that 'specific learning difficulties be examined in the context of personal experiences and interpersonal relationships, recognizing the emotional impact of a prolonged struggle with literacy' (*ibid*, 73).

My study at a special school for dyslexic students (Pollak, 1993) was partly a response to this. I found that by the end of their first year, new students' self-esteem had improved markedly. Using personal construct psychology, the study revealed that they associated reading and writing with positive aspects of their lives. Personal construct psychology also showed that the staff construed the students in widely differing ways, but that they acknowledged that such constructs were 'part of the informal baggage they [brought] into the classroom' and that 'a child's progress depends on how good s/he feels' (Pollak, 1993).

In what was probably the first published response to Pumfrey and Reason's call for further research into socio-emotional aspects, Edwards (1994) examined the 'emotional reactions' of eight 16- to 17-year-old boys who were also attending a special school for dyslexic students. Her case studies reveal uniformly negative relationships with subjects' previous teachers; two thirds of them had been physically attacked, and all had 'suffer[ed] inadequate help or neglect' (Edwards, 1994: 161). On the basis of the boys' response to 'special' schooling, she concludes that 'failure and scarring is not an innate and integral feature of the dyslexic' (*ibid*, 162). However, both this and Pollak (1993) focused on students who had been extracted from mainstream schools and given intensive attention, including deliberate efforts to boost their self-esteem.

Riddick's *Living with dyslexia* (1996), sub-titled 'The social and emotional consequence of specific learning difficulties', also responds to Pumfrey and Reason. She points out that many studies of self-esteem and 'learning difficulties' (such as Butkowsky and Willows, 1980) have focused on reading delay rather than dyslexia and have studied self-esteem only in relation to reading competence.

Riddick (1995) points out that the relationship between teachers and parents of younger students can be particularly stressful for all three parties when there is disagreement over the nature of a child's difficulties. Part of the problem can be, as Pollock and Waller (1994) observe, that the concept of dyslexia is rather like a religion: people are either believers or they are not.

A notable exception to studies which focus only on reading is Rawson's *Dyslexia over the lifespan – fifty-five-year longitudinal study* (Rawson, 1995). This study is of 56 boys, both dyslexic and not, who attended a small private school in Pennsylvania. Rawson states:

> The problem of low self-concept was more prevalent and persistent among the boys who were diagnosed and given help after they had experienced failure, for then it was hard for them to believe that they were as capable and likely to succeed as the accumulating evidence of their competence indicated. (*ibid*, 58)

This appears to contradict Miles' belief in the value of the dyslexic label, although the potential problem might be avoided if screening for dyslexia were a normal, non-stigmatising procedure. Rawson adopts a medical view of dyslexia, quoting in full what was then the Orton Dyslexia Society's definition with its reference to a 'neurologically-based disorder', and stating that the 'diagnosis' must be 'clinical' (*ibid*, 149). So it is not surprising that some of her students did not at first believe they could succeed.

However, it seems that Rawson's school adopted the same philosophy as those referred to above (Pollak, 1993; Edwards, 1994):

> It may be that one of the school's most valuable contributions was to the self-concepts of the dyslexic boys, a persistent faith in their intelligence and capacity to achieve, transmitted to the boys directly and indirectly. (Rawson, 1995: 110)

Bat-Hayim (1997) reports on a course at an American college designed to tackle learned helplessness in students with 'learning disabilities' and 'by-pass long-standing emotional and linguistic barriers to learning'. She refers to one student who failed the course, and later thanked the tutors for the fact that 'he was not permitted to use his well remediated dyslexia as a crutch' (*ibid*, 230).

Hales (1994) attempted a quantitative study of 'some personal aspects of the personal functioning of dyslexic people', using a personality factor questionnaire. He found that infants appeared tense and frustrated, children in the middle school years showed low motivation and high anxiety, whereas at secondary school they wanted to be as unobtrusive as possible. Hales found an inverse relationship between anxiety and IQ, which tends to counter the common belief that intelligent dyslexic children find school life more difficult than their peers.

More than twenty years earlier, a report in the *British Medical Journal* (Saunders and Barker, 1972) had found 'a recognisable neurotic pattern' in a group of dyslexic adults. One had said: 'I want to be a normal person'. This comment may hide a great deal. It suggests a kind of Hawthorne effect in which the experience of being the subject of such research makes people feel abnormal and anxious. Rourke *et al* (1989) listed nine 'neuropsychological characteristics' of children with 'nonverbal learning disability' and used such words as disability, disorder, dysfunction and disease. Their subjects were found to be depressed and suicidal in later years.

Some studies show depression in dyslexic children and adolescents. Maag and Behrens (1989) found that of a sample of 465 high school students, 21 per cent experienced severe depression, although this finding, based on self-report inventories, is complicated by the fact that some of the students had already been identified as 'seriously emotionally disturbed'. A Texas inquiry (Wright-Strawderman and Watson, 1992) found that 35 per cent of the subjects (aged 8 to 11) scored in the depressed range, again using a self-report inventory.

Michaels and Lewandowski (1990) used structured reports by the parents of child subjects. They found that a greater than average proportion of boys with 'learning disabilities' were at risk of developing 'psychological adjustment problems' such as anxiety, depression and obsessive-compulsive behaviour. On the other hand, an Israeli study (Lamm and Epstein, 1992) which used a 'symptom checklist' filled in by teachers, found no difference in terms of 'emotional status' between a dyslexic group of young adults, psychiatric patients or controls. All this supports Little's (1993) strictures as regards generalisability.

Emotional support in higher education

Gilroy (1995), an experienced educational practitioner, makes a practical, realistic contribution. Her chapter in the book *Dyslexia and stress* is called 'Stress factors in the college student'. She writes of the effect of past experiences like these on self-concept:

> … having been branded as 'thick', … being ridiculed and misunderstood, … having struggled hard at school without efforts being recognized. (Gilroy, 1995: 66)

In conversation between members of a student support group at her university, Gilroy notes the frequency of expressions such as 'hopeless at', 'could never' and 'typical me'. She observes that:

> There are certain times in a university career that are particularly stressful for the dyslexic student. The very early days at university can place heavy demands on memory, organisation, orientation. There is the stress of the new environment and the anxiety of coping with new names, relationships, activities and a new lifestyle. (*ibid*, 59)

But this is true for all new students, as others have pointed out (Raaheim *et al.*, 1991; Earwaker, 1992; Peelo, 1994). A recent report by a British Heads of University Counselling Services Working Group (Rana *et al.*, 1999: 1) found that there was 'broad agreement from counselling services that the severity of emotional and behavioural disturbance amongst university students is increasing'. Peelo (2000a, 2000b) believes that learning support tutors must address not only cognitive processes but also affective and social ones.

Gilroy (1995: 56) argues that dyslexic students have 'a specific language disability' the history of which, when combined with associated working memory difficulties, makes them liable to develop stress symptoms more quickly. She admits that those who regard themselves as dyslexic sometimes fail to see that all students must accept negative criticism in order to develop academically. They may 'blame everything on dyslexia' (*ibid*, 62):

> Dyslexia is ever-present in the students' minds; it makes them egocentric, and they cannot think out from themselves. As a result, they become quite demanding over their 'rights' and may go bluntly into a tutor's room to seek 'justice'. (*ibid*, 62)

Goodwin (1996) suggests that tutors need counselling skills to help students 'move on from' feelings of bitterness and anger, as well as from fearing that they will not succeed. She believes (Goodwin, 1998) that individual counselling for dyslexic students should be of the humanistic or 'person-centred' type, as Rogerian positive regard and empathy are essential for clients who are experiencing anxiety and self-doubt. On the other hand, McLoughlin *et al* (1994: 47), while acknowledging the importance of Rogers' 'core conditions', propose that what they call 'generalist' as opposed to 'specialist' counsellors might successfully use a cognitive approach. They explain that 'a dyslexic's understanding of the nature of their difficulties is central to overcoming those difficulties' and that 'maladaptive feelings are caused by irrational beliefs' such as that most other students are very good at spelling or rapid reading.

McLoughlin *et al* go on to describe a vicious circle, in which the memory of being called unintelligent by significant others such as relatives or teachers increases negative feelings; this in turn leads to poor self-esteem and lack of confidence, which reduces motivation; this is then interpreted by others – and probably by the student as well – as evidence of low intelligence. They posit four levels of awareness in adult dyslexic people, claiming that supporting them requires consciousness of their starting point:

> People at level 1 are not aware of their weaknesses and have developed no strategies to overcome them.

> People at level 2 are aware of their weaknesses but have not developed strategies to overcome them.

> People at level 3 are aware of their weaknesses and have developed compensatory strategies, but have developed them unconsciously.

> Finally, people at level 4 are aware of their weaknesses and they have consciously developed strategies to overcome them. (McLoughlin *et al*., 1994: 50)

As regards 'starting points', the report of the NWP differentiates between counselling newly enrolled students and such work with newly identified students. The suggestion is that identification as dyslexic is central: newly admitted students may have recently experienced stressful dyslexia assessment, or be fearing that they will have to go through it, whereas those who have just been identified may need emotional support because 'they need to come to terms with new aspects of themselves' (Singleton, 1999: 134).

> The discovery that one has dyslexia can produce feelings of relief, but it can also generate anxieties. Students exhibit confusion and loss of confidence *because they have only a vague understanding of the nature of the condition at this early stage*. (*ibid*, 134 – author's emphasis)

This part of the Singleton report raises two issues. One is concerned with the use of the word 'identify'. In some quarters, it has become the norm to try to avoid medical language in connection with dyslexia in adults (Hunter-Carsch, 2001; Hunter-Carsch and Herrington, 2001; McLoughlin *et al*, 2002); the Singleton report itself states that the term 'diagnosis' 'will be avoided as far as possible because of "disease" connotations' (*ibid*, 81). The preferred term is 'identification', the root word of which has clear implications for the present study. Yet on the same page as this passage, the NWP report uses the expressions 'students with dyslexia' and 'a student has dyslexia'; in its preferred definition, it refers to dyslexia as a 'condition'. The other issue is the assumption that it is necessary to expound a discourse of dyslexia to a student; the report also recommends that this should be done as part of staff development (*ibid*, Chapter 13). [...]

References

Andersen, S (1987) The role of cultural assumptions in self-concept development. *Self and identity: psychosocial perspectives* edited by K Yardley and T Honess. Chichester, John Wiley

Bat-Hayim, M (1997) Learning to learn: learning therapy in a college classroom. *Annals of Dyslexia* 47: 203–235

Battle, J (1990) *Self-esteem: the new revolution*. Edmonton, James Battle Associates

Benson, N, Gurney, S, Harrison, J and Rimmershaw, R (1994) The place of academic writing in whole life writing. *Worlds of Literacy* edited by D Barton, M Hamilton and R Ivanic. Clevedon, Multilingual Matters

Burns, R (1979) *The self-concept: theory, measurement, development and behaviour*. London, Longman

Butkowsky, IS and Willows, DM (1980) Coginitive-motivational characteristics of children varying in reading ability: evidence for learned helplessness in poor readers. *Journal of Educational Psychology* 72(3): 408–422

Clark, R and Ivanic, R (1997) *The politics of writing*. London, Routledge

Coopersmith, S (1967) *The antecedenents of self-esteem*. San Francisco, Freeman

Craib, I (1998) *Experiencing identity*. London, Sage

Earwaker, J (1992) *Helping and supporting students*. Milton Keynes, Open University Press

Edwards, J (1994) *The scars of dyslexia*. London, Cassell

Fairclough, N (1989) *Language and power*. London, Longman

Fairclough, N (1992) *Discourse and social change*. Cambridge, Polity Press

Franklin, A and Naidoo, S (1970) *Assessment and teaching of dyslexic children*. London, Invalid Children's Aid Association

Gee, JP (1990) Social linguistics and literacies: ideology in discourses. Basingstoke, Falmer. Cited in Boughey, C (2002). 'Naming' students' problems: an analysis of language-related discourses at a South African university. *Teaching in Higher Education* 7(3): 295–307

Gerber, P, Ginsberg, R and Reiff, HB (1992) Identifying alterable patterns in employment success for highly successful adults with learning disabilities. *Journal of Learning Disabilities* 25(8): 475–487

Gerber, P, Reiff, HB and Ginsberg, R (1996) Reframing the learning disabilities experience. *Journal of Learning Disabilities* 29(1): 98–101, 97

Gilroy, D (1995) Stress factors in the college student. *Dyslexia and stress* edited by T Miles and V Varma. London, Whurr

Goffman, E (1959) *The presentation of self in everyday life*. Harmondsworth, Penguin

Goodwin, V (1996) *Counselling of dyslexic students in H.E.* Dyslexia in higher education – practical responses to student and institutional needs, University of Huddersfield

Goodwin, V (1998) *Person-centred counselling for the dyslexic student*. Dyslexia in higher education: learning along the continuum, University of Plymouth

Hales, G ed (1994) *Dyslexia matters*. London, Whurr

Hickey, K (1977) *Dyslexia. A language training course for teachers and learners*. Bath, Better Books

Humphrey, N (2002) Teacher and pupil ratings of self-esteem in developmental dyslexia. *British Journal of Special Education* 29(1): 29–35

Hunter-Carsch, M ed (2001) *Dyslexia: a psychosocial perspective*. London, Whurr

Hunter-Carsch, M and Herrington, M eds (2001) *Dyslexia and effective learning in secondary and tertiary education*. London, Whurr

Ivanic, R (1998) *Writing and identity*. Amsterdam, John Benjamins

Kelly, GA (1955) *The psychology of personal constructs*. New York, WW Norton

Kirschenbaum, H and Henderson, V eds (1990) *The Carl Rogers reader*, London, Constable

Klein, C (1993) *Diagnosing dyslexia*. London, ALBSU

Lamm, O and Epstein, R (1992) Specific reading impairments – are they to be associated with emotional difficulties? *Journal of Learning Disabilities* 25(9): 605–615

Lawrence, D (1996) *Enhancing self-esteem in the classroom*. London, Paul Chapman

Linde, C (1993) *Life stories*. Oxford University Press

Little, S (1993) Nonverbal learning disabilities and socioemotional functioning: a review of recent literature. *Journal of Learning Disabilities* 26(10): 653–665

Maag, J and Behrens, J (1989) Depression and cognitive self-statements of learning disabled and seriously emotionally disturbed adolescents. *Journal of Special Education* 23(1): 17–27

Markus, H and Nurius, P (1987) Possible selves: the interface between motivation and the self-concept. *Self and identity: psychosocial perspectives* edited by K Yardley and T Honess. Chichester, John Wiley

Marsh, H (1992) Content specificity of relations between academic achievement and academic self-concept. *Journal of Educational Psychology* 84(1): 35–42

McLoughlin, D, Fitzgibbon, G and Young, V (1994) *Adult dyslexia: assessment, counselling and training*. London, Whurr

McLoughlin, D, Leather, C and Stringer, P (2002) *The adult dyslexic: interventions and outcomes*. London, Whurr

Mead, M (1934) *Mind, self and society*. Chicago, University of Chicago Press

Michaels, C and Lewandowski, L (1990) Psychological adjustment and family functioning of boys with learning disabilities. *Journal of Learning Disabilities* 23(7): 446–450

Miles, T (1970) *On helping the dyslexic child*. London, Methuen

Miles, T (1988) Counselling in dyslexia. *Counselling Psychology Quarterly* 1(1): 97–107

Miles, T (1993) *Dyslexia: the pattern of difficulties*. London, Whurr

Naidoo, S (1972) *Specific dyslexia*. London, Pitman

Newton, M and Thomson, M (1974) *Dyslexia: a guide to teaching*. Birmingham, University of Aston

Peelo, M (1994) *Helping students with study problems*. Milton Keynes, Open University Press

Peelo, M (2000a) Learning support in universities: counselling or teaching? *Newsletter and Journal of the Association of University and College Counsellors* 4

Peelo, M (2000b) Learning reality: inner and outer journeys. *Changes* 18(2): 118–127

Pollak, D (1993) Increasing staff awareness of the effect of social and emotional factors on the learning of pupils at a special school for children with specific learning difficulties. Unpublished MA, Institute of Continuing and Professional Education, University of Sussex

Pollock, J and Waller, E (1994) *Day-to-day dyslexia in the classroom*. London, Routledge

Pumfrey, P and Reason, R (1991) *Specific learning difficulties (dyslexia) – challenges and responses*. Windsor, NFER-Nelson

Raaheim, K, Wankowski, J and Radford, J (1991) *Helping students to learn*. Buckingham, Open University Press

Rana, R, Smith, E and Walkling, J (1999) *The impact of increasing levels of psychological disturbance amongst students in higher education*. London, Heads of University Counselling Services Working Group

Ravenette, T (1979) Specific reading difficulties: appearance and reality. *Association of Educational Psychologists Journal* 4(10): 1–12

Rawson, M (1995) *Dyslexia over the lifespan: a fifty-five year longitudinal study*. Cambridge, Mass, Educators Publishing Services, Inc

Riddick, B (1995) Dyslexia: dispelling the myths. *Disability and Society* 10(4)

Riddick, B (1996) *Living with dyslexia*. London, Routledge

Rogers, C (1951) *Client-centred therapy*. Boston, Houghton Mifflin

Rourke, BP, Young, GC and Leenaars, AA (1989) A childhood learning disability that predisposes those afflicted to adolescent and adult depression and suicide risk. *Journal of Learning Disbilities* 22(3): 169–175

Salzberger-Wittenberg, I, Henry, G and Osborne, E (1983) *The emotional experiences of learning and teaching*. London, Routledge and Kegan Paul

Saunders, W and Barker, M (1972) Dyslexia as a cause of psychiatric disorder in adults. *British Medical Journal* 4: 759–761

Schunk, D (1990) Self-concept and school achievement. *The social psychology of the primary school* edited by C Rogers and P Kutnick. London, Routledge

Singleton, C ed (1999) *Dyslexia in higher education: policy, provision and practice.* Report of the National Working Party on Dyslexia in Higher Education, University of Hull

Stevens, R ed (1996) *Understanding the self.* London, Sage

Stuart, M and Thomson, A eds (1995) *Engaging with difference: the 'other' in education.* Leicester, NIACE

Summerfield, P (1998) *Reconstructing women's wartime lives.* Manchester, Manchester University Press

Wilson, A (1999) Reading a library – writing a book: the significance of literacies for the prison community. Unpublished PhD thesis, University of Lancaster

Winter, D (1992) *Personal construct psychology in clinical practice.* London, Routledge

Wright-Strawderman, C and Watson, B (1992) The prevalence of depressive symptoms in children with learning disabilities. *Journal of Learning Disabilities* 25(4): 258–264

Part 5

Social Justice, Equity Issues and Learning Disabilities

16

Special Education's Changing Identity: Paradoxes and Dilemmas in Views of Culture and Space

Alfredo J. Artiles

[...]

U.S. classrooms today look dramatically different than they did thirty years ago, before the federal government passed its first comprehensive special education legislation – the Education for All Handicapped Children Act – in 1975. This law was reauthorized as the Individuals with Disabilities Education Act (IDEA) in 1990. Although educators now have theoretically more sophisticated and effective interventions at their disposal for serving students with disabilities, their work also is far more complex and challenging. For instance, as the population of students with disabilities and the proportion of minority students grow rapidly, we are witnessing the inexorable convergence of two of the most important developments in special education's contemporary history, namely, the inclusive education movement[1] and the overrepresentation of racial minority students in special education.[2] The increasing complexity of diversity in terms of racial background and ability level poses significant challenges to the refinement of special education services, the improvement of policies, and the development of a knowledge base, particularly when we acknowledge that the research literature on racial and linguistic minority students is rather thin (Donovan & Cross, 2002; Gersten, Baker, & Pugach, 2001). Moreover, minority overrepresentation and inclusion pose important challenges to special educators' understandings of culture, the role of culture in visions of disability, and the creation of a research ethos that is mindful of cultural differences.

Inclusion and overrepresentation will undoubtedly influence the transformation of special education's identity. Let us remember that a cornerstone of special education's original identity was grounded in a civil rights discourse for people with disabilities. As a result, IDEA was passed to ensure free and appropriate public education, parents' rights to be informed of evaluation and placement decisions (including the right to due process hearings), individualized and nondiscriminatory assessment, individualized educational and related services, education in the least restrictive environment, and federal assistance to support states' and school districts' efforts to educate students with disabilities (Smith, 2001).

The passage and refinement of IDEA was a major accomplishment in the history of special education that has made a difference in the lives of millions of people with disabilities.

From: *Harvard Educational Review*, 73 (2), 2003, pp. 164–202.

However, given ongoing societal and professional transformations, the special education field must still address the following questions:

- How will special education's identity change as this system serves more racially diverse students with disabilities in general education contexts?
- How will understandings of culture be infused in special education's identity?
- How will this field acknowledge race and language background in research practices and how will researchers place these constructs in dynamic grids of cultural influence?
- As understandings of inclusion shift from a spatial location (the general education classroom) to the alignment of educational philosophies with visions of organizational arrangements, how will the new identity of the field account for racial differences, culture, and space?

It is imperative that the discourse communities working on inclusion and overrepresentation begin to craft a dialogue across their respective discourse boundaries to reflect on the implications of their labor for a new, emerging systemic identity.[3] Unfortunately, these discourse communities rarely reflect on their growing overlapping foci or on the implications of such convergence. Hence, in this [chapter], I discuss the intersection of inclusion and overrepresentation as it affects school-age individuals with high-incidence disabilities (particularly learning disabilities). I focus on this group because it comprises the United States' largest segment of the school population with disabilities.[4]

I build my analysis of the literatures on inclusion and overrepresentation on two ideas. First, current special education developments ought to be examined in the context of larger cultural and political processes located in educational reforms and society at large. This examination must include an analysis of the power differentials and struggles that shape the educational outcomes of racial minorities and students with disabilities. Second, the convergence of the inclusion movement and the overrepresentation of minorities in special education create paradoxes and dilemmas that can interfere with the development of socially just educational systems in a democratic society.

In this [chapter], I present the preliminary findings of an analysis of the inclusion and overrepresentation literatures, namely 1) silence about racial diversity in the implementation of inclusive models, 2) lack of vision for a culturally responsive educational system, 3) inadequate attention to sociohistorical context and the complexity of culture, 4) limited definitions of space, and 5) problematic views of difference. I conclude with a discussion of the implications of this analysis for a new generation of inclusion and overrepresentation research. Before developing these ideas, I situate overrepresentation and inclusion in the current cultural politics of educational reform.

The cultural politics of current educational reforms

As I witness the ongoing debates about inclusive education and minority representation in special education, I cannot ignore the contexts in which these conversations are taking place. The most immediate is the sociopolitical context of general education reform. For example, the recent neoconservative tide of reforms largely assumes that schools should produce human capital (Apple, 1996). Neoconservative reformers reason that, in an era of increasing global competition and unprecedented economic progress, schools must produce a skilled and competitive labor force. Apple argues that this premise is ingrained in a larger and more complex cultural agenda that values individualism and competition. Implied in this premise is the idea that the educational system will have winners and losers (see also Varenne & McDermott, 1999).

Policymakers and the general public have generally concluded that in order for the United States to be competitive in this era of globalization, schools must produce the human capital necessary to meet the demands of the new economy. This commitment has generated a number of popular reform ideas, including the incorporation of national standards, curricula, and testing and privatized choice plans (see Apple, 1996, and McLaughlin & Tilstone, 1999, for analytic overviews of these reforms). Due in part to concerns over poor outcomes and low expectations for students with disabilities, the most recent reauthorization of IDEA has incorporated several accountability provisions that align with general education reforms. Examples of such provisions include performance goals and indicators, school-based improvement plans, participation in large-scale assessments, access to the general education curriculum, and greater collaboration between general and special education personnel (McLaughlin & Tilstone, 1999). It is feasible that general and special educators' potentially divergent views of effective instruction might create contradictions in the implementation of these policies (McDonnell, McLaughlin, & Morison, 1997). For example, it is not clear whether the new emphasis on standards-based reform for all students will shortchange students with disabilities as teachers feel compelled to cover content and promote more sophisticated forms of learning, thus leaving less time for teachers to support students who lag behind. Confused about when to modify curriculum versus when to provide instructional accommodations in order to access the curriculum, teachers often feel unprepared to apply this new accountability framework to special education populations (McLaughlin, Henderson, & Rhim, 1998; McLaughlin & Tilstone, 1999).

Apple (1996) argues that neoconservative reforms help to maintain economic and political security for the dominant group, preserve the dominant group's traditional values, and legitimize dominant definitions of knowledge and competence. These reforms ratify a politics of difference that favors neoconservatives because such reforms afford them the privilege to construct and impose exclusionary insider and outsider identities (i.e., 'we' and 'them'). 'We' are homogeneous, hard working, and English speaking, and 'we' do better in all labor, educational, and health outcome measures. In contrast, 'they' are lazy, dirty, heterogeneous, misuse English, and take advantage of the government and the 'We' (Apple, 1996). The consolidation of deficit views about 'them' has drawn attention to issues of difference in education and beyond at a time when the nation is experiencing unprecedented cultural diversification.

Areas in which we observe the interplay between conservative educational reforms and their implicit pursuit of a cultural agenda that privileges dominant groups are language and literacy reform, particularly in the debates over bilingual education and the English-only movement. As these debates polarized, we witnessed the abolition of bilingual education programs in states including California, Arizona, and Massachusetts. These policies have had dreadful consequences as they became embodied in what some call 'backlash pedagogies' (Gutiérrez, Asato, Santos, & Gotanda, 2002), which aim to maintain the status quo that assumes inequality is a natural state of affairs in educational practice and reform. Backlash pedagogies disregard the history of oppression and marginalization suffered by minority populations (Gutiérrez et al., 2002) and are ultimately grounded in colonialist views of literacy and learning.

As we witness the initial implementation of standards, accountability reforms, and English-only initiatives, we must consider the consequences for historically marginalized racial and linguistically diverse groups. For instance, will referrals of English language learners (ELLs) to special education increase? (Artiles, Rueda, Salazar, & Higareda, 2002). How will special education placement for ELLs influence access to the general education curriculum and affect dropout, graduation, or special education exit rates? How will the principles of the inclusive education movement be operationalized when placing ELLs in special education, considering that (a) ELLs are likely to be taught by teachers without credentials (Gándara et al., 2000), (b) there is a dramatic shortage of special education and bilingual teachers (García, 1996; Reynolds & York, 1996), (c) most teachers receive poor training on the influence of language and culture in children's learning (Zeichner & Hoeft, 1996), and (d) teachers have limited experience with collaborative and/or team-teaching arrangements (Smith, 2001)?

These are the cultural politics enclosing the special education field in which an emphasis on individualism and competition, views of competence and literacy that privilege certain groups, and a troubling politics of difference intermingle. We must not lose sight of these cultural politics as we move toward a more inclusive special educational system and grapple with the overrepresentation of minority students in disability programs. An exhaustive analysis of inclusion and overrepresentation is beyond the scope of this [chapter]. Therefore, in the next section, my goal is to sketch their boundaries and highlight key issues as a means to identify paradoxes and dilemmas that exist within and between these literatures.

Outline of the inclusive education movement

Special education legislation requires that students with disabilities be educated in the least restrictive environment (LRE). Although this notion is a fundamental and identifying principle of contemporary special education, it is also one of the most controversial constructs in the field (Smith, 2001). In its early years, special education was provided in self-contained classrooms and separate schools. During the 1970s and 1980s, the LRE requirement allowed schools to mainstream students with disabilities in general education classrooms for a portion of the day, though this practice was done on a voluntary basis (Brantlinger, 1997). In the mid 1980s, Madeline Will, then director of the federal Office of Special Education Programs, challenged the field to transform traditional practices so that more students with disabilities would be integrated into general education classrooms (Will, 1984). These efforts were called the Regular Education Initiative. Although the law requires that LRE be individually determined and that services be available across a continuum of options from most to least integrated, debates ensued between parents, practitioners, policymakers, and researchers about best practices for implementation (Smith, 2001). These debates evolved from discussions about integration (as embodied in the REI) to the development of proposals based on the concept of inclusive education.

The inclusive education movement aims to change a school's ethos and practices to promote truly inclusive models and ultimately to promote student academic learning, social competence, social skills, attitude change, and positive peer relations. In its early years, the movement stressed full inclusion and focused primarily on students with severe disabilities; however, it has steadily expanded to include students with high-incidence disabilities (Fuchs & Fuchs, 1994). The inclusive education movement embodies several important characteristics and beliefs focusing on the student, the teacher, and the system. For example, the movement argues that all children can learn, that learning is supported by a strong sense of community, and that services are based on need rather than limited by location. Also, the movement promotes schoolwide approaches, such as teacher collaboration, enhanced instructional strategies, curriculum accommodations and modifications, and additional supports in general education settings. Finally, the movement focuses on the system, asserting that neighborhood schools enroll natural proportions of students with disabilities and demonstrate a concern for standards and outcomes for all students (Lipsky & Gartner, 1999).

Despite these common characteristics and beliefs, unclear goals and multiple definitions of inclusion seem to permeate the movement's discourse and research practices (Dyson, 1999; Fuch & Fuchs, 1994). For instance, definitions can range from students with disabilities' part- or full-time placement in a general education classroom to the transformation of a school ethos or the construction of entire educational systems based on an inclusive education philosophy (Dyson, 1999). The diversity of definitions and goals of the movement contribute to the creation of multiple discourses. Dyson argues that discourses about inclusion can be organized along two dimensions: (a) the *rationale* for inclusion and (b) the *realization* of inclusion.

Rationale for inclusion

With regard to the rationale dimension, Dyson (1999) identifies two discourses: 1) the rights-and-ethics discourse and 2) the efficacy discourse. The rights-and-ethics discourse uses a civil rights discourse to argue that individuals with disabilities have the fundamental human right to be educated, ideally alongside nondisabled peers (Brantlinger, 1997). This basic right is grounded in ethical principles of fairness and social justice (Lipsky & Gartner, 1999; Skrtic, 1991). According to Dyson (1999), the rights-and-ethics discourse derives from structuralist analyses that suggest that societal inequalities are reproduced in educational systems. Individuals and groups who possess cultural capital have advantages over marginalized or oppressed people with educational and labor opportunities, since educational systems are built on the knowledge and values of dominant groups. When applied to people with disabilities, this critique asserts that special education, a historically segregated system parallel to general education, further privileges certain groups by separating and marginalizing students deemed problematic or difficult. The existence of this system in turn establishes general education as the norm and special education as deviant, and conceals the underlying need to restructure societal conditions. Therefore, the argument follows, special education placement decisions are inextricably linked to issues of equity and social justice. According to the rights-and-ethics discourse, the maintenance of a segregated special education system is incongruous with socially just educational systems, and ultimately with democratic ideals.

Despite the clear logic of this critique, particularly with regard to equity issues, we must acknowledge that competing definitions of social justice that permeate this discourse and the special education field add confusion to an already complex process (Christensen & Rizvi, 1996). For instance, current reforms based on notions of free market and choice, which in turn are grounded in individualistic meritocratic principles, define social justice as fairness of opportunity for individuals. As such, 'social justice is no longer "seen as linked to past group oppression and disadvantage" judged historically, but represented simply as a matter of guaranteeing individual choice under the conditions of a "free market"' (Rizvi & Lingard, 1996, p. 15).

Conversely, within the rights-and-ethics discourse, social justice is defined as the access to and the redistribution of general education resources for students with disabilities. Unfortunately, as Rizvi and Lingard (1996) argue, even this distributive view is limited, for it does not 'account adequately for either contemporary politics of difference, or the various complex ways in which exclusion and discrimination are now practiced, in both their individual and institutional forms' (p. 21). This is indeed a major shortcoming of this discourse in light of the growing overrepresentation of minorities in special education, which I take up in more detail in the following section.

The rationale based on the efficacy discourse is closely aligned with the rights-and-ethics thesis. This rationale cites evidence that suggests that students with disabilities who are placed in segregated programs do not exhibit greater educational gains than comparable peers educated in integrated contexts. Evidence is also cited about the lack of differentiation between the instructional practices observed in programs for various disabilities and general education classrooms (Lipsky & Gartner, 1996). This discourse's underlying view of social justice is also based on the aforementioned arguments of access and equity. Unfortunately, access does not guarantee meaningful participation, full membership, or more comparable outcomes (Rizvi & Lingard, 1996).

Realization of inclusion

In addition to the discourses advanced to justify the creation of an inclusive educational system, visions of how such a system ought to be realized have been proposed. Dyson (1999) labels these discourses political and pragmatic. The political discourse is concerned with developing forms of resistance against the interest groups that uphold the traditional special education system. For example, the inclusion movement has faced strong resistance from segments of the special education professional community and it has spurred heated debates in professional journals and conferences. Some of these discussions revolve around technical issues, such as empirical bases of arguments or lack of specificity in proposed models (Fuchs & Fuchs, 1994; Kauffman & Hallahan, 1995; Wang & Walberg, 1988). Others are ideological or rhetorical, focusing on values and beliefs about learning, teaching, disability, research, and meanings of expressions such as 'all children' (Brantlinger, 1997; Gartner & Lipsky, 1987; Pugach & Lilly, 1984; Stainback & Stainback, 1991).[5]

The pragmatic discourse has received by far the most attention from researchers. This discourse addresses what inclusive education programs and schools do and should look like. Some scholars have developed profiles of inclusive schools related to the ethos, structures, and processes in such contexts, while others have offered conceptual analyses of the fundamental differences between inclusive and non-inclusive schools (Skrtic, 1991; Villa & Thousand, 1995). It is common to find within this discourse practical materials and guides for teachers and administrators interested in developing inclusive programs and schools (Dyson, 1999). A potentially damaging consequence of the pragmatic discourse is that educators might become overly concerned with how to allocate human and material resources, carry out procedures, or create regulatory stipulations aimed at compensating for or avoiding discriminatory practices (Slee, 1996).

A review of research based on the pragmatic discourse reflects the following findings about the inclusion of students with disabilities in general education contexts (U.S. Department of Education, 1999): (a) higher frequency of interactions with nondisabled peers; (b) larger and more enduring nondisabled peer networks; (c) improved social and communication skills (e.g., initiation, self-regulation, choice, contact termination); (d) variations in relationships and status similar to friendships observed among nondisabled students; (e) contingent upon the types of assistance provided, adults as positive mediators of friendships between students with and without disabilities; (f) gains in some academic areas; and (g) success with cooperative learning and peer tutoring, although the impact of mixed-ability grouping on disabled student learning is inconclusive. Some studies that focus on students with learning disabilities find that these students do not always participate meaningfully in general education classrooms. They also show that instruction for this group is undifferentiated. Overall, the results of research 'to improve the quality of instruction provided to students with disabilities in general education classrooms ... have been mixed' (Gersten et al., 2001, p. 699). A few studies suggest that the presence of students with disabilities in inclusive contexts does not have a negative effect on nondisabled students' developmental or academic outcomes (e.g., Staub, 2000). Some argue that gains for nondisabled students is the most consistent finding in this line of inquiry (Manset & Semmel, 1997).

Overview of minority representation in special education

The special education population is increasingly segregated along racial lines, as reflected in the disproportionate representation of these minorities in such programs (Donovan & Cross, 2002; Dunn, 1968). While both over- and underrepresentation patterns are associated with disproportionality (Artiles & Trent, 2000), overrepresentation has by far received the most attention in the literature. African Americans and American Indians are most affected by overrepresentation, mostly in the high-incidence disability categories such as LD, MMR, and ED (see note 4).

Considerable efforts and resources have been spent to understand and address this problem, perhaps with more intensity in recent years. Over the last three decades, insights and alternative solutions to this problem have come about through litigation, new legal requirements, active lobbying and advocacy from professional state, and civil rights groups, two National Research Council (NRC) reports (Donovan & Cross, 2002; Heller, Holtzman, & Messick, 1982), and increasing attention and support from the federal government (e.g., funding of research, technical assistance, and training projects,[6] coverage in recent annual reports to Congress, and attention from high-level administrators in official speeches, reports, and statements) (Hehir, 2002). Unfortunately, the problem is still reflected in current enrollment statistics (Losen & Orfield, 2002).

Although few question whether overrepresentation exists, there is some disagreement about the causes and magnitude of the problem, and some have even asked why overrepresentation is a problem (see Artiles, Trent, & Palmer, 2004). Proposed causes cover a wide range; at opposite extremes of this range we find institutional racism and child poverty. The institutional racism thesis is based on social reproduction theory and argues that minority groups' overrepresentation in special education reflects their oppressed and marginalized status in society. Child poverty has also been offered as the cause of this predicament. The latest NRC report (Donovan & Cross, 2002) devoted a great deal of attention to this issue and summarized an extensive literature on the association between poverty and risk for disability. Unfortunately, to our dismay, 'we know precious little about the intervening dynamics that connect socioeconomic status to disability' (Fujiura & Yamaki, 2000, p. 196). Sociological and cultural analyses about the connection between child poverty and disability are rarely conducted in the special education field, and thus we rarely consider the historical, cultural, and structural antecedents of the systematic link between poverty, race, and disability (Slee, 1996). A result of this is the implementation of deficit-based studies that overlook the forces that can protect children's development even when they live in dreadful conditions (McLoyd, 1998). Research that aims to document children's deficits also ignores the structural correlates of poverty – for example, schools that serve poor minority students have significantly fewer material and financial resources, lower teacher and instructional quality, and bleak school climates. The existing literature in this field generally falls into two categories: research on placement patterns and research on the precursors to placement, both of which I discuss next.

Racial minority overrepresentation: placement patterns

The bulk of the overrepresentation literature focuses on special education placement patterns in various disability categories. Findings suggest that overrepresentation patterns vary, depending on whether the data are disaggregated by geographic location, ethnicity, or disability program. Overrepresentation trends can also vary according to ethnic representation in the school population, year, and indicator used (Artiles et al., 2002; Donovan & Cross, 2002; Finn, 1982; Reschly, 1997).

Based on 1998 data, the latest NRC report (Donovan & Cross, 2002) indicates that at the national level, 12 percent of all students are served in special education, whereas the risk indices by ethnic group are as follows: 13.1 percent for American Indians, 14.3 percent for African Americans, 11.3 percent for Latinos/as, 5.3 percent for Asian Americans, and 12.1 percent for Whites. When racial minorities' placement rates are compared with White students (using odds ratios)[7] across all disabilities, only African Americans (1.18) and American Indians (1.08) are overrepresented (Donovan & Cross, 2002). There is some variability when the data are disaggregated by disability category. African Americans are overrepresented in mental retardation (MR) (2.35), LD (1.08), ED (1.59), and developmental delay (2.06). These patterns reiterate a consistent finding over the history of this problem regarding African Americans. American Indians are also overrepresented in MR (1.07) and LD (1.2) programs. Latinos are slightly overrepresented in LD (1.12), and Asian Americans are underrepresented in all high-incidence categories.[8]

Several caveats relate to the analysis of placement patterns such as problems with the procedures used to collect data for national datasets, variability in the definition and eligibility criteria for disability across states, and lack of data on factors that could deepen understanding of the contexts of overrepresentation (e.g., teachers' and administrators' beliefs, school climate, quality of instruction, and quality of prereferral interventions). For example, based on data gathered in New York's urban schools, Gottlieb, Alter, Gottlieb, and Wishner (1994) concluded that the fact that '1 in 6 students with LD have IQ scores that could render them eligible for classification as mentally retarded calls into question the definition of learning disabilities that is being applied' (p. 455). Thus, it seems that the LD category, which used to be reserved mostly for White middle-class students, may be becoming a repository for poor ethnic minorities, many of whom come from immigrant or migrant families (Gottlieb et al., 1994). Sometimes these placement decisions may be made to avoid accusations of bias due to the greater stigma of the MMR category or out of fear of litigation: other times, as Gottlieb et al. suggest, decisions are based on the need to use scarce resources for low-achieving students.

Racial minority overrepresentation: precursors to placement

An alternative strand of overrepresentation research is concerned with the precursors to special education placement. Thus, studies have examined referral, assessment, and decisionmaking processes (Artiles & Pak, 2000; Harry, Klingner, Sturges, & Moore, 2002; Mehan, Hartwick, & Meihls, 1986; Varenne & McDermott, 1999). Some studies have examined bias in referral and placement decisions as associated with teacher gender, race, classroom management ability, and beliefs, whereas other work has assessed the influence of examiner and test (content and development) biases in disability diagnoses (see Donovan & Cross, 2002, for a review of this literature).

Overrepresentation has received closer scrutiny in recent years and a new wave of evidence on the potential antecedents of placement is emerging (e.g., Losen & Orfield, 2002). For instance, funding seems to be associated with minority placement patterns. Parrish (2002) concluded that:

> variation in the type of special education funding system suggests that funding systems based on category of disability are particularly prone to troubling patterns of minority overrepresentation and resource distribution. These systems appear much more likely to show overrepresentation of minority students into the disability category mental retardation, while at the same time providing greater special education funding to districts enrolling the lowest percentages of minority students. (p. 33)

Studies have also begun to document the complex interactions between school location, disability category, ethnic group, poverty, and proportion of minority school enrollment. For instance, Oswald, Coutinho, Best, and Singh (1999) documented interactions between demographic variables and overrepresentation patterns and found that Black overrepresentation in MR programs is associated with an increase in poverty, while overrepresentation in the ED category is associated with a decrease in poverty (Oswald et al., 1999). More recently, Oswald, Coutinho, and Best (2002) reported that American Indians were overrepresented in predominantly minority communities, most visibly in ED. Furthermore, 'as communities become increasingly Nonwhite, however, white students are substantially less likely to be identified as LD. For Black students, particularly Black male students, living in a community with few Nonwhite students is a substantial risk factor for MR and SED [serious emotional disturbance] identification' (p. 9).

Another factor that could shape placement patterns is the availability of alternative programs (e.g., bilingual education), proportional representation in the district population, and district size. There is evidence, for instance, that Latino overrepresentation as MR was sizable in small districts with high Latino enrollment (i.e., over 70%) (Finn, 1982). Finn reported that overrepresentation was negatively related to the proportion of students placed in bilingual programs. A significant gap in the recent NRC report (Donovan & Cross, 2002) was the discussion of ELL placement in special education; there is indeed an urgent need to conduct more research with this population (Artiles et al., 2002; Ortiz, 1997).

Several important reforms are being implemented in general and special education that may ultimately influence placement in special education. Three such reforms include standards, high-stakes testing, and zero tolerance policies. Minority students are predicted to be most affected by these initiatives, but we are only beginning to study the impact of these reforms (Advancement Project & Civil Rights Project, 2000). For instance, we need more research to understand the impact of high-stakes tests on minority students and on the referral rates to special education. The results of these tests should be examined in conjunction with other indicators such as dropout rates (paying attention to who was included/ excluded in this index) and grade retention rates (Heubert, 2002). Impact assessments of these tests should also verify who was included or excluded in the tests, the procedures used to give the tests (particularly with minority students), and the potential impact of inappropriate accommodations (Heubert, 2002). Although increasing numbers of students with disabilities are passing high-stakes tests in recent years, these students continue to lag behind their nondisabled peers.

The specter of bias is always (tacitly or explicitly) present in discussions and analyses of this problem. Unfortunately, little unequivocal evidence is available. In this vein, the latest NRC report concluded that 'the evidence available is insufficient to support a claim that *either* discrimination does or does not play a significant role' (Donovan & Cross, 2002, p. 78, emphasis in original). Nevertheless, given the historical legacies of discrimination and racism in our society, we cannot afford to ignore the potential mediating effect of bias on overrepresentation. Two key tasks for future efforts include addressing bias explicitly in research efforts and broadening the conceptualization of bias. As we suggested recently, 'bias is not restricted to the actions and decisions of individuals. Bias can also take the form of historical residue and can be found in the social structures of educational settings and institutional regulations and practices that shape institutional discrimination' (Artiles et al., in press).

Overrepresentation is a multidimensional predicament with deep historical and systemic roots, and there are many areas and factors that need to be studied and initiatives that need to be pursued. Perhaps the two most urgent areas of action are the production of more and better data to understand this problem and the need to enforce IDEA'S mandates to monitor and prevent it.[9] However, it is beyond the scope of this [chapter] to discuss future directions (see Artiles et al., in press; Donovan & Cross, 2002; Losen & Orfield, 2002).

To conclude, it is important to ask, what is at the heart of the overrepresentation problem? Would the problem be solved with quotas so that racial minority students are proportionally represented in general and special education? Is overrepresentation a symptom of massive bias toward racial minorities? Is racial minority overrepresentation justified, given the higher poverty rate in these populations? Why is special education placement deemed negative if it embodies desirable features (e.g., individualized education, higher per-pupil expenditures, smaller teacher–student ratio) (Reschly, 1997)? Answers to these questions are not straightforward. The problem will not be solved with quotas, and it is an oversimplification to blame it on either massive bias or child poverty. Part of the problem is whether we are adequately addressing students' educational potential and needs; from this perspective, false positives and negatives are equally problematic. Let us remember that special education placement is a highly consequential decision, as disability labels carry visible stigma and have other high-cost repercussions. It adds another layer of difference to racial minorities, restricts their access to high-currency educational programs and opportunities, and further limits their long-term educational outcomes, as special education populations have lower graduation, higher dropout, and lower academic achievement rates than their general education counterparts. We should be aware, however, that the overrepresentation debate affords us the opportunity to shift our gaze inward and examine our assumptions about culture. We need to ask tough questions about the role of culture and power in learning and dis/ability and the visions that inform the work we do with students who have historically faced great adversity because of their skin color or the language they speak. My expectation is that such introspection will contribute to the creation of a pluralistic educational system that informs its research knowledge base with a historical and cultural consciousness. The analyses presented in this [chapter] represent one step in this direction.

Silence in the inclusion and overrepresentation discourses

A troubling fact evident in the preceding review of the overrepresentation and inclusion scholarship is the silence in and between these literatures. Special education is indeed engaged in an active process of identity transformation as it strives to make services and policies more inclusive. However, such efforts seem to portray educators and students as devoid of sociohistorical identities, even though a sizable segment of the special education population comes from nonmainstream racial, social-class, and linguistic backgrounds. Furthermore, the majority of students entering the special education system in the largest U.S. school districts are ethnic and linguistic minorities. The scholarship on minority placement in special education is silent about the implications of the inclusive education movement. The fact that there is silence in both the overrepresentation and inclusion literatures suggests that it is socially shared. But how can we interpret these silences? And what can we learn from theorizing silence?

The silence on issues of race in the implementation discourse of inclusive education is a major oversight, considering that the history and status of minority groups in our society play major roles in minority students' educational experiences and outcomes. Historically, minority students have been perceived as lacking the skills, experiences, and dispositions to be successful in general education, and, indeed, we know academic achievement is correlated with ethnicity, language background, and social class (Valencia, 1997). Thus, minority students exit general education and move into special education with a deficit identity that foregrounds the aforementioned markers of difference. When diversity is summoned in the inclusion literature (mainly in the rationale scholarship), it is generally associated with diversity of ability level – indeed an important aspect of diversity – but the plight of minority students is tangentially recognized in the implementation discourse. It is paradoxical that, as the inclusive education movement represents the emergence of empowered voices about disability rights and better educational services for this population, it has been painfully silent about the plight of minority students.

It is also paradoxical that, due to the inclusion movement, minority students might be returning to general education, but with an identity that adds an additional layer of difference – that is, a label adding ability to the composite of racial, linguistic, and social-class markers.[10] This new identity dispensed by the special education system legitimizes the surveillance of these students through legal and technical means (Erickson, 1996). It can also help to perpetuate the poor school outcomes of minorities, since disability status (particularly MR) is correlated with high dropout rates, low school completion rates, low special education exit rates, and poor employment outcomes (Gottlieb et al., 1994; U.S. Department of Education, 1997; Wagner et al., 1993).

Moreover, let us remember that minority students with disabilities are returning to a general education system that is fraught with paradoxical policies and reform pressures, as reflected in the tensions between the push for individual entitlement to the same treatment (same standards and curriculum access) and entitlement to differential treatments (individualized education) (McLaughlin, Fuchs, & Hardman, 1999). It is not clear how this paradoxical situation will be resolved, and it will be interesting to trace whether these reforms are enforced differentially with various segments of the population with disabilities (e.g., minority v. nonminority students) or whether these reforms will benefit certain groups (e.g., nonminority students).

Scholars working on overrepresentation (including myself) are guilty of a silence on the implications of the realization of inclusion for minority students. Although culture (as a way of life) is acknowledged, the dominant overrepresentation discourse seems to favor a deficit view of traditionally silent groups – that is, racial minority groups (Donovan & Cross, 2002). There is a conspicuous silence about the oppressive weight of structural discrimination and about the cultural power, legitimacy, and competence of minority groups; furthermore, this scholarship is painfully devoid of the voices of minority families and students. However, as Sheriff (2000) warns, silence should not be interpreted as oppressed groups' 'acceptance of dominant ideology' (p. 118). I argue that we will enhance our understanding of overrepresentation as we scrutinize the contradictory explanations of this predicament and face the silences that emerge from such analyses.

The discourse on the realization of inclusion, on the other hand, assumes White middle-class student experience as the norm, because race and student cultural practices are rarely mentioned. If we consider that the history of a field is built in part through the production of scholarship, we cannot deny that inclusion will be regarded in the future as a critical era in the history of special education. But how will we explain to the future generation of educators and the families they serve that those who benefited from inclusion had no race, class, or culture? We must contest this approach to the production of collective memory.

One potentially fruitful path is to analyze these silences as forms of cultural censorship. Sider explains that 'the creation of culture is also, simultaneously and necessarily, the creation of silence ... We can have no significant understanding of any culture unless we also know the silences that were *institutionally* created and guaranteed along with it' (cited in Sheriff, 2000, p. 118, emphasis in original). Historically, the research community has created a silence about ethnic, racial, class, gender, and linguistic differences, as evidenced in a major analysis of contemporary special education research. Less than 3 percent of the empirical research published in four peer-reviewed special education journals over a 22-year period (1975–1994) examined data across ethnic and social class lines (Artiles et al., 1997).[11]

An important implication of this finding is that we must strive to understand the goals and functions of the institutionalization of silences about difference in the culture of special education scholarship. Walker (1999) explains that questions about culture are kept on the periphery of educational researchers' socialization. Future researchers are taught that culture should be controlled, that it amounts to variance that ought to be held constant, or worse, it is ignored because the lessons learned from White middle-class samples are assumed to be universal. Similar to the process of historical production (Trouillot, 1995), silences enter research processes at various crucial points: the moment of question formulation or problem statement, the moment of source identification or participant recruitment, the moment of fact creation or assembly (design of data collection tools and actual data collection), or the moment of fact retrieval and retrospective significance (data analysis and final writing).

As I acknowledged at the beginning of this [chapter], special education researchers have made important advances in the development of a scientific knowledge base. However, as this analysis suggests, researchers need to make visible the object of analysis, the language of analysis, and the position of the analyst (Geertz, 1983) to interrogate the identified silences and begin the critique and transformation of the existing knowledge base, the curricula, and the apprenticeship systems of doctoral and teacher education programs. Critiques and analyses of past research efforts should be mindful of the fact that there is always a presence in the past; as Trouillot (1995) reminds us, 'It could not just be The Past. It had to be someone's past' (p. 142). Whose past is represented in the special education scholarship? What is the presence that authored the special education scholarship? To conclude, we find ourselves in a situation in which culture or 'culturally different' students are 'overlooked' (Bhabha, 1994) in the double sense of social surveillance, as in the overrepresentation literature and of invisibility as in the inclusion scholarship. We must end these silences so that we better inform future analysis of inclusion and overrepresentation and deepen our understanding of the processes that lead to and the consequences of overrepresentation patterns in inclusive contexts.

Visions of culture

The inclusion and overrepresentation discourse communities are concerned with issues of culture: the former in terms of issues of professional and organizational cultures, the latter of cultural issues related to student characteristics. Culture, however, is not easily defined, as is reflected in its multiple definitions. In fact, Williams (1983) states that culture is one of the most complicated notions in the English language. In his review of the concept, Brightman (1995) concludes: 'Unstable in meaning and reference both synchronically and over time, the culture construct has exhibited exceptional lability' (p. 539). Space constraints prevent me from presenting an exhaustive analysis of this construct (see reviews in Brightman, 1995; Eagleton, 2000; Eisenhart, 2001; Erickson, 2001; Gallego et al., 2001; Rogoff & Angelillo, 2002; Varenne, 1984). Instead, I discuss the most common views of culture that permeate scholarship on inclusion and overrepresentation. I frame this discussion in the context of a description of culture's five primary underlying dimensions: cohesion, stability, location, temporality, and power.[12]

The cohesion and stability of culture

Culture's underlying dimensions of cohesion and stability embody dialectical tensions between culture as homogeneous v. variable, ahistorical v. ever-changing, and reproductive v. improvisational (Brightman, 1995; Rogoff & Angelillo, 2002; Varenne, 1984). The scholarship on overrepresentation and inclusion favors distinct poles in each of these dialectical tensions.

Culture is assumed to be cohesive, to embody characteristics that are distinctive and clearly differentiate cultural groups. Group patterning serves a critical function, for it provides a sense of identity; it allows members of a group to recognize who is and who is not a member of their group (Erickson, 2001). It is also important to recognize that within-group diversity exists in every culture, as individuals are not mere replicas of their cultural histories. Individuals use their agency as they cope with life circumstances to create unique life histories, and such a process contributes to the creation of within-group and within-individual diversity (Anzaldúa, 1999). Culture is also assumed to be stable and can be regarded as fossilized. In such cases, culture is both cohesive and stable, since it is conceptualized as if there is a bounded culture that never changes. Although culture must be transmitted across generations so that newcomers can build on their ancestors' legacies, it is equally critical that cultures evolve and change in order to survive (Erickson, 2001).

An important insight is that cohesion and stability of culture embody dialectical tensions between group traits and within group diversity and between enduring legacies and cultural change. Disparate conceptions of culture emerge, depending on whether scholars privilege certain elements of these dialectical tensions over others. For instance, a common conception of culture in special education scholarship is 'culture as a way of life.' According to this view, the work of researchers is to document the cohesion and stability of a group's culture. A key assumption is that culture has effects that are independent from other potentially salient variables, which 'warrants reification and essentialization' (Handwerker, 2002, p. 108); moreover, culture represents a successful adaptation to relatively constant external conditions. It is further assumed that such a cohesive 'way of life' (culture) is transmitted to the next generation through socialization processes (e.g., child rearing). Thus, unless external conditions vary, culture remains stable over time; culture is seen as cohesive and stable.

The overrepresentation scholarship tends to stress two distinct analyses of the problem that ultimately rest on the view of culture as a way of life. One argument is that minorities are disproportionately placed in special education because these groups have distinctive cultures that are incongruent with the school culture.[13] This thesis assumes that misunderstandings and conflict arise when groups that have developed different ways of life come into contact (see Heath, 1983; Vogt, Jordan, & Tharp, 1993, for discussions of this theory in general education contexts). Prescriptions, interventions, and models have been advanced (and often succeeded) to bridge these discontinuities and improve minority students' experiences and outcomes in school (Eisenhart, 2001). The second argument is that racial minority students are disproportionately exposed to the culture of poverty that hinders their development and may put them in a situation that merits special education interventions (Donovan & Cross, 2002).

In turn, the inclusion discourse community uses various perspectives on culture. Let us remember that this literature focuses on the rationale and implementation of inclusion (Dyson, 1999). The work on the rationale tends to focus on the culture of institutions (e.g., schools, classrooms, groups), particularly their histories, assumptions, and traits, and bases its arguments on a view of culture as cohesive and stable over time. Schools organize activities, define roles for teachers and students, and create rules to privilege nondisabled middle-class students. Procedures and other institutional processes are orchestrated to instill in students particular (affective, cognitive) dispositions that reproduce their status in society. A critique of this view is that it is deterministic; the agent is stripped of strategy and improvisation (Brightman, 1995).

Although not always articulated explicitly, this literature relies on a social reproduction thesis. Social reproduction theory is grounded in Marxist precepts of the role of social class in society. Individuals relate to the means of production in routine activities and by assuming particular occupations. Over time, constellations of groups and families develop a shared history of relations to these means of production, which in turn produces a collective cosmovision, 'a set of symbolic and conceptual forms by which a group's social class circumstances are made to seem reasonable and "natural"' (Eisenhart, 2001, p. 212). This view of culture privileges a sociological imagination and foregrounds how cultures are reproduced across generations so that groups maintain their status; school is regarded as a primary site where reproductive processes take place (Anyon, 1997; Bowles & Gintis, 1976; Willis, 1977). This strand of the inclusion literature does not do justice to the perennial tension between cultural reproduction and cultural transformation. Instead, the rationale discourse privileges the reproduction thesis to justify inclusion.

In contrast, the implementation discourse is concerned primarily with cultural change as inclusionists strive to transform the culture of traditional schools. Because there is hardly any acknowledgement of the presence of minorities in special education in the inclusion implementation literature, and considering the history of marginalization of racial minorities in our society, I argue that attention to cultural reproduction processes is imperative. The implementation of inclusion must take into account the reproduction of the historical circumstances that marginalize minority students in the general education system and society at large. This means inclusion scholarship ought to transcend notions of difference based on ability and acknowledge more structural forces that shape minority students' experiences in general and special education alike.

Interestingly, the implementation-of-inclusion literature is grounded in two perspectives of culture, namely, a way-of-life and an interpretivist view. The former is reflected in descriptions of the cohesive and stable cultures of inclusive schools or in comparisons between inclusive and non-inclusive schools. This perspective highlights distinctive structures and processes, with prescriptions for practitioners for the engineering of cogent school cultures that are mindful of inclusion. The interpretivist perspective holds that individuals can actively transform the meanings brought from home as they negotiate their place and roles in the groups they encounter in schools and other contexts (Erickson, 1996); as a result, new meanings, ways to interpret the world, and practices (i.e., idiocultures) can be created. The inclusion work in this tradition either describes inclusive conditions/experiences or assesses the impact of interventions by looking at the meaning-making processes between disabled and nondisabled students in general education instructional (e.g., peer tutoring, cooperative learning groups) or social contexts (e.g., peer networks, communication skills, status, friendships, types of assistance to mediate interactional processes and outcomes). A vision of culture as a meaning-making process privileges the situatedness of social events and implicitly honors the within-group diversity embodied in the individual-in-action (though it does not disregard cohesion). Culture as a meaning-making process opens a space for cultural transformation since it concentrates on the unpredictable construction of local processes.

The location of culture

Depending on its definition, culture can be located internally and externally.[14] The former locates culture in the values, beliefs, worldviews, schemas, and knowledge that people develop locally to navigate the world, solve problems, and attain goals. When located internally, culture is ideational: it is inside the mind of individuals. The work on overrepresentation relies heavily on the internal location of culture. This 'subjective knowledge' view assumes that membership in a given ethnic racial, gender, social-class, ability, or linguistic group will produce distinctive patterns of beliefs, behaviors, customs, values, and so forth. It follows that such groups possess distinctive and homogeneous cognitive, communication, and relational patterns (Cole, 1996); a popular example is the idea of minorities' unique learning styles (see a critical review of the learning styles literature in Irvine & York, 1995). The interactions between markers of difference (e.g., race, ability, gender, language background, social class) are not explored. The scholarship on overrepresentation either argues that educators must be mindful of the distinctive traits of racial groups to avoid misunderstandings that lead to special education placement, or that the distinguishing cognitive and social deficits that characterize poor racial minorities explain their greater need for special education.

Culture can also be located externally, in the historical residues of institutional rules and practices, in the routines and expected ways of using language and nonverbal behavior, and in the social rituals, practices, and predictable means to coordinate actions. Note that these 'external' aspects are typically invisible to members of a cultural group, for they have grown accustomed to them (Cole, 1996). The external or 'material practices' view is applied to any group that interacts over time; studies of the dominant discourse in U.S. classrooms along with its concomitant social and cognitive consequences illustrate this perspective. The inclusion literature has used an external view of culture as the characteristics, values, and practices of either traditional or inclusive school organizations are identified. The internal/external dichotomy oversimplifies the complex locations of culture.

The temporality of culture

Culture has temporal properties. Researchers study the cohesion, stability, and location of culture across time. To illustrate, we know that changes in a group's culture (cultural history) occur at a faster speed than changes in the history of a species (phylogeny), while cultural historical change proceeds at a slower pace than changes in the life history of an individual (ontogeny) (Cole, 1996). Moving down one level in this hierarchy of temporal scales to the microgenesis of events (moment-to-moment history), one could ask, 'How do moments add up to lives? How do our shared moments together add up to social life as such?' (Lemke, 2000, p. 273). Lemke uses the term *temporal heterarchy* to describe the 'interdependence of processes at very different timescales … of an organizational hierarchy in a complex self-organizing system' (p. 280). These levels of history unfold simultaneously and are interdependent (Scribner, 1985).[15]

The integration of these scales enables us to depict the temporality of culture (see Figure 16.1). The vertical axis represents the time scales that correspond to phylogenetic (the history of a species), cultural historical (the history of a group, institution, or society), ontogenetic (history

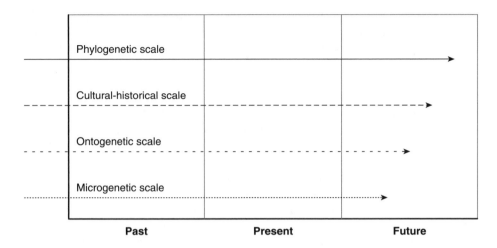

Figure 16.1   Distribution of Culture across Time Scales (adapted from Cole and Engestrom, 1993)

of an individual over his or her lifespan), and microgenetic (the history of moment-to-moment lived experience) levels. The vertical axis also suggests that there is a hierarchy of embedded temporal scales that vary according to the level of temporal aggregation at which we examine culture. The horizontal axis depicts the temporality of culture with respect to the past, present, and future, which allows us to conduct synchronic (at a given point in time) and diachronic (across time) analyses; in this vein, Cole and Engestrom (1993) remind us that 'only a culture-using human being can' "reach into" the cultural past, project it into the future, and then "carry" that (purely conceptual) future "back" into the present in the shape of beliefs that then constrain and organize the present sociocultural environment' (p. 21).[16]

This differentiation of time scales contributes to explanations of cultural reproduction and cultural change. The cultural historical level represents the cultural patterning of a group, community, institution, or society that is reproduced from one generation to the next via apprenticeship processes (e.g., child-rearing practices).[17] When culture is studied at the cultural historical level, we find an emphasis on aspects such as ethnic groups' distinctive traits (e.g., learning or cognitive styles), or the distinctive features of 'school cultures,' 'classroom cultures,' or even 'the culture of a reading group' (Jacob, 1995). The microgenetic level enables us to understand how an individual both acquires and reproduces such patterns. Individuals also have the potential to contribute to the transformation of cultural history as they exert their agency, though as we know, cultural change is a slower and more complex process. Depending on how one deals with the tensions between reproducing culture and crafting one's own life trajectory, individuals end up composing unique ontogenetic pathways and, ultimately, contribute to within-group diversity. In other words, inherent in ontogenetic development is the tension between normative views of developmental trajectories (i.e., what members of the cultural group are expected to achieve at different life stages) versus the hybridity of individuals (i.e., the within-individual diversity of a person).

The scholarship on overrepresentation tends to emphasize the cultural historical level. For example, recommendations from this discourse community exhort sensitivity toward the cultural historical characteristics of minority groups (e.g., dialect and language preferences, learning styles). It is paradoxical that, in their attempt to affirm cultural diversity, these suggestions end up advocating for essentialist and more static views of culture and cultural history. Furthermore, the risk of stressing a cultural historical view of minorities is that it might implicitly suggest that group traits are immutable features with no previous histories – that is, cultural reproduction is stressed.

Let us contrast the overrepresentation discourse community's traditional views of cultural history with a more dynamic perspective (Cole, 1996). In the case of Latinos/as, for example, we often ignore the fact that Latin America's evolution is fraught with political instability, oppression, ethnic, political, and religious conflict, and fragmented identities (Comas-Díaz, Lykes, & Alarcón, 1998). As a result, generations of Latinos/as, particularly in nations with sizable indigenous or Black populations, have been raised under savage economic, social, and educational inequalities and brutal repression; thus many of them (particularly members of racial minorities) have learned to live with fear, distrust, and/or despair (Galeano, 1989; Seed, 2001). However, these communities have not been merely passive recipients. They have developed and maintained incredible resiliency and perseverance to survive in such adverse circumstances (Comas-Díaz et al., 1998; Poniatowska, 1985).

When Latinos/as who have lived for generations under these conditions migrate to the United States, they engage in a complex process of coping and adapting to the host society that is inextricably intertwined with the cultural histories crafted in their homelands. Meanwhile, let us not forget that the cultural history of the dominant U.S. society has also influenced the evolving cultural histories of Latinos/as. In this process, recent immigrants begin to compose new cultural histories. As these immigrants weave new hybrid cultural histories in the context of U.S. society, generational differences emerge between themselves and their fellow ethnic peers who have lived in the United States for generations. Generational differences also arise between the recent immigrants and their own children as they are raised in the United States (Delgado-Gaitán, 1994; Suárez-Orozco & Suárez-Orozco, 1995). The result is that we find different combinations of stances (e.g., submission, resistance, assimilation, accommodation) among Latinos/as toward the values, institutions, and demands of the U.S. mainstream society, depending on their previous cultural histories, generation in the country, and the nature of experiences and contacts with dominant and subjugated communities (Suárez-Orozco & Suárez-Orozco, 1995).

This more complex perspective on the cultural histories of Latinos/as differs dramatically from the static view that permeates the overrepresentation discourse. It is indeed imperative that this discourse community take into account the interplay between historical legacies of domination and oppression in the U.S. society and the role of coping strategies, resilience mechanisms, and social and cultural capital in the construction of hybrid cultural histories in Latino and other minority communities. More importantly, researchers need to ask how these insights can inform research on placement patterns and the precursors of overrepresentation.

The inclusion literature, in turn, tends to focus on two time scales, namely, the cultural historical and ontogenetic levels. As explained above, inclusion has concentrated on the culture of traditional or inclusive schools (cultural history of institutions) or on the impact of inclusion on individuals' development or adaptation at certain ages and/or grade levels (ontogenesis); this work has examined one scale at a time (either cultural history or ontogenesis), and most investigators have preferred cross-sectional analyses. This is not surprising, given that special education research relies heavily on developmental psychology, which is inherently organized around chronological age as the primary index of the passage of time (i.e., ontogenetic development). Inclusion scholars face at least two major challenges. The first is to avoid an exclusive focus on single time scales so that the multiple developmental trajectories of students (ontogenetic level) that emerge within the cultural history of a given inclusive school can be documented. The second is to add complexity by acknowledging the racial, ability, language, gender, and class dimensions of students' and teachers' identities. Both challenges call for more complex research designs, as investigators will need to maintain a focus on both time scales throughout data collection and analysis activities while simultaneously considering multiple dimensions of identity.

Power in culture

Even as we complicate the notion of culture around the dimensions identified thus far, we run the risk of grasping only a partial understanding of the construct if we do not include the role of power and its link to historicity. Gallego et al. (2001) define culture as 'the socially inherited body of past human accomplishments that serves as the resources for the current life of a social group ordinarily thought of as the inhabitants of a country or region' (p. 362). From this perspective, culture is constituted in the sedimentation of historical experience and it is at the intersection of history and social processes that the political nature of culture emerges. As Erickson (2001) explains:

> We live in webs of meaning, caring, and desire that we create and that create us, but those webs also hang in social gravity. Within the webs all our activity is vested in the weight of history; that is, in a social world of inequality all movement is up or down. (p. 38)

Note that this view of culture embodies visible and invisible elements, and its production and reproduction are achieved in social interactions 'from the partial and mutually dependent knowledge of each person caught in the process. It is constituted, in the long run, by the work they do together' (Varenne & McDermott, 1999, p. 137).

Let us remember, though, that the maintenance of domination (i.e., hegemony) by a segment of society is achieved by 'supplying the symbols, representations, and practices of social life in such a way that the basis of social authority and the unequal relations of power and privilege remain hidden' (McLaren, 1989, p. 174). Thus, the dominant culture is naturalized and used as a reference point against which all other cultural practices are compared and evaluated. This explains why groups' cultural practices have differential status and prestige in a given society and opportunities to learn valued practices are restricted and controlled. Various groups learn disparate portions or sets of culture and occupy dissimilar power positions. The processes by which culture is unequally distributed across individuals, groups, and generations is the result of profoundly political processes (Erickson, 2001).

Research and scholarship on racial minority placement in special education has overlooked issues of power and history. The bulk of this literature is concerned with placement patterns of discretely defined groups in disability categories or programs. Although some work is mindful of the political dimension of special education placement, we have a long way to go in this area. This oversight is even more intriguing if we consider that work in this area involves cultural groups that have a long history of oppression in U.S. society. Although reviews of the literature and the research base continue to report mixed evidence about bias and discrimination, I argue that overrepresentation scholarship must be mindful of the legacy of deficit thinking about racial minorities in U.S. history that continue to inform policy and scholarly writings (Artiles, 1998). We must acknowledge that unidimensional and deficit-based views of racial minorities permeate societal perceptions and thus mediate educators' and schools' ideologies. The challenge becomes how to develop research approaches that enable us to disentangle and examine the role of power in the construction of minority overrepresentation in special education.

Inclusion, on the other hand, features power to support the rationale for inclusive educational systems. Critiques of the traditional educational system grounded in a disability rights perspective are exemplary in this regard, as they denounce the power differentials and discriminatory assumptions and practices that curtail people with disabilities' access and outcomes in mainstream society. Research on the implementation of inclusion, however, has ignored power issues. Although some work on the social dimension of inclusion (e.g., social status in classrooms, friendships) has the potential to shed light on power issues, most studies neither theorize nor problematize the compelling force of power issues in inclusive classroom and school cultures.

Space: discontinuities in understanding and uses

A limited conception of space plays a critical role in the discourses on overrepresentation and inclusion. One central concern in the inclusion movement is access to general education spaces. Placement data suggest that, despite important variations across states, the nation's students with disabilities are increasingly educated in general education schools and classrooms, particularly students with LD (McLeskey, Henry, & Axelrod, 1999). We also know that discussions and investigations about minority overrepresentation are concerned with placement in various programs and the level of integration of such programs. It is important, therefore, to discuss the theoretical underpinnings of the concept of 'space' and examine the inclusion and overrepresentation scholarships from this notion.

Systematic theorizing about space has intensified in recent years, particularly within the study of social life (Daniels & Lee, 1996; Foucault, 1986; Keith & Pile, 1993; Soja, 1996). I use the notion of space from the perspective of social geography to transcend the idea of space as simply physical location or destination. This perspective calls for 'the study of physical space and human constructions, perceptions, and representations of spatiality as contexts for and consequences of human interaction' (Hargreaves, 1995, p, 7). Lefebvre (1991) argues for the creation of a 'science of space,' a unitary theory that aims to bridge the separation between the conception and analysis of space as physical/perceived space and the conception of space as conceived/mental space. Soja (1996) refers to the former as 'FirstSpace' and to the latter as 'SecondSpace.' In this view, space is simultaneously physical, ideal, and the product of social translation and transformation (Lefebvre, 1991; Soja, 1989). The notion of space I am working from, therefore, transcends the traditional view of an a priori fixed entity and is conceived as 'an achievement and an ongoing practice' (Shields, 2000, p. 155).

FirstSpace in the inclusion and overrepresentation literatures

FirstSpace refers to physical space that is perceived; it entails the processes and forms of social 'spatiality.' The social or spatial practice of a society 'is thus presented as both medium and outcome of human activity, behavior, and experience' (Soja, 1996, p. 66). Space structures and is structured by people's actions; that is, there is a dialectical tension between the deterministic force of space and people's agency to counter its reproductive weight. As Soja (1989) explains, 'We make our own history and geography, but not just as we please; we do not make them under circumstances chosen by ourselves, but under circumstances directly encountered, given and transmitted from the historical geographies produced in the past' (p. 129).

FirstSpace represents our commonsense understanding of space in which physical/perceived space (or what is readily visible) plays a significant role. FirstSpace analysis thus 'concentrates on the accurate description of surface appearances … [or] searches for spatial explanation in primarily exogenous social, psychological, and biophysical processes' (Soja, 1996, p. 75). Inclusion research has assumed that placement of special education students in the physical spaces of general education classrooms has an effect on disabled and nondisabled students' learning and development. Studies that are concerned with the description of practices in inclusive classrooms or that test the impact of instructional approaches on student learning (e.g., Baker & Zigmond, 1995; Mortweet et al., 1999), focusing on human activity, behavior, and/or experience, are examples of research that conceptualize the space of inclusive classrooms simply in terms of FirstSpace. It is not uncommon that researchers assess such practices using data from published research or address process variables (e.g., participation in cooperative groups) indirectly through statistical analysis (Elbaum, Vaughn, Hughes, & Watson-Moody, 1999). Researchers have also examined parents', teachers', administrators', and students' understandings (cognitive/social skills, perceptions) of the physical spaces of inclusive classrooms. These studies have been conducted in an attempt to assess the viability of inclusive models, anticipate potential constraints, and inform inclusion approaches (e.g., Cook et al., 1999; Soodak, Podell, & Lehman, 1998).

Although it is important to address parents' and students' understandings of physical/perceived spaces of inclusion, it is also necessary to obtain detailed or moment-to-moment accounts of the construction processes of academic and social outcomes in those spaces. Evidence of the need for this line of research is apparent in studies reporting mixed results. In such instances, the authors allude to contextual aspects. For example, in the case of the outcomes of mixed-ability groups, it was reported that 'factors such as partner selection, teacher monitoring, and the establishment of a cooperative ethic appeared to influence the outcomes. Clearly, the structure and support are essential to the success of these arrangements' (U.S. Department of Education, 1999, p. III–29). Another example of studies that conceptualizes classrooms simply in terms of physical space is found in the research on the mixed impact of program models on students with disabilities; the reviewers conclude that such findings underscore 'the need to pay greater attention to specific organizational and instructional practices in heterogeneous classrooms' (p. III–22).

The bulk of the overrepresentation literature is equally concerned with FirstSpace analyses as reflected in the almost exclusive attention to placement patterns for various ethnic groups in disability programs. Outcomes (i.e., placement patterns) are foregrounded in these analyses, and static markers of difference (e.g., ethnic labels) are included in studies to discern their association with various physical spaces (e.g., school location, type of special education program). For example, researchers have studied whether placement patterns are differentially shaped by student race, poverty level, academic achievement level, and school location (urban v. suburban) (Artiles et al., 1998; Oswald et al., 1999). With a few exceptions, the social practices that precede placement decisions are ignored. The understandings of physical/perceived spaces by teachers and other school personnel are also assessed (generally via surveys and questionnaires), typically to test a bias hypothesis (Donovan & Cross, 2002). Given the strong social desirability associated with measures of cultural bias, it is not surprising that this evidence is mixed.

SecondSpace in the inclusion and overrepresentation scholarship

SecondSpace refers to space as conceptualized by people; it encompasses conceived spaces and includes 'representations of power and ideology, of control and surveillance … It is the primary source of utopian thought and vision' (Soja, 1996, p. 67). SecondSpace is 'the ideological content of codes, theories, and the conceptual depictions of space linked to production relations' (Shields, 2000, p. 163). Lefebvre (1991) referred to it as 'conceptualized space, the space of scientists'(p. 38). There are far-reaching conceptualizations (conceived space) of inclusive education that situate the meaning and place of special education in larger societal and historical contexts (e.g., Ferguson, 1995; Lipsky & Gartner, 1996). These conceptualizations emphasize complexity, are comprehensive and ambitious, and generally suggest a revamping of the educational system's premises, values, and practices (Ferguson & Ferguson, 1997). Interestingly, these frameworks contrast with the more outcome-oriented focus of the inclusion research literature. In other words, there seems to be a discontinuity between the representations of inclusive education (the SecondSpace dimensions of space) and the actual examination of inclusion processes and outcomes (FirstSpace).

Unlike inclusion, the overrepresentation discourse has devoted hardly any effort to developing conceptualizations and visions of the types of spaces needed by students in inclusive classrooms. Given that Secondspace is 'entirely ideational, made up of projections into the empirical world from conceived or imagined geographies' (Soja, 1996, p. 79), the lack of utopian thinking or imagination in the overrepresentation discourse has potentially devastating consequences. This scholarship runs the risk of merely accumulating descriptions of spatial practices that are not guided by a theoretical imagination about the role of cultural differences in education or a vision of an ideal state of affairs in a pluralistic society. Unlike the inclusion discourse, the scholarship devoted to address solutions to this problem tends to lack a transformative bent.

There are gaps in the spaces examined by the inclusion and overrepresentation discourse communities. Although both communities tend to concentrate on the production of spatial practices (on space as FirstSpace), the inclusion community seems to be guided by visions of an inclusive education system (space conceptualized as SecondSpace). In contrast, overrepresentation lacks such conceived space. Without finding a way to bring the two literatures together, special educators risk reconstructing the educational system based on visions that ignore the history and implications of racial, ethnic, class, and linguistic differences in the social organization of learning in culturally and politically charged contexts. Likewise, we cannot afford to reconstruct the system without a vision of what we want to achieve in a heterogeneous educational system to consolidate a socially just society.

Challenges for a new generation of inclusion and overrepresentation research: the productions of culture, lived spaces, and difference

The convergence of inclusion and overrepresentation exposes the fact that the educational system may be educating more students with disabilities in general education contexts, but many of those being included are poor racial and linguistic minorities that have additional ability deficits superimposed onto their identities. It seems that both phenomena have stressed a technical perspective. The inclusion movement has focused on a redistribution of resources so that students with disabilities are educated in a presumed new breed of general education, whereas overrepresentation has been largely reduced to the study of placement proportions. These discourses have also emphasized legalistic issues. Inclusion has focused on new requirements for placement in general education, access to the curriculum, and accountability, while overrepresentation has pushed for the creation of antidiscriminatory regulations generally enforced by the Office for Civil Rights (Losen & Orfield, 2002). However, I argue that the overrepresentation and inclusion literatures have used partial perspectives on culture, have not adequately theorized space, and have been silent about difference. Future research cannot afford to ignore these aspects as we live in an increasingly pluralistic society.

Beyond 'ways of life' and places: the productions of culture and lived spaces

Both inclusion and overrepresentation scholarship need to adopt more complex and dynamic conceptions of culture and multiple time scales (cultural, historical, ontogenetic, microgenetic) in order to obtain a deeper understanding of human development as situated in cultural, historical, and social contexts. Traditional views of culture have faced mounting criticism due to the limits of their assumptions and premises. Scholars have criticized traditional views because they project an image of culture that (a) privileges group patterns at the expense of within-group diversity, (b) portrays culture as stagnant in time with clearly demarcated boundaries between groups, (c) ignores individual agency, and (d) overlooks the role of power in cultural processes (Eisenhart, 2001). Researchers face the challenge of incorporating 'the fact of constant individual creativity into a theory of culture' (Varenne, 1984, p. 282). At the same time, we must avoid dichotomizing the individual and the society. As Rosaldo (1984) warns us, the 'view of the repeated struggle between sacred individualism and sociological wisdom reduces complex historical processes to timeless conflicts' (p. 294).

One of the most ambitious projects that aims to transcend the limits of traditional views of culture is represented in the so-called cultural productions turn (Eisenhart, 2001). This view accounts for individual (e.g., beliefs, values) and societal (e.g., structures) cultural forces, and it argues that the convergence of such forces must be examined as situated in and shaped by the local social conditions of everyday practice. From this perspective, culture not only constrains but also enables individual performance. It constrains in the sense that a person enters a context where a culture is represented in the structural and historical legacies embedded in the artifacts, rules for interaction, and prescribed roles available in the setting. The subject, therefore, is constrained to operate with those elements and pressured to reproduce cultural tradition. At the same time, the individual's agency enables her to use artifacts in novel ways, challenge prescribed roles, and modify established rules. In this sense, culture can also enable the individual to disrupt tradition and promote change (see examples of this research in Engestrom, Miettinen, & Punamaki, 1999; Nespor, 1994).

The cultural productions view uses a unit of analysis that requires researchers to study classroom cultures 'as a hybrid of the local and the social historical levels of analysis' (Gallego et al., 2001, p. 957). That is, it uses a unit of analysis that accounts for cultural acquisition, use, reproduction, and change. The recent work on cultural productions enhances our understanding of 'how local practices of cultural production become meaningful and consequential to participants; differentiate otherwise similar individuals; make similar otherwise different people; are connected to wider processes of nationalism, stratification, globalization, and professionalism; and sometimes motivate change' (Eisenhart, 2001, p. 218). This perspective on culture, therefore, can help researchers generate knowledge that honors the complexities of the spaces, histories, and cultural practices of both overrepresentation and inclusion.

Similarly, inclusion and overrepresentation scholarship can benefit from a new science of space, building on knowledge of how First- and SecondSpaces interact and influence one another in the lived spaces of inclusive classrooms. Within the interactions between FirstSpace and SecondSpace, a ThirdSpace is created, capturing lived space, or spaces of representation (Soja, 1996). Lived space both encompasses and is distinct from the other two spaces. ThirdSpace is the 'habitus of social practices, a constantly shifting and changing milieu of ideas, events, appearances, and meanings' (Kahn, 2000, p. 7). According to Soja (1996), counterspaces or spaces of resistance can be created in ThirdSpace because it is filled with ideology and politics, with relations of dominance and subordination, with the intricate interdependency of the real and the imagined. ThirdSpace is a powerful tool because it enables us to question simplifications of space as 'site' or 'destination' and to transcend dichotomies of representations such as insiders and outsiders. At the same time, ThirdSpace is a dynamic construct that surfaces as a result of the dialectic of the physical and the mental, the concrete and the abstract; it contains the perceived and conceived spaces simultaneously (Soja, 1996; Tejeda, 2000).

At a time when politically and ideologically charged reforms will likely have devastating consequences for poor and racial minority students, future research ought to focus on the genesis and transformation of ThirdSpaces – the site where attention to ideology and politics is prominent and where resistance is created. Attention to ThirdSpaces will inevitably compel us to be mindful of social justice as issues of power, subordination, and dominance are central. Researchers must conduct participatory research with teachers, families, and students and focus explicitly on the role of institutional forces in their lived experiences in schools, households, and communities.

Beyond diversity: toward an understanding of difference and perspective

Ultimately, inclusion and overrepresentation researchers face dilemmas related to underlying assumptions about difference. Both discourse communities tend to use the notion of cultural 'diversity,' which is typically defined as 'the recognition of pre-given cultural contents and customs' (Bhabha, 1994, p. 34). Two problems exist with this notion. First, the notion of diversity embodies a 'transparent norm' (Alsayyad, 2001, p. 7) that essentializes culture and 'turns the other into something monolithic, partly out of not only ignorance but also fear' (Viswanathan, 2001, p. 238). Second, racism is very much alive in *all* societies precisely because 'the universalism that paradoxically permits diversity masks ethnocentric norms, values, and interests' (Bhabha, cited in Alsayyad, 2001, p. 7).

Cultural difference in turn questions binary distinctions (diverse, nondiverse) and foregrounds 'the problem of the ambivalence of cultural authority' (Bhabha, 1994, p. 34). Minow (1990) stated that difference has been equated with deviance or stigma, and thus sameness is a prerequisite of equality. Therefore, it is not surprising that traditional treatments of difference ultimately reaffirm difference and offer options that signal the deficits or disadvantages typically associated with difference – it is paradoxical then that to recognize 'difference reinforces hierarchy' (Abu-Lughod, cited in Brightman, 1995, p. 532). Special education has historically faced the dilemma of affirming or ignoring difference. On the one hand, it was argued that equal instructional treatment was unfair, institutionalizing an individualized educational system. On the other hand, the inclusion movement has argued that equal access to general education spaces, curriculum, and accountability standards are just. The former strategy recognizes difference while the latter diffuses it; ultimately, both are organized around it. In the case of minorities, we observe a similar ambivalence in the solutions offered to the dilemma of difference – again, the underlying question has been whether we should ignore or affirm it. Indeed, access to the same (integrated) educational contexts was a major achievement for racial minorities in the civil rights era while linguistic minorities have fought for differential treatment in the form of bilingual education programs.

The inclusion and overrepresentation discourses have offered ambivalent and even conflicting responses to the question of how to handle difference due to their underlying assumptions. A first step is to make explicit the underlying assumptions of difference and counter them with alternative assumptions. As we use more complex views of culture in the discourses of inclusion and overrepresentation to address issues ultimately concerned with difference, we must ask: when does a difference count, under what conditions, in what ways, and for what reasons? (Varenne & McDermott, 1999).

Attention to culture and space as a way to understand notions of difference demands that we acknowledge the role of power in the creation of borders. It particularly calls our attention to the perspective of the observer, an issue that has been historically invisible and unquestioned in research practices. Implications of the role of perspective are twofold. First, the perspective of the observer or analyst (e.g., teacher, researcher) must be recognized. Second, we can gain greater insight from examining how people use notions of difference to create borders during social interactions in particular institutional contexts rather than studying the distinctive features of a group's cultural history (Barth, 1969). This is a particularly important theoretical insight, as overrepresentation and inclusion focus on borders, such as race, that possess great historical currency in U.S. society. As Rosaldo (1984) explains: 'Race relations in North America involve a blend of assimilationist efforts, raw prejudice, and cultural containment that revolves around a concerted effort to keep each culture pure and in its place' (p. 212).

In turn, systematic attention to culture in research practices will force us to be aware of and disclose our assumptions about difference (e.g., researchers' understandings of development, time, space, and culture). Such heightened awareness will compel us to envision difference as produced in relationships and rooted in comparisons between a person and culturally based norms that can be unveiled, evaluated, and contested (Minow, 1990). Minow also challenges us to enable those who have been dispensed identities of difference, such as disability, to share alternative perspectives that are not always aligned with culturally based norms and expectations. This practice will allow us to reflect on the culturally based assumptions that underlie the design and implementation of school rules, curricula, and assessment practices. The practice of honoring multiple perspectives on inclusion and overrepresentation will also enable us to read these knowledge bases (borrowing from Said) 'contrapuntally, to use the metaphor from music. [This practice would enable us to go] over the same history but from a different point of view' (Viswanathan, 2001, p. 245). This way, we could transcend the traditional dilemmas of difference (e.g., to provide equal or preferential treatment). Instead, analysis of culture-based notions of difference should focus on 'the ways in which institutions construct and utilize differences to justify and enforce exclusions – and the ways in which such institutional practices can be changed' (Minow, 1990, p. 86). The potential role of institutional histories and contexts must be taken into account in such analyses; this is why it is critical to situate overrepresentation and inclusion analyses in the larger cultural politics of special education reforms.

Overrepresentation and inclusion are ultimately about how educators and educational systems deal with 'difference' in politically and culturally charged contexts. I argue that we must examine these phenomena beyond special education placement issues, using more sophisticated views of culture and space. The present emphasis on reporting only the number of students with disabilities being educated in general education classrooms and schools is creating the illusion that the inclusive education movement is consolidating. This emphasis also disregards both the historicity and sociality of who is being identified as disabled and the sociocultural roots of disability constructions. As the complexity of the cultural politics of educational reform surfaces and as its influence on special education transformations intensifies, we must concern ourselves with the study of disability, inclusion, and overrepresentation in an elaborate cultural medium, mediated by multiple scales and planes of space and time. In this manner, disability and special education scholarship will transcend the traditional individualistic perspective and infuse a social justice dimension so that the improvement of educational experiences and life opportunities for historically marginalized students are of central concern.

Notes

1 'The term inclusion has been used so widely that it has almost lost its meaning' (Skrtic, Sailor, & Gee, 1996, p. 149). Some definitions stress physical placement – for example, 'placement (full or partial) of students with mild disabilities in general education classrooms' (Cook, Semmel, & Gerber, 1999, p. 207). Others stress the notion of inclusive schools, which, according to Skrtic, Sailor, and Gee (1996), 'are those designed to meet the educational needs of all their members within common, yet fluid, environments and activities' (p. 149). Inclusion is also seen as a process of developing a unified educational system that serves students with disabilities and their nondisabled peers 'as active, fully participating members of the school community; that views diversity as the norm; and that ensures a high-quality education for students by providing meaningful curriculum, effective teaching, and necessary supports for each student' (Ferguson, 1995, p. 286).

2 Overrepresentation is defined as 'unequal proportions of culturally diverse students in [special education] programs' (Artiles & Trent, 2000, p. 514); typically, this phenomenon is calculated in relation to a group's representation in general education or in reference to the representation of a comparison group (e.g., White students).

3 I use the notion of 'discourse community' to describe groups (e.g., researchers, practitioners) that coalesce around a common interest or an object of study or labor. A discourse community devotes efforts and resources to produce knowledge about its object 'and establishes conditions for who speaks and what gets heard … Because it is institutionally sanctioned, their discourse is powerful … its "regime" or "politics of truth" sets standards for the field' (Brantlinger, 1997, p. 432). Although the notion of discourse community emphasizes cohesion, note that there are diverse perspectives within the overrepresentation and inclusion discourse communities.

4 Special education relies on a categorical model of disabilities. High-incidence disabilities include learning disabilities (LD), emotional disturbance (ED), mild mental retardation (MMR), and speech or language impairments; students with LD comprise about half of the special education population (Smith, 2001). Low-incidence disabilities include autism, deafness/hearing

impairments, multiple disabilities, visual impairments, other health impairments, deaf-blindness, orthopedic impairments, and traumatic brain injury.

5   To the dismay of debate participants, general education hardly pays attention to these deliberations. To this day, large-scale efforts to monitor the implementation of major general education reforms 'have generally ignored the issue of disability and ... the information that is available has been collected in a piecemeal fashion' (Vanderwood, McGrew, & Ysseldyke, 1998, p. 366).

6   For instance, the federal government in recent years has funded the National Longitudinal Transition Study (Wagner et al., 1993), the COMRISE and LASER Projects, the National Institute for Urban School Improvement, and the National Center for Culturally Responsive Educational Systems (among others) to support research and technical assistance activities with an explicit attention to race and minority special education placement and urban education issues.

7   The risk index offers a measure of the proportion of students from a group that is placed in a disability category. It is calculated 'by dividing the number of students in a given racial or ethnic category served in a given disability category by the total enrollment for that racial or ethnic group in the school population' (Donovan & Cross, 2002, pp. 42–43). The odds ratio divides the risk index of one racial/ethnic group by the risk index of another racial/ethnic group in order to provide a comparison. If the risk indices are identical for two groups, the odds ratio will equal 1.0. Odds ratios greater than 1.0 indicate that the minority group students are at greater risk for identification, while odds of less than 1.0 indicate that they are less at risk (Donovan & Cross, 2002). To illustrate, let us assume that a comparison of Latino and White student LD identification in a given district results in an odds ratio of 1.36. This means Latino students would be 36 percent more likely than White students to be given the LD label in that school district.

8   Based on OSEP data, the NRC report concluded there is no 'evidence that minority children are systematically represented in low-incidence disability categories in numbers that are disproportionate to their representation in the population' (Donovan & Cross, 2002, p. 61).

9   The reauthorization of IDEA in 1997 strengthened the nondiscriminatory requirements of the law, which include using nondiscriminatory assessment, collecting and monitoring placement data by race and class, providing educational services for expelled students or for school-age youngsters in correctional facilities, providing procedural safeguards for parents, and documenting the quality of instruction and opportunity to learn prior to special education referrals (Hehir, 2002; Smith, 2001).

10   As stated above, data are scarce on the types of placement contexts (segregated v. integrated) in which minority students with disabilities are being placed.

11   Artiles et al. acknowledged that 'although we are not advocating the use of ethnicity or race as the most important proxies of culture in LD research, we chose to examine the research using these proxies to obtain baseline information about this knowledge base' (p. 83).

12   The five dimensions of culture are intricately interrelated, and I discuss them separately for heuristic purposes.

13   Several objections have been made to the cultural discontinuity hypothesis (Gallego et al., 2001; Varenne & McDermott, 1999). One criticism is that cultural discontinuities do not always result in miscommunications and school failure for minorities. Ogbu (1992), for instance, argues that groups create cultural frames of reference based on their unique histories (e.g., immigration, societal power status), which explains why various groups sometimes exhibit distinct responses to similar external conditions. This explains why a minority group that experiences a discontinuity between its own culture and the school's culture still exhibits educational success. Another criticism of the way-of-life view is that it is overly deterministic, as it assumes that home or group culture defines what people do when they enter new contexts.

14   Scholars have taken issue with the internal–external dualism and have advanced more complex views (Erickson, 2001; Gallego et al., 2001). I differentiate these locations to explain that many definitions of culture artificially create this dichotomy and tend to privilege one location over the other.

15   Researchers are only beginning to investigate the embeddedness of multiple historical domains and their mutual influences to understand the temporal distribution of culture in human development

(Cole, 1996; Dien, 2000). For examples of this emergent scholarship, see Cole and Engestrom (1993), Cole (1996), Lemke (2000), and Dien (2000).

16 See Artiles, Gutiérrez, and Rueda (2002), Cole (1996), and Stone (1993) for discussions of prolepsis and other processes that can help us understand how culture mediates learning.

17 Note that cultural history also embodies the transformed elements of cultural legacies that result from cultural change processes.

References

Advancement Project & Civil Rights Project. (2000). *Opportunities suspended: The devastating consequences of zero tolerance and school discipline policies.* Cambridge, MA: Civil Rights Project at Harvard University. Retrieved on December 10, 2000, from http://www.law.Harvard.edu/groups/civil rights/conferences/zero/zt_report2.html

Alsayyad, N. (2001). Hybrid culture/hybrid urbanism: Pandora's box of the 'third place.' In N. Alsayyad (Ed.), *Hybrid urbanism: On the identity discourse and the built environment* (pp.1–18). Westport, CT: Praeger.

Anyon, J. (1997). *Ghetto schooling: A political economy of urban educational reform.* New York: Teachers College Press.

Anzaldúa, G. (1999). *Borderlands/La frontera: The new mestiza* (2nd ed.). San Francisco: Aunt Lute Books.

Apple, M.W. (1996). *Cultural politics and education.* New York: Teachers College Press.

Artiles, A.J. (1998). The dilemma of difference: Enriching the disproportionality discourse with theory and context. *Journal of Special Education, 32,* 33–36.

Artiles, A.J., Aguirre-Muñoz, Z., & Abedi, J. (1998). Predicting placement in learning disabilities programs: Do predictors vary by ethnic group? *Exceptional Children, 64,* 543–559.

Artiles, A.J., Gutiérrez, K., & Rueda, R. (2002, April). *Teacher education in a culturally diverse inclusive era: Implications of a cultural historical vision for teacher learning research.* Paper presented at the annual meeting of the American Educational Research Association, New Orleans.

Artiles, A.J., & Pak, M. (2000, July). *Becoming an inclusive education teacher in an urban multicultural school: Tensions, contradictions, and implications for inclusion research.* Paper presented at the International Special Education Conference, Manchester, England.

Artiles, A.J., Rueda, R., Salazar, J., & Higareda, I. (2002). English-language learner representation in special education in California urban school districts. In D.J. Losen & G. Orfield (Eds.), *Racial inequity in special education* (pp. 117–136). Cambridge, MA: Harvard Education Press.

Artiles, A.J., & Trent, S.C. (2000), Representation of culturally/linguistically diverse students. In C.R. Reynolds & E. Fletcher-Jantzen (Eds.), *Encyclopedia of special education, Vol. I* (2nd ed., pp. 513–517). New York: John Wiley.

Artiles, A.J., Trent, S.C., & Kuan, L.A. (1997). Learning disabilities research on ethnic minority students: An analysis of 22 years of studies published in selected refereed journals. *Learning Disabilities Research and Practice, 12,* 82–91.

Artiles, A.J., Trent, S.C., & Palmer, J. (2004). Culturally diverse students in special education: Legacies and prospects. In J.A. Banks & C.M. Banks (Eds.), *Handbook of research on multicultural education* (2nd ed., pp. 716–735). San Francisco: Jossey-Bass.

Baker, J., & Zigmond, N. (1995). The meaning and practice of inclusion for students with learning disabilities: Themes and implications from the five case studies. *Journal of Special Education, 29,* 163–180.

Barth, F. (1969). *Ethnic groups and boundaries: The social organization of culture difference.* Boston: Little Brown.

Bhabha, H.K. (1994). *The location of culture.* London: Routledge.

Bowles, S., & Gintis, H. (1976). *Schooling in capitalist America: Educational reform and the contradictions of economic life.* New York: Basic Books.

Brantlinger, E. (1997). Using ideology: Cases of nonrecognition of the politics of research and practice in special education. *Review of Educational Research, 67,* 425–459.

Brightman, R. (1995). Forget culture: Replacement, transcendence, relexification. *Cultural Anthropology, 10,* 509–546.

Christensen, C., & Rizvi, F. (Eds.). (1996). *Disability and the dilemmas of education and justice.* Buckingham, Eng.: Open University Press.

Cole, M. (1996). *Cultural psychology: A once and future discipline.* Cambridge, MA: Harvard University Press.

Cole, M., & Engestrom, Y. (1993). A cultural-historical approach to distributed cognition. In G. Salomon (Ed.), *Distributed cognitions: Psychological and educational considerations* (pp. 1–46). New York: Cambridge University Press.

Comas-Díaz, L., Lykes, M.B., & Alarcón, R.D. (1998). Ethnic conflict and the psychology of liberation in Guatemala, Peru, and Puerto Rico. *American Psychologist, 53,* 778–792.

Cook, B.G., Semmel, M.I., & Gerber, M.M. (1999). Attitudes of principals and special education teachers toward the inclusion of students with mild disabilities. *Remedial and Special Education, 20,* 199–207.

Daniels, S., & Lee, R. (Eds.). (1996). *Exploring human geography: A reader.* New York: Halstead Press.

Delgado-Gaitán, C. (1994). Socializing young children in Mexican-American families: An intergenerational perspective. In P. Greenfield & R. Cocking (Eds.), *Cross-cultural roots of minority child development* (pp. 55–86). Hillsdale, NJ: Lawrence Erlbaum.

Dien, D.S. (2000). The evolving nature of self-identity across four levels of history. *Human Development, 43,* 1–18.

Donovan, S., & Cross, C. (Eds.). (2002). *Minority students in special and gifted education.* Washington, DC: National Academy Press.

Dunn, L.M. (1968). Special education for the mildly retarded: Is much of it justifiable? *Exceptional Children, 35,* 5–22.

Dyson, A. (1999). Inclusion and inclusions: Theories and discourses in inclusive education. In H. Daniels & P. Garner (Eds.), *World yearbook of education 1999: Inclusive education* (pp. 36–53). London: Kogan Page.

Eagleton, T. (2000). *The idea of culture.* Oxford: Blackwell.

Eisenhart, M. (2001). Changing conceptions of culture and ethnographic methodology: Recent thematic shifts and their implications for research on teaching. In V. Richardson (Ed.), *Handbook of research on teaching* (4th ed., pp. 209–225). Washington, DC: American Educational Research Association.

Elbaum, B., Vaughn, S., Hughes, M., & Watson-Moody, S. (1999). Grouping practices and reading outcomes for students with disabilities. *Exceptional Children, 65,* 399–415.

Engestrom, Y., Miettinen, R., & Punamaki, R. (Eds.). (1999). *Perspectives on activity theory.* New York: Cambridge University Press.

Erickson, F. (1996). Inclusion into what? Thoughts on the construction of learning, identity, and affiliation in the general education classroom. In D.L. Speece & B.K. Keogh (Eds.), *Research on classroom ecologies* (pp. 91–105). Mahwah, NJ: Lawrence Erlbaum.

Erickson, F. (2001). Culture in society and in educational practices. In J. Banks & C.M. Banks (Eds.), *Multicultural education: Issues and perspectives* (pp. 31–58). New York: Wiley.

Ferguson, D.L. (1995) The real challenge of inclusion: Confessions of a rabid inclusionist. *Phi Delta Kappan, 77,* 281–287.

Ferguson, D.L., & Ferguson, P.M. (1997). Debating inclusion in Synecdoche, New York: A response to Gresham and MacMillan. *Review of Educational Research, 67,* 416–420.

Finn, J.D. (1982). Patterns in special education placement as revealed by the OCR surveys. In K.A. Heller, W.H. Hollzman, & S. Messick (Eds.), *Placing children in special education: A strategy for equity* (pp. 322–381). Washington, DC: National Academy Press.

Foucault, M. (1986). Of other spaces. *Diacritics, 16,* 22–27.

Fuchs, D., & Fuchs, L.S. (1994). Inclusive schools movement and the radicalization of special education reform. *Exceptional Children, 60*, 294–309.

Fujiura, G.T., & Yamaki, K. (2000). Trends in demography of childhood poverty and disability. *Exceptional Children, 66*, 187–99.

Galeano, E. (1989). *Las venas abiertas de América Latino.* Mexico DF: Siglo Veintiuno Editores.

Gallego, M.A., Cole, M., & Laboratory of Comparative Human Cognition. (2001). Classroom cultures and cultures in the classroom. In V. Richardson (Ed.), *Handbook of research on teaching* (4th ed.). Washington, DC: American Educational Research Association.

Gándara, P., Maxwell-Jolly. J., García, E., Asato, J., Gutiérrez, K., Stritikus, T., & Curry, J. (2000, April). *The initial impact of Proposition 227 on the instruction of English learners.* Santa Barbara: University of California Linguistic Minority Research Institute.

García, E. (1996). Preparing instructional professionals for linguistically and culturally diverse students. In J. Sikula (Ed.), *Handbook of research on teacher education* (pp. 802–812). New York: Macmillan.

Gartner, A., & Lipsky, D.K. (1987). Beyond special education: Toward a quality system for all students. *Harvard Educational Review, 57,* 367–395.

Geertz, C. (1983). *Local knowledge: Further essays in interpretive anthropology.* New York: Basic Books.

Gersten, R., Baker, S., Pugach, M., with Scanlon, D., & Chard, D. (2001). Contemporary research on special education teaching. In V. Richardson (Ed.), *Handbook of research on teaching* (4th ed., pp. 695–722). Washington, DC: American Educational Research Association.

Gottlieb, J., Alter, M., Gottlieb, B.W., & Wishner, J. (1994). Special education in urban America: It's not justifiable for many. *Journal of Special Education, 27,* 453–465.

Gutiérrez, K., Asato, J., Santos, M., & Gotanda, N. (2002). Backlash pedagogy: Language and culture and the politics of reform. *Review of Education, Pedagogy, and Cultural Studies, 24,* 335–351.

Handwerker, W.P. (2002). The construct validity of cultures: Cultural diversity, culture theory, and a method for ethnography. *American Anthropologist, 104,* 106–122.

Hargreaves, A. (1995). Toward a social geography of teacher education. In N.K. Shimahara & I.Z. Holowinsky (Eds.), *Teacher education in industrialized nations* (pp. 3–40). New York: Garland.

Harry, B., Klingner, J., Sturges, K.M., & Moore, R.F. (2002). Of rocks and soft places: Using qualitative methods to investigate disproportionality. In D.J. Losen & G. Orfield (Eds.), *Racial inequity in special education* (pp. 71–92). Cambridge, MA: Harvard Education Press.

Heath, S.B. (1983). *Ways with words: Language, life and work in communities and classrooms.* Cambridge, Eng.: Cambridge University Press.

Hehir, T. (2002). IDEA and disproportionality: Federal enforcement, effective advocacy, and strategies for change. In D.J. Losen & G. Orfield (Eds.), *Racial inequity in special education* (pp. 219–238). Cambridge, MA: Harvard Education Press.

Heller, K.A., Holtzman, W.H., & Messick, S. (Eds.). (1982). *Placing children in special education: A strategy for equity.* Washington, DC: National Academy Press.

Heubert, J.P. (2002). Disability, race, and high-stakes testing of students. In D.J. Losen & G. Orfield (Eds.), *Racial inequity in special education* (pp. 137–165). Cambridge, MA: Harvard Education Press.

Individuals with Disabilities Education Act Amendments of 1997 (IDEA), 20 U.S.C. § 1400–87 (1997) (1994 & Supp. V 1999) (originally enacted as the Education for All Handicapped Children Act of 1975, Pub. L. No. 94–142, 89 Stat. 773).

Irvine, J.J., & York, D.E. (1995). Learning styles and culturally diverse students: A literature review. In J.A. Banks & C.A. McGee Banks (Eds.), *Handbook of research on multicultural education* (pp. 484–497). New York: Macmillan.

Jacob, E. (1995). Reflective practice and anthropology in culturally diverse classrooms. *Elementary School Journal, 95,* 451–463.

Kahn, M. (2000). Thaiti intertwined: Ancestral land, tourist postcard, and nuclear test site. *American Anthropologist, 102,* 7–26.

Kauffman, J.M., & Hallahan, D.P. (Eds.). (1995). *The illusion of full inclusion.* Austin, TX: Pro-Ed.

Keith, M., & Pile, S. (Eds.). (1993). *Place and the politics of identity.* New York: Routledge.

Lefebvre, H. (1991). *The production of space.* Oxford: Blackwell.

Lemke, J.L. (2000). Across the scales of time: Artifacts, activities, and meanings in ecosocial systems. *Mind, Culture, and Activity,* 7, 273–290.

Lipsky, D.K., & Gartner, A. (1996). Inclusion, school restructuring, and the remaking of American society. *Harvard Educational Review,* 66, 762–796.

Lipsky, D.K., & Gartner, A. (1999). Inclusive education: A requirement of a democratic society. In H. Daniels & P. Garner (Eds.), *World yearbook of education 1999: Inclusive education* (pp. 12–23). London: Kogan Page.

Losen, D.J., & Orfield, G. (Eds.). (2002). *Racial inequity in special education.* Cambridge, MA: Harvard Education Press.

Manset, G., & Semmel, M.I. (1997). Are inclusive programs for students with mild disabilities effective? A comparative review of model programs. *Journal of Special Education, 31,* 155–180.

McDonnell, L., McLaughlin, M.J., & Morison, P. (Eds.). (1997). *Educating one and all: Students with disabilities and standards-based reform.* Washington, DC: National Academy Press.

McLaren, P. (1989). *Life in schools.* New York: Longman.

McLaughlin, M.J., & Tilstone, C. (1999). Standards and curriculum: The core of educational reform. In M.J. McLaughlin & M. Rouse (Eds.), *Special education and school reform in the United States and Britain* (pp. 38–65). London: Routledge.

McLaughlin, M.J., Fuchs. L., & Hardman, M. (1999). Individual rights to education and students with disabilities: Some lessons from U.S. policy. In H. Daniels & P. Garner (Eds.), *World yearbook of education 1999: Inclusive education* (pp. 24–35). London: Kogan Page.

McLaughlin, M.J., Henderson, K., & Rhim, L.M. (1998, September). *Snapshots of reform: How five local districts are interpreting standards-based reform for students with disabilities.* Alexandria, VA: Center for Policy Research.

McLeskey, J., Henry, D., & Axelrod, M.I. (1999). Inclusion of students with learning disabilities: An examination of data from reports to Congress. *Exceptional Children, 66,* 55–66.

McLoyd, V.C. (1998). Socioeconomic disadvantage and child development. *American Psychologist, 53,* 185–204.

Mehan, H., Hartwick, A., & Meihls, J.L. (1986). *Handicapping the handicapped: Decision-making in students' educational careers.* Stanford, CA: Stanford University Press.

Minow, M. (1990). *Making all the difference: Inclusion, exclusion, and American law.* Ithaca, NY: Cornell University Press.

Mortweet, S.L., Utley, C.A., Walker, D., Dawson, H.L., Delquadri, J.C., Reddy, S.S., Greenwood, C.R., Hamilton, S., & Ledford, D. (1999). Classwide peer tutoring: Teaching students with mild mental retardation in inclusive classrooms. *Exceptional Children, 65,* 524–536.

Nespor, J. (1994). *Knowledge in motion: Space, time, and curriculum in undergraduate physics and management.* London: Falmer Press.

Ogbu, J.U. (1992). Understanding cultural diversity and learning. *Educational Researcher, 21*(8), 5–14.

Ortiz, A.A. (1997). Learning disabilities occurring concomitantly with linguistic differences. *Journal of Learning Disabilities, 30,* 321–332.

Oswald, D.P., Coutinho, M.J., & Best, A.M. (2002). Community and school predictors of overrepresentation of minority children in special education. In D.J. Losen & G. Orfield (Eds.), *Racial inequity in special education* (pp. 1–13). Cambridge, MA: Harvard Education Press.

Oswald, D.P., Coutinho, M.J., Best, A.M., & Singh, N.N. (1999). Ethnic representation in special education: The influence of school-related economic and demographic variables. *Journal of Special Education, 32,* 194–206.

Parrish, T. (2002). Racial disparities in the identification, funding, and provision of special education. In D.J. Losen & G. Orfield (Eds.), *Racial inequity in special education* (pp. 15–37). Cambridge, MA: Harvard Education Press.

Poniatowska, E. (1985). *Fuerte es el silencio.* Mexico DF: Ediciones ERA.

Pugach, M., & Lilly, S. (1984). Reconceptualizing support services for classroom teachers: Implications for teacher education. *Journal of Teacher Education, 35,* 48–55.

Reschly, D.J. (1997). *Disproportionate minority representation in general and special education. Patterns, issues, and alternatives.* Des Moines: Iowa Department of Education.

Reynolds, M.C., & York, J.L. (1996). Special education and inclusion, In J. Sikula (Ed.), *Handbook of research on teacher education* (pp. 820–836). New York: Macmillan.

Rizvi, F., & Lingard, B. (1996). Disability, education and the discourses of justice. In C. Christensen & F. Rizvi (Eds.), *Disability and the dilemmas of education and justice* (pp. 9–26). Buckingham, Eng.: Open University Press.

Rogoff, B., & Angelillo, C. (2002). Investigating the coordinated functioning of multifaceted cultural practices in human development. *Human Development, 45,* 211–225.

Rosaldo, R. (1984). Comments. *Current Anthropology, 25.*

Rueda, R., Artiles, A.J., Salazar, J., & Higareda, I. (2002). An analysis of special education as a response to the diminished academic achievement of Chicano/Latino students: An update. In R.R. Valencia (Ed.), *Chicano school failure and success: Past, present, and future* (2nd ed., pp. 310–332). London: Routledge/Falmer.

Scribner, S. (1985) Vygotsky's uses of history. In J.V. Wertsch (Ed.), *Culture, communication, and cognition* (pp. 119–145). New York: Cambridge University Press.

Seed, P. (2001). *American pentimiento.* Minneapolis: University of Minnesota Press.

Sheriff, R.E. (2000). Exposing silence as cultural censorship: A Brazilian case. *American Anthropologist, 102,* 114–132.

Shields, R. (2000). *Lefebvre, love and struggle: Spatial dialectics.* London: Routledge.

Skrtic, T.M. (1991). The special education paradox: Equity as the way to excellence. *Harvard Educational Review, 61,* 148–206.

Skrtic, T.M., Sailor, W., & Gee, K. (1996). Voice, collaboration, and inclusion: Democratic themes in educational and social reform initiatives. *Remedial and Special Education, 17,* 142–157.

Slee, R. (1996). Disability, social class and poverty: School structures and policing identities. In C. Chrisiensen & F. Rizvi (Eds.), *Disability and the dilemmas of education and justice* (pp. 96–118). Buckingham, Eng.: Open University Press.

Smith, D.D. (2001). *Introduction to special education: Teaching in an age of opportunity* (4th ed.). Boston: Allyn & Bacon.

Soja, E. (1989). *Postmodern geographies: The reassertion of space in critical social theory.* New York: Verso.

Soja, E.W. (1996). *Thirdspace: Journeys to Los Angeles and other real-and-imagined places.* Oxford, Eng.: Blackwell.

Soodak, L.C., Podell, D.M., & Lehman, L.R. (1998). Teacher, student, and school attributes as predictors of teachers' responses to inclusion. *Journal of Special Education, 31,* 480–497.

Stainback, W., & Stainback, S. (1991). Rationale for integration and restructuring: A synopsis. In J.W. Lloyd, A.C. Repp, & N.N. Singh (Eds.), *The Regular Education Initiative: Alternative perspectives on concepts, issues, and models* (pp. 225–239). Sycamore, IL: Sycamore.

Staub, N. (2000). *On inclusion and the other kids: Here's what research shows so far about inclusion's effect on nondisabled students.* Retrieved on March 1, 2001, from http://www.edc.org/urban

Stone, C.A. (1993). What's missing in the metaphor of scaffolding? In E.A. Forman, N. Minick, & C.A. Stone (Eds.), *Contexts for learning: Sociocultural dynamics in children's development* (pp. 169–183). New York: Oxford University Press.

Suárez-Orozco, C., & Suárez-Orozco, M. (1995). *Transformations: Migration, family life, and achievement motivation among Latino adolescents.* Stanford, CA: Stanford University Press.

Tejeda, C. (2000). *Mapping social space: A study of spatial production in an elementary classroom.* (Doctoral dissertation, University of California, Los Angeles, 2000). Ann Arbor: UMI 2001, Microform 9993008.

Trouillot, M. (1995). *Silencing the past: Power and the production of history.* Boston: Beacon Press.

U.S. Department of Education. (1997). *Nineteenth annual report to Congress on the implementation of the IDEA.* Washington, DC: Author.

U.S. Department of Education. (1999). *Twenty-first report to Congress on the implementation of the IDEA.* Washington, DC: Author.

Valencia, R. (Ed.). (1997). *The evolution of deficit thinking.* London: Falmer.

Vanderwood, M., McGrew, K.S., & Ysseldyke, J.E. (1998). Why we can't say much about students with disabilities during education reform. *Exceptional Children, 64,* 359–370.

Varenne, H. (1984). Collective representation in American anthropological conversations: Individual and culture. *Current Anthropology, 25,* 281–291.

Varenne, H., & McDermott, R. (Eds.). (1999). *Successful failure: The school America builds.* Boulder, CO: Westview Press.

Villa, R.A., & Thousand, J.S. (Eds.). (1995). *Creating an inclusive school.* Alexandria, VA: Association for Supervision and Curriculum Development.

Viswanathan, G. (Ed.). (2001). *Power, politics, and culture: Interviews with Edward W. Said.* New York: Pantheon.

Vogt, L., Jordan, C., & Tharp, R. (1993). Explaining school failure, producing school success: Two cases. In E. Jacob & C. Jordan (Eds.), *Minority education: Anthropological perspectives* (pp. 53–65). Norwood, NJ: Ablex.

Wagner, M., Blackorby, J., Cameto, R., Hebbler, K., & Newman, L. (1993). *The transition experiences of young people with disabilities: A summary of findings from the national longitudinal transition study of special education students.* Menlo Park, CA: SRI International.

Walker, V.S. (1999). Culture and commitment: Challenges for the future training of education researchers. In E.C. Lagemann & L.S. Shulman (Eds.), *Issues in education research: Problems and possibilities* (pp. 224–244). San Francisco: Jossey-Bass.

Wang, M.C., & Walberg. H.J. (1988). Four fallacies of segregationism. *Exceptional Children, 55,* 128–137.

Will, M. (1984). Let us pause and reflect – but not too long. *Exceptional Children, 51*(1)*,* 11–16.

Williams, R. (1983). *Culture and society.* New York: Columbia University Press.

Willis, P. (1977). *Learning to labor: How working class kids get working class jobs.* New York: Columbia University Press.

Zeichner, K.M., & Hoeft, K. (1996). Teacher socialization for cultural diversity. In J. Sikula, T.J. Buttery, & E. Guyton (Eds.), *The handbook of research on teacher education* (pp. 525–547). New York: Macmillan.

17

The Cultural Work of Learning Disabilities

Ray McDermott, Shelley Goldman and Hervé Varenne

[...]

Since about 1850, first in Europe and then in the United States, classifying human beings by mental ability, accurately or not, has been a politically rewarded activity. Those with power have placed others, usually the downtrodden, into ability and disposition groups that they cannot escape. The practice has prospered even where the groupings are, as is usually the case, ill defined and, as is always the case in human cultures, arbitrary, in the revealing sense that groupings could be defined differently. People who live together in a culture must struggle constantly with the constraints and affordances of the systems of classification and interpretation that are used in the culture. This is so even when the identifications are selectively deleterious to many involved. In a badly divided society, the bad effects can appear to be the very purpose of the classifications.

Culture against children

Consider the case of learning disability (LD) labels in the politics of mainstream educational institutions and minority groups in the United States. Three patterns are well known: (a) a higher percentage of minority children than of White children are assigned to special education; (b) within special education, White children are assigned to less restrictive programs than are their minority counter-parts; and (c) the data – driven by inconsistent methods of diagnosis, treatment, and funding – make the overall system difficult to describe or change (Losen & Orfield, 2002; National Research Council, 2002). A half-century of ethnographic studies has shown that American education is compulsively competitive. In American classrooms, every child not only has to learn, but has to learn better or faster than his or her neighbors (Varenne & McDermott, 1998). Hence American education is well organized to make hierarchy out of any differences that can be claimed, however falsely, to be natural, inherent, and potentially consequential in school. By means of the same competitive impulse, American education is well organized to have the problem of mixing and matching LD and minority status.

From: *Educational Researcher*, 35 (6), 2006, pp. 12–17.

For an illustration, we describe a group of boys adjusting to the demands of the moment in a mathematics classroom where their behavior is fodder for the cultural practice of interpreting and explaining children as disadvantaged, deprived, at risk, slow, LD, ELL (English Language Learner), ADD (Attention Deficit Disorder), emotionally disturbed, and so forth. Their behavior is quite normal in two senses of the term: one, their actions make sense as responses to the environments provided by adults; and, two, the same behavior can be found in most classrooms around the country. The labels are not so much facts about specific children as they are mirrors to what happens in classrooms run by the survival-of-the-show-off-smartest logic of American education. Because it is always possible to celebrate or disparage another person's cognitive abilities, and because schools magnify and record for eternity – in file cabinets, anyway – the measured pluses and minuses of every child, LD labels are as much resources in struggles over access to credentials as they are descriptions of a child's inner properties. Add to this the ambiguities of racial, ethnic, and linguistic labels and the competitive and politically consequential agendas for which the labels are made relevant, and the ties between LD and minoriry status become both intertwined and systematically unsteady enough for political intrigue (Artiles, 2003). The same cultural arrangements and tensions that make racial and linguistic borders into variables correlating with school success are also background for the fast growth of the LD industry.

Units in a cultural analysis

Our goal is to present a way of thinking about LD as a cultural preoccupation and production. We present no original findings on specific LD children and no new arguments based on available demographic trends. We heavily stress the cultural world in which LD designations live, and we try to say as little as possible about individual children. In Toni Morrison's first novel, *The Bluest Eye* (1970), she portrayed an African American child put-upon and abused in every way imaginable and left with only a deep desire for having blue eyes. Decades later, Morrison critiqued her own effort:

> … [T]he weight of the novel's inquiry on so delicate and vulnerable a character could smash her and lead readers into the comfort of pitying her rather than into an interrogation of themselves for the smashing … many readers remain touched but not moved. (1994, p. 211)

In keeping with Morrison's complaint, we are interested in spotlighting not so much the children as their adults, not so much minorities as the larger system of which they are a part.[1] We are not as interested in LD behavior as in the preoccupations – as seen from the level of classroom organization – of all those adults who are professionally poised to discover LD behavior. We limit our description to classroom events in which the explanation of children as LD, ADD, low IQ, at risk, culturally deprived, and so on might come alive. We are less interested in the characteristics of LD children than in the cultural arrangements that make an LD label relevant; we are less interested in minds and their moments than in moments and their minds.[2]

A cultural analysis takes individuals seriously by focusing on their environments and rarely allows a single person to bear the undue burden of being targeted, accused, labeled, explained, worried about, remediated, or even rehabilitated without an account of the conditions in which he or she lives. A cultural approach to LD does not address LD directly but instead addresses arrangements among persons, ideas, opportunities, constraints, and interpretations – what others call the discursive practices of LD (Artiles, 2004; Dudley-Marling, 2004; Reid & Valle, 2004) – that allow or even require that certain facts be searched for, discovered, measured, recorded, and made consequential as label relevant (McDermott & Varenne, 2006; Varenne, 1998). Responses and interpretations are the primary focuses. The individual child can be the unit of concern, but not the unit of analysis.

Anthropologist Conrad Arensberg (1982, p. 109) identified the analytic biases behind disciplinary approaches to the description of behavior: for psychology, the minimal unit of analysis is one person doing something; for sociology, the minimal unit is two people interacting; and for anthropology, the minimal unit is three – two people interacting and one person interpreting them. It takes constant interpretive work for people to create the ground where certain behaviors stand out in ways that ate consistently and institutionally consequential. As a cultural fact, LD demands more than just some children with learning difficulties and more than just some adults to notice, diagnose, and remediate them. The cultural work of LD is embedded in the concerted activities of millions of people engaging in a surveillance system consisting of professionals – doctors, psychologists, lawyers, educators – and parents, all of whom are involved and at the ready before the children show up. All of these people are looking for and producing evidence of LD in educational settings designed to make symptoms of LD visible.

LD as a kind of mind

LD is a newcomer to the stock of identified cultural selves. One could not be LD in 1900. One could be a 'laggard' in an American school, or a 'lazy idle little loafer' (Joyce, 1916/1956, p. 51) in an Irish school. By 1940, it was possible to suffer from *strephosymbolia,* an early term for what, by approximately 1960, became *dyslexia,* which in turn, by 1970, became often subsumed by the more generalized LD label. All of these terms are part of a larger preoccupation with mental capacities as a determinant of both school and social success. For 150 years, the West has been rife with rumors about intelligence, primitive minds, and inherited genius, all differentially distributed across kinds of people by race, class, gender, and national character. The rumors have encouraged oppression by explanation: some can, some cannot, and this is why some have and some have not. Contemporary parents, teachers, and researchers are recipients of a cultural preoccupation with mental incapacities.

When the National Research Council produced a helpful volume (2002) on the difficult-to-analyze data on minority and LD labels, it called for better data – with more controls – but did not ask cultural questions. For example: what is the rhetorical importance of LD such that researchers are paid to produce and then to settle for so much bad data? What are the classroom conditions that make educators desperate to label children LD? Will new data solve the problems? Instead of more data on individual LD students, why not search for data on conditions that make LD look promising as a way to save children? Can new data help to change classrooms enough that LD will cease to be a necessary fact? A cultural analysis focuses less on LD minds and more on LD situations. At any given moment in a cultural arrangement, just what interpretations are available and called into use?

Genius and LD as kinds of mind

We circumscribe a cultural analysis of LD with a portrait of the modern West as a machine shop for the production of ever-shifting labels for kinds of mind. Around 1700, for example, 'genius' was transformed from a guiding spirit (a tradition starting in ancient Rome) to a stable property of creative persons in market economies. Shakespeare, Galileo, Pascal, and Newton were celebrated tokens of the type, and modern exemplars were hailed for making knowledge subordinate to procedural rationality, science, and strategic planning. A century later, full-sail colonialism tied biological definitions of race to emerging ideas of intelligence and personality (Baker, 1998; Smedley, 1993). Francis Galton (1865) lit this conceptual fire with claims of inherent genius, especially for upper-class, White, British males – a perspective eventually fueled by genetics. Kinds of minds defined by ability began to define kinds of persons by race, gender, language, and even sexual orientation. Genius became a display board for indignities imposed on those deemed inherently not smart enough, usually women or people of African descent (from past victims of eugenics to current victims for whom the bell curve tolls), or those deemed inherently too smart, usually homosexuals or Jews (Elfenbein, 1999; Gilman, 1996). Even good ideas about creativity can turn dangerous. For better and often worse, genius and LD are labels with which students, teachers, and researchers must make their peace (DeNora & Mehan, 1994; McDermott, 2006).

A thumbnail history of LD in the United States, like the history of genius in Europe, says more about American culture than about schoolchildren, more about the interpretations available for talking about children than about the children themselves. After decades of neurological speculation on dyslexia, the very idea of selective disabilities found a niche in the 1960s as an explanation of why children of privilege and intelligence could not learn to read as expected. Based on flimsy diagnostic criteria, LD became a convenient fiction applicable to almost anyone and consequential by the demands of the latest trends in diagnosis and record keeping. By 1980, White children were labeled LD and, with an ugly lack of crossover, minorities were labeled emotionally disturbed or retarded. Legal briefs were filed, government warnings rendered, and LD was momentarily spread more evenly across groups (Coles, 1987). Schools were quickly overrun with LD children and budget deficits for their care. With increasing competition, a new use for LD was found in the 1990s – securing more time for labeled children on examinations. Mediating smart versus slow, LD became a defense against threats to sustained high prestige, and it now serves the wealthy with legitimate escape routes from low test scores. Those without access to the best schools – whether labeled as disabled and forgotten, or not labeled and forgotten nonetheless – remain stuck in place. As Artiles (2003) says, 'false positives and negatives are equally problematic' (p. 174). Attempts to measure, diagnose, and treat LD have aided the production of inequities.

Across decades of classroom research, we have never set out to study LD, but classroom practices make interpretations of LD sometimes a thing to notice. We have generally found children called LD – the ones on our classroom videotapes over the past 30 years – to be far more capable than claimed. By a play of rumors, facts, and concerns, in real classrooms LD children have to spend their time avoiding getting caught not knowing something. Facing the double job of doing school tasks while arranging to not look incompetent, children who are ripe to be categorized as LD often have their struggles magnified (Hood, McDermott, & Cole, 1980; McDermott, 1993). The same thing happens to children spotlighted by racial and linguistic categories. Under current conditions, the search for LD results in documentation mostly of what many children cannot do. Parental demands that individual children be allowed to learn unconstrained by pressure to do better than everyone else have been remade into tools for the suppression of their children.

A problematic success

The easy assumption that children are LD requires that many people systematically fail to attend to what children can do (Hood, McDermott, & Cole, 1980; McDermott, 1993; Mehan, 1993, 1996). In this article, we offer, instead, an account of schoolchildren knowing and doing more than a glance, a test, and a label might reveal. Our example erases simplistic questions about what is wrong with the children and initiates more complex questions about how American classrooms organize occasions for children to look unsuccessful, and then to blame their behavior on disabilities inside their heads and/or incapacities brought on by their race, gender, language, or social class.

We observed a middle-school classroom for three months as part of field-testing a reform-based, technology-integrated mathematics curriculum (Goldman, Knudsen, & Latvala, 1998; Greeno et al., 1999). Our observations focused on a group of three boys, each with an LD story sometimes told, sometimes not. We intentionally withhold the labels applied to the boys for three good reasons: (a) although the teacher had access to their files, she tried to forget everyone's official diagnosis; therefore, who was called what was not a factor in this classroom; (b) we are trying to keep the reader focused on the classroom as a site for invoking LD stories; and (c) we are trying to keep the analysis of LD more open than is possible once labels stand in as proxies for complex and multilayered behavior across persons over time.

Boomer was a high-intelligence 'star' on entry to middle school but had a focus and 'attitude' problem that kept him from high achievement. In class, he alternated between yelling at teachers and tackling academic questions. Teachers who worked with him talked about making an 'investment.' They tried to keep him in class, but he was often on 'office suspension,' with staff members watching him while he did schoolwork. In a wealthier district, Boomer and his teachers might have had more assistance.

Hector was 'a nice kid' but in trouble academically. He stayed away from teachers, and they, perhaps, from him. He never raised his hand in a class discussion, rarely volunteered an answer, and spent as much time as he could visiting the pencil sharpener. He did not hand in assignments or keep work papers. He was sociable and expert in teenage banter but usually missing at performance relevant moments. Ripe for several interventions, he received no services. The teacher said she could not remember if he was LD or low IQ.

Ricardo was a model student at first glance, sitting quietly, socializing appropriately, and working. He was soon transferred to another school for sending a death threat to a teacher.

Officially and unofficially, all three boys were sometimes described and treated as kinds of minds and ability sets. Unofficially, they were also talked about in terms of their home cultures: Boomer was African American, and Hector and Ricardo were immigrants from Mexico.

Teachers called the boys 'at risk.' Just what does 'at risk' mean in situ, in the actual unfolding of any child's behavior in relation to other children, teachers, or special needs personnel? We studied the 'at risk' stories in comparison with our daily video records thoroughly enough to question, reject, or verify each story. New stories emerged. We saw Hector, the 'unengaged' student, working hard, organizing group activities, and mastering new math concepts and operations. We saw Ricardo paying careful attention despite his upcoming removal from the school. We saw Boomer, the 'promising' student, performing smartness for the teacher and building his academic image at the expense of Hector and Ricardo. Then we saw Hector, no matter how hard he worked, avoiding official and public assessment. His image as slow and unengaged remained unchanged, even as he successfully completed assignments. We videotaped for six weeks as the boys completed a simulation-based math unit requiring that they design, heat, and finance a research station for scientists in Antarctica. Hector and Boomer finished the required task. Hector became expert with the modeling software and created a floor plan for his group's research center, and they produced a proficient analysis. The mismatch between their behavior and the school's story about them invited a more careful look. Although their teacher was happy that the boys were working steadily, the particulars of their achievements were hardly noticed.

We watched the video carefully and saw how the boys handled their assignments. The students had a scale problem when imagining a meter length in the real world as they designed the research station for scientists in Antarctica. One meter in the world was surprisingly larger than one meter measured by dots on paper or by tiny lines on a computer screen. After the boys created a 6-by-6-meter room on paper, Hector went to get a ruler for a comparison. He put the stick on the ground and marked the floor to designate each meter until he had six lengths. Meanwhile, his group-mates worked on floor plans at their desks. Boomer looked at Hector and asked, 'Is that six meters?' The answer came quickly, but in a difficult exchange. Hector led a monologue for three:

Hector: Here! [Stands up and goes to the spot.] Six!
Boomer: That's big enough.
Hector: From that thing. [Points to where he started at door.] That's BIG!
Hector: That's bigger than my whole house! [Laughs.]

Back at his desk, next to the other boys, Hector counts meters on his paper, picks up the assignment, reads it, and writes on his paper. Ricardo looks at Hector's writing.

Hector: They're going to sleep in an area six-by-six. That's big! [Gestures 'big' with his hands.]

Ricardo asks how many rooms are modeled in their floor plans. Hector joins the conversation but seems more concerned that the rooms are too big. (*R* is a researcher.)

Hector: This was a living area. No mas una. Puerta grande.
Boomer: [Boomer looks over at Hector.] Everybody should have their own room.
Hector: Eh. ... so I made a big room. [The boys talk quietly among themselves.]

Hector:	Four and a half. … [Boomer is looking at his own work.]
Hector:	I'm going to leave it like that. [Plays with a pen on his desk and looks at Ricardo's paper.]
Hector:	Pues, una grande, ja!
R:	We need to start cleaning up.
Hector:	This time I'm gonna make little small rooms. [Picks up a towel to erase the board and reworks his design.]
Hector:	That's good. Look. [Turns to Ricardo with his paper, then to the camera.]

Ricardo doesn't look at the paper. Hector moves closer to get his attention, puts his picture on the desk, and closes his pen.

| *Hector:* | Now we clean this up. [To a researcher] We erase everything we did to this, right? |
| *R:* | No, no, no, no. [Hector leaves the design on the desk.] |

Hector carried the lesson, investigating the scale details with more accuracy than the other boys, yet offering to erase his work before it could be seen. As the work went on, he became the group's expert on measurements and scale translations, compared meters on paper and in the software with meters on the floor and at home, and convinced his group to make bedrooms smaller than 6 by 6 meters. He and Boomer interrogated their data, made graphs of insulation values and heating costs, and realized how the graphed quantities varied inversely. Hector learned to graph data, mastered the software, and entered all floor plan requests for the group. Modeling and revising the station took six classes, and most of the work was based on Hector's model. We saw both boys engaged, and only after we tracked tasks over time did we discover the negative relation between Hector and assessment.

Children against their culture

Hector hid his learning, and Boomer announced his. Twice Hector had to report his group's work, and twice he avoided success. With both Ricardo and Boomer suspended and absent, Hector was asked to give a tour of his group's research station – his specialty – in a class-wide design review. He pointed at the monitor displaying the research station but gave little information and even claimed not to know much about it. He made jokes. The class laughed hysterically, and Hector sat down. At the final presentation, Boomer did most of the talking, and he called Hector 'stupid' a few times. When classmates noticed a mistake – a 3-meter bed – Hector left the front of the room to fix it. The computer crashed. The presentation unraveled. The teacher tried to help. While Hector worked on the computer, Boomer continued to call Hector names, and six weeks of good work evaporated. Boomer's charts and graphs were the only project materials handed in, even though we saw Hector ask Boomer to safeguard his papers.

Across weeks of work, the teacher assumed that the group's achievement belonged solely to Boomer. When she visited the boys at their table, Boomer did most of the talking, and the teacher turned toward his papers and ignored Hector's correct contribution. Even when he was accomplishing classroom work, Hector was not seen as working capably. This was so even when the teacher was intentionally trying to avoid treating students by their classifications. While watching tapes with us, the teacher saw Hector's accomplishments She gave him an A for the project – the first unit he passed that year. Hector's brief success gave way when he was placed in remedial algebra for high school. Boomer was assigned to college-bound algebra.

The American classroom is well organized for the production and display of failure, one child at a time if possible, but group by group if necessary. The groups can consist of kinds of person by race, gender, or class, and/or by kinds of minds described through simple contrasts such as smart/dumb or gifted/disabled. Even if the teacher manages to treat every child as potentially capable, the children can hammer each other into negative status positions; and even if both teacher and children can resist dropping everyone into predefined categories, the children's parents can take over, demanding more and more boxes with which to specify and proliferate kinds of kids doing better than other kinds of kids. In such a classroom, if there were no LD categories, someone would have to invent them.

The Illusive LD compromise

To counteract the cultural inclination to focus on what is wrong with individual children, we must seek data showing children more skilled than schools have categories or time to notice, describe, diagnose, record, and remediate. Even this is an incomplete goal, for such data can leave us still embedded in the assumptions and practices of the culture that we are trying to change, the culture of people institutionally preoccupied with measured success or failure for individual children. When we show children knowing more than expected, personal disability disappears as an object, but the arrangements that defined the problem and invited the LD interpretations stay in place. We can be sure that in other cultures, in other times, arrangements were different, and so was education research. By our analytic position, gone is the disability – because human beings are all exactly the same, not because some cannot be found learning things more slowly or with great difficulty, but because LD comes to practical existence inside a school system designed to measure how much faster or slower various children learn. Change the school, and LD becomes less relevant. LD is made consequential by gatekeepers assigning children to fixed positions. Without an institutional apparatus for measuring individual differences and kinds of minds, research into the consequences of misidentification would be superfluous. Without an apparatus for measuring individual minds, demonstrations that 'failing' students are 'really' attentive and knowledgeable might not be taken as still another call for better assessment tools or teacher training.

The political logic of LD and minority status is clear in the inverse cases of minority LD and upper-class LD. If the market separates adults with access to resources from those without, then grades, degrees, and diagnoses do the same to their children. If people complain about the injustice done to lower-class and minority children by any categorization, the category can be extended to a wider, and Whiter, population with the proviso that those with resources must have a higher-echelon label. This division can be so thick that upper-class White parents now seek the diagnosis of LD for the extra allowances it offers their children (Sireci, Scarpati, & Li, 2005). Who gets called LD, when, by whom, and with what results is organized by demographic and political conditions. LD is less a kind of mind, and more a method for differentiating people and treating them differently. Being treated differently can be good, or dangerous, depending on the cultural preoccupations with which it is aligned.

In a cultural analysis, isolated facts are rarely as important as the preoccupations that elicit them and give them consequence. In 1850, Ralph Waldo Emerson (1850/1995) used a question and answer to initiate a cultural analysis. Question: '[I]s not the fact but the rumor of some fact?' Answer: 'A fact is only a fulcrum of the spirit. It is the terminus of past thought, but only a means now to new sallies of the imagination and new progress of wisdom' (p. 177). For 50 years, American education has been rife with rumors about LD; built on the anxieties of parents and teachers of children in trouble, the 'fulcrum of the spirit' has run ahead of research and practice and made LD a common possibility in classrooms. In an early ethnography of schooling, Jules Henry remade the Emersonian point: 'School metamorphoses the child, giving it the kind of Self the school can manage, and then proceeds to minister to the Self it has made' (1963, p. 292). LD is a kind of self that American education knows how to produce, and so too are the supposed selves from named racial, ethnic, and linguistic backgrounds (Varenne, 1998). American schools are not always better off for their careful attention to kinds of children, but they do relentlessly create conditions under which rumors of disability and disadvantaged background are attended to and their persons counted, theorized, explained, and remediated. It's rumors all the way down.

Notes

The authors wish to thank Deborah Stipek for commenting on this article.

1   See Morrison's analysis of American racism based on peripheral African American characters in the novels of major White American authors.
2   We alter here a phrase by Goffman (1967), who wrote of 'moments and their men.'

References

Arensberg, C.A. (1982). Generalizing anthropology. In E.A. Hoebel (Ed.), *Crisis in anthropology* (pp. 109–130). New York: Garland.
Artiles, A. (2003). Special education's changing identity. *Harvard Educational Review, 75,* 164–202.
Artiles, A. (2004). The end of innocence: Historiography and representation in the discursive practice of learning disabilities. *Journal of Learning Disabilities, 37,* 550–555.
Baker, L. (1998). *From savage to Negro.* Berkeley: University of California Press.
Coles, G. (1987). *The learning mystique. A critical look at 'Learning Disabilities'.* New York: Pantheon.
DeNora. T., & Mehan, H. (1994). Genius: A social construction. In J. Kitsuse & T. Sarbin (Eds.), *Constructing the social* (pp. 157–173). Thousand Oaks, CA: Sage.
Dudley-Marling, C. (2004). The social construction of learning disabilities. *Journal of Learning Disabilities, 37,* 482–489.
Elfenbein, A. (1999). *Romantic genius.* New York: Columbia University Press.
Emerson, R.W. (1995). *Representative men.* New York: Marsilio Press. (Original work published 1850)
Galton, F. (1865). Hereditary talent and character. *Macmillan's Magazine, 12,* 157–166.

Gilman, S.L. (1996). *Smart Jews: The construction of the image of Jewish superior intelligence.* Lincoln: University of Nebraska Press.

Goffman, E. (1967). *Interaction ritual.* New York: Anchor.

Goldman, S., Knudsen. J., & Latvala, M. (1998). Engaging middle schoolers in and through real-world mathematics. In L. Leuzinger (Ed.), *Mathematics in the middle* (pp. 129–140). Reston, VA: National Council of Teachers of Mathematics.

Greeno, J.G., McDermott, R., Cole, K., Engle. R., Goldman, S., Knudsen, J., et al. (1999). Research, reform, and the aims of education. In E. Lagemenn & L. Shulman (Eds.), *Issues in education research* (pp. 299–335). San Francisco: Jossey-Bass.

Henry, J. (1963). *Culture against man.* New York: Vintage.

Hood, L., McDermott, R., & Cole, M. (1980). 'Let's try to make it a good day.' *Discourse Processes, 3,* 155–168.

Joyce, J. (1956). *A portrait of the artist as a young man.* New York: Viking Press. (Original work published 1916)

Losen, D., & Orfield, G. (Eds.). (2002). *Racial inequity in special education.* Cambridge, MA: Harvard Education Press.

McDermott, R. (1993). The acquisition of a child by a learning disability. In S. Chaiklin & J. Lave (Eds.), *Understanding practice: Perspectives on activity and context* (pp. 269–305). Cambridge, UK: Cambridge University Press.

McDermott, R. (2006). Situating genius. In Z. Bekerman, N. Burbules, & D. Silberman-Keller (Eds.), *Learning in places* (pp. 285–302). Bern: Peter Lang.

McDermott, R., & Varenne, H. (2006). Reconstructing culture in educational research. In G. Spindler & L. Hammond (Eds.), *Innovations in educational ethnography* (pp. 3–31). Mahwah, NJ: Lawrence Erlbaum.

Mehan, H. (1993). Beneath the skin and between the ears. In S. Chaiklin & J. Lave (Eds.), *Understanding practice* (pp. 241–269). New York: Cambridge University Press.

Mehan, H. (1996). The construction of an LD student. In M. Silverstein & G. Urban (Eds.), *Natural histories of discourse* (pp. 253–276). Chicago: University of Chicago Press.

Morrison, T. (1970). *The bluest eye.* New York: Holt, Rinehart, and Winston.

Morrison, T. (1994). Afterword. In *The bluest eye* (pp. 209–216). New York: Plume.

National Research Council. (2002). *Minority students in special and gifted education* (Committee on Minority Representation in Special Education, M.S. Donovan & C.T. Cross. Eds., Division of Behavioral and Social Sciences and Education). Washington, DC: National Academy Press.

Reid, D.K., & Valle, J.W. (2004). The discursive practice of learning disability. *Journal of Learning Disabilities, 37,* 466–481.

Sireci, S., Scarpati, S., &. Li, S. (2005). Test accommodations for students with disabilities: An analysis of the interaction hypothesis. *Review of Educational Research 75,* 457–490.

Smedley, A. (1993). *Race in North America.* Boulder, CO: Westview.

Varenne, H. (1998). Diversity as American cultural category. In C. Greenhouse (Ed.), *Democracy and ethnography* (pp. 27–32). Albany: State University of New York Press.

Varenne, H., & McDermott, R. (1998). *Successful failure: The school America builds.* Boulder, CO: Westview.

Index